The 100 Best Small Towns in AMERICA

Norman Crampton

Prentice Hall

New York • London • Toronto • Sydney • Tokyo

PRENTICE HALL GENERAL REFERENCE
15 Columbus Circle
New York, NY 10023

Copyright © 1993 by Norman Crampton
All rights reserved
including the right of reproduction
in whole or in part in any form

A Prentice Hall Book

PRENTICE HALL and colophon are
registered trademarks of Simon & Schuster, Inc.

Crampton, Norman.
    The 100 best small towns in America / Norman Crampton.—1st ed.
      p. cm.
    ISBN 0-671-84671-X
      1. Cities and towns—United States—Ratings. 2. Cities and towns—
United States—Statistics. 3. Social indicators—United States. 4. Quality
of life—United States—Statistics. 5. United States—Rural conditions.
6. United States—Social conditions—1980– I. Title. II. Title: Hundred
best small towns in America.
HT123.C68   1993   92-8214
307.76'0973—dc20   CIP

Designed by M.R.P. Design
Manufactured in the United States of America

2 3 4 5 6 7 8 9 10

Acknowledgments

Statistics and other data in this book have come from various sources, including libraries, schools, hospitals, and town clerks, to name only a few. Special thanks also are due the many chambers of commerce and industrial development offices that provided demographic profiles.

Gathering deeper insights about the towns involved more than 500 telephone interviews with local residents. Practically without exception, my phone calls were received warmly and enthusiastically. In an age when the telephone may be viewed as an instrument of torture, my small-town contacts cheerfully tolerated long interviews, and many took the time to follow up by mail. I'm extremely grateful to them.

Finally, I wish to acknowledge my family—Mary Alice, Frederick, and Abigail Crampton—without whose advice, patience, encouragement, and love this book simply would not have been possible.

Greencastle, Indiana   **N.C.**

Contents

In praise of small-town America.

You don't have to be small-town bred to have a soft spot for America's small towns. For at least half our history, we were mostly a nation of microcenters surrounded by farms. In 10,000 Centervilles scattered across the land, the American idea took root, flourished, and fed the nation. You can still catch a glimpse of this old America from the window seat of a jetliner on a clear night, spotting small clusters of light across whole time zones.

The 1990 Census contained no real surprises for small-town America. Many of the rural lights have dimmed and some have flickered out, a long-term trend that is well understood, if not well accepted. When the old family homestead is gone and good jobs are elsewhere, people move away. In 1950, 44 percent of the U.S. population still lived on farms or in small towns; by 1990, that segment was down to 23 percent.

Ask small-towners what their place contributes to the national economy and they'll tell you, with a mixture of pride and sadness: our kids. You can forget about those bumper crops of corn and beans and truckloads of beef and machinery—the big export item of small-town America always has been people, mostly young people, and mostly reared in an environment where traditional values of family, community, faith, hard work, and patriotism remain strong. Small wonder we put our small towns up on a pedestal—they're helping to preserve the American dream.

But as their numbers and size dwindle, how long can we expect small towns to perform this vital service for the nation? And why are some of these places thriving while others, the majority, decline? To find some answers, we began a search for the 100 best small towns in America. One hundred is just a number, and the choices are bound to raise objection. Everyone's small hometown is "best" for unassailable reasons. We simply wanted this selection of places to illustrate, one way or another, the qualities of the classic small American town. (The process of finding the 100 towns is explained in Chapter 2.)

If this small sample is any indication, there's good news: The American dream is still coming alive in the countryside, in places such as Penn Yan, New York; Glenwood Springs, Colorado; Grand Rapids, Minnesota; West Plains, Missouri; and Douglas, Wyoming. Come along for a quick tour.

Penn Yan, population 5,248, is named for the original Pennsylvania Yankee settlers. It's in the Finger Lakes region, about 56 miles southeast of Rochester—a very pretty part of western New York State, with vistas of farms and orchards on rolling hills.

It's also a hard place to make a living. Penn Yan lost jobs in the mid-1980s, during the same time its farmers watched prices drop to Depression levels. They were practically giving sweet corn away when Penn Yan business-man Ron Nissen decided, enough! He called a meeting of old friends, towns-people and farmers to make a new plan for Penn Yan. They knew they had assets—a wide variety of skills and an old acquaintance with sweat equity. They also knew they had plenty of good things to sell—fruits, vegetables, meats, crafts. They could see a huge potential customer base in the Rochester–Syracuse area; all they needed was a big, attractive marketplace. It was easy to visualize. Someone suggested a name: Windmill Farm and Craft Market.

Then came the hard part: money. Organized as the Yates County Country Cooperative, Nissen and the 12 other founders figured it would take at least $125,000 to buy land and put up two simple but sizeable pole buildings to house the market. When the state turned down their request for financial help, the Penn Yan group and their neighbors tapped their own resources, sold shares, and raised $55,000. That paid for a 26-acre site and several loads of building materials, but not for labor. Nissen, a tire dealer, asked a few of his Mennonite farmer customers whether they could help.

Asking was all it took. As in an old-time barn raising, farmers and towns-people built the frame and roof of two 60-by-100-foot buildings in one day. Dozens of people who just happened to be driving by on that May weekend in 1988 hopped out of their cars and lent a hand.

Open Saturdays only, May through Christmas, the Windmill Farm has drawn as many as 12,000 customers in one day. Sales topped $1 million the first year and exceeded $2 million in 1991. Nissen figures the enterprise has created about 115 new jobs.

The Windmill has an elusive, special quality, Nissen believes. "The vendors are so friendly and enjoying themselves that it radiates across the counters to the public," he says. "There's no admission, no charge for parking. It's the old-fashioned country shopping, and we have about anything you want to buy." His own specialty is penny candy. Down the aisle, Mennonite artisans sell beautiful quilts, with stunning price tags.

Penn Yan's wonderful Windmill has become a model for other small towns, and the sweetest part for Penn Yan residents is that they did it all themselves.

Self-reliance is a key quality of the best small towns. The willingness to look problems square in the eye probably comes first. When Glenwood Springs, Colorado, took a hard look at itself about a decade ago, "we didn't have a clear vision of what we were going to become," Mayor Ted O'Leary remembers. " 'What is our strength?' we asked." As many suspected, the answer was location—a gorgeous setting in a Rocky Mountain river valley, within 50 miles of two world-class ski resorts, Vail and Aspen. But if Glenwood expected to capitalize on its location, it had to put on a prettier face. The downtown area needed sprucing up. And there were more basic problems, such as affordable housing for the town's low-income residents who commuted to motel, resort, and restaurant jobs in the area.

As usual, there wasn't much money. Glenwood, no different from many small towns, pays its bills mostly from property taxes on homes, including the homes of numerous older residents on fixed incomes. Raising property taxes was out of the question, but raising a little more tax revenue was OK with residents, so Glenwood gritted its teeth and passed a three-quarter-cent sales tax. That bought such basics as new sidewalks, trees, and flower beds, and even some bike paths. Then, to raise promotional funds without pinching local pocketbooks any more, Glenwood passed a 1-percent tax on motel rooms.

To increase its stock of affordable homes without getting into the expensive and risky housing business itself, Glenwood passed an ordinance to make the town more attractive to qualified builders—and spread the word.

Before long, Glenwood Springs was talking seriously with the Denver Archdiocese of the Catholic Church. Mayor O'Leary was impressed by the housing projects the Archdiocese had been running on the Eastern Slope—"by any standard a model," he said. Glenwood expects to have some 50 new units, complete with playgrounds and day care.

Small towns have just about all the problems of big cities, including drugs, crime, child abuse, homelessness, and teens in trouble. But the scale of problems is often so much smaller that they are not absolutely overwhelming. And in the best small towns, there are always volunteers ready to make a difference.

For example, Brattleboro, Vermont—population 12,241—needed a teen center. "They were looking for someone really kid-oriented, and I filled the bill," said Nancy Hagstrom, a high school teacher, who provided not only the adult perspective but also, along with neighbors, pledged personal assets to finance the project. Luckily, the perfect building was available—a bankrupt nightclub with dance floor and all the required amenities. But it needed work. "We probably had 2,500 volunteer hours from the kids," Hagstrom said. Local contractors supervised vocational–technical students in carrying out the plumbing and electrical work. The place was finished, and the idea has clicked with Brattleboro teens, who are well represented on the board of directors.

A policeman is stationed at the front door—not to control internal activity, Hagstrom explained, "but to discourage the conglomeration of sleaze, as the kids call them, who follow around trying to sell them drugs or whatever." It's not a perfect world, and the teen center doesn't promise that, Hagstrom said. "But so far it's worked. Last Friday night we had 320 seventh through ninth graders."

Small towns can be mind-expanding, as Dan McCandless discovered when he moved from New York City to Carlinville, Illinois, population 5,416. McCandless is a reporter at the Macoupin County Enquirer and his spouse teaches at Blackburn College. He recalled the shock of plunging into a small town environment. "In New York, you learn to lock everything up and mind your own business," McCandless said. In Carlinville? If it were anyplace else, he admits, he might say "Butt out!" to questions concerning what church he belongs to—or why he did or did not do something on a certain day.

McCandless has learned to accept these probes as a normal part of small-town everyday care and concern. And the absence of serious crime is liberating. "For the first time, we haven't consulted the most-stolen list before buying a car," he said. "We bought a Renault Encore in New York because nobody ever steals them." But they still drive their Manhattan car, he added. "That is another thing about small towns—you don't have a whole lot of money, but you find you don't need a lot of it. Once you adjust to that, everything seems to fall into place."

Small towns generally are not rich places. But they have a resource money cannot buy—hospitality—as Al Pinder has shown in Grinnell, Iowa. Pinder is editor and publisher of the Grinnell Herald-Register, a twice-weekly newspaper in the college town of 8,902 people. One day, some years ago, the publisher of the daily newspaper in Taipei arrived in Grinnell during a two-month tour of the United States arranged by the State Department. Pinder and his wife, Dorothy, did the customary small-town thing, inviting the visitor for an honest Iowa supper of fried chicken, fresh tossed green salad, and homemade rolls. Surrounded by his hosts and the Pinder tribe of six young kids, the man from the Far East exclaimed, "This night is the most special one!" Pinder asked why. "Because," he said, "this is the first American home I have been inside of."

Pinder wondered how anyone could see America without seeing an American household of the small-town variety. He wrote to the State Department, suggesting that small towners are natural diplomats, taking time with guests "to show them where they work, where they play, where they worship—learn their hopes, their fears, their plans for the future," he recalled. Soon, whole delegations of foreign journalists began arriving in Grinnell. No problem—Pinder had a ready list of town volunteers willing to open their homes and lives to travelers.

The best small towns teach civics lessons, with a lot of heart. Bill and Margaret Sottile and their two kids moved from suburban Chicago to Houghton, Michigan, population 7,498, where Bill became director of the Upper Peninsula Laboratory of the Michigan Department of Health.

One of the qualities of Houghton is somewhat less obvious than the 200-plus inches of snow that pile up each winter. Bill explained, "In Chicago, there were impoverished areas. We would go through them every day. But in a suburban lifestyle, one became insulated from other people's problems. Here, if you want something to happen you have to roll up your sleeves and make it happen. Community action begins at home—you cannot escape the conclusion. And I find I like that," Bill said. In this community spirit, Margaret Sottile and a friend, Patricia Wood, have set up a drop-in center at a local church for mothers of infants and toddlers, one morning a week.

As Dan McCandless has learned in Carlinville, churches form the social fabric of small towns. The Rev. Don Dunn, rector of St. Paul's Episcopal Church in Elko, Nevada, will testify to this. Nearing a population of 15,000, Elko practically doubled in size during the 1980s. The big draw: gold mining, ranching, and the casino industry. To jobless people elsewhere, Elko looked like an oasis in the high Nevada desert.

"Often I would have 15 to 20 transients at the door each day—people who came out here searching for a job," Fr. Dunn said. What to do? The county had once provided temporary help to newcomers. But then budget restraints forced it to cut back all emergency aid except for medical services. Elko's churches just had to respond.

The solution was FISH—Friends in Service Helping, a coalition of Elko churches with a budget of $60,000, raised entirely from the member churches and used to provide a helping hand to new arrivals in need. "It's difficult to find a job if you are dirty or unshaven," Fr. Dunn said.

Small towns can be rich in contradictions. Frank Martin, editor and publisher of the West Plains, Missouri, *Daily Quill*, was reminded of that in a university-sponsored discussion about the uniqueness of his part of the country. In the Ozarks of south central Missouri, West Plains, population 8,913, is, by local description, about 100 miles from anything. It was once a pit stop for Jesse James and the Ma Barker gang.

"We listed the best and worst traits of the typical Ozark native," Martin said. It came as only a partial surprise that the number one item on both lists was the same: the fierce feeling of independence and resistance to change that natives have inherited as a tradition. "The result is we have something between a fairly stable economy and planned progress," said Martin. "I don't mean a mindless Babbittism but a well reasoned approach to growth."

Small towns preserve good manners. "The smaller the town, the more likely it is that you know the other people moving around," says Peter Viemeister, a retired vice president of Grumman Corporation, who now lives in Bedford, Virginia—population 6,073. "You do not have that anonymity that allows you to be rude, hostile, aggressive, pushy. You know everybody and everybody knows you. You're kind of on your good behavior."

Good behavior does not mean avoiding controversy, however. Describing what they term "entrepreneurial rural communities," professors Cornelia and Jan Flora of Virginia Polytechnic Institute say these places accept controversy as normal and are willing to talk about it in the local newspaper. They're not afraid of politics and don't let personalities get in the way. "Policies, not people, are the focus of discussion," the VPI professors have written.

The Floras have found that entrepreneurial small towns like to win in academics as much as in athletics. These towns also have some surplus to reinvest in town projects, and they're willing to tax themselves to maintain public services. They have the vision to see beyond city limits and the confidence to share leadership with one another and with newcomers.

But small-town residents can't survive by taking in each other's laundry, simply performing services. They have to make real things for sale elsewhere. "Adding value in rural areas is the key to our future success," says Todd Driscoll, of Grand Rapids, Minnesota, a paper-mill town with a population of 7,976. The big Blandin Mill in town adds value by converting cheap wood fiber into premium paper for printing magazines like *Time* and *Newsweek*. Driscoll's model works well in farming. He says, "If we can take milk and make cheese, or corn and make syrup, that's the future."

The future seemed assured in Douglas, Wyoming, when Diane Harrop and her husband, Randy, arrived in 1976. Douglas is what analysts in faraway places call an "energy impacted" town, meaning it's surrounded by rich deposits of coal, uranium, and oil but is unable to regulate the mining of this great wealth—world markets and national agendas do that. Unless the community springs to life and takes charge, a place like Douglas is like a marionette, with people far away pulling the strings.

But in 1976, Douglas was single-minded—mobilizing to produce energy for an anxious nation. Everybody figured the town, then a place of about 5,000 people, would double, or possibly triple, in size. The Harrops, a viable combination of pharmacist and schoolteacher, were immigrants from the urban Kansas City area. They were prepared for anything.

Diane arrived in Wyoming with experience as a high school debate coach and teacher of speech and English. She made a temporary career change, working in the bank. "And then we bought the store," she said. Now known as R-D Pharmacy & Books, the store is a rare retail hybrid, purveying "tonics for the body and tonics for the mind," in Diane's words. The bookstore part of the business shows how survival in small towns may require thinking big. The Douglas energy boom went bust after six or seven years. After a quick run-up to 10,000, the population fell back to an official 5,076 in the 1990 Census.

"There are three drugstores, and you can't make a living here with just a drugstore," Diane said. "One thing that did not exist was a full-line bookstore." For good reason, perhaps. As she learned, it takes a population of at least 20,000 to support a bookstore. Resourceful, Diane decided to create a retail niche, specializing in Western histories and diaries, regional titles, and children's books, "because that's where there's a real opening in the market, plus special ordering." After three years, the bookstore looks like the right Rx for the pharmacy, and vice versa.

Meanwhile, Diane and other Douglas residents are helping the town bounce back. She was elected to the city council and has served as mayor, guiding a downtown renewal project. "I see a return to optimism. I think that's vital," she said. "There was a kind of refusal to look ahead, to take a leap of faith on behalf of ourselves. That happens in small towns—people fool themselves into thinking they can keep things just the same, and that isn't valid. There is no standing still. I grew up in larger places, but in none of those places was I ever really tempted to get involved to change things for the better. I've come to learn in this small place that I have a lot of abilities, that I have a lot to give."

Jimmy Stewart, in the small-town movie fable *It's a Wonderful Life*, has a chance to see what life would have been like without him and learns that Bedford Falls would have been a poorer place in many ways. The danger in small towns is exactly the same—that ordinary people of ordinary means will fail to see, or fail to be shown, what a difference each one of them could make. The wonder in so many American small towns is that so many people do see and do make that difference.

2

How the 100 places were selected.

Entry Criteria

The process began by defining *small town* as a place with between 5,000 and 15,000 inhabitants, an arbitrary decision that undoubtedly removed many very nice small places from consideration. Unfortunately, there exists no commonly accepted definition of the term by population alone, not even at the Census Bureau. In the bureau's *County and City Data Book: 1988*, a major source of data for this book, population centers of between 2,500 and 25,000 are called "places." At the 25,000 threshold, however, the Census Bureau begins using the word "city." That point might be considered the extreme outer limits of "town." We felt, based on some experience living in a rural community of 9,000 and conversations with more experienced small-towners, that "small town" simply can't be stretched past 15,000.

What is the lower limit of "town"? More precisely, how small can a place be and still be considered a fairly independent social and economic unit, providing some range of employment, services, and institutional support to the populace? We didn't think 2,500 was large enough to pass those tests; thus, the bottom was raised to 5,000.

The second criterion after size was location. We were looking for communities that have their own economic base, places that offer jobs and employ a significant proportion of the local population. We were not looking for bedroom towns (although some of the 100 do have sizeable groups of commuters).

We wanted stand-alone economies, towns that were making good because of their own initiative. Thus, all towns located within what the Census Bureau calls an MSA—Metropolitan Statistical Area—were removed. MSAs are clusters of counties around big cities, and the smaller towns within MSAs are suburbs. There are therefore no suburbs among our 100 Best.

The next step was to apply a very broad test of vitality—to select places that are growing, according to the 1990 Census. The simple fact that a place is growing says a lot about its economic vitality and attractiveness. The vast majority of small, rural U.S. towns are not growing but shrinking; it is no small feat for a small town simply to hold its population constant. We did not adhere 100 percent to the population test: 14 towns on the list lost population during the 1980s. But all of these places scored well in other ways; and there were extenuating circumstances on the population matter, as with towns that have depended very heavily on the oil and gas industry, or other kinds of mining, and were hard hit when companies in those industries closed local operations.

SEVEN SELECTORS

After applying the entry test of size and location, and noting 1990 Census numbers, each town was measured by seven additional criteria:

1. Per capita income.
2. Proportion of black and other nonwhite population.
3. Proportion of population in the 25- to 34-year age group.
4. Number of physicians per 100,000 residents.
5. Number of serious crimes known to police per 100,000 residents.
6. Percentage of local population with a four-year college education or more.
7. Local government spending for public education.

All of this information came from Census Bureau data. However, the range of data specifically concerning places with populations between 5,000 and 15,000 is limited. Because none of the seven selectors except per capita income is measured directly by the Census Bureau, we used county data, reasoning that the towns are population centers within their counties. Many, in fact, are the largest town in the county. In any case, the county numbers should fairly reflect the towns.

A State-by-State Approach. In a nationwide search for the best small towns, the proper approach might be a nationwide ranking, looking at all the candidates irrespective of state lines, so that Texas towns compete with Vermont towns and Georgia towns go head to head with those in Utah. We decided against one national ranking and took a state-by-state approach, with a spreadsheet for each state, measuring how the candidates looked in comparison to others within the same state. This was another arbitrary decision, but we felt that cutting the universe down to state level was one way within an objective selection process to acknowledge that good small towns can be found in many places.

Now let's look at the selectors in more detail.

Per Capita Income

Income defines strength, buying power. It also is a relative number—relative to income of the surrounding area. Thus, in each case, per capita income is expressed both in dollars and in percentage of state average.

Percentage of Nonwhite Population

We were seeking small towns that reflected racial diversity, just as the nation does. However, small towns in general do not reflect the heterogeneity of cities. For the most part, blacks, Native Americans, and other people of color are not well represented in the towns on this list compared to their respective proportions of the total U.S. population.

Age Group 25 to 34

We selected this band of the population as a yardstick because people in this age group largely have completed their formal education—at least the first round—and are going to work, getting married, having children, and buying goods and services. Furthermore, 25-to-34-year-olds are the new recruits for local leadership. They are the young volunteers. Some are the young elected local officials. For all these reasons, this age group seems important to a town.

Physicians per 100,000 Population

This number was used as a broad measure of the availability of health care.

Serious Crimes Known to Police per 100,000 Residents

Serious crimes are defined as murder, nonnegligent manslaughter, forcible rape, robbery, and aggravated assault.

Percentage of Population with 16-Plus Years of Formal Education

Again using a number for the whole county in which the town is located, this is a measure of four-year college graduates. We used this number as a broad indicator of the kind of employment available in the area.

Local Government Expenditures for Public Education

This is an investment in human capital, through the elementary and secondary schools. Frequently it's a heavy investment and a long-term commitment.

The appendix of this book contains tables ranking each of the 100 towns by the seven selectors, as well as by growth rate.

FIVE MORE MEASURES

To cut the list of candidates further, we established a five-item checklist. We asked:

1. Is the town a county seat?

2. Does it have a newspaper, and if it does, is it weekly or daily?

3. Does it have an institution of higher learning—a college, junior college, or university?

4. Is it in an area that could be called scenic?

5. How close is the town to an MSA—a Metropolitan Statistical Area—for access to the services, goods, and diversions that cannot be found locally?

County Seat

County seats have a survival advantage. Legally speaking, there's no doing away with them, small though they may be. The county seat is a center of government; it draws traffic for that reason alone. People coming into town to conduct government business may shop and use other services, as well. We can't prove that being a county seat makes one town better than another, but 80 percent of the towns on this list are county seats.

Newspaper

The local newspaper is a very important institution in a small town. It serves as the public forum and unifying force. Under the best editors and publishers, small-town newspapers can be the single most influential force operating in a community. Also, the size and frequency of the newspaper are pretty good indicators of community vitality. Thirty-four of the 100 towns in this book have a weekly; 65 have a paper appearing between three times a week and daily. The one town without its own newspaper is covered by a neighboring town.

Institution of Higher Learning

The presence of a two- or four-year college or a university has at least two important effects. Beyond simply creating jobs and bolstering the local economy with student and staff spending, the better colleges also create or import ideas, through lectures and concerts, for example. Forty-eight percent of the 100 towns are home to a two-year or four-year college or a university. A few have more than one institution of higher learning.

Scenery

Part of the charm of a small town is its setting. Towns located in obviously scenic places, such as the seashore or the mountains, and others situated on roads that the *Rand McNally Road Atlas* designates as scenic, were given credit in this category. We also took note of proximity to scenic places, such as state and federal parks.

Proximity

This final objective measure gives an advantage to towns that are within 40 miles of a metropolitan area, meaning 40 miles or less from the border of an MSA county.

INTERVIEWS

The next step after identifying candidate towns with the objective criteria was to interview town residents. The candidates for these interviews were nominated by local newspaper editors, library directors, chamber of commerce officials, and other knowledgeable residents. The purpose of the interviews, which were conducted by telephone, was to reveal the town's personality. We wanted to hear people talk about what makes them proud concerning their town, how problems get solved, and what the future looks like.

We also wanted to make sure the objective selection process hadn't turned up any duds, such as places that appeared to be dealing inadequately with large problems or just seemed to lack the resolve to deal with them. Even the best small towns have problems; it's their willingness to respond that sets the best places apart.

To conclude, we have attempted to select these 100 places on an objective basis. But objectivity goes only so far in a small town. Very quickly, you run out of things to measure and must fall back—more aptly stated, plunge ahead—to the unquantifiable but nonetheless very real character of the place, revealed through its people and their care and concern about one another and the community at large. We hope the interviews reveal at least a little bit of the essence of each town. We believe all the towns are good places, for 100 different reasons.

The Towns

THE 100 BEST SMALL

WA
- Anacortes
- Kalispell
- Moses Lake
- St. Helens
- Lincoln City
- Newport

OR

MT

ND
- Devils Lake

ID
- Rexburg

SD
- Pierre

WY
- Lander
- Douglas

NE
- York

NV
- Yreka
- Elko
- Ukiah

UT
- Vernal
- Cedar City

CO
- Glenwood Springs
- Montrose
- Durango

KS
- McPherson
- Winfield

CA

AZ
- Page
- Bisbee

NM
- Silver City

OK
- Tahlequah
- Poteau

TX
- Mt. Pleasant
- Stephenville
- Carthage

TOWNS IN AMERICA

Grand Rapids · Houghton ·

· Bemidji

MN

Marshall ·

WI

Baraboo ·

Red Wing ·

· Monroe

IA

· Grinnell

· Nevada

Washington ·

IL

Greencastle ·

Carlinville ·

MO

Bolivar · · Rolla

Marion ·

West Plains ·

Harrison ·

· Batesville

AR

Oxford ·

Cleveland ·

West Point

LA

Franklin ·

MS

MI

· Petoskey

· Elkhorn Hastings

Warsaw · · Bryan **OH**

· Celina

· Crawfordsville

Wilmington ·

IN

· Jasper

Bardstown ·

Pikeville

· Danville

KY

Somerset ·

WV

Greeneville · Boone ·

Hendersonville ·

TN

Crossville ·

Hartselle · Cartersville ·

Fort Payne ·

AL

Brewton ·

GA

· Tifton

FL

Arcadia ·

Littleton

Lebanon

St. Albans ·

Middlebury ·

ME

Plymouth ·

· Rockland

· Bath

VT **NH**

· Franklin

NY

Brattleboro ·

Geneva ·

Penn Yan ·

Williamstown ·

MA

CT

RI

Essex ·

PA

Lewisburg ·

Shippensburg ·

NJ

· Smyrna

Martinsburg · **MD**

DE

· Easton

VA · Culpeper

Bedford ·

· Elizabeth City

Mount Airy ·

NC

Newberry ·

SC · Georgetown

· Beaufort

Anacortes, WA 98221

Location: On Fidalgo Island, across Deception Pass from Whidbey Island, in Puget Sound, 72 miles north of Seattle, 89 miles south of Vancouver, British Columbia.

Population: 11,451 (1990).

Growth rate: 12% since 1986.

Per capita income: $11,207 (1985), 3% above state average ($10,866).

Geography/climate: Scenic seacoast island bounded on 3 sides by Puget Sound; often called "Gateway to the San Juan Islands." Temperate marine climate, usually cool, seldom extremely hot or very cold. January average temperatures: low, 33; high, 46. Trace to 3 inches snow. Frequent light rain, but location in the "rain shadow" of the Olympic Mountains keeps annual precipitation to about 25 inches, 10 inches less than Seattle. July averages: low, 50; high, 73. Warm, dry summers. Air conditioning unnecessary. No mosquitoes.

Economic base: Commercial fishing and seafood processing; seaport shipping logs, lumber, sulphur, petroleum coke to Pacific Rim; oil refining, marinas, tourism, retirees. Large payrolls: Texaco Refining & Marketing, 393 employees; Shell Oil, 324; Island Hospital, 260; Anacortes School District, 252; Dakota Creek Industries, shipbuilding, 200; Custom Plywood, sheeting, 130; Sugiyo USA, seafood, 190; Specialty Seafoods, smoked salmon, 125; Trident Seafoods, fish processing, 125.

Newspaper: *Anacortes American*, 901 Sixth Street, Anacortes, WA 98221. 206-293-3122. Weekly, Wednesday. Leighton Wood, publisher. Mark Carlson, editor and general manager. $30 a year.

TV, radio: Local AM station. Cable carries network TV from Seattle, CBC from Vancouver. NPR received off-air from Seattle.

Health Care: Island Hospital, 44 beds, 6-room emergency treatment center. 44 physicians, 11 dentists in local practice. Heliport. Hospital at Mt. Vernon, 14 miles southeast, treats head injuries, burns.

Schools: 4 elementary (K–5), 1 middle (6–8). In 1988, Fidalgo Elementary School was one of 7 statewide named a "School for the 21st Century." Anacortes High School enrolls 661, sends 40% to college. ACT composite score not available. High school was one of 244 nationwide selected for Excellence in Education Award, 1988–89, from U.S. Department of Education.

Educational level: 13.2% of Skagit County residents have 16 or more years of formal education; state average, 19%. County per capita expenditure for public education, $499; state average, $498.

Library: 52,000 volumes, 7,000 card holders. Expansion bond issue in 1987 won 75% approval.

Recreation: 4 city parks plus Community Forest Lands total 2,500 acres. Campsites, boat launching, ball fields, hiking trails. Fishing in 7 freshwater lakes on Fidalgo Island, 18-hole public golf course. Olympic-size pool. 5 marinas with 2,200 moorages. Charter fishing and boating. Community Theater, Anacortes Museum in old Carnegie library building, annual waterfront and arts-crafts festivals. Bowling alleys. 2 movie theaters. 2-hour drive to ski country in Cascade Range.

3 BR, 2 BA house: New, $125,000. Older houses sell in $80,000 to $90,000 range.

Cost of electricity: $.055 per kilowatt hour.

Cost of natural gas: $.50 per therm.

Sales tax: 7.5%

State income tax: None.

Churches: 15. Denominations: Assembly of God, Christian, Christian Reformed, Church of Jesus Christ of Latter-day Saints, Community, Episcopal, Foursquare, Lutheran, Presbyterian, Religious Science Center, Roman Catholic, Salvation Army, United Church of Christ, United Methodist.

The symmetry would have been beautiful—New York on the East Coast, Anacortes on the West Coast. After all, both were ocean ports and both were islands. The parallels may have run out some short distance beyond that point, but the dream was so vivid to civic leaders of the booming mill town above Seattle that they began to lay out Fidalgo Island just like Manhattan, with main north–south avenues and smaller east–west streets.

Anacortes (pronounced "Anna-COURT-iss") didn't turn out like Manhattan, but that doesn't bother anyone. This small island town in Puget Sound has contributed, on a per capita basis, commercial vitality that stands up to New York's, residents believe. First a lumbering center, then a fishing center, then a ferry port terminal connecting the mainland to scattered settlements on the San Juan Islands, then an oil refining center with the construction of big plants by Shell and Texaco, Anacortes has evolved. Lumbering has been replaced mostly by marinas. Tourism is big. Burl Ives has moved to town. Real estate prices are rising as people discover this pretty place with salt water in the air and fresh water from the Skagit River.

What residents say . . .

Leighton Wood, publisher, **Anacortes American:** "This used to be a workingman's town. Now there is a whole new group of people in Anacortes running the city. . . . Has the character changed much? Not really. It's just a nice place to be. Pretty even politically. . . . Conservatives rear up every once in a while. Some screwballs precipitated three months of argument last spring over certain ideas they found in school books, references to witches and devils. . . . Anacortes is the frontier. It's kind of the end of the line."

W.H. "Nick" Nichols, retired mechanic, retired ski instructor: "I'm a native of New York State, then Vermont, then here. My wife is the real native. She has lived here all her life. . . . Commercial Avenue is the main street in Anacortes, two miles long. . . . We have hills. I guess you would call them mountains back east. There's a paved road all the

19

way up Mount Erie, which is 1,400 feet. You get a fine view up there. . . . The fishing industry is still real strong. They've turned the old lumber mills into marinas. . . . Yeah, I still ski , at Stevens Pass. It's two hours 15 minutes and 114 miles from here."

Mrs. W.H. Nichols: "Like any small town, Anacortes is full of cliques . . . including people, Californians, if you really want to know . . . who move in because it's beautiful and then they want to change it to what they moved away from. Californians buy here and raise the cost."

John Donaldson, former resident of Orcas Island: "The whole area receives less rain than Seattle. The difference could be 10 inches a year. . . . It's cloudy a lot and drizzles. You either get used to it or you don't."

Jack Irion, principal, Anacortes High School: "Our district extends out into the San Juan Islands. This fall we have seven freshmen coming from Shaw Island. The ferry gets them here an hour late, so we have a taxi pick them up at the terminal. They're here for second period. We came up with an alternative learning plan for them. . . . They get a lot of homework done going back and forth. . . . Regardless of where you work in the Skagit Valley you can almost pick anyplace to live. More and more, parents are shopping schools. Increasingly each year, I receive calls about our school . . . from Maine, California, Oregon, the Midwest."

Jim Rice, mayor: "It's a fulltime job, the pay is $39,000 a year. . . . I'm on my fourth term and I love it. I like people. I like dealing with people. . . . The big project is our new sewer plant, started about two years ago. [Sewer] rates are up, to about $38 a month. Before, $4. There was quite a bit of controversy over that, but it's nationwide. We're not the only town doing this. . . . Real estate is up. There

are no vacancies as far as rentals go. It's difficult for young people. Hard to make it financially. Lack of affordable housing is the big problem. . . . Burl Ives is a good neighbor. He's lived here about three years. He did a benefit for the hospital a few months ago. . . . Everybody's a celebrity in my home town."

Mark Carlson, editor, **Anacortes American:** "There's a lot to lose here if growth is not managed correctly. . . . Anacortes has been at the forefront. We're the first city in the county to meet requirements of the [Washington] Growth Management Act."

Doug Everhart, director, Anacortes Public Library: "We have one of the highest per capita utilization rates in the state, approximately 14 books per person read per year. Last year the national average was something like five. . . . I think it is because this has been a maritime community. Traditionally, people associated with the sea have always read. . . . It goes all the way back to Melville . . . a long time without anything else to do but read. . . . You had to be able to read to navigate. . . . In addition, there is a very high emphasis on education, a large educated populace, and not an awful lot of distractions. . . . For our size, we have one of the largest children's libraries in the country, percentagewise. . . . Another thing, we do fine printing of poetry, with hand-set type, handmade paper, and printing on a platen press. It's called The Co-Op Press. The latest book is a 300-copy collection of Denise Levertov titled *Double Image.* . . . Basically, the idea is to continue the tradition of fine printing and its relationship to poetry. Some of our editions are in major university libraries. . . . Anacortes reminds me of Steinbeck's *Cannery Row.* It is very much like Monterey in the late '40s, transported into the '90s." ∎

Arcadia, FL 33821

Location: 49 miles southeast of Sarasota, 125 miles northwest of West Palm Beach, at the junction of U.S. 17 and Fla. 70, in southwestern Florida.

Population: 6,488 (1990).

Growth rate: 8% since 1980.

Per capita income: $7,150 (1985), 63% of state average ($11,271).

Geography/climate: Low, level land; elevation 56 feet. Subtropical climate. Mild winters with bright, warm days. January average temperature: 61 degrees. August is warmest month: 82 average. Hot, humid, and stormy June through September, with daily highs in the 90s. Most of annual rainfall of 53 inches falls during this period. Average relative humidity: 76%. Frequent fog during late evenings in fall.

Economic base: 60% of DeSoto County's 636 square miles covered by cattle ranches. Estimated 50,000–55,000 head generate $70 million in annual sales. Citrus is largest industry, producing $80 million. County ranks 7th in statewide production of oranges, grapefruit, tangelos, temples, tangerines. State hospital, $35 million budget, is largest single employer. Major private-sector payrolls: Central Moloney, transformers, 326 employees; Winn-Dixie, grocery, 160; Orange-Co, citrus, 128; Wal-Mart, retail, 125. Arcadia is seat of DeSoto County, a retail center.

Newspapers: *The Arcadian*, P.O. Box 670, Arcadia, FL 33821. 813-494-2434. Weekly, Wednesday. Clark Young, editor. $14.45 a year. *DeSoto County Times*, 128 W. Oak Street, Arcadia, FL 33821. 813-494-7600. Weekly, Wednesday. Patti Magee, editor. $27.82 a year.

TV, radio: Local AM/FM station. TV can be received off-air from major Gulf-coast cities as far as Tampa, 83 miles. NPR from Fort Myers.

Health care: DeSoto Memorial Hospital, 82 beds. 20 physicians, 7 dentists in local practice.

Schools: 2 elementary (K–5), 1 middle (6–8). DeSoto County High School enrolls 947, sends about 40% to higher education. 1991 composite SAT scores: math, 477, verbal, 447.

Educational level: 8.2% of DeSoto County residents have 16 or more years of formal education; state average, 14.9%. Per capita expenditure for public education, $466; state average, $384.

Library: DeSoto County Library, 16,000 volumes.

Recreation: 4 municipal recreation centers equipped with ball fields, tennis courts, shuffleboard courts. Also volleyball, gymnastics, basketball, aerobics programs. DeSoto County Youth Athletic Association offers baseball, football, softball for kids 6–15. Adult Athletic Association also organizes team sports. 2 golf courses, country club, boat ramps, movie theater. Peace River stretches 47 miles through county. Access just west of Arcadia on State Road 70. Wilderness river offers canoeing, camping, fishing, rapids-running.

3 BR, 2 BA house: $60,000 to $70,000 for conventional house in town. Mobile homes are popular.

Cost of electricity: $.08 per kilowatt hour.

Cost of propane: $1.59 per gallon.

Sales tax: 6%.

State income tax: None.

Churches: 51. Denominations: Apostolic, Baptist (18), Bible Covenant, Brethren, Christian church, Church of Christ, Church of God, Church of Jesus Christ of Latter-day Saints, Church of the Nazarene, Episcopal, Gospel Assembly, Jehovah's Witnesses, Methodist, Mt. Zion AME, Pentecostal, Presbyterian, Roman Catholic, Seventh-Day Adventist, Upper Room.

During the 1890s, while other places perfected their Victorian manners, Arcadia was staging some real, shoot-'em-up range wars. Beef cattle was big business, rustling was common, and cowboys were being shot dead. Thanks to a string of undeclared skirmishes over cattle, Arcadia became known as one of the wildest towns in Florida. Frederic Remington captured the action in a series of canvases based on the Arcadia of that era.

A disastrous fire on Thanksgiving Day 1905 leveled much of downtown. It was rebuilt quickly—and refurbished many years later in the Arcadia Main Street Program, one of the first downtown improvement programs in Florida. More than 370 homes and businesses are on the National Registry of Historic Places, many of them built during the Roaring Twenties. Today, cattle are fattened on industrial-size ranches around Arcadia, and citrus and watermelon are grown in the spaces in between. For excitement, everybody comes to town for the Arcadia All-Florida Championship Rodeo each March and July. It is billed as America's most dangerous contest, on a par with running as a Republican in DeSoto County.

What residents say . . .

R.V. Griffin, chairman, DeSoto County Board of Commissioners: "This is my 17th year as county commissioner. I'm a Democrat. If you're not a Democrat in this county you kind of miss out on election. Everything is settled in the primary. . . . Our growth from retirees has come from the working-class people who don't like either coast. Coming here they can live a little cheaper and have access to the coast at any time they want. . . . Our growth factor has not been exceedingly high, as it has on the coasts. Growth is good to a certain extent, but growth never takes care of itself costwise. . . . We're still oriented towards agriculture. Citrus groves and cattle. . . . I consider us still a small town. To some extent you could call it a little clannish, too. . . . When you move in you got to kind of prove yourself before you're accepted. That's not all bad, because you never know about a person moving in. . . . You should be down to earth, not a coat-and-tie man. Being a Baptist does not hurt at all. Southern Baptist, that is."

Adrian Cline, superintendent, DeSoto County Schools: "At our middle school, we have interdisciplinary teaching teams. It is not team teaching, which means two or more teachers in a classroom. We have clusters of teachers grouped together in . . . a suite of classrooms. Teachers get to know their students very well. We provide the teachers with common planning time so they can discuss common needs. . . . What we have seen is an increase in our achievement test scores. . . . The largest organization on the middle school campus is the National Honor Society. . . . At the elementary level, we serve limited English proficiency students and we serve the needs of our gifted. We do have a migrant population in this county . . . approximately 23 percent black, 4 percent migrant Hispanic, and the remaining white. . . . We have a complete guidance program. . . . Six years ago, 18 percent of our high school students went on to college. Last year approximately 48 percent went to college, due largely to making the course work accessible. The community college that serves this area has established a satellite campus here in Arcadia, and we've entered a dual enrollment agreement. . . . One good thing about working in a community where you've grown up all your life, you have a very good working relationship with the people. . . . Football is always the big sport. And we have basketball, volleyball, softball, baseball, track. . . . That's real important in a small community. We don't have an overabundance of recreational facilities. So the school becomes an even bigger focal point after the school day ends."

Sherri Ambler, administrator, health and rehabilitation services: "The schools have a pretty well-rounded athletic program. We have an athletic association that is basically parent driven and supported . . . a very strong 4-H program, lots of recognition for those youth. . . . When there's a need, this community is responsive in terms of volunteering in the schools, or the Red Cross shelter, or driving patients for appointments. It is a caring community, very much so. . . . Neighbors watch out for one another. And then you have very strong churches that provide for their members and the extended family. . . . What are the big needs? Within resources, raising healthy children, educated to compete, physically healthy and mentally having it together."

Eugene Hickson, Sr., city council member, funeral director: "I've been in the funeral-home business for 31 years. My grandmother owned it prior to me. Hickson Funeral Home. It's a service rendered to the town not only when a person is deceased but living. . . . We take people to town, take them to the post office. You're involved in the community. . . . I happen to be treasurer of the NAACP. It's a very active program to try to get justice for the black community. . . . It's improving, but it'll be like that the rest of your life. . . . Arcadia is a very unique town in that in 1971, when I was the first black elected to the City Council, out of eight candidates I was the top vote-getter in every precinct. . . . When I became mayor in 1979, the City of Arcadia had never had a black secretary. I made sure we got one. Also the Fire Department and Police Department, the Planning and Zoning Board and the Housing Authority. So there was a change when I became mayor, and the change has held fast. . . . It tells you you've got good and bad, but I think the good overrides the bad." ■

23

Baraboo, WI 53913

Location: 100 miles west of Milwaukee, 41 miles northwest of Madison, 200 miles southeast of Minneapolis-St. Paul, in south central Wisconsin.

Population: 9,203 (1990).

Growth rate: 12% since 1980.

Per capita income: $10,858, 5% higher than state average ($10,298).

Geography/climate: To the west, gently rolling plain, deeply cut by streams and broken by occasional hills or ridges. To the east, glacial landscape of moraines, bogs, and marshes. Pleasant summers; long, severe winters. January daily average high, 25 degrees; low, 8. Average 164 days below freezing, 25 days below 0. July daily high, 81; low, 59. 12 days into the 90s. Annual rainfall, 32 inches; snowfall, 39 inches.

Economic base: Tourism, manufacturing, agriculture. Devil's Lake State Park attracts up to 1.5 million visitors a year. Larger payrolls: Almet/Lawnlite, lawn furniture, 312 employees; Badger Ordinance-Olin, ammunition, 158; Baraboo Sysco Foods, wholesaler, 537; Flambeau Plastics, 420; Industrial Coils, 147; Perry Printing, 340; Teel Plastics, 185; Seneca Foods, 140; Baraboo Public Schools, 324; St. Clare Hospital, 257. Baraboo is seat of Sauk County.

Newspaper: *Baraboo News-Republic*, 219 First Street, Baraboo, WI 53913. 608-356-4808. Monday through Saturday morning. James A. Shawback, publisher. $72 a year.

TV, radio: Local AM station. 5 TV stations received off-air. Cable carries network TV,

PBS from Madison, Milwaukee, Chicago. NPR from Madison.

Health care: St. Clare Hospital, 100 beds. 18 physicians, 11 dentists in local practice.

Schools: 6 elementary (K–6), 1 junior high (7–9). Baraboo High School enrolls 597, sends 57% to 4-year college. Two 1990 graduates were National Merit scholars. Composite ACT, 21.3. St. John's Lutheran School, St. Joseph Catholic School (K–8). University of Wisconsin Center–Baraboo, 2-year campus, enrolls 350.

Educational level: 11.2% of Sauk County residents have 16 or more years of formal education; state average, 14.8%. Per capita expenditure for public education, $504; state average, $476.

Library: Baraboo Carnegie Free Library, 30,000 volumes.

Recreation: 11 city parks total 104 acres. Swimming pool, 6 lighted tennis courts, 3 ice-skating rinks. Devil's Lake State Park, 3 miles south, offers rock-climbing, scuba-diving, hiking, swimming, boating, fishing, camping, cross-country skiing. Circus World Museum. Al Ringling Theatre, movie house on the town square, built 1915 and proclaimed "America's Prettiest Playhouse." Wisconsin Dells, 15 miles north, is state's most popular vacation destination. 165 miles of snowmobiling trails in county.

3 BR, 2 BA house: $80,000 to $90,000.

Cost of electricity: $.06 per kilowatt hour.

Cost of natural gas: $.53 per therm.

Sales tax: 5%.

State income tax: 4.9% to 6.93%.

Churches: 20. Denominations: Assemblies of God, Baptist, Christian, Christian Science, Church of Christ, Church of God, Church of Jesus Christ of Latter-day Saints, Church of the Nazarene, Episcopal, Jehovah's Witnesses, Lutheran ELCA, Lutheran-Missouri Synod, Presbyterian USA, Roman Catholic, United Church of Christ, United Methodist, Wesleyan.

As every member of the older generation should know, Baraboo is where the circus spent its winters. Hometown of the Ringling brothers—Al, Alf T., Charles, John, and Otto—Baraboo kept the elephants and big cats and other regulars of The Ringling Brothers and Barnum & Bailey Circus between seasons. Though that era has ended, this Wisconsin town retains its title as "Circus City of the Nation." Circus World Museum, owned by the State Historical Society of Wisconsin, is a big tourist draw. And the movie house in town is the Al Ringling Theatre, a small version of the Great Opera Hall of Louis XIV's palace at Versailles. "The Al" is on Courthouse Square and shows first-run and classic films.

After the circus, Baraboo is known for Devil's Lake State Park, a spectacular gift of nature just three miles south of town. In return, Baraboo gives Mother Nature a helping hand by providing refuge and a breeding center for the rarest and most beautiful species of cranes in the world.

What residents say . . .

George Archibald, co-founder, International Crane Foundation: "Scientists on our staff travel to foreign countries to study cranes and develop educational programs to better assure the protection of the birds. We breed endangered cranes in captivity and send birds for rearing and release in the wild. We have about 130 cranes now, 15 species. . . . We're the only place in the world that deals with all types of cranes. We have many volunteers from the community, and many of our foreign guests stay at homes of people in Baraboo."

Tim Miller, superintendent, Devil's Lake State Park: "Devil's Lake is probably the largest and busiest state park in Wisconsin, and perhaps the Midwest. The property is about 11,000 acres . . . 415 campsites . . . between 1.3 and 1.5 million visitors a year. . . . We have this fairly pristine lake, used for scuba diving a lot. It's real clear, 20-feet visibility underwater . . . surrounded by 500-foot quartzite bluffs. There's a lot of rock climbing. People train here before they go on long climbs out west. . . . This year I was elected president of the Chamber of Commerce, kind of a first for any park superintendent in Wisconsin. . . . Devil's Lake pours millions of dollars into the local economy. My estimate is $10 million a year. . . . We have a mixture of the blue collar and white collar, internationally recognized industry, tourism, which gives you a very good retail base, plus a lot of dairying . . . and beef, Herefords . . . a couple of canning companies . . . corn, peas, and beans. . . . I live up in the bluffs and have a view of 25 miles to the north. This year's colors were the best I've seen in many years."

Sue Moore, branch manager, Baraboo National Bank: "We're from Long Island. About 20 years ago we lived in the little town of Oyster Bay. It was becoming citified and getting to be quite a problem. So we looked in upstate New York, traveled as far as the Mississippi. We stopped here to visit somebody and absolutely fell in love with Baraboo. After the first six months of homesickness, we've never regretted it. . . . There are three banks, two commercial and one savings. Our bank is locally owned and the largest bank in the county. I feel a good part of the reason we are at least twice the size of the other banks is that we are locally owned. . . . We have high taxes, comparatively, but we wouldn't trade it for anything. We have a very good school system, very excellent park facilities, good streets. We even have a zoo. It's not a Greater Milwaukee Zoo, but it's growing every year."

John Taapken, owner, Glacier Ace Hardware; chairman, Baraboo Improvement District: "The Wisconsin Legislature thought they needed to give downtowns a tool to work with. It's a special assessment based on the valuation within a defined area. Ours is a nine-square-block area. At 86 cents a thousand, it nets $20,500 annually. The money is used for promotions in the downtown area or face lifts or things the board feels will enhance the downtown. . . .

One thing we've done is make 'Open' signs. When the store is open you put out your sign. It's on a pole that projects from the face of the building at a 45-degree angle, a bright yellow triangle with red lettering, 'Open.' . . . Downtown can get real quiet all of a sudden. They're very effective. On our block, maybe six of these splashes of color, and you know somebody's alive."

Jeff Smith, general manager, radio station WRPQ: "We're locally owned and controlled, the only media in the community which is. Our primary focus is our city. We employ a full-time news director who spends most of her time in the community gathering stories . . . three local newscasts a day. In addition, we carry all the local Baraboo Thunderbird sports. . . . We're 24 hours a day, 250 watts during the day and 6.4 watts at night. It covers the entire city and a five-mile radius. It is an AM-stereo operation, the first in Wisconsin. . . . We play adult contemporary. Starting November first, we'll play soft hits, a mellower approach. . . . 95% of our music comes in via satellite from Dallas. . . . Downtown revitalization and bringing the business district back are ongoing big problems and will continue to be. The government is mayor and council . . . just beginning to consider hiring a city administrator. That is a hot potato, because of Baraboo's makeup of politicians. . . . Our prospects for the future are excellent based on the recent past. We have had good growth, stable industry, above average people coming in. Baraboo is viewed as a very good place to live. Real estate prices have skyrocketed in the past three to four years. . . . Even though we may not always agree with what is happening at City Hall, the town has done very well." ■

Bardstown, KY 40004

Location: 34 miles south of Louisville via I-65 and Ky. 245.

Population: 6,801 (1990).

Growth rate: 6% increase since 1980.

Per capita income: $9,650 (1986), 12% higher than state average ($8,614).

Geography/climate: On a hill, in hilly Kentucky country called the Knobs. Continental climate with 4 distinct seasons. Moderately cold winters with average 15 inches of snow. Warm, humid summers with average 26 days of 90 degrees or higher. 44 inches of rain a year. Intense rainstorms common in spring and summer.

Economic base: Industry, tourism, agriculture. Major payrolls: American Greetings, 763 employees; Inoac International, 470; Nu-Kote, 382; Owens-Illinois, 392; Barton Brands, 290; Heaven Hill, 300. Site of Stephen Foster's "Old Kentucky Home." Bardstown is seat of Nelson County, the "Kentucky Bourbon Capital of the World."

Newspaper: *The Kentucky Standard*, 110 W. Stephen Foster Avenue, Bardstown, KY 40004. 502-348-9003. Monday, Wednesday, Friday. Steve Lowery, publisher. $30 a year.

TV, radio: One AM, one FM station. Cable system, city-owned, brings in 36 channels, networks from Louisville, PBS.

Health care: Flaget Memorial Hospital, 52 beds. 28 physicians, 18 dentists in local practice.

Schools: Early Childhood Development Center enrolls 120; 1 elementary (K–4), 675; 1 middle (5–8), 490; 1 high school, 380. 1991 composite ACT at Bardstown High School: 19.8. 65% of graduates go to college.

Educational level: 10% of Nelson County residents have 16 or more years of formal education; state average, 11%. Per capita expenditure for public education, $349; state average, $314.

Library: Nelson County Public Library, 46,000 volumes, 8,500 card holders.

Recreation: Parks and Recreation Center includes Olympic-size pool, tennis courts, football and baseball fields, indoor skating, bowling. Bernheim Forest—10,000-acre wildlife refuge, arboretum, nature center. My Old Kentucky Home State Park has golf course, camping, and picnic areas. Twin cinema in town.

3 BR, 2 BA house: $100,000 to $125,000.

Cost of electricity: $.06 per kilowatt hour.

Cost of natural gas: $.40 per therm.

Sales tax: 6%.

State income tax: Graduated 2% to 6%.

Churches: 24. Denominations: AME Zion, Apostolic, Assembly of God, Baptist (7), Church of Christ, Church of God, Christian, Episcopal, Jehovah's Witnesses, Methodist, Presbyterian, Roman Catholic (3), United Methodist.

When Stephen Foster visited Bardstown in 1852, he was inspired to write "My Old Kentucky Home." In 1990, an estimated 101,000 visitors came to Bardstown perhaps in search of that same inspiration and in the process left about $12 million with local shopkeepers, restaurants, and inns. Though tourism ranks second to industry in economic importance to the town, it is far more visible.

Small wonder. Bardstown is a little jewel, frequently described as a pristine, picture-postcard paradise for nostalgia buffs. It is as clean and clear as a Disney re-creation, except these cobblestone streets and eighteenth-and-nineteenth-century mansions are the real thing.

Bardstown is also thoroughly modern. In 1966 it became the first Kentucky town to pass ordinances prohibiting racial discrimination in employment and housing. The municipally owned utilities generate an abundance of revenue, rare these days in small towns. And on warm, still days downtown, the air is sweet with the aroma of sour mash wafting up from the whiskey distilleries. Stephen Foster, take a note.

What residents say ...

Dixie Hibbs, member of City Council, town historian: "We have always been on the road to somewhere . . . always had lots of travelers, and many did stay. Our position as a district court of appeals in the 1800s brought us very good legal talent. . . . When you have professional people, lawyers and doctors, you also have education. We had St. Joseph College, used by young men from all over the South. . . . Sitting here in the middle of Kentucky, we were not isolated but absorbed things from other countries, other cultures. . . . We have four Japanese plants and an influx of Japanese people as residents. I'm going next week and take a Japanese language course. . . . We have been very fortunate in city government to look ahead and see what would be in the best interests of the community, and the community has been very supportive. We are very comfortable financially. Our bond-

ing ability is very good. . . . It's a lot of dumb luck, but first of all we had a mayor here for 25 years, Guthrie Wilson. His political contacts in the state, our location on a major highway between two north–south interstates, his ability to work with politicians, manufacturers, state government. . . . It's hard to believe we have all of this here. We're not a tourist trap at all."

Steve Lowery, publisher, **The Kentucky Standard:** "The forefathers in this community had extremely good foresight. The problem in most small towns is they lack money. Bardstown purchased the electric utility and has had this revenue base. The cable system eventually will be a major money-maker. . . . We had the benefit of a mayor who is probably the best politician I've ever been associated with. Gus Wilson, he owns a Chevrolet dealership. He has tremendous 'getalong' . . . a very articulate guy who can disagree without being disagreeable. . . . This community hasn't been incestuous. It has had the benefit of new blood, new ideas."

Celia Keeling, librarian, Nelson County Public Library: "Nelson County was a melting pot in the late 1700s. We have a large genealogy collection . . . Virginia, Pennsylvania, Maryland records, as well as Nelson County. We had a big reunion here last year of people whose ancestors had come from St. Charles, Maryland, in 1790. They came from everywhere, 500 to 600 people. . . . Our Tourist Commission has been giving us $1,000 a year for the last five years to build our collection up."

Robert Smotherman, superintendent of schools: "Our little school system is a 45-acre campus. All the schools are located on the same campus. . . . We are about 23 percent black, about 40 percent either free or reduced lunch, which indicates some sort of deprivation. We also have about 65 percent going on to college, the highest of any around here. There are a number of quite affluent families who send their kids to Bardstown. A pretty diverse student body. . . . The Early Childhood program is the first of its kind in Kentucky. Quite simply it is a five-day-a-week program for four-year-olds, nine to 12 and one to four. We run all the bus transportation to and from day-care centers . . . almost a necessity from the standpoint of working moms."

Lynn Ledford, president, Farmer's Bank & Trust, national commanding general of the Honorable Order of the Kentucky Colonels: "There are in excess of 200,000 Kentucky Colonels. It was founded back in the 1800s as private guards commissioned by the governor, more like bodyguards before you had real, paid security . . . an honorary thing, the way a local sheriff might appoint nonpaid deputies. Then in the late thirties it was revived and we got into the traditional dinner before the Kentucky Derby. . . . To become a Colonel you have to be active and to have done something in your community. Sometimes politics is involved. . . . A lot of Japanese recently became Colonels because of locating plants in Kentucky. Up until General Schwarzkopf came this last year, Mr. Toyota himself probably caused the most excitement at our annual dinner. . . . We are the largest nondues-paying organization in the world. . . . Everything we give away is to Kentucky-based charities. We hit a million dollars two years in a row."

Kim Kirkpatrick, director, Downtown Development Commission: "Our objective is to basically nip in the bud any problems that could arise downtown. We are fortunate right now we have a very vital downtown. Because we are historic . . . our downtown itself is an attraction. If we can only get people coming downtown to sightsee to shop in our stores as well. . . . We get funding from our Tourist Commission, a 1 percent meal tax. We also have a 3-percent lodging tax . . . and private funding. . . . We've hired a landscape architect to come in and do a streetscape study . . . lighting, benches, sidewalk pavement. We also had three gentlemen from the National Historic Trust come in and meet with 40 local residents, basically develop a plan of action for Bardstown. We've used it like a bible. It's working. . . . There is a real distinct pride in this community. I've never lived anyplace else except college." ∎

Batesville, AR 72501

Location: 80 miles northeast of Little Rock, 115 miles northwest of Memphis, on U.S. Hwy. 167.

Population: 9,187 (1990).

Growth rate: 1% since 1980.

Per capita income: $8,982 (1986); state average, $8,389.

Geography/climate: Rolling hill country approaching the Arkansas Ozarks. Elevation 365 feet. Long, warm summers including some high humidity and heat waves. Short, mild winters but with occasional ice and sleet. Annual average rainfall, 49 inches. Snowfall, 4 inches.

Economic base: Seat of Independence County, population 31,000. Retail trading center for large region—87,000 people live within a 30-minute drive. Poultry processing is the major industry, employing more than 2,000 people. Arkansas Eastman Co., maker of industrial chemicals, employs 630, including many professionals. Home of Arkansas College, a private, 4-year, liberal arts institution enrolling 800.

Newspaper: *Batesville Guard*, 258 W. Main St., Batesville, AR 72501. 501-793-2383. Daily, Monday through Friday. Jeff Porter, editor. 3-month subscription, $12.

TV, radio: 2 local AM, 2 FM stations. TV by cable brings in Little Rock, Pine Bluff, Jonesboro stations, networks, PBS. NPR available.

Health care: White River Medical Center, 136 beds. 32 physicians and surgeons, 14 dentists in local practice.

Schools: 4 elementary (K–4), 1 middle (5–6), 1 junior high (7–9) with 550 students, 1 high school (10–12) with 500 students. 52% of high school graduates seek higher education. Composite ACT, 21.3.

Educational level: 8.2% of Independence County residents have 16 or more years of formal education; state average, 10.8%. Per capita expenditure for public education, $374; state average, $350.

Library: White River Regional Library, serving a 6-county area, 127,870 volumes. Arkansas College library, 85,000 volumes.

Recreation: 5 city parks totaling 130 acres. Baseball is big, soccer and tennis are growing. Hunting for upland game, duck, deer, turkey. Boating, swimming, water-skiing on White River. 45 minutes by car to fishing and water sports at Bull Shoals State Park.

3 BR, 2 BA house: $50,000 to $75,000.

Electricity: $.095 per kilowatt hour.

Natural gas: $.52 per therm.

Sales tax: 5½%.

State income tax: Graduated 1% to 7%.

Churches: 41 Protestant, including Adventist, Baptist, Charismatic, Church of Christ, Episcopal, Lutheran, Methodist, Presbyterian; 1 Roman Catholic.

The busiest intersection in all of Arkansas is in Fayetteville, boom town of more than 50,000 inhabitants in the robust northwest corner of the state. The second busiest intersection is the corner of St. Louis and Harrison, in Batesville, population 9,187. By official traffic count, 20,000 cars pass through this small-town crossroads on a weekday. "There are many, many more people here during the working day," says Jeff Porter, editor of the daily *Batesville Guard.* "They all go home in the evening."

Batesville has jobs, and people drive 30 or more miles to fill them. Though the city proper has grown very little in the past decade, its importance as an employment and shopping center in northern Arkansas has multiplied. Batesville was chosen by the big Arkansas-based retailer as the site of the state's first "Super Center"—a 178,000-square-foot emporium extraordinaire. Porter describes it as "a cross between a Sam's Wholesale Club and a regular Wal-Mart store."

Having integrated one ordinary Wal-Mart some years ago with only minor damage to local retail enterprises, Batesville expects to coexist with the new addition. Porter notes that highway improvements will help speed people into town—and out again, too soon. What Batesville needs now, he says, is a tourist attraction.

What residents say . . .

Darrell Loyless, vice president and fundraiser for Arkansas College: "I would describe Batesville in four words. The first is beauty. It is a very pretty area with four distinct seasons, none of them incessant. Our fall can be glorious. Spring is the prettiest. The second word is history. Batesville is the second oldest town in Arkansas. We have some beautiful old houses with fish-scale siding and gables. The college is the oldest in the state, founded in 1872, and has a strong program. . . . The town is very plural . . . old families that have been here since the earth cooled, college professors from all over the nation, chemists, blue-collar, white-collar. The only thing we are not is racially plural, and in my mind that is a drawback. . . . The third word is civil-

ity. That doesn't mean we don't have a large slice of parochialism. The symphony comes up twice a year to play here, there is a community theater. Over and above all that, the average citizen of Batesville can go duck hunting, fishing in the White River. The last word I'd use to describe Batesville is creativity. How can we continue to provide jobs for our people—and make sure they are not jobs that pollute our environment? How do we open up to new experience?"

Sarah Cumnock, mobile librarian, White River Regional Library: "We moved here in 1976 from North Little Rock. We both wanted to move away from the city, in a sense, back to the land. Mike found employment. . . . In 1980, I took a job as book-mobile librarian. We serve Independence County and five other counties. One year we traveled 14,000 miles and checked out 14,000 books! Things have changed since '76. Batesville was much slower-paced then. . . . It's pretty country. A lot of the area I travel spring and fall is breathtakingly gorgeous."

Mike Cumnock, social worker, Arkansas Sheriffs' Ranches: "For kids here, a primary goal is to get old enough to have a car—or have friends who have a car!. . . . Small-town America is a stronghold of drug dealing because it's easier not to get caught bringing drugs into a small town. . . . A curfew was put in place two or three years ago at the suggestion of a juvenile judge. . . . Kids who have family or a support system, we make sure they can hunt and fish. Kids are hunting and fishing as soon as their dads will take them. If you're nine or 10 years old and get your first deer, you drive around town with it on the hood of the car."

Alma Ann DeSio, supervising nurse practitioner: "Baseball—that's what all the kids do. The boys play and the girls go watch, mainly."

John Saltzman, locomotive engineer, technical director of Batesville Community Theatre: "This season we have done *The Velveteen Rabbit*, a big success. Next is *The World of Carl Sandburg*, pretty close to a reader's theater piece. Since this is our 20th anniversary, we're doing *Rave Review*, a one-night show free to the public with pieces from musicals we've done over the years, a lot of Broadway music. I work for the Union Pacific railroad . . . handle coal trains. I was born in Mountain Home,

moved here in '77. . . . This is Hometown, America. It's a hard place to leave."

Jeff Porter, editor, **Batesville Guard**: "The big business here is poultry. We have two large poultry-processing plants . . . that industry is getting better all the time . . . they don't have enough chickens to keep them busy. . . . I think we're seeing a pretty good economy here. Diversity helps . . . agriculture in the southeast portion of the county, industrial firms in the northwest."

Diane Tebbetts, founder of Main Street Arkansas, consultant to small towns: "Batesville tended to be settled by gentry out of Virginia and Maryland. From the very beginning it was a trade center. . . . Our success has been in large part due to our leadership. Excellent mayor the last 10 to 12 years, excellent county judges, responsible fiscal management, looking ahead and seeing the end of revenue sharing. Batesville has two nationally registered historic districts, Downtown and East Main, and maybe a dozen other properties on the Register."

Terrell Tebbetts, professor of English at Arkansas College: "Batesville was isolated for so very, very long that it grew to be self-sufficient. Thus, the foundation of the college by the local Presbyterians. Like an Andy Hardy movie, 'We'll do it right here!' The only reliable link to the outside was the river. We had no paved roads out of this town until after World War II."

Dick Nelms, personnel manager, Arkansas Eastman Co.: "Batesville has a very large United Way campaign for its size—$200,000. It's money put back into the community that helps make the area more self-sufficient." ■

Bath, ME 04530

Location: One-third of the way up the Maine coast, on the Kennebec River, 35 miles northeast of Portland, 109 miles southwest of Bangor.

Population: 9,799 (1990).

Growth rate: 4% decline since 1980.

Per capita income: $9,238 (1985), 2% higher than state average ($9,042).

Geography/climate: Elevation 70 feet. Surrounding area is rolling farmland, forests, islands, peninsulas, bays, and beaches. Moderate climate influenced by proximity to ocean, about 15 miles southeast. Winter temperatures range from 0 to 40; summer from 50 to 85. Average rainfall, 40 inches; snowfall, 75 inches. Very pleasant summers; brilliant falls when foliage becomes red, orange, and gold.

Economic base: Bath Iron Works, shipbuilder, is Maine's largest employer, with payroll up to 10,000. Many residents work at the U.S. Navy station in Brunswick. Tourism, retirement living are important props to economy.

Newspapers: *Coastal Journal*, 361 High Street, Suite 3, Bath, ME 04530. 207-443-6241. Weekly, Wednesday. Richard Denzer, publisher. $20 a year. Daily paper serving the area is the *Times Record*, Industry Road, Brunswick, ME 04011. 207-729-3311. Monday through Friday. Terry Shaw, managing editor. $70.80 a year.

TV, radio: Local AM station. TV, NPR can be received off-air from Portland. Cable carries Boston stations.

Health care: Mid-Coast Hospital-Bath, 55 beds. 29 physicians, 9 dentists in local practice.

Schools: 2 elementary (K–4), 1 middle (5–6), 1 junior high (7–9). Morse High School (10–12) enrolls 567 students. 38% of class of 1991 went to 4-year college, 7% to 2-year college, 7% to technical schools, 41% to employment, 7% to armed forces. Average SATs: math, 477; verbal, 419. Bath High School Alumni Association, 100 years old, has raised half a million dollars in scholarship fund. Bath Regional Vocational Center, on high school campus, enrolls 251.

Educational level: 15.1% of Sagadohoc County residents have 16 or more years of formal education; state average, 14.1%. Per capita expenditure for public education, $484; state average, $398.

Library: Patten Free Library, 40,000 volumes.

Recreation: YMCA, with swimming pool, racquetball, fitness program. Lighted tennis courts, 18-hole golf course. Boating on the Kennebec River. Deep-sea fishing. Jogging, walking at junior high school. Outdoor skating at Goddards Pond. Rec Department schedules team sports winter and summer.

3 Br, 2 BA house: $85,000 to $95,000.

Cost of electricity: $.115 per kilowatt hour.

Cost of fuel oil: $.88 per gallon ("if it goes over $1, people start burning wood . . . lots of old, drafty houses").

Sales tax: 6%.

State income tax: 2% to 8.5%.

Churches: 14 Denominations: Alliance, Assemblies of God, Baptist, Christian Science, Episcopal, Foursquare Gospel, Nazarene, New Jerusalem, Roman Catholic, Salvation Army, Seventh-Day Adventist, United Church of Christ, United Methodist.

Synagogues: 1.

The first sight you see as you enter Bath is the giant crane, soaring 400 feet, at Bath Iron Works, the famous shipyard. The crane lifts and positions welded steel sections as heavy as 220 tons for merchant and military ships. It is Bath's hook to the world. Shipbuilding in the area dates from 1762, when Captain William Swanton launched *The Earl of Bute*. Hundreds of vessels have rolled down the ways since, among them, the gunboat U.S.S. *Vicksburg*, in 1897; the U.S.S. *Drayton*, in 1936; and the *Nevada*, in 1976. Since then, numerous other enterprises have been launched on Front Street, in downtown Bath.

What residents say ...

Craig Burgess, owner, Burgess Market, grocery; Burgess Computers: "The stores are side by side, in two separate buildings. The grocery store has a real old background. My grandfather in the '20s was a peddler off a truck. He used to sell groceries downriver . . . drive 15 miles down the peninsula. Then in 1941, he and my grandmother started the grocery. . . . It's 10,000 square feet, what we call a small store. We try to focus on personal service. At our meat counter there is no prepackaged meat at all. When people walk in, every customer is waited on individually. That's our edge over the large chains. . . . Downtown has been great for us . . . being downtown and in close proximity to the Bath Iron Works and most of the people. The national trend is that people shop daily. Households with two working adults don't have time to spend two hours shopping. They want to stop on the way home to pick up fresh produce, in and out in five minutes. . . . My education is in electrical engineering and computer systems. After I graduated from college in 1980, I went to work for Procter & Gamble and got heavily involved in computers. After working for them five years I really wanted to get back to Maine. I bought out the grocery business from my father, and I saw another potential market in Bath for the computer business. . . . There is a natural connection to the grocery business. You're not going to survive today, big volume, low profit, if you don't have state-of-the-art scanners, direct-store delivery systems. . . . Bath has a strong business district. It's doing well because of the uniqueness of the shops downtown. Nothing downtown is duplicated in the shopping center or mall. There are no vacant storefronts, that speaks to the uniqueness. All owner-operated. . . . I'm literally going back and forth . . . continually jumping from the grocery store to the computer store. . . . I like them both. But at the grocery store you've got people. 10,000, that's our customer count. When you consider the population of Bath is 10,000, I see just about everyone once a week."

John G. Morse, Jr., sawmill owner, real-estate investor: "Like a lot of rural towns in Maine, usually there are one or two families that have been important to the community in one way or another. We've been here as a family ever since the Revolution. Yeah, I guess we've taken a reasonably important part in the growth of the community. Our business is rather varied but basically started in 1801 as a sawmill. We still run one today, not the same one. The family was engaged in wooden ship–building, as most everyone was in the Bath area. In recent years we've become involved in real estate. . . . Shipbuilding, be it steel or wood, has always been an extremely cyclical industry, booming today and tomorrow it isn't anything. Bath Iron Works, ever since the 1930s, has seemed to be able to buck that trend. The employment level has gone up and down, but nonetheless the yard has been able to operate and prosper. In that industry, that is a very unusual thing. It is a fine company and the salvation of this part of Maine."

Mary Ella Rogers, founder Sagadahoc Preservation, Inc.: "Our mission was to document every building built before 1920. But since that included practically the whole town, we surveyed the placement of each building. The older ones, we guessed at when the house was constructed. The organization has had a great influence. Twenty-five years ago Bath was very much undiscovered as a quite unchanged nineteenth-century town. It wasn't at all fashionable in those days. . . . In the late 1960s, the big stores moved out to the shopping malls and there was nothing downtown except lawyers and banks. But John Morse, Jr., who owns most of the property down-

town, he was very supportive in getting the downtown plan through. In fact, I worked with him on an ad hoc committee. Bath authorized a $500,000 bond issue that paid for this . . . celebrating the nineteenth-century architecture of downtown. The City Council and my organization did receive an award from the National Trust for Historic Preservation. We were one of the very first to carry out this kind of preservation. . . . During the last 10 to 15 years, people have been attracted here because they like the town and its atmosphere. They've taken a house that's run down and put a lot of time and money into fixing it up. . . . Like many old towns, the churches are still quite important. If a person comes here and joins a church, they find a very warm welcome. I think that's true here."

Di Francis, acting director, Center for the Arts: "Two Congregational churches merged in the 1970s and left two of the most beautiful churches. Our [Center] is called The Chocolate Church because it's an old wooden gothic church painted chocolate brown. . . . We had to jack the whole church up and put in a new foundation, remove the pews and install theater seats . . . 296 seats, in the balcony 75 more . . . a very nice art gallery downstairs. We do lots of Maine artists, a folk group, Schooner Fare, they sing sea chanties . . . the Brunswick Choral Society, they do Gilbert and Sullivan every fall. They've just done *The Gondoliers*. We present the Portland Symphony Orchestra Kinderconcerts for children from the Bath school system. . . . We had the percussion in October, brass is tomorrow, March is woodwinds, April is strings. Most of the children are under six and have never been in a theater or heard a symphony orchestra. We figure they are going to be our future audience and supporters." ∎

Beaufort, SC 29901

Location: 67 miles southwest of Charleston, 38 miles northeast of Savannah, Georgia, just up from Hilton Head, on Atlantic Ocean.

Population: 9,576 (1990).

Growth rate: 4% since 1986.

Per capita income: $10,802 (1985), 22% higher than state average ($8,890).

Geography/climate: Georgia Lowcountry: elevation 21 feet. Town is an island—in a county of 64 major islands and hundreds of smaller ones. Maritime, nearly subtropical climate. Mild winters; hot, humid summers. Average growing season, 293 days. Average temperature: January: high, 59; low, 38. July: high, 89; low, 71. Possible sunshine averages 63% year-round; April and May are sunniest. Annual rainfall, 50 inches.

Economic base: Military personnel, dependents, and retirees; civilian employees of military; tourism; retail; county-seat services; some small-scale manufacturing. Military payrolls at Marine Corps Recruit Depot, Parris Island; Marine Corps Air Station; and U.S. Naval Hospital total $140 million. Civilian payrolls add another $34 million. Tourism attracted 260,000 visitors to Beaufort County in 1989–90, generating $61 million in local revenue. Estimated 3,500 tourism-related jobs total $16 million in payroll. Industrial payrolls: NWL Control Systems, aircraft flight and engine controls, 256 employees; Parker Dye Casting, aluminum and zinc castings, 91.

Newspaper: *The Beaufort Gazette,* 1556 Salem Road, Beaufort, SC 29901. 803-524-3183. Monday through Friday, Sunday. James Cato, editor. $62 a year.

TV, radio: 2 AM, 3 FM stations, including NPR affiliate. Local PBS-TV station. Network TV received off-air from Savannah. Cable available.

Health care: Beaufort Memorial Hospital, 99 beds. 42 physicians, 16 dentists in local practice.

Schools: 4 elementary (1–5), 1 middle (6–8). Beaufort High School, enrollment 1,200 is 65% black, 35% white, sends approximately 40% of graduates to 4-year college. Advanced placement courses in calculus, chemistry, U.S. history, English. Composite SAT scores of "around 1,000," with several students at 1,250 or above. League-leading football, wrestling teams. Private schools: Beaufort Academy (K–12) enrolls 385; Eleanor Christensen School (pre-K–6). University of South Carolina, Beaufort Regional Campus. Technical College of the Lowcountry (2-year program).

Educational level: 21.9% of Beaufort County residents have 16 or more years of formal education; state average, 13.4%. Per capita expenditure for public education, $283; state average, $403.

Library: Beaufort County Library, 90,000 volumes.

Recreation: 13 public parks and playgrounds, with ball fields, boat landings. Waterfront Park along Beaufort River has playground, pavilion, crafts market. 3 marinas in sight of downtown; 9 tennis courts, 7 local-area golf courses. Bowling, 5-screen cinema, community theater. Hunting Island State Park, directly east of Beaufort on the ocean, has 3 miles of beaches, boat-launching sites, camping.

3 BR, 2 BA house: $70,000.

Cost of electricity: $.06 to $.07 per kilowatt hour.

Cost of natural gas: $.53 to $.66 per therm.

Sales tax: 5%.

State income tax: 3% to 7%.

Churches: 34 total. Denominations: African Methodist Episcopal, Apostolic, Assem-18blies of God, Baptist, Independent Baptist, Southern Baptist, Christian, Disciples of Christ, Church of Christ, Church of Jesus Christ of Latter-day Saints, Episcopal, Holiness, Jehovah's Witnesses, Lutheran, Methodist, Nondenominational, Pentecostal, Pentecostal Holiness, Presbyterian, Roman Catholic, Salvation Army, Seventh-Day Adventist, United Methodist, United Pentecostal.

Synagogues: 2.

You may have seen Beaufort and not known it. *The Great Santini, The Big Chill,* and *Prince of Tides* all were filmed in the area. Beaufort translates romantic Southern movie-set qualities into municipal terms: live oaks draped with Spanish moss, antebellum houses, and water everywhere. They call it "Beautiful Beaufort by the Sea," and the message has not been lost on tourists and retirees, who are discovering Beaufort in growing numbers.

Spanish sea captain Pedro de Salaza discovered the place first, in 1514. After the Spanish Conquistadores came French Huguenots, English privateers, and even pirates. Plantations of the Lowcountry produced indigo and long-staple cotton for world trade in the nineteenth century. The Civil War brought an occupying army and ruined the economy, but otherwise left Beaufort relatively unscathed. Today, old plantations are back in business as the centerpiece of private resorts. Some days, the whole area appears to be switching onto the fast track, and that has some people worried.

What residents say ...

Lolita Huckaby, president, League of Women Voters; newspaper reporter: "The growth along the coast has been just phenomenal in this county. More and more truck farmers are selling off the land to small single homes, subdivisions, putting real pressure on the county government for infrastructure services. I think they're trying to handle it pretty well. . . . But the Republican [majority] don't seem to have a good grasp for spending and how to control it. When the majority first took over five years ago, they just held the line and everything got behind. Recently they started a building program, now $34 million . . . another courthouse, an administration building. That's a real sore point with a lot of people. Property taxes keep going up."

Ojars Jurjans, retired Marine: "I'm a Yankee transplant. I retired out of Marine Corps Air Station in 1979 . . . typically middle-class military retiree who's got an interest in the community and the plans for it, rather vocal in my criticism of local projects, mostly because of their negative long-range effect. . . . It was a quiet, gentle, picturesque area here which is slowly being commercialized, where there are traffic problems now and it's getting slightly congested. . . . The price we're afraid we're going to end up paying is the way that Myrtle Beach is going. It is almost impossible to imagine unless you were in Myrtle Beach in the '50s and are there now, it is so commercialized. We have passed zoning laws to prevent uncontrolled expansion. . . . Fishing and hunting here is terrific. We've got fresh water and salt water. . . . The deer season begins the 15th of August and ends January 1 because we are terrifically overpopulated. . . . Inland property is still reasonable. You can afford a nice lot and a couple of acres and still be within access of [boat] landings. If I were young enough to have any now, this would be the ideal place to raise children."

Julie Zachowski, director, Beaufort County Library: "We're at a real turning point. We're building a new library and will end up with 21,000 square feet on the first floor, another 10,000 on the second. We have been operating in a building of 5,600 square feet for 30 years. We are not automated and in the beginning phases of getting that implemented. . . . I grew up here. I've been with the public library 18 years. . . . The physical environment of Beaufort is beautiful. We are still blessed with natural resources though I think the community needs to be very careful about protecting them. It's still kind of a low-key place. . . . It can be very hot in the summer. . . . We have the usual pests . . . mosquitoes, and what we call roaches, which are really palmetto bugs. . . . We have a lot of history. Beaufort survived the Civil War because it was occupied. Therefore the houses were not burned down or removed."

Mary Jo Richter, president, Beaufort Little Theatre: "We're opening the season with *The Good Doctor*, by Neil Simon. In January, *Steel Magnolias*. Then a co-production between ourselves and the Raphael Sabatini company, *Electra*, the first Greek that's ever been tried around this town. The final production will be *My Fair Lady*, in the spring. . . . [Beaufort] is not an easy place to make a living. But you have to sacrifice that in order to get the lifestyle."

Ken Cowart, former president, Running Club of Beaufort: "This is probably everybody's favorite running route: a 12-K, starts at Waterfront Park, crosses the bridge to Lady's Island, goes a couple of miles along Meridian Road, covered by big oak trees with Spanish moss, real shady, then breaks across McTeer Bridge back into Beaufort. You can run more or less any time of the year down here. . . . Myself, I got out of the Marine Corps and work for an aerospace manufacturer in Savannah. I have two kids, one 10 and one three."

Patti Cowart: "Dean, my 10-year-old, is a straight-A student . . . and a black belt in karate. He's in the Beaufort County Gifted Program. . . . They meet once a week . . . teach the children how to find their own information so they become more resourceful, a lot of independent work. Up to this point I've been very satisfied. South Carolina has got a bad reputation [for education], as you know. Part of the problem is test scores. . . . We've been here 15 years and it has snowed twice. The nicest time of the year is March and April, and October." ■

Bedford, VA 24523

Location: 29 miles east of Roanoke, 24 miles west of Lynchburg, 210 miles southwest of Washington, DC, on the Piedmont Plateau of west central Virginia.

Population: 6,073 (1990).

Growth rate: 1% since 1980.

Per capita income: $9,356 (1985), 79% of state average ($11,894).

Geography/climate: Mild, mid-Atlantic climate, with moderate temperatures and well-defined seasons. Elevations range from 800 feet in southern half of county to 4,200 feet on Flat Top Mountain, in far northwest. Bedford is in geographic center. Blue Ridge mountain barrier buffers cold winter air from the north. January temperature averages: high, 46; low, 28. July: high, 87; low, 65. Average annual rainfall, 45 inches; snowfall, 17 inches.

Economic base: Diverse manufacturing, retirement living, bedroom town for Lynchburg, Roanoke. Agricultural products include tobacco, apples, peaches, dairy, beef cattle. Large payrolls: Rubatex/Bondtex, rubber products, 900 employees. Georgia Pacific, Bedford Memorial Hospital, over 300 each. Payrolls of 200–299: Piedmont Label; Sam Moore Furniture; Bedford County; Frank Chervan, furniture. 100–199: Gunnoe Sausage; Bunker Hill, food products; Bedford Weaving; City of Bedford; Coleman-Adams Construction; Elks National Home, retirement center. Galileo Electro-Optics, fiber optics; Jamco, truck brokerage, employ 50–99. Bedford County Schools, over 1,000. Bedford is county seat, retail hub.

Newspaper: *Bedford Bulletin*, 202 E. Main Street, Bedford, VA 24523. 703-586-8612. Weekly, Wednesday. Rebecca Jackson-Clause, editor. $18.95 a year.

TV, radio: Local AM station. Cable available. Network TV, PBS, NPR can be received off-air.

Health care: Bedford County Memorial Hospital, 352 beds. 22 physicians, 8 dentists in local practice.

Schools: 1 primary (K–2), 1 elementary (3–5), 1 middle (6–8). Liberty High School enrolls 966, sends about 40% to higher education. SAT/ACT scores not available.

Educational level: 10.3% of Bedford County residents have 16 or more years of formal education; state average, 19.1%. Per capita expenditure for public education, $413; state average, $430.

Library: Bedford Public Library, 30,000 volumes. Annual circulation approaching 300,000.

Recreation: Liberty Lake Park, 59-acres, is center of recreational program in town. 9 staffed recreational locations throughout county. Smith Mountain Lake, 20 miles southwest, has 500 miles of shoreline, 1,500-acre state park. Boat ramps, camping, trails, swimming beach. Blue Ridge Parkway, Appalachian Trail pass 15 miles to northwest.

3 BR, 2 BA house: $90,000 to $130,000.

Cost of electricity: $.055 per kilowatt hour.

Cost of propane: $.96 a gallon.

Sales tax: 4½%.

State income tax: 2% to 5.75%.

Churches: 21. Denominations: Assemblies of God, Baptist, Free Will Baptist, Independent Baptist, Missionary Baptist, Southern Baptist, Church of God, Church of Jesus Christ of Latter-day Saints, Episcopal, Jehovah's Witnesses, Presbyterian, Roman Catholic, United Methodist.

When Peter Viemeister began searching for the ideal small town, he set some standards. "I used taxes per capita. I didn't care what kind of taxes they were. If they spend it they've got to collect it one way or another. . . . Climate, I wanted not too unlike what I was accustomed to on Long Island, New York. . . . Absence of tornadoes, rare frequency of earthquakes. . . . I didn't use crime rate—I used school truancy rate. I also used the percentage of people who own their own homes, which is an indication of self-reliance. . . . Then there was access to higher education, on the rationale that culture generally swirls around centers of education."

He chose Bedford.

What residents say . . .

Jack Gross, city manager: "We're a combination of things. A bedroom community for Lynchburg and Roanoke, a retirement mecca. Lots and lots of folks move down here from New York and New Jersey. Bedford looks like what a small town should look like. We've just completely renovated downtown . . . considered one of the most successful renovations in the state, it capitalizes on existing, turn-of-the-century architecture. . . . Like most communities, the budgeting process is a little tight. Nevertheless, it's a thriving community. . . . Bedford owns its own electric system. The electric operation returns a contribution in lieu of taxes to our general fund. Taxes in general are one of the lowest of any city in the Commonwealth. On the other hand, our service level is about twice as high. We collect garbage twice a week . . . brand-new park opened a few years ago . . . racquetball court. . . . We have a skateboard facility, unusual for a municipality. Our insurance carrier assisted with the design. If you don't provide a safe place for kids to skateboard they're going to skateboard anyway. The project actually involved the kids. Every year we have a mock City Council, students from the middle school. They said they needed a skateboard facility so we would stop harassing them on the sidewalks. It's worked out very nicely. . . . The city owns and maintains the school buildings. We contract with the county to provide educational services. To understand what that means, you have to understand [that] independent cities are not part of counties. . . . It can become a very adversarial situation, very antagonistic. Annexations are extremely painful and dragged out, often referred to as annexation wars. To say that the city and county cooperate is quite unusual. . . . I've been city manager for nine years. Before that I was in Tennessee for 13 years . . . native of Wisconsin."

Rebecca Jackson-Clause, editor, **Bedford Bulletin:** "I was one of those back-to-the-landers in search of a quiet, peaceful place to live. Originally, my father's side of the family landed here in the 1600s. . . . We came back here sight unseen. We quit our jobs in Phoenix and loaded up the furniture. We drove to Lynchburg and stopped at the first real-estate agency we saw. Come to find out the realtor had a farm for sale. . . . We want to attract more clean industry to the area, generating jobs for young people, who have a tendency to go away to the larger cities. . . . When I came here 12 years ago we had only one little cafe downtown. Now there are four or five, including a very nice Chinese restaurant. . . . Main Street did a survey. Everybody wanted a Chinese restaurant. They went out and found a fellow in a neighboring city, Willis Yang, helped him locate here on North Bridge Street. . . . Bedford County is becoming more and more less rural . . . a lot of young professionals attracted to the area. . . . Our circulation is over 9,000 and growing. We'll be going to twice a week, as early as next year."

Barbara H. Ring, executive director, Chamber of Commerce: "Do you know about our famous buried treasure? We've been on *Unsolved Mysteries.* It's called the Beale Treasure. Some say Thomas Beale buried a hoard of gold and silver coins in the county in 1819, then died without recovering them. There's a code which supposedly tells where it is. It was written up in *Smithsonian.* It's amazing the number of people who come here, shovel in hand, thinking they are going to find it."

Peter E. Viemeister, author, antique dealer, activist: "I had been president of Grumman Data Systems Corporation, then ultimately vice president of Grumman Corporation. I left there when I was 50, which was 1979. . . . I've gotten in a lot of volunteer things, chairman of the city–county museum, officer of the local health foundation. But I have a small antique shop and an office in the back, where I write, slowly. I wrote *The Historical Diary of Bedford, Virginia, USA.* I also wrote *Beale Treasure: History of a Mystery.* . . . The folks here are Democrats and Republicans, but they are conservatives. They believe in family. . . . There tends to be a strong commitment to local churches, probably less than [there was] 50 years ago but more than in your usual urban situations. . . . One of the things true here and a general observation on my part: the smaller the town, the more likely it is that you know the other people moving around. You do not have that anonymity that allows you to be rude, hostile, aggressive, pushy. . . . You're kind of on your good behavior. . . . One of the most important goals we should have is to recapture the benefits of smallness. That's true not just in communities but in business and industry and government. . . . In smallness you have folks accepting more responsibility for themselves and the outcome of what they do. If that concept could be nurtured in public school and news programs and woven into TV entertainment, we could go a long way towards being more competitive internationally. Ultimately it comes back to the economic health of our society and the well-being of people . . . rooted in manners and basic values and ethics. The only place we hear about it anymore is in church." ◼

Bemidji, MN 56601

Location: 229 miles northwest of Minneapolis, 110 miles east-southeast of Grand Forks, North Dakota, in north central Minnesota.

Population: 11,245 (1990).

Growth rate: 3% since 1980.

Per capita income: $7,792 (1985), 59% of state average ($13,212).

Geography/climate: Elevation 1,356 feet. Generally flat, wooded terrain, with many lakes. "Bemidji is not the 'icebox of the nation,'" the Chamber of Commerce wants everyone to know. "There are colder spots elsewhere through the northern tier of states. . . . Lack of wind and low humidity also help make the cold temperatures less disagreeable." January average temperatures: high, 12 degrees; low, 11 below zero. July: high, 78; low, 55. Average number of days over 90, 3. Average rainfall, 41 inches; snowfall, 41 inches. A Continental Divide marker 12 miles north of Bemidji, at elevation 1,397 feet, indicates where lakes and streams flow north 3,200 miles to Hudson Bay, and south 1,800 miles to the Gulf of Mexico.

Economic base: Public services, tourism, wood products, retail. Agricultural products include sunflower seeds, potatoes, hay. Larger payrolls: Bemidji Public Schools, 800 employees; North County Hospital, 645; Bemidji State University, 587; County Government Office, 481; Potlatch, panelboard, 200; Johanneson's, retail, 152; Northwood Panelboard, 141; Bemidji Clinic, 120; DSC Nortech, computer components, 90. Bemidji is the seat of Beltrami County.

Newspaper: *The Pioneer*, Neilson & Pioneer Streets, P.O. Box 455, Bemidji, MN 56601. 218-751-3740. Monday through Friday, Sunday. $72 a year.

TV, radio: 2 AM stations; 3 FM stations, including NPR. Cable carries PBS, network TV from Minneapolis, Duluth, Fargo.

Health care: North County Regional Hospital, 89 beds. 33 physicians, 16 dentists in local practice.

Schools: 7 elementary (K–5), 1 junior high (6–8). Bemidji Senior High School enrolls 1,400, sends 60% of graduates to 4-year college. Minnesota offers College Options Program, enabling students to take college-credit courses tuition-free while in high school. High school is 3 blocks from university campus. SAT averages termed "above state." Catholic, Lutheran, Seventh-Day Adventist schools (K–8), Heartland Christian Academy (K–6). Bemidji State University enrolls 5,000. Oak Hills Bible College. Concordia Language Village, a foreign-language training center for elementary, secondary school students, located on Turtle River Lake, north of Bemidji.

Educational level: 17.3% of Beltrami County residents have 16 or more years of formal education; state average, 17.4%. Per capita expenditure for public education, $974; state average, $554.

Library: Kitchigami Regional Library, 24,000 volumes.

Recreation: 11 parks totaling 150 acres, with facilities for cross-country skiing, ice-skating, swimming, tennis. Picnic areas, boat-launching sites, curling rink, ball fields. 3 18-hole golf courses. Downhill skiing at Buena Vista, 12 miles north. Casino and bingo establishments on Indian reservations north and south of town. 3 theaters, 1 drive-in. Snowmobiling trails start in town and fan out in all directions. 6 million acres of lakes, forest lands in area; camping, fishing sites abound.

3 BR, 2 BA house: $60,000 to $110,000.

Cost of electricity: $.065 to $.07 per kilowatt hour.

Cost of natural gas: $.50 per therm.

Sales tax: 6%.

State income tax: 6% to 8.5%.

Churches: 30, including 8 Lutheran (AFLC, ELCA, LC-MS, Wisconsin Synod). Other denominations: Assemblies of God, Baptist, Southern Baptist, Christian Science, Church of Christ, Church of Jesus Christ of Latter-day Saints, Episcopal, Evangelical Covenant, Evangelical Free, Independent, Jehovah's Witnesses, Free Methodist, United Methodist, Nondenominational, Pentecostal, Presbyterian, Roman Catholic, Seventh-Day Adventist.

The name Bemidji is derived from the Ojibway, or Chippewa, phrase *Bay-me-ji-ga-maug*, meaning "a lake with water flowing through." The water flowing through is none other than the Mississippi River, which originates here. If the concept of a river flowing through a lake is difficult, consider the giant standing by the lake: Paul Bunyan, the great outdoorsman, who must be regarded as Bemidji's favorite son. He watches over his city along with Babe the Blue Ox.

What residents say . . .

Rosemary Given-Amble, nurse, author, former member of City Council: "I am a self-published writer of family history and city history. I had a fascinating mother. I and my children were the only ones who heard her stories of homesteading in Dakota, early Bemidji, and as a nurse in the front lines with the Mayo brothers. . . . Back in the late 1800s this was all Indian land, occupied by what was then called Chippewa, now Ojibway. The Indians were indebted to some of the fur traders. To satisfy that debt, the Indian chiefs agreed to give a portion of their land to the government.

The Reservation line was moved from below Bemidji to 30 miles north, opening this land to homesteading. The majority of people that took homesteads, including my family, were Scandinavian people who had come to take land on the prairie. When they found there was land in the woods, like their land back home, they escaped the flat, open prairie. . . . They were strong people with minds of their own. That characteristic still stands. I don't know whether you'd call it feisty. . . . In the early 1900s thousands of lumberjacks arrived, shortly after the railroad. The lumber companies were stripping the land of huge Norway and white pines. . . . You had the group of homesteaders, very Christian, very pious, very home-loving, on the one hand, and a town full of lumberjacks on Saturdays after being in the woods all week, drinking up all their earnings. That's a generalization, they were not all like that. As mother would put it, they were most gentlemanly when you met them on the street. . . . Beginning in 1907 there was a competition among towns up here for the site of the new normal school of the northern tier, Bemidji Normal School. . . . The Bemidji Townsite & Improvement Corporation had laid out the town, avenues running north and south beside the lake, and the names in the sequence of how they fit into our history. . . . Bemidji right next to the lake, where Paul Bunyan stands; next, Beltrami, the county; then Minnesota, America, Mississippi. . . . Right now I'm very much involved in water-testing of the Mississippi River. The river and the pollution start in Bemidji. We are very much concerned that we do not contribute to the latter. . . . It's a hard-working people. It is not a prosperous area. When you average the total income of Beltrami County, it must be lower than Appalachia. We have some who are a little better off, but we have no very wealthy people here. . . . We are in a constant recession here. We don't have a high economy but it's a stable one . . . logging and wood products, government jobs, the university, tourism . . . when one is up another is down. . . . We have learned long ago, to do anything we have to work together. I think we have more volunteers in our community than in most. A few years ago we honored our volunteers. We se-lected one person to represent each group and had a banquet of over 200 people. We can't have a beautiful, progressive city without someone putting a shoulder to the wheel. . . . That's a large part of the character of the community. . . . Graduates of the university will stay here even though there is nothing for them. They stay, anyhow, and make their little niche. . . . The story behind Paul Bunyan: as the loggers came across from Quebec, Paul Bunyan just kept moving further west . . . until he got as far as California, when he decided where he wanted to spend eternity. He came back to Bemidji. . . . Needless to say, I was chairman of the all-school reunion in 1987, the 50th anniversary of the Paul Bunyan statue."

Larry Young, executive director, Joint Economic Development Commission: "We haven't been doing smokestack chasing. We've been trying to find businesses that have potential and determining what it would take to expand. . . . I think overall the community has done fairly well considering the nation is in a recession. I work primarily with manufacturing companies. From what I see and hear, their sales have continued to hold very well. . . . We tend to be in an area of in-migration. This year we reached one of the highest employment levels. Again, that's not supposed to be happening in a time of recession. . . . Bemidji has never gone for the home run when it comes to industry and development. We've had a strategy of trying to diversify and encourage locally grown business. We think they're around much longer when that happens." ∎

Bisbee, AZ 85603

Location: 100 miles southeast of Tucson, 35 miles east of Sierra Vista, 4 miles from the Mexican border, in extreme southeastern Arizona.

Population: 6,288 (1990).

Growth rate: 12% loss since 1980.

Per capita income: $8,595 (1985), 81% of state average ($10,561).

Geography/climate: 5,300-foot-high canyon town in the Mule Mountains. Dry, sunny climate most of year. January averages: low, 34; high, 57. Snow, sleet, hail totaling 4.5 inches. "Last winter, I didn't even get my winter coat out," says Mayor Laverne Williams. "We never get below zero." July averages: low, 64; high, 89. Usually 15–20 degrees cooler than Phoenix, Tucson. 16 inches of rain a year, most in brief, heavy Mexican monsoons during July, August.

Economic base: Government services, tourism. Seat of Cochise County. Former copper-mining town now a center for artists, writers, silver- and goldsmiths. Growing retiree population. 31% of jobs are in public administration, 29% in services, 24% in wholesale and retail trade. Phelps Dodge, the copper-mining company, retains mineral rights and could restart operations. Trade across Mexican border is another long-term economic development possibility.

Newspaper: *The Bisbee Observer*, Warren Plaza, Suite K, 7 Bisbee Road, Bisbee, AZ 85603. 602-432-7254. Weekly, Thursday. Candace Ketchum, managing editor and general manager. $20 a year.

TV, radio: Cable carries Tucson TV stations.

Health care: Copper Queen Community Hospital, 49 beds. 29 physicians, 5 dentists in local practice.

Schools: 1 elementary (K–5), 1 junior high (6–8). Bisbee High School enrolls 435 (52% Hispanic, 48% Anglo), sends 30% to college. ACT composite score not available.

Educational level: 13.8% of Cochise County residents have 16 or more years of formal education; state average, 17.4%. Per capita expenditure for public education, $461; state average, $453.

Library: Copper Queen Library, 12,000 volumes.

Recreation: 7 public parks. Warren Ball Park has baseball, football, basketball, 4 Little League fields. Swimming pool. 10 tennis courts, 4 lighted. 9-hole golf course. 3 museums, 9 art galleries, 6 RV parks. Host to annual La Vuelta de Bisbee, a US Cycling Federation event on the final weekend of April.

3 BR, 2 BA house: $30,000 to $75,000 in Old Bisbee.

Cost of electricity: $.08 to $.14 per kilowatt hour.

Cost of natural gas: $.60 per therm.

Sales tax: 7%.

State income tax: 3.8% to 7%.

Churches: 19. Denominations: Assemblies of God, Baptist (Conservative, Independent,

Southern), Church of Christ, Church of Jesus Christ of Latter-day Saints, Episcopal, Jehovah's Witnesses, Lutheran Missouri Synod, United Methodist, Nazarene, Pentecostal, Presbyterian USA, Religious Science, Roman Catholic, Seventh-Day Adventist.

A century ago, the United States was being wired for electricity, and Bisbee, Arizona, was cashing in. Bisbee had huge deposits of copper for wire-making. The big mining companies plowed big money into the remote bordertown. Soon, a thoroughly modern turn-of-the-century community sprang up in Tombstone Canyon and the surrounding hillsides. It even had an electric streetcar.

When large-scale mining became unprofitable in the early 1970s, Bisbee fell on very hard times. The population plummeted. Victorian houses could be bought for back taxes. Today, Bisbee believes it is on the road back, nurturing a new economy based on tourism, retirement living, and the arts. But the biggest asset is Old Bisbee, the original town, which remains virtually unchanged from the building boom of 1904 to 1910 and is so full of Old World charm that it's frequently used as a movie location. The apparent big loss in population reported by the 1990 Census is worrisome—but may be a mirage, says Mayor Laverne Williams. "We are a border town and feel there are people here who did not want to be counted," she says.

What residents say . . .

Larry Tanner, director, Bisbee Mining & Historical Museum: "It's a small museum but we are just completing a major permanent exhibit that interprets the early history of Bisbee, the first 40 years, from 1877 to 1917. . . . We had a very sophisticated urban center here in the middle of nowhere. Bisbee was bigger than Phoenix or Tucson . . . investors coming in from New York on private railroad cars, a sizeable management class. It had all the amenities. The exhibit is funded by the National Endowment for the Humanities. We got a total of $152,000. This is really rare for a small museum. They thought the project was exceptional and have used it as a model for other museums. . . . Bis-bee's black eye was 'The Bisbee Deportation,' in 1917, July 12 to be exact. We're just two months into World War I when the miners go on strike. The price of copper had skyrocketed because of the war and the companies were missing out on huge profits. The copper companies got the sheriff . . . to deputize a whole mess of loyalists. . . . 2,000 people were rounded up at gunpoint, not only miners but sympathizers, marched to Warren, where they were held in the ball park. Before a kangaroo court, they were given an opportunity to swear loyalty . . . 1,200 still remaining were loaded onto cattle cars and deported to New Mexico. The train stopped out in the middle of nowhere. They were left there and told never to come back to Bisbee. They were finally rescued by the Army.... This is how things end, the last part of the exhibit.... Many descendants here of people who were deported still look at it as a grave injustice. The problem is it was never resolved. People will get in arguments about it even today, and of course the company feels guilty and sensitive.... The town is such a little jewel it can't go anyplace but up. It remains largely undiscovered. It could conceivably go the path of Santa Fe because it has such a rich historic fabric that's still intact. The local people take this for granted."

Valerie Miller, coffee-shop owner: "I heard about Bisbee when I was still living in Germany ... 'You must visit this little town. It's kinda neat, kinda cute, but you wouldn't want to live there because it's full of hippies' ... I'll never forget. We came to Bisbee. I was walking along the street. Somebody came towards me and said, 'Hi!' I looked behind me since this person obviously didn't know me. But it was me.... I thought, if people are going to talk to perfect strangers, how is it going to be when they get to know you? ... We do have older hippies. They're 40-on-up, kind of settled down.... To get into Bisbee you have to come through a tunnel. One of our artists wrote in great big writing, 'Time Tunnel.' Unfortunately, the city didn't see the humor or pathos and had it whitewashed out. What a shame! A lot of people come here and feel all of a sudden they've gone back 20, 30 years.... There is a great feeling of community here.... We have public transport, a bus run by Catholic Community Services, and the city kicks in so much money. But this year the city has had to cut back. So, today is the Bisbee

Bus Fund Raiser at the Elks Lodge, an all-you-can-eat chicken dinner. Almost everything has been donated. Every member of the City Council will have to sit in one of those dunking booths."

Stan Dupry, owner, recreational-vehicle park: "I've been here seven years. I was part owner of a couple of bicycle shops in Denver.... I fell in love with the town ... one of those emotional moves I haven't regretted. It's more than just the architecture and European feel. It has also attracted a unique blend of people. To say they are for the most part fairly eccentric would be an understatement. We get some real characters, a lot of gray matter in this town, and a wonderful blend of artists because the housing is still fairly inexpensive.... I'm in charge of advertising Bisbee.... We're very careful about this. We realize tourism up to a certain point can be a wonderful, clean industry. But past that it creates traffic problems and you find the standard of living for people living there actually goes down.... Approximately 80 percent of all the birds that can be spotted in the United States come through our area. It is probably no surprise that birding is a very lucrative market. Birders for the most part have a fairly nice level of discretionary income and don't deny themselves too much. What you have to do is create an environment. People who are into birding can stay in Bisbee. We are working right now on a couple of different projects...."

Lise Gilliland, librarian: "I grew up here but came back.... It's not an easy place to work, difficult to find a full-time job. I was on the verge of leaving when the library job opened up.... Our immediate plan is to move some of the collection down to the second floor. We're up on the third floor now. It's a three-story building that's been here since the 1900s."

Stan Strebel, city manager: "I came here three years ago. I'm the first city manager. Quite frankly, the adoption of the new city charter was quite attractive. It gave me the opportunity to establish a new form of government. Bisbee is a very challenging place to be. Much of the community is over 100 years old. Streets are old, sewer system is old. One of the most fascinating places you could be from a public-works standpoint. . . . This is a very unique place. Tombstone, which markets itself, is mostly manufactured and not very authentic. Sierra Vista, our big sister city about 30 miles from here, is a plastic place with every conceivable fast-food restaurant all on one street. Bisbee is really the only true community of the three, in my opinion." ■

Bolivar, MO 65613

Location: 150 miles southeast of Kansas City, 210 miles southwest of St. Louis, 30 miles north of Springfield, in the Osage Lakes region of southwestern Missouri.

Population: 6,845 (1990).

Growth rate: 9% since 1986.

Per capita income: $7,497 (1985), 73% of state average ($10,283).

Geography/climate: Gently rolling terrain, elevation about 1,000 feet. Modified continental climate generally without winter–summer extremes. Average temperatures: January: high, 44; low, 22. July: high, 92; low, 66. Average annual rainfall, 42 inches, with June the wettest month. Snowfall average, 16 inches. January is the driest month.

Economic base: Agriculture, manufacturing, health care, education. Polk County ranks among top 5 in Missouri for beef cattle, dairy cattle, hay. Southwest Baptist University employs 313; Citizens Memorial Hospital, 469. Other major payrolls: Teters Floral Products, artificial flowers, 250 employees; Wal-Mart, 195; Tracker Marine, boats, 178; Micro Magic Systems, computer software, 116; Southwest Electric Cooperative, 70; Liber-Tees, T-shirts, 40.

Newspaper: *The Bolivar Herald-Free Press*, 335 S. Springfield, Bolivar, MO 65613-0330. 417-326-7636. Weekly, Wednesday. Dave Berry, publisher. $52 a year.

TV, radio: Local AM, FM stations. TV networks and PBS received off-air from Springfield and on cable. NPR from Springfield.

Health care: Citizens Memorial Hospital, 60 beds. 2 clinics. 27 physicians, 6 dentists in local practice.

Schools: 1 elementary (K–5); 1 middle (6–8). Bolivar High School enrolls 455, sends 65% of graduates to college. Recent composite ACT, 21. 8 seniors in 1991 placed in top 3% of ACT nationally. Private Christian school (K–12) enrolls 25. Southwest Baptist University enrolls 1,732. Some public high school students take classes at university under a dual-enrollment policy.

Educational level: 9.8% of Polk County residents have 16 or more years of formal education; state average, 13.9%. Per capita expenditure for public education, $351; state average, $378.

Library: Southwest Regional Library, 116,000 volumes.

Recreation: 2 public parks, indoor and outdoor swimming pools, 10 tennis courts, golf course, fitness center. Stockton and Pomme de Terre lakes, both within 15 miles, provide water sports, camping, nature trails. Movie theater, bowling alley, 2 baseball fields, art gallery, 2 museums, community concert association. Major reservoirs about an hour distant include Truman, Table Rock, Lake of the Ozarks.

3 BR, 2 BA house: $45,000 to $55,000.

Cost of electricity: $.04 per kilowatt hour.

Cost of propane: $.50 per gallon.

Sales tax: 6¼%.

Income tax: 1.5% to 6%.

Churches: 16. Denominations: Berean Baptist, Baptist-American, Baptist-Southern, Christian, Church of Christ, Church of God, Episcopal, Pentecostal, Roman Catholic, Seventh-Day Adventist, United Methodist, Word of God Fellowship, Zion Lutheran.

The name is Bolivar, as in Simon, liberator of South America. It is a good thing the news of his triumphs reached into the heartland, for the Polk County seat of justice needed a name with some authority, and Bolivar seemed ideal. The name was formally adopted in 1835. Authentic pronunciation was not part of the deal, however. The Spanish sound is "See-MOAN Bowl-EE-var." But in southwest Missouri, they say "SY-mon BAHL-ih-ver."

If the accent is slightly askew, so are the streets, canted approximately 22 degrees off true north–south. The explanation, according to local historians, is that the settlement that was to become Bolivar was an early way station along the old Overland Stage trail, which inclined southwest.

Many years later, a native son of Bolivar named David Delarue inclined west to San Francisco, where he made a small fortune in stocks and, like a guardian angel, sent a bundle back to his old hometown at a time of particular need. Newspaper publisher Dave Berry sets the scene.

What residents say ...

Dave Berry, publisher, **The Bolivar Herald-Free Press**:   "People who have moved away but still subscribe read the paper more thoroughly than the people who still live here. They're probably more interested in information between the lines. [David Delarue] has long remained a subscriber to the paper and was aware that the economy here had taken a downturn. We'd had a local garment factory closed down. At its peak it employed over 300 people . . . left a building vacant and left us without a few jobs. He, being aware of that, made the first gift . . . some stocks that amounted to about $118,000. . . . Later he came through with a trust fund of $3 million that benefits the city, county, and six school districts. . . . Through reading the paper he realized a stately old house was available for purchase, in what he knew to be a good central location. So he bought the property and gifted it to the city for a new city hall. Then he came along with a pledge in excess of $300,000 to actually build the building. . . . He absolutely refused to have anything named for him. . . . Most newspapers in small towns do a 'progress' issue once a year. Most do it in January. We call ours 'Pride & Progress.' It's not every year you're going to be able to measure progress in a small town. That is why we incorporate the word 'pride.' "

Nina Jester, historical society: "Oby and Nina Jester, we are the unpaid curators of two museums, The Old Jail Museum and Northward Museum. . . . We just recently had a series of three programs on the Civil War times. The last one was called 'Baptizings, Hangings, and Funerals'. . . . We have some neat shops in Bolivar . . . Hacker's

Dress Shop, Horton's, Jester's, the one we used to own but don't anymore, a gift and glass shop. There's only two furniture stores downtown, both of them new. The one thing this town lacks downtown is a good grocery store. We have good banks. There's been a little airport. . . . I should mention the college. . . . It has been a wonderful business for Bolivar. The hospital is also good business. . . . The biggest business started in my brother's basement. My dad ran a nursery and greenhouse. His dream was to have an artificial flower business. The [Teters] boys took that idea and started in the basement of the big old house on East Broadway. They made sprays and wreaths and flower arrangements. They outgrew that pretty quick."

H.W. "Bud" Godfrey, CEO, Teters Floral Products: "In 1965, the Teters family started to move the business to Springfield. A group of men in town raised $500,000 to keep Teters in Bolivar. . . . They used to pay their help in silver dollars, so everybody in town would realize how much they were committing to the community. In 1966, the company I was associated with bought them out. I was one of the first outsiders in management . . . to build a sales force. I became president in 1976. We've gone from around $5 million when I joined, to $42 million. . . . We dropped the plastic flowers in 1977–78. Silk flowers are not really silk but polyester. . . . We have been very fortunate to be connected with two successful chains, K-Mart and Wal-Mart . . . like hitching your wagon to a rising star. . . . All of my marketing and sales people live in Springfield and commute. We have a four-lane highway. It's an easy commute. . . . The college brings a lot of cultural activity that probably would not be available without them. . . . Faculty wives teach in our school system, and that's good for the schools. . . . Have you heard about when Harry Truman spoke here? It was in 1948 and the president of Venezuela was visiting, so they picked out the largest town in the United States named after Simon Bolivar. Standing in the hot sun, Truman suffered third-degree burns on his head, and two of his bodyguards keeled over in the heat. Years later he wrote, there's only one place hotter than Hell, and that's Bolivar, Missouri."

L.D. Silvey, head of the Industrial Development Authority: "The economy is pretty stable, never affected as much as the fluctuations on either coast . . . because of diversification. . . . Many of the work force here live on small farms. They have some farm income, then one or both spouses work in town. . . . We've helped five or six manufacturers come to town. We sell them the land and take back a note for it, then give them credit for each new full-time job they provide. If they meet their employment objectives, the land costs them nothing."

Joe Lemmon, proprietor, Lemmon's Conoco Service, former mayor: "I served from '73 to '91, got beat in the last election. . . . You bet your boots I own a service station, and I'm proud of it. . . . A number of people away from here think that's something to grin about. But the mayor of any town if he's worth his salt volunteers his time and has to make a living. If he don't make it honest he makes it dishonest. . . . In 1973, when I was elected we had only four streets paved north–south and east–west. Every other street was dirt, gravel, mud, potholes. I attempted to get a sales tax passed and got it the second time by a 102-vote margin. We started rebuilding our streets in 1975. This year we have about 60 miles finished." ■

51

Boone, NC 28607

Location: 85 miles west of Winston-Salem, 95 miles northeast of Asheville, 15 miles from the Tennessee border, in northwestern North Carolina.

Population: 12,915 (1990).

Growth rate: 18% since 1986.

Per capita income: $6,935 (1985), 73% of state average ($9,517).

Geography/climate: Situated in a long valley within the Appalachian Mountains at 3,333 feet elevation. Temperate, humid climate. Average temperatures: January: high, 42; low, 21. July: high, 81; low, 60. Annual average snowfall, 36 inches; rainfall, 53 inches. Growing season, 158 days.

Economic base: Education, government services, industry, tourism, agriculture, retail. Appalachian State University has annual budget of $115 million, employs 1,725 people, county's largest single payroll. Tourism accounts for 2,500 jobs, generates $95 million. Other large payrolls: Watauga County Board of Education, 521 employees; Watauga County Hospital, 441; IRC, resistors, 252; Shadowline, ladies lingerie, 260; Watauga County Offices, 196; Town of Boone Offices, 133; Carroll Leather Goods, 148; Ribbon Textiles, 110. Boone is the seat of Watauga County.

Newspaper: *Watauga Democrat*, 300 W. King Street, Boone, NC 28607. 704-264-3612. Monday, Wednesday, Friday. Armfield Coffey, editor. $62 a year.

TV, radio: Local AM/FM station. Cable carries network TV, PBS from Charlotte, Johnson City, Bristol, Winston-Salem.

Health care: Watauga County Hospital, 141 beds. 49 physicians, 17 dentists in local practice.

Schools: 3 elementary (K–8). Watauga High School enrolls 1,250. Dropout rate, 3–4%. 40% of graduates go on to some form of higher education. 1991 SAT composite score, 914, second highest in state. Private schools: Anderley Academy (pre-K–12); Appalachian Christian School (K–8); Mountain Pathways School (pre-K–6). Appalachian State University enrolls 11,500. Caldwell Community College & Technical Institute, a 2-year institution.

Educational level: 20.9% of Watauga County residents have 16 or more years of formal education; state average, 13.2% . Per capita expenditure for public education, $312; state average, $390.

Library: Watauga County Library, 35,000 volumes.

Recreation: 4 city parks. Watauga Recreation Complex has 3 swimming pools, including indoor; 4 lighted tennis courts, basketball and volleyball areas, horseshoe court, tot lot, 4 playing fields, walking trail. Parks Department offers classes in dance, karate, gymnastics, various sports. 4 18-hole golf courses in county. Blue Ridge Parkway runs just south of Boone, links many recreational areas of the North Carolina High Country, a popular vacation site. Downhill and cross-country skiing, hunting, fishing, camping, hiking, birdwatching. Craft shops and museums. In town, 4 movie theaters have total of 14 screens. Bowling alley, roller-skating rink. Appalachian State University artist and lecture series. Equity Professional Theatre at Blowing Rock has a summer season.

3 BR, 2 BA house: $45,000 to $200,000. Median price home in area, $80,000.

Cost of electricity: $.08 per kilowatt hour.

Cost of propane heating fuel: $1.33 per gallon.

Sales tax: 6%.

State income tax: 6% to 7%.

Churches: 32. Denominations: Baptist, Independent Baptist, Southern Baptist, Christian, Christian & Missionary Alliance, Church of Christ, Episcopal, Foursquare Gospel, Interdenominational, Jehovah's Witnesses, Lutheran, Methodist, United Methodist, Nondenominational, Presbyterian, Presbyterian-American, Roman Catholic, Seventh-Day Adventist, Unitarian Universalist.

Synagogues: 1.

Alfred Adams, chairman of the First Union Bank, describes Boone as "The Second Garden of Eden." The evidence is irrefutable, as he has often explained to local audiences. Consider this: The first Garden of Eden was thought to lie 40 miles from Damascus. Can it be only coincidence that Boone, North Carolina, is located 40 miles from Damascus, Virginia? What's more, from the original Garden of Eden, "there rose four rivers," Mr. Adams points out. "One flowed north, one south, one east and one west." And identically the same phenomenon occurs at Grandfather Mountain, the 5,964-foot peak south of Boone. Mr. Adams also observes that residents of Boone, elevation 3,333 feet, are much closer to heaven than mortals who reside at sea level. On the other hand, if you're heading towards Satan's abode, "you can delay your entrance . . . by that much travel time," he writes, "and the way traffic gets in Boone, it's worth considering."

What residents say . . .

Robert E. Snead, assistant to the chancellor, Appalachian State University: "With the university about the same size as the town . . . we live fairly close together. When you have that many students in a small town, parking and traffic are the two things that cause the most difficulties. . . . About 88 percent of our students are from North Carolina. We are a teaching institution. We do public service and research, but by and large we teach. Full professors teaching freshmen classes. In terms of beauty, there is no prettier spot in the Southeast, and I'm not native of these mountains. Grandfather Mountain, a little more than a mile high, is one of the oldest in the world. . . . The reason they are called the Blue Ridge Mountains, part of that is pollution. It is not ours but comes from the industrial Piedmont as prevailing wind backs it up. . . . Appalachian enjoys the reputation of being a very friendly campus. Everyone is on a first-name basis, from chancellor on down to janitor. . . . I think it is the look of this place. Howard's Knob and Rich Mountain, they literally go straight up out of the main street of Boone. Wherever you look you see green. It is tranquil and peace-ful-looking. That relaxes people and makes them more friendly."

Rogers Whitener, emeritus professor of English, Appalachian State University: "I did a folk column called 'Folkways & Folk-speech' for about 19 years. It was initiated by the Appalachian Consortium . . . moun-tain colleges and universities and others in-terested in trying to save what was worth saving in the mountains . . . traditions, ma-terial things. . . . A lot has fallen by the way. TV has made inroads, obviously. Modern ve-hicles have brought our mountain kids into consolidated schools. . . . At one time when Appalachian University was a much smaller place, in speech classes in particular, the pro-fessors oftentimes ridiculed the speech of freshmen and sophomore students and in so doing eliminated a lot of very effective folk expressions. Very colorful type of speech was supplanted by Standard English. . . . Now we're trying to recover those things. . . . We were at one time tabbed 'The Lost Prov-inces' in this area because the roads were so bad and we were so isolated here. We were really cut off from cultural opportunities ex-cept those manufactured locally."

Armfield Coffey, editor, **Watauga Democrat:** "The issues? The ecology, primarily. We're near national forests, and the clear-cutting of forests is a concern. Also, preservation of the rivers, and overdevelopment, trying to control development in the whole area. It's been slip-shod in the past, but now the county and town are zoning areas. We have a lot of people mov-ing here from Florida. It's a nice climate, es-pecially in the summer. . . . Downtown Boone is very viable. King Street is the main street. We have a couple of outlying shop-ping centers and the Boone Mall. . . . We need some four-lane highways into the city."

Sherri Carreker, principal, Watauga High School: "Eight elementary schools feed into the high school. It's the only high school in the county. Changing to middle school was voted down by the community. We'd have to have two middle schools, and kids would be riding out of their commu-nity for quite some time. So we have a mid-dle school concept within each elementary school. . . . Some students coming to us were used to having 18 members in their eighth grade. With a ninth-grade class of 389, we have to help them make the transition. . . . We were ranked second in the state on SAT scores. Being second to Chapel Hill, we are very excited. Students come back to us and say they are very well prepared for college. . . . A lot of attention has always been paid to college-bound and students with special needs. We are now fo-cusing on our middle majority students, preparing them to enter the work force or community college. Often they just don't get real clear direction. We're beginning to look at the curriculum and evaluate it, do away with what is not pertinent. Some of our students can receive community-college credit before they leave. We are now put-ting Algebra I in elementary school and Probability and Statistics at the senior level. . . . The 'Stay In School' program just started August 1 with our Chamber of Commerce. Community businesses are signing agreements with local schools. If they know a student is thinking about dropping out, they're encouraging them to work no more than four hours a day. Stu-dents who drop out tend to come back. . . . We always seem to have a surplus of excel-lent teachers who apply for positions here. That has a lot to do with the fact we are a university town. I attribute some of it to the geographic area. People move here." ■

Brattleboro, VT 05301

Location: 120 miles northwest of Boston, 15 miles southwest of Keene, New Hampshire, in southeastern Vermont.

Population: 12,241 (1990).

Growth rate: 3% since 1980.

Per capita income: $10,667 (1985), 11% higher than state average ($9,619).

Geography/climate: Valley town of the Connecticut River, elevation 310 feet, bounded by 1,351-foot Mt. Wantastiquet on the east and 1,500-foot hills approaching the Green Mountains on the west. Average January high, 29 degrees; low, 6, but with 16 days sub-zero. Annual snowfall, 68 inches. July average low, 56; high 81, but with 11 days at 90 or above. Annual rainfall, 42 inches.

Economic base: Trading center for population of 45,000 to 50,000 at the junction of Vermont, New Hampshire, Massachusetts. Cultural center of tri-state region. Wholesale food distribution point. Tourist stop-off on I-91 New England axis. 10 largest payrolls: Brattleboro Retreat, psychiatric hospital; C&S Wholesale Grocers; Vermont National Bank; Vermont Yankee Nuclear Power Company; Brattleboro Memorial Hospital; Brattleboro School Department; The Book Press, book manufacturers; Specialty Paperboard; G&S Precision, instruments; Stow-Mills, natural foods. Apple growing, maple sugar, dairying.

Newspaper: *Brattleboro Reformer*, Black Mountain Road, P.O. Box 802, Brattleboro, VT 05301. 802-254-2311. Mornings, Monday through Saturday. Stephen Fay, editor. $10 a month.

TV, radio: 2 local AM/FM stations. Cable carries network TV from Boston, New York, Hartford, and Portland, Maine. NPR from Windsor, Vermont; Amherst, Massachusetts.

Health care: Brattleboro Memorial Hospital, 100 beds. 35 physicians, 20 dentists in local practice.

Schools: 4 elementary (K–6), 1 middle (7–8), 326 students. Brattleboro Union High School enrolls 938, sends 45% to 4-year college, 15% to 2-year college. 2 National Merit Finalists. Composite SAT scores: math, 494; verbal, 460. Advanced-placement courses offered.

Educational level: 19.7% of Windham County residents have 16 or more years of formal education; state average, 19.0%. Per capita expenditure for public education, $528; state average, $468.

Library: Brooks Memorial Library, 150,000 volumes. Annual circulation, 345,000, one of the highest in state.

Recreation: 390-acre Living Memorial Park has swimming pool, lighted softball diamonds, Small Fry baseball field, basketball and tennis courts, ice-skating rink, cross-country ski trail, 15-meter ski jump, 1,200-foot ski lift, outdoor amphitheater. Canoeing, fishing in Connecticut and West rivers. Swimming holes along both rivers. Daily-fee 9-hole golf course; 3 18-hole courses nearby. Numerous cross-country and alpine skiing sites. Mount Snow, Stratton, Haystack, Maple Valley. Harris Hill Ski Jump, 70 meters, attracts U.S., European ski jumpers to annual competition each Washington's Birthday week.

3 BR, 2 BA house: $100,000 to $150,000.

Cost of electricity: $.10 to $.11 per kilowatt hour.

Cost of propane: $1 per gallon.

Sales tax: 5%.

State income tax: 2.5% of modified federal income tax liability.

Churches: 20. Denominations: Baha'i, Baptist, Christian Fellowship, Christian & Missionary Alliance, Church of Christ, Congregational, Episcopal, Jehovah's Witnesses, Lutheran, Pentecostal, Roman Catholic, Seventh-Day Adventist, Society of Friends, Unitarian Universalist.

Synagogues: 1.

Residents speak of the diversity and variety of Brattleboro. That quality is immediately apparent on Main Street, which is barely five blocks long and neatly anchored at each end by a small park. Packed cheek-by-jowl along this short commercial strip are, to name only the prominent residents, Gothic Revival, Southern, Victorian, High Victorian Gothic, Second Empire, Art Deco, and Italianate Revival. The walking-tour leaflet calls it "a wonderful hodgepodge of 170 years of architectural styles, shapes, and ideas."

"Downtown is vibrant," says longtime resident Hugh Bronson. "As soon as one store is gone another comes in."

Comings and goings to Brattleboro are facilitated by Interstate 91. It runs about a mile west of Main Street, hooking this small Vermont town to the economic and cultural mainstream of New England, including heavy winter ski traffic. There are seven colleges in the immediate area. It's an exceptional place in many ways, familiar in others.

What residents say ...

Martha O'Connor, member, Board of Selectmen: "I think the major challenge is the same as it is in many towns, finances. The town provides a lot of services to its people. The major source of funding is the property tax. How can we continue to have all the services we want and pay for them with the property tax? Some people say we have to provide less services. . . . Social services and human services are provided at a very high level. Whether those should be taken out of taxes and funded by voluntary sources, I don't know. . . . The people in Brattleboro seem to have a very great sense of caring. Whether for a social or political cause, people get together and work hard. . . . Just recently we hosted the state bicentennial parade. There were no state funds. It was going to cost about $40,000 to have this parade. A committee was put together and the money was raised. . . . Most of your people are blue-collar people.

They work hard, but they believe in giving to others. . . . I was president of the State Board of Education for six years. I'm presently president of the Vermont State Literacy Board . . . just formed to make sure that by the year 2000 all Vermonters are literate. . . . I cannot remember when a school budget has been defeated in this area. . . . In small towns people have a chance to stop and think about where we're going . . . time to talk and visit with one another. We meet often and we talk about all sorts of things. I think that contributes. . . . I don't think we think there is a problem we can't solve. . . . In large cities, that doesn't happen, at least not as often."

Hugh Bronson, former selectman, real-estate agent: "Probably the only problem, our tax rates are tremendously high. I've got a house appraised for $140,000. I pay $1,125 per quarter in taxes. But again, I don't worry too much because the services are magnificent."

Glenn Hill, town manager: "I grew up in southern California. What attracted me first and foremost was the job opportunity . . . and the area, its location close to cultural centers. . . . Brattleboro is the only town in Vermont that has the representative town-meeting format. Instead of everybody participating, we have elected representatives from each of the four wards. . . . My impression is it tends to add a little more efficiency to operation of the town meeting. Certainly it has its detractors, folks who believe everyone should have a right to be a participant. . . . They can speak to the meeting but just not vote. . . . I think Brattleboro is seen as a progressive community in the state . . . its commitment to the selectman-town manager system since World War II . . . real consistency in approach to municipal

issues. . . . I guess the underlying principle in Brattleboro is great respect for varying thoughts and opinions, a real blend of talent and experience."

Nancy Hagstrom, president, Brattleboro Area Teen Community Center: "Four and a half years ago, when the idea first came up, they were looking for someone really kid-oriented, and I filled the bill. . . . Many teen centers fail because they haven't been responsive to kids themselves, so we decided to have five kids on the board of directors. Also, a teen advisory committee works with the director, giving us the feedback to keep up with the times. . . . Admission is $3 Friday, $4 Saturday. Kids who can't afford it can apply to the director in private for a scholarship or can work for their admission. . . . On Friday nights they're not allowed to leave the Center until a parent comes for them or until closing time, at 10:30. . . . A policeman is stationed at the front door, not to control internal activity but to discourage the conglomeration of sleaze, as the kids call them, who follow around trying to sell them drugs or whatever. . . . They also have to leave any belongings, including coats and purses, at the cloakroom. This eliminates most possibilities of alcohol and drugs coming into the Center. . . . It's not a perfect world, and we don't promise that. But so far it's worked. Last Friday night we had 320 seventh through ninth graders. On Saturday night, we're averaging between 60 and 100 for grades 10 through 12. . . . I believe the real freedom we give to kids is setting the limits they need to have the freedom to grow. If you don't do that, they are so busy looking for the limits that they get themselves into trouble. The teen center provides those limits." ∎

Brewton, AL 36427

Location: 98 miles southwest of Montgomery, 60 miles north of Pensacola, Florida, in extreme southern Alabama.

Population: 5,885 (1990).

Growth rate: 12% decrease since 1980.

Per capita income: $10,348 (1985), 19% higher than state average.

Geography/climate: Pine forest flatlands. Long, hot summers. Short, mild winters. Growing season of 220–240 days. Average annual rainfall, 70 inches.

Economic base: Historically, forest products, drawing on abundance of southern yellow pine. Largest payrolls: Container Corporation, 550 employees; Brewton Fashions, ladies' blouses, 400; T. R. Miller, wood products, 425; Alabama Ductile Casting, 250; Frit Car & Equipment, rail-car maintenance, 75. Oil and gas production in Escambia County. Brewton is county seat.

Newspaper: *The Brewton Standard*, P.O. Box 887, Brewton, AL 36427. 205-867-4876. Monday, Wednesday. Jeff Stumb, editor. $28 a year.

TV, radio: Local AM, FM stations. Mobile, Pensacola TV stations can be received locally. 34 channels on cable.

Health care: D. W. McMillan Hospital, 91 beds. 13 physicians, 5 dentists in local practice.

Schools: Brewton City School System enrolls 597 in elementary (K–5), 498 in middle (6–8), 468 at T. R. Miller High School. Also, Southern Normal, parochial school of the Reformed Church. Composite ACT score at public high school, 21.3. 72% of graduates go to college. Jefferson Davis State Junior College enrolls 850 students.

Educational level: 7.2% of Escambia County residents have 12 or more years of formal education; state average, 12.2%. Per capita expenditure on public education, $396, 22% higher than state average of $324.

Library: Brewton Public Library, 32,616 volumes; Jefferson Davis Junior College, 30,000 volumes.

Recreation: 2 public parks, 15 tennis courts, 8 ball fields. New YMCA open 7 days a week has Olympic-length pool, Nautilus room, indoor track, racquetball and handball courts, group lessons, day camps. Private country club with 9-hole course. Fishing and hunting in 180,000-acre wildlife preserve in area. Gulf Coast beaches are about an hour's drive.

3 BR, 2 BA house: High $40s to high $50s.

Cost of electricity: $.075 to $.08 per kilowatt hour.

Cost of natural gas: Based on volume. For info call 205-869-3281.

Sales tax: 6%.

State income tax: 2% to 5%.

Churches: 52 total.

Once upon a time, Brewton was known as the richest little town in the South. Some local residents say it was the richest in the nation (though there are other contenders for that distinction, including Bryan, Ohio, for example). Brewton's high per capita income was created by a small number of "Lumber Barons," as they are remembered, who arrived at the tail end of the last century to cut pine and stayed to build extraordinary homes along Belleville and Evergreen avenues. They were generous people, and their descendants have carried on the tradition, funding many public improvements over the years—most recently, a $1 million YMCA completed in 1989.

Some of the wealth in more recent decades has flowed from oil and gas fields in Escambia County. When that industry took a nose dive in the early 1980s, Brewton suffered, losing 12 percent of its population over 10 years.

To stabilize, Brewton must remain connected with the economy of the region. It may be only symbolic, but the successful campaign to get the Amtrak train to stop in Brewton on its run from Birmingham to Mobile is seen as a major victory.

What residents say . . .

Jim Hart, attorney: "Initially they said Brewton was going to be one of the stops. But that didn't pan out. The train stopped at Evergreen, 30 miles north. . . . Our local Rotary Club took this on as a project, and it soon got to be a community-wide effort. We had hoped to get the stop at timetable change in October 1990, but they added a community 30 miles south of us. So we kept on plugging. We went to Washington and met with Amtrak personnel. We had a lot of input from our senators. But I suppose what did it was the little demonstration we staged along the track six weeks ago as the Mobile train came through. We knew the Amtrak president was going to be on the train. In fact he was in the engine and saw all our folks holding signs . . . 'We need Amtrak!' Obviously, he was impressed. . . . The service begins June 1. . . . We're building a boarding platform. . . . We think having Amtrak will help promote the community . . . and now you can leave Brewton and go all the way to Washington, New York, Boston."

Lee Bain, artist, teacher, manager of the Brewton Arts Festival: "It's a juried show, a high-quality show. It does include some crafts, good pottery and stained glass. . . . It's in a good location, on the campus of T. R. Miller High School, in a little pecan orchard. We limit it to 60 exhibitors. We have enough space to put 500 out there, and in the past we've had as many as 120. But that's too many. We limit it and all the artists sell a little better. We have a great party on Saturday night. People in Brewton love parties. Artists have told us they don't care if they don't sell anything but the party's so good they don't want to miss the show. We've had them from as far away as Texas and way down in Florida. But mostly it's Alabama, Mississippi, Louisiana. . . . There's quite a bit of money here . . . college-educated people who have traveled all over the world. They come back home and want some of the finer things here, too."

Robbie Cotton, top-ranked amateur golfer: "I started playing when I was 10. . . . Went to Troy State University, played golf there four years and made All American twice. . . . Graduated with a degree in marketing and now I work for Southern Pine Electric Cooperative. . . . I usually play 10 or 12 tournaments a year. . . . Just stepped in the door from the Montgomery Country Club Invitational. . . . I'm in sixth place after two days. . . . I'm married and have a three-week-old daughter. . . . My dad, he's principal at the high school. My mother teaches home ec and family living. . . . Brewton is just a small town, but we're not a country town. In a country town people sit on the front doorstep of the Five and Dime. . . . We do have a social class above the rest. . . . It's a real nice town. Most everybody knows everybody. . . . Kind of hard to find the opposite sex if you're single. But we're only 45 miles from Pensacola, only 80 miles from Mobile. . . . The main thing we need here is something for the younger kids to do."

Ethelene Harold, senior local office representative, Alabama Power: "For such a long time we've had just the same opportunities for employment. . . . It's changed having Container Corporation here. These young families who came with Container have really had a lot of input into the city. . . . I can remember when we had very few fund-raisers, and when we did we didn't do very well. Yesterday we had 'The Longest Day of Golf.' They got pledges, started at

seven and played all day. We thought in our wildest dreams they might raise $4,000. They raised $7,000 for the Cancer Society."

Doris Bruner, secretary to State Representative F.P. "Skippy" White: "I was born here. . . . I started out as a feature writer at the newspaper, and I was editor two years. Reporters don't stay here long enough to learn people's names. You will have a person to die who maybe has served 20 years in an important post here, and that person at the newspaper may not know it. That's general opinion. . . . Brewton is not a farm-oriented community as much as so many of the towns are in the South. We are timber-oriented. It's sort of an intangible thing, but it does make a difference. Not that one is better than another."

Eugene Stallworth, educator, first black member of City Council: "I just came back from my 50th reunion at Stillman College, in Tuscaloosa. . . . This is my second term on the council. I retired in 1986 from the county school system. I taught for 36 years, was administrator in the middle school for 14 years, art supervisor for four years. . . . I don't think kids are serious enough about school. If they do not have any help at home, you have an automatic problem. . . . We find so many foreign students excelling in the classrooms. They are taught so extensively at home. . . . Brewton is 40 percent black. I would think the relationship with whites is good. On the whole we've gotten along pretty good, and I'm going back to the 1930s. . . . I think there's room for improvement in the area of wholesome recreation. I would like to see public transit. . . . Presently we are seeking ways and means to improve our highway system. I-65 is within 17 miles. It would be wonderful if we could get a closer connection." ■

Bryan, OH 43506

Location: 60 miles southwest of Toledo, 56 miles northeast of Fort Wayne, Indiana, in northwestern Ohio.

Population: 8,348 (1990).

Growth rate: 4% since 1986.

Per capita income: $10,664 (1985), 3% above state average ($10,371).

Geography/climate: Flat farmlands. Cold winters, hot and humid summers. Average temperatures: January: high, 33 degrees; low, 18. July: high 84; low, 62. 140 days at freezing or below, 14 at 90 or above. Ground usually snow-covered 30 days through winter. Annual rainfall, 34 inches; snowfall, 34 inches.

Economic base: Seat of Williams County, retail center serving farm country. Diversified industry. Large payrolls: Aro Corp, tools, 715 employees; Bryan Custom Plastics, 425; Spangler Candy Company, 342; General Tire, 326; Challenge-Cook Brothers, 319; Ohio Art Company, 305; Bard Manufacturing, furnaces, 239; Allied Molded Products, 238. Hayes-Albion Corporation, 158; Tomco Plastics, 151.

Newspaper: *The Bryan Times*, 121 S. Walnut, Bryan, OH 43506. 419-636-1111. Daily, Monday through Saturday. Chris Cullis, managing editor and publisher. $83 a year.

TV, radio: 1 local AM/FM station. TV can be received off-air from Lima, Toledo, Bowling Green, Fort Wayne. NPR from Toledo, Fort Wayne.

Health care: Community Hospitals of Williams County, 70 beds. 20 physicians, 5 dentists in local practice.

Schools: 1 elementary (K–5), 1 middle (6–8). Bryan Senior High School enrolls 717, sends 70% to higher education. Recent composite ACT, 21.9.

Educational level: 8.3% of county residents have 16 or more years of formal education; state average, 13.7%. Williams County per capita expenditure on public education, $471; state average, $445.

Library: Bryan Public Library, including 5 branches, 255,000 volumes.

Recreation: City parks total 170 acres. Baseball diamonds, 2 swimming pools, tennis and basketball courts, playgrounds, picnic areas, ice arena. Public golf course. Country club. New YWCA has swimming pool, fitness areas, gym, running track, 2 handball courts.

3 BR, 2 BA house: $50,000 to $60,000.

Cost of electricity: $.05 per kilowatt hour.

Cost of natural gas: $.52 per therm.

Sales tax: 6%.

State income tax: 0.734% to 6.9%.

Churches: 24. Denominations: Alliance, Apostolic, Assembly of God, Baptist, Brethren, Calvary Chapel, Church of Christ, Church of Jesus Christ of Latter-day Saints, Episcopal, La Hermosa Concilio Latino Americano, Lutheran, Methodist, Miracle Revival Center, Nazarene, Pentecostal, Prayer Chapel, Presbyterian, Roman Catholic, Seventh-Day Adventist.

If a town is what a town does, Bryan must know how to please kids. One of its oldest industries is the Spangler Candy Company, maker of those kid-pleasing Dum-Dums, Saf-T-Pops, and Circus Marshmallow Peanuts. Another company, with the nondescript name of Ohio Art, is the source of that classic toy called Etch-A-Sketch, the little red box with two knobs and an aluminum-gray drawing surface.

Etch-A-Sketch was first manufactured for the Christmas season of 1960. According to a company history, it was an instant hit—so popular that the assembly line didn't quit until noon on Christmas Eve, when a last-minute order was shipped to Santa-helpers in California. Thirty-some years later, Ohio Art has dispatched more than 52 million units of Etch-A-Sketch to a world market. Many of the 38 employees dedicated to Etch-A-Sketch production have worked there since the 1960s.

Bryan takes pride in being far-sighted. "That's why the town has remained a nice place," says Chris Cullis, third-generation publisher of *The Bryan Times*. "We didn't wait until a mall arrived in town before we decided we better do something about downtown. Hence, we don't have a mall. We have a very strong downtown." To ensure the town retains its vision, Jeri Adams, at the Bryan Area Chamber of Commerce, has organized "Leadership Williams County," an annual program to educate 15 local men and women about the problems and prospects for the community, and instill a willingness to serve. The course runs from September to May, requires eight hours a month of each class member, and costs $400, of which the participant personally pays at least $100. Corporate sponsorship is limited to $300.

Bryan believes it has the oldest city concert band in Ohio. On Wednesday nights in summer, when the band strikes up a Sousa march on the courthouse lawn and townfolk gather to listen beneath the trees, the picture is museum-quality Americana.

What residents say ...

Tom Voigt, general manager, **The Bryan Times:** "I was on the original committee formed to put a new face on the downtown. Bryan was one of these typical midwestern small towns ... gloomy ... every building a different color, every one with a neon sign. we hired Ohio State University to do a study, $18,000 up front, and they told us it was a heck of a bargain. $6,000 came from the Chamber of Commerce, $6,000 from industry, $6,000 from retail merchants, a united effort. . . . When people go to a town they look at the downtown. It's really the image of the community. I don't care how many beautiful schools and churches you have. People are going to drive downtown and say, 'Well, this is Bryan,' or 'This is Greencastle.' . . . Our key was to have downtown viewed as a whole. Not one building should stand out. We wanted to eliminate visual chaos. . . . The first thing was a sign ordinance. We volunteered to have all the overhanging signs taken down, and 28 came down in one swoop. We just paid a local sign guy to do it for us. . . . We had some pretty nice buildings. You take the best of the old and trim them up. . . . We got rid of the parking meters. Meters don't make money, anyway, and they look like hell. Besides, we have good off-street parking. . . . Of course, being with the newspaper, we gave it a lot of PR. A newspaper that is really supportive has a lot to do with how well a community does."

Stanley Day, director, Bryan Municipal Light & Water Utility: "We purchase our power from the Ohio Power System for about two and a half cents a kilowatt hour and sell it for up to five cents. . . . If you were on the Toledo Edison system as a homeowner you'd pay about 12 cents. . . . There are a lot of things you can do with a municipal electrical system. We can be flexible with our rates in helping to attract industry, that's one good thing. We bought 88 acres of land for an industrial park through savings in the electric and water department. . . . We supply about $250,000 in free electric service to the city. Street lighting, traffic signals, things the city would have to pay for if it was an investor-owned utility."

Richard Reed, president, Bryan Area Foundation: "We like to seed projects for the community. We gave a sizeable donation to the YWCA when it was started, $100,000. Over time, we'll give to virtually every civic organization. . . . We're 20-some years old and have about two million three. We in-

vest the principal and only disperse interest . . . running $125,000 to $150,000 this year. Probably half of our funds go for 75 or 80 memorial funds. People like to know their name is going to go forward, and in a community foundation the funds will be managed forever. We get money from people we didn't know existed. People die with no relatives. We just recently picked up one, $110,000. We've had people living in Arizona, out of this town for many years, left $20,000 to start a memorial fund. . . . In the beginning we established a charter donor fund . . . become a charter donor for $25. We didn't pick up a lot of dollars but involved a lot of people, and we published all the names in the newspaper. . . . There is a feeling, I think, that there is not enough money in small communities, but people have seen what's being done here and started seven or eight community foundations in the area."

Grant Brown, retired civic leader: "I got out of the Army in December 1945. In June 1946, I opened the first drive-in between Jackson, Michigan, and Lima, Ohio, and Toledo and Fort Wayne. Brownie's Drive-In, corner of Walnut and Butler streets. Hamburgers and french fries. I had the first business with a parking lot in Bryan, and the first business with air conditioning, a big squirrel fan that pulled air over a wet straw mat. It didn't work very well in hot, muggy weather when you needed it most. . . . I had that business for 30 years. It was a nice place. The reason I enjoyed it, I like to be with people. . . . I was on the City Council, president of Rotary, Chamber of Commerce, president of the Ohio County Commissioners Association, involved in the Methodist Church. . . . Bryan is an outstanding small community.

You don't find very many of them. It takes an awful lot of work by a lot of people. We've been fortunate for years to have a lot of people give an awful lot of themselves."

Phyllis Goldstein, retired jewelry-store owner: "Just for an instance, I have recently remarried and my husband is from New York City. He loves Bryan. He was given a chance to go back to the company, but he has decided he wants to live in Bryan, Ohio, rather than New York City. . . . There's a caring here. . . . I pick up *The Bryan Times* and see where a family has lost all its belongings in a fire and there's not enough insurance. . . . I call up and find out what I can do for them, what we can do to help. It's being aware. We may not know these people personally, but they're part of us." ■

Carlinville, IL 62626

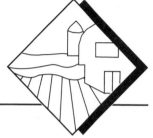

Location: 60 miles northeast of St. Louis, 223 miles southwest of Chicago, in southwestern Illinois.

Population: 5,416 (1990).

Growth rate: 1% since 1986.

Per capita income: $9,136 (1985), 81% of state average ($11,302).

Geography/climate: Mostly flat farmland north of town, quite hilly south, along Macoupin Creek. Tree-shaded streets in town. Continental climate. Strong seasonal swings. 119 below-freezing days, 8 below-zero days. 18 inches of snow. Average temperatures: January: high, 39; low, 19. July: high, 87; low, 66. Summers are sunny, often hot and humid. 28 days of 90 or above. Annual rainfall, 38 inches.

Economic base: Seat of Macoupin County. Home of Blackburn College. Agricultural economy supplemented by several major industrial employers: Monterey Coal Company, 425 employees; Prairie Farms Dairy, a "Fortune 500" company, 125; Central Illinois Steel, 100. Also, KarmaK, Software, an "Inc. 500" company. Carlinville Area Hospital employs 175; Blackburn College, 100.

Newspapers: *Carlinville Democrat*, 118 N. West Street, Carlinville, IL 62626. 217-854-2561. Weekly, Wednesday, Thomas E. Hatalla, Sr., editor. $12 a year. *Macoupin County Enquirer*, 125 E. Main Street, Carlinville, IL 62626. 217-854-2534. Weekly, Wednesday. Chris Schmitt, editor and publisher. $12 a year.

TV, radio: 1 local AM, 3 FM stations. TV, NPR can be received off-air from St. Louis, Springfield, Ill.

Health care: Carlinville Area Hospital, 50 beds. 7 physicians, 5 dentists in local practice.

Schools: 3 elementary (1 kindergarten only); others, 1–5. Junior, senior high share building, 6–12. Carlinville Senior High School enrolls 500 students, sends 60% to college. 1991 composite ACT, 24.1.

Educational level: 7.9% of Macoupin County residents have 16 or more years of formal education; state average, 16.2%. Per capita expenditure for public education, $462; state average, $442.

Library: Carlinville Library, 27,000 volumes.

Recreation: Neighborhood parks with tennis courts, lighted ball fields, swimming pool. Private country club with 18-hole course, tennis, swimming. Health Promotion Center. Carlinville Lake: boating, swimming, fishing, 50 camping hookups. Beaver Dam State Park, 7 miles southwest. Twin movie theater. Bowling alley. Senior citizens center. Second largest county fair in Illinois.

3 BR, 2 BA house: $40,000 to $60,000.

Cost of electricity: $.07 to $.09 per kilowatt hour.

Cost of natural gas: $.41 per therm.

Sales tax: 6.25%.

State income tax: 3.5%.

Churches: 15. Denominations: Assemblies of God, Baptist, Southern Baptist, Southern Baptist Convention, Christian, Episcopal, Lutheran, United Methodist, Nazarene, Presbyterian, Roman Catholic, United Church of Christ.

The Macoupin County Courthouse, built in 1867, was only supposed to cost about $300,000. The final tab was $1.3 million for possibly the largest courthouse in the United States at that time. Some people think this extravagant edifice ("a little Ionic, a little Greek, a little this and a little that, with a huge dome," says Lucy Klaus, president of the historical society) was designed to saddle local residents with so much debt that they couldn't afford to secede from Illinois. Another theory is greed, possibly explaining the mysterious disappearance of the county clerk. At least he left the vital records behind in Carlinville's "Million Dollar Courthouse."

The other celebrated local institution is Blackburn College, founded in 1837, enrollment about 500. Recognized as one of the strongest liberal arts colleges in the nation, Blackburn is known for its work program. Each student works 15 hours a week at some job essential to running the college: maintenance, cafeteria, office work, construction, etc. The program keeps costs down. Tuition, room, and board for 1990–91 totaled $8,750.

What residents say . . .

Miriam Pride, president, Blackburn College: "It has not been an easy road for Blackburn. Historically the college has struggled. But because of the work program we have been attractive to donor-foundation support and get some help that way . . . 90 percent of our students qualify for some form of financial aid. . . . It's been a remarkably good relationship with the community. We've educated teachers who are now teaching in the Carlinville school system. We've got students who work as emergency medical technicians for the ambulance service. We've got, I think, 50 students volunteering in the community . . . part of a mentoring program for junior high, working in nursing homes, at the recycling center. . . . The town and the college just share all kinds of facilities. They've helped us to be able to afford some facilities . . . night lights for our athletic fields. . . . I think in Carlinville you

still find a strong sense of the values associated with middle America. Family is still important. Kids are still really important here. The church figures largely in the community. Historically, the Catholic Church has been important to this town. People still work hard. We're very close to the agricultural economy and all the values that go with that. You're dependent on the weather and knowledgeable about the seasons. I think people here have a very strong sense of history . . . a strong sense of connectedness to the place."

Lydia Forbes, librarian, Blackburn College: "When the town really stops to think that Blackburn is one of their major industries, fine. . . . But, you know, college students can get on people's nerves. [Miriam] Pride has been doing a yeoman job of getting us together. She goes down and hollers at the Rotary Club. . . . You really have to be born here. The hierarchy is pretty emphatic, no different from any other town. A certain number of people all know each other, are all related, and live in each other's pockets. The college is a separate community. But we get on fine and go to each other's tea parties."

Donna Heinz, observer: "You can quote me as saying it's very similar to Sinclair Lewis's *Main Street.* We're talking old money and old families versus the new. If you remember, Doc and Carol Kennicott. The newcomer to the town has a lot of great ideas . . . but they didn't conform to a one-horse town. It didn't hit me until I was married. I looked around at Carlinville and said, 'By God, I know all these people.' "

Clay Heinz, funeral-home director: "My grandfather's family came over from Germany and got into the cabinet and furniture business at a time when there was a natural progression of furniture stores into the undertaking business . . . the ability to make a casket and a team of horses to haul it. . . . In a smaller town, other than in business, you learn to know people by a birth, a death, a marriage. It's a closer contact than city-dwellers enjoy, which can have positive and negative aspects. It does tend to widen the basis of acquaintants, and that can be supportive. . . . I know from doing an internship in a large town, even prominent people would not have more than 50 to 100 people show up for a funeral or visitation. For a well-known person in a small town, 500 to 800 will be there. . . . Carlinville is where I was raised. I don't think you could find a better place. . . . I know in my upbringing, the level of security here is very good. Kids can go to friends without parents shadow-

ing them. . . . Carlinville is a town of joiners. I have caught the negative aspects, that it is a very cliquish town. But it is also a very friendly town if you put yourself in a mood to meet people. If you're standoffish, Carlinville can be standoffish. . . . I was never enthralled by the job of being an undertaker. But it's a family business and because it's in Carlinville, the trade-offs seem to have an advantage."

Randolph Tinder, school superintendent: "I've only been superintendent since July 1. . . . I'd been looking at this superintendency for a number of years because of the reputation it has. . . . On the 13th of September 1987, the high school building burned completely. Rather than raze it and build new, we have the original facade and a brand-new building inside. It's bright, airy, carpeted and air-conditioned. . . . There are a lot of farm kids, coal miners' kids. Monterey Coal has its headquarters in Carlinville. It's a division of Exxon. They have a lot of white-collar people move in here from all over the world. . . . It's a good mix. . . . This just seems a very, very good place to raise children. That's one of the reasons I moved here. . . . My children are in sixth and ninth grades. . . . People value education here and are willing to pay for it."

Dan McCandless, reporter, Macoupin County Enquirer: "I lived in New York City for about six years. Coming here was a big shock, but it's been a pleasure. . . . My wife works at the college. . . . In New York, you learn to lock everything up and mind your own business. Here, you find people asking you questions that if it were anyplace else you'd say, 'None of your damn business.' Just outrageous questions like what church do you belong to, or why you did or didn't do something on a certain day. . . . A friend of a friend visited here, walked around the town square, and became really paranoid. . . . 'Why is everyone smiling at me? What do they know about me?'. . . . But to my father-in-law, who lives in England, it was like quintessential America. He loved it. . . . For the first time, we haven't consulted the most-stolen list before buying a car. We bought a Renault Encore in New York because nobody ever steals them. . . . We still have it. This is another thing about small towns: you don't make a whole lot of money. But you find out you don't need a lot of it. Once you adjust to that, everything seems to fall into place." ■

Cartersville, GA 30120

Location: 42 miles northwest of Atlanta, 24 miles southeast of Rome, Georgia, off I-75 in northwest Georgia.

Population: 12,035 (1990).

Growth rate: 18% since 1986.

Per capita income: $10,138 (1985), 99% of state average ($10,191).

Geography/climate: Rolling terrain. Hot, stormy summers; mild winters. Average temperatures: January: high, 50; low 31. Seasonal average of 60 days at or below freezing. Spring begins in February. July: high, 87; low, 68. Average 20 days into the 90s. Fall begins mid-October. Annual rainfall, 48 inches; snowfall, 3 inches.

Economic base: Once mainly a farm community, now industrial as well, with growing contingent of commuters to Atlanta. Larger payrolls: Shaw Industries, carpet, 1,407 employees; First Brands, plastic film, 634; Georgia Power, generating plant, 554; Goodyear Tire & Rubber, tire cord, 550; Spring City Knitting, apparel, 428; Cartersville Spinning, yarn, 350; Nantucket Industries, apparel, 350; Atlantic Steel, rolled steel, 292. Anheuser-Busch is building a plant. Cartersville is seat of Bartow County.

Newspaper: *Daily Tribune News*, 251 S. Tennessee Street, Cartersville, GA 30120. 404-382-4545. Monday through Friday. Charles Hurley, publisher. $95 a year. Same company publishes a weekly, Thursday, paper—*Herald-Tribune*—containing same news as Tuesday daily. $20 a year.

TV, radio: Local AM, FM stations. Cable available. TV from Atlanta can be received off-air. NPR from Atlanta.

Health care: Humana of Cartersville, 80 beds. 43 physicians, 20 dentists in local practice.

Schools: 1 primary (K–2), 1 elementary (3–5), 1 middle (6–8). Cass High School enrolls 697, sends 75% to college. 15 to 20 students taking SAT score 1,000 or better. Overall SAT above state average. Advanced placement courses in Spanish, calculus, U.S. history, English. Student can acquire 30–45 college credits in English, social studies through program in cooperation with Floyd Junior College, Rome.

Educational level: 6.3% of Bartow County residents have 16 or more years of formal education; state average, 14.6%. Per capita expenditure on public education, $451; state average, $389.

Library: Bartow County Library, 60,000 volumes.

Recreation: 6 vest-pocket, neighborhood parks with playgrounds. Dellinger Park, the main recreational center, has 13 tennis courts, 6 softball/baseball fields, football and soccer fields, 5 tot lots, Olympic-size pool, 20-station Vita course stretching 1.3 and 2.0 miles, 4 picnic shelters, 19-hole put-put golf, 4-acre lake with gazebo. 3 other ball fields in town.

3 BR, 2 BA house: $86,000 to $105,000, higher in select areas.

Cost of electricity: $.08 per kilowatt hour.

Cost of natural gas: $.53 per therm.

Sales tax: 6%.

State income tax: 1% to 6%.

Churches: 57. Denominations: Assemblies of God, Baptist (18), Grace Missionary Baptist, Independent Baptist, Southern Baptist, Charismatic, Christian, Church of Christ, Church of God, Church of God in Christ, Episcopal, Full Gospel, Independent, Interdenominational, Jehovah's Witnesses, Lutheran Missouri Synod, Methodist, United Methodist, Nazarene, Nondenominational, Pentecostal, Pentecostal Holiness, Presbyterian, Roman Catholic.

Statistics tell part of a town's story. For example, Cartersville is the seat of Bartow County, and the county ranks 23rd among 159 Georgia counties determined by personal income, sales-tax receipts, motor-vehicle tags, and assessed property taxes. (Although doubtless an accurate measure of performance, such a ranking does not—yawn—scintillate. Let's try for something warmer, homier. OK, how about. . . .) Cartersville public school kids continually score among the top 10 percent of 186 school systems in Georgia on the Criterion-Referenced Tests and Norm-Referenced Tests. (Better. Got any more?) There are only three opera companies in the state of Georgia, and one is The Grand Theatre Opera, in Cartersville. (Now, there's a statistic that sings!)

What residents say . . .

Jonalyn Bew, director, The Grand Theatre Opera: "My husband and I moved here from Florida, and we're experienced in the operatic field. I've studied and sung in Europe and he's done the same. He's the keyboard person and composer. . . . To tell you the truth we didn't intend to settle here but it just happened. We had purchased property in Marietta so we could be close to the airport, but my husband declared Marietta unlivable. We came here to visit my sister when The Grand Theatre was being renovated. I understand it was the first opera house in the South after the Civil War, but it had been converted to a movie theater. . . . People thought we were crazy for trying to start an opera company in Cartersville. I went and spoke to the Rotary . . . they got together and raised enough money for our first season. *La Traviata, Amahl and the Night Visitors, Madame Butterfly.* . . . It's funny, people at first thought we were talking Grand Ole Opry. . . . This is a singing community, so it was not that difficult to put together a chorus. My lead tenor was a local the first season. . . . This season we'll do *Magic Flute, Amahl,* and *Tosca.* . . . Our accompaniment is probably quite unique. What my husband does, he literally plays on a synthesizer all the notes that an orchestra would play, into a computer. Then the computer plays it back live. So you get a full orchestral spectrum, authentic orchestral song. As far as we know, he is the only one to have done this with classical music. Due to our budgetary constraints, he just decided to do this because it was necessary. It is possible for us to have opera without a plunkety-plunk piano. . . . This last performance was quite a wonderful surprise. We drew people from out of state, and a lot of our audience was out of Atlanta. . . . Tickets are $10, $15, and $25. Mostly my $25 section is sold out before the season begins. . . . The community has responded very well. The house is three-fourths full for most of our performances. It depends whether we're up against the Florida–Georgia game."

Nancy Haight, CEO, A.S. Haight & Co.:
"We are apparel printers. What that means is, the fabric comes to us from the dye house. We put the pattern on it and ship it off to the cut-and-sew plants. We turn out about 400,000 to 500,000 yards of fabric a week. We are very, very busy. Luckily, business is rebounding for us. . . . This is a family business. We've been in various aspects of the textile business since 1868, and I am the fifth generation. My grandfather purchased the Cartersville mills in the late 1920s; however, I'm the first member of my family to actually make this my home. I've been here six years. . . . I moved down from Massachusetts. . . . Life is much gentler. I'm not sure I would say it's any slower. There's a kindness here that maybe doesn't exist in New England, and I grew up in New England. We're rather clipped [there] and to the point. . . . This community has a very strong sense of volunteerism. Coming from the Northeast, I am really amazed at the commitment to this community by its citizens. Everyone I know volunteers for something. There's a lot of local talent. . . . Cartersville is poised to explode. There will be an outer perimeter around Atlanta, and we will be in the outer perimeter."

Woodrow Bradley, newspaper columnist:
"One of our chief assets is Dellinger Park, a beautiful park, a good place to walk and ponder nature. One cold day this week I met a lady who said, 'I thought I was the only fool out walking—until I ran into you!' So I wove that into the column. I try to add a little humor to it. And I went on to comment on communing with nature, and when we reach a time in life we begin to think of the cycle of life like the seasons. The column is called 'Comments,' and it appears on Thursday. I also write the 25- and 50-years-ago stuff for the paper. . . . I've been instrumental in some of the growth of Cartersville during my years here. . . . I had just come back from overseas in 1945 and bought a little business here. One of the councilmen wanted to appoint me on the school board. . . . We were a small, rural town. I found there were some inequities. So we decided . . . to open it up. We went through a very, very bitter fight that eventually changed our entire city . . . changed our school system from just a college-entrance course to a system that embraced the welfare of every child."

Susie Wheeler, retired teacher: ". . . I worked with the small, rural black schools. After we integrated our schools I worked as curriculum director until I retired . . . 1965–67, that is when we integrated. All our youngsters go to the same schools now. . . . The county below us is in the metro area. We are getting a lot of people coming out to live here, people who commute into Atlanta or surrounding areas. . . . Cartersville still has its own identity. In fact, people have fought becoming part of metro Atlanta. . . . We think we are one of the best." ■

Carthage, TX 75633

Location: 168 miles east of Dallas, 42 miles southwest of Shreveport, Louisiana, in East Texas.

Population: 6,496 (1990).

Growth rate: Barely 1% since 1980.

Per capita income: $10,625 (1985), 2% higher than state average ($10,373).

Geography/climate: Rolling hills, town elevation 282 feet. Mild winters, pleasant springs; hot, steamy summers; long falls, stretching into December. Average temperatures: January: high, 57; low, 38. July: high, 94; low, 73. Average 87 days at 90 or above. Annual rainfall, 44 inches; snowfall, trace.

Economic base: Historically a center of natural gas production, Panola County was hard hit in the '80s by collapse of oil and gas prices. Carthage fared better than other East Texas towns because of manufacturing base, lignite mining. Gas prices have rallied; county ranked 2nd in state gas production during 1991. Large local payrolls: Texas Utilities Mining, lignite, 1,200 employees; Tyson Foods, chicken, 700; Drew Woods, contractor, 200; Carthage Cup, plastic cups, 110; Louisiana-Pacific, lumber, 110; United Gas Pipeline, 58; Union Pacific Resources, gas processing, 75.

Newspaper: *Panola Watchman*, 109 W. Panola, Carthage, TX 75633. 903-693-7888. Wednesday, Sunday. Lloyd Grissom, editor and publisher. $32 a year.

TV, radio: Local AM station. Cable carries network TV, PBS from Shreveport, Dallas. NPR from Shreveport.

Health care: Panola General Hospital, 91 beds. 10 physicians, 5 dentists in local practice.

Schools: 1 primary (K–1); 1 elementary (2–3); 1 elementary (4–6); 1 junior high (7–8). Carthage High School enrolls 860, sends about 60% to 4-year college plus a number to Panola Junior College, in town. Composite SAT scores reported to exceed 1100 past 3 years.

Educational level: 9.5% of Panola County residents have 16 or more years of formal education; state average, 16.9%. Per capita expenditure for public education, $512; state average, $441.

Library: Sammy Brown Library, 45,000 volumes.

Recreation: 2 city parks, with swimming pool, tennis courts. Public golf course, country club. Lake Murvaul, 10 miles southwest, provides fishing, boating, skiing. Toledo Bend Reservoir, about 15 miles southeast, and Sabine River have fishing well-regarded by fishermen. Bowling alley, roller-skating rink, twin-screen cinema.

3 BR, 2 BA house: $35,000 to $48,000.

Cost of electricity: $.055 per kilowatt hour.

Cost of natural gas: $.40 per therm.

Sales tax: 6.25%.

State income tax: None.

Churches: 15. Denominations: Assemblies of God, Baptist, Free Will Baptist, Missionary Baptist, Southern Baptist, Episcopal, Interdenominationl, Methodist, United Methodist, United Pentecostal.

Carthage has sent two native sons to the top of the charts in country music—Jim Reeves and Tex Ritter. Gentleman Jim Reeves rose to national and international fame in the 1950s and 1960s. He was a regular on Grand Ole Opry, had his own show on ABC-TV, and was a frequent guest of Ed Sullivan, Steve Allen, and Dick Clark on "American Bandstand." Woodward Maurice Ritter, later "Tex," began studying for a law degree at the University of Texas, but soon was making a career as "The Texas Cowboy and His Song." He made his Broadway and radio debut in the 1930s, signed with Columbia Records in the '40s, and struck a major pop hit with his recording of "High Noon," the title song of the Gary Cooper classic film, in 1952.

It is not reported that Reeves or Ritter made much music while students at Carthage High. Today, they could barely escape the program: out of a total enrollment of 850 students, Carthage High School is proud to present the largest marching band in the state of Texas—240 players.

What residents say . . .

Mack Wheat, superintendent of schools:
"We're the largest Class 4-A band, I'm sure, in the state, and perhaps in the nation. We were named the Number One band in our class this year . . . just a lot of pride in that organization. . . . There are several values to band. Music is a lifetime activity, and any time we have students involved in extracurricular organizations they tend to do better in school. Also it's a good behavior-control system. . . . Generally we make a trip every second year. We've been to Orlando to a big music festival there, to Gatlinburg, to Los Angeles. All of that is paid for by the Band Booster organization. . . . The Carthage High School Bulldogs are undefeated in football. This Saturday night we're playing in the regional finals in Texas Stadium, in Dallas. It's been a good year. We're in the playoffs fairly regularly, but this is the first time in the school's history we've won 12 games in a row. . . . Our industrial arts program has been selected as one of the outstanding programs in the state for five consecutive years. . . . We do a lot of things with computer design. . . . Academically we do well, the last two years we won our University Interscholastic League academic competition, the counterpart to athletics."

Jerry Hanszen, owner, radio station KGAS: "Carthage was the gas capital of the nation in the late '40s and '50s. We're still recognized as a gas-related community though we're trying to diversify. . . . We are a very tight-knit group of people, just like a big family, many of us all kin to each other. . . . We are supporters of anything for a good cause. For example, we just had a lock-in for kids to raise money for multiple sclerosis. They raised right at $9,000, more than almost every town in the district. . . . The community will muster together if the need is there."

Donresia Henigan, member of the board, Sammy Brown Library: "The Junior Service League group in Carthage had several projects but finally settled on building a library because Panola County did not have one. It opened in 1962, a small, frame building, 40 by 36 feet, that had belonged to the telephone company. . . . We're just now finishing our third addition. . . . After the library was established and running, the Service League was paying for everything. We made a deal with the county judge . . . deeded the property to the county, and the county and city jointly pay the salary of our librarian. We now have one librarian and two other paid staff, plus two senior citizens who work 20 hours a week. . . . Last year we changed the name to Sammy Brown Library because she is the only charter member. . . . We won the J. Frank Dobie Award for libraries. Fifty-one libraries in the state applied and we won. . . . Our library was made possible by some women who have stuck to it. . . . Our old jail restoration is another wonderful thing that has brought people together."

Leila Belle LaGrone, retired teacher, author: "The genealogy library, I'm the mama of that one. It was the old jail, the oldest building in the town still standing, built in 1891, and it looked like it was going to go down, just losing from vandalism, standing open and not in use. The city manager is one of my former students. He wanted so much for someone to do something about it. I had a group interested in establishing a genealogical library. . . . We have a fine city library, but this was a special thing. We needed a roof over our heads and also needed to save that building. We organized the Panola County Historical and Geneaological Association. . . . There was not a window, not a door left except the iron front door.

The floors were all decayed and gone. The architect back in 1980 said it would cost $96,000 to restore. We have completed it for two-thirds of that, done much of the work ourselves as volunteers. . . . Governor Ann Richards was here to help us with the dedication. We had a big blowout for that. . . . The name of the library is the Leila Belle LaGrone Family History Center. . . . Family records, family histories, documents that had been put away in old trunks, medical records as early as 1852, census records, tax records. You name it, we have it. It's a search for family roots. . . . We have not bought a single book. Everything is donated. We donated the building to the people of the county, free and debt free. The Lord himself was in the work, every bit of it. . . . I am 82 years old. I was a teacher for 50 years, in 12th grade. I have scattered over the world at least 10,000 ex-students. Don't think they haven't come to my rescue on this project. . . . This is an interesting part of Texas. I have done 11 volumes on area history and I'm working on a manuscript right now concerning a feudal war that was fought right here, the Regulator–Moderator War. The Regulators organized themselves in Texas Republic days. There was a lot of horse-thieving. A bunch of people thought lawlessness needed to be curbed. The Regulators started chasing down anybody who had an accusation, but they didn't go through the courts. People who thought that was going too far, the Moderators, organized to support the courts, and open warfare lasted four years. It took the state president and his army to stop it. This used to be in the textbooks, but modern warfare has taken so much room it has been forgotten. . . . They're pressuring me to get this done." ■

Cedar City, UT 84720

Location: 270 miles south of Salt Lake City, 170 miles north of Las Vegas, in the foothills of southwestern Utah.

Population: 13,443 (1990).

Growth rate: 18% since 1980.

Per capita income: $7,095 (1985), 83% of state average ($8,535).

Geography/climate: Elevation, 5,800 feet. 10,000-foot mountain peaks rise to the southwest, in Pine Valley Mountains; and to the east, in Dixie National Forest. 4-season, semi-arid climate. Temperatures range from lows in teens to highs in 40s during the winter; lows in 50s to highs in 80s during the summer. Average rainfall, 10 inches, heaviest in March, July, October. Average snowfall, 40 inches, generally occurring in storms of short duration and melting between storms.

Economic base: Education, tourism, federal agencies, manufacturing. Largest employer is Southern Utah State University. Others employing more than 100 each: Iron County School District; T.W. Recreational Services; Goer Manufacturing, shelving for supermarkets; Wal-Mart; U.S. Forest Service; Coleman Outdoor Products; Valley View Medical Center, Iron County; Pizza Hut; Utah Power & Light; Matrixx Marketing; Western Electro Chemical, rocket fuel.

Newspaper: *The Daily Spectrum*, 403 S. Main Street, Cedar City, UT 84720. 801-586-7646. Published seven days a week. $12 a month for Monday through Saturday subscription; $6 a month for Sunday paper. Danny Stewart, editor.

TV, radio: 2 AM, 2 FM stations. Cable carries network TV, PBS, NPR from Salt Lake City.

Health care: Valley View Medical Center, 48 beds. 16 physicians, 15 dentists in local practice.

Schools: 5 elementary (K–5), 6th-grade center, 1 middle school (7–8), 9th-grade center. Cedar City High School enrolls 1,300, sends 66% to college. Composite ACT, 20.5. Trinity Lutheran Christian School (K–6). Southern Utah University, enrollment 4,400, is a 4-year liberal arts institution with master's program in accounting, elementary education.

Educational level: 19.9% of Iron County residents have 16 or more years of formal education, same as state average. Per capita expenditure for public education, $676; state average, $508.

Library: Cedar City Public Library, 41,000 volumes.

Recreation: 2 city parks, 12 ball fields, 18-hole municipal golf course, horse racetrack and rodeo arena, public swimming pool, tennis courts. Bowling alley, skating rink, fitness center, 2 movie theaters. Utah Summer Games held in Cedar City last week of June each year. Bryce Canyon National Park, 77 miles east; Zion National Park, 60 miles south. Home of American Folk Ballet, Utah Shakespearean Festival.

3 BR, 2 BA house: $70,000 to $80,000.

Cost of electricity: $.07 per kilowatt hour.

Cost of natural gas: $.66 per therm.

Sales tax: 6%.

State income tax: 2.55% to 7.2%.

Churches: 34 wards in 4 states of the

Church of Jesus Christ of Latter-day Saints. Other denominations: Assemblies of God, Baptist, Bible, Church of Christ, Episcopal, Jehovah's Witnesses, Lutheran, Presbyterian, Roman Catholic.

Along with glossy brochures and maps, the Chamber of Commerce of Cedar City, Utah, distributes a second-generation photocopy of city-police crime statistics for the previous year. It makes interesting reading, especially for immigrants from places like Los Angeles, a mere day's drive down Interstate 15.

Cedar City is the seat of Iron County, home of Southern Utah State University, site of a celebrated Shakespearean festival, home of the American Folk Ballet, center of spectacular natural beauty—and an awfully dull place when it comes to crime. During 1990, there were no homicides. Three rapes were reported, but two were unfounded and the other was reduced to sexual assault. One kidnapping ended in the arrest of two suspects. There was one robbery, 59 burglaries, 478 thefts, 26 auto thefts, and 70 assaults. The dollar loss attributed to these crimes was $176,000, of which $140,000 was recovered. There were 487 traffic accidents in the county during the year, or a little more than one accident per day on average. In some metro areas, by comparison, there may be 487 accidents over one long weekend, but that is not Cedar City's problem.

So far as mayhem, intrigue, and violence are concerned, Cedar City residents and visitors have to settle for reasonable facsimiles by the Bard of Avon, in selected performances of Shakespeare on the University stage, from June to September. *Julius Caesar* and *King Lear* ought to fill the bill.

What residents say . . .

Harold Hiskey, vice president for regional services, Southern Utah State University:
"Many people would call us a liberal arts school because of our Shakespeare festival. But we are a comprehensive university. Training business graduates and teachers . . . those are our two biggest departments. We started out as a normal school and have been training teachers for years. We supply nearly all of the rural parts of the state. We're known for the quality of teachers we produce. Our business program is growing rapidly. We serve 15 rural counties of southern Utah . . . where about 70 percent of our students come from. They come with a good work ethic and have grown up in homes that are fairly conservative. . . . Tourism is becoming a popular industry, one we can't really keep out because of the attraction of this beauti-

ful scenery . . . but we need to plan better for it. This year we had over 100,000 people attend the Shakespearean festival. . . . Being isolated as we are, we travel a lot. I was on the highway late at night, listening to a talk show that made me wonder what Cedar City could be known for. I thought, maybe we should be 'The Festival City.' The City Council liked the idea. We changed the logo on our letterhead and trucks and city buildings, and now we're known as 'The Festival City.' "

Alan Hamlin, City Council member, professor of economics: "I moved here from San Diego in 1981. . . . I had listed 22 important things I wanted in a community to raise my kids in . . . small-town flavor, college, good hospital, a lot of culture. We looked at the western United States and narrowed it down to Logan or Cedar City. . . . Cedar City at that time was still in an economic slump. The major employer in Iron County was the iron mines. Up to 1980 they were extremely important. They collapsed in 1981. We lost 600 jobs, which, for a town of 9,000 people, is just devastating. That took eight years to rebound from. One of the things I tried to do was bring in industry . . . 11 companies have moved here in the last three years. We're now in great shape. . . . We do not like to promote the inexpensive wages in this area, but it's true . . . plus inexpensive land prices and good quality of life. . . . Just in the last years we've got a housing problem. We've had quite a few people move here. We've rezoned 400 acres to accommodate apartments and we're trying to revitalize the downtown area. . . . One other thing, according to the American Chamber of Commerce cost-of-living index, our cost is 89 to 90 percent of the national average."

Elloyd Marchant, developer: "We're right at the edge of the desert and at the foot of the mountains. In 15 minutes we can be into the mountains . . . and we lose elevation going south toward Las Vegas, 3,000 feet in 50 miles. We most certainly have winter but it is not extreme. Summers are delightful. Probably the best time of the year is [October] till Christmas because we see bright sunny days. We see lots of the sun."

Harold Shirley, mayor, high school English teacher: "We have been growing at the rate of 2 percent to 4 percent a year. I think that is clearly manageable. If we get above 6 percent, we can't keep up. . . . We're going to have to build a bigger sewage-treatment plant. Some streets are in terrible shape. Water development is always necessary. We get only six to 10 inches of rain a year, and four out of the five past years we've had drought. But we own enough water for a town of 60,000 people. . . . This is my 25th year as a teacher of English at Cedar High. I was elected mayor two years ago, after literally 40 people asked me to run. I was on the Council twice before. . . . I ran the Rec Department for the city, so I know the departments in and out. . . . I am also on the Bishopric of my church . . . one of the three guys that leads the local congregation. . . . I have a lawn-care and landscaping business on the side. . . . I'm a Democrat and this is a super-Republican area. They sing 'Hail to the Chief' every morning! This is anti-environment-enforcing, rural conservative, redneck country. . . . I have taught between 3,000 and 4,000 people here, and a lot of those people voted for me. I think of the kids I taught, I probably got eight out of 10 votes. . . . There's a real care and concern in small towns. . . . That kind of thing we lose in big towns. As a nation we really need some of that lifestyle to take us into the 21st Century, more of that trust. . . . I think what small towns contribute is an attitude. I think people have a greater faith in democracy in small towns. They live on the same street with the mayor or councilman, whereas in the big city you may never see an elected official. . . . Hey, I can't hide! I wear a pager on my waist. So, that's maybe a big-city thing, but it also makes me accessible." ■

Celina, OH 45822

Location: 120 miles southwest of Toledo, 100 miles northwest of Columbus, in northwestern Ohio.

Population: 9,650 (1990).

Growth rate: 5% since 1980.

Per capita income: $9,516 (1985), 92% of state average ($10,371).

Geography/climate: Flat midwestern farmland, with town situated at northwestern end of Grand Lake St. Marys, largest man-made lake in the eastern United States (17,000 acres, 52-mile shoreline). Mid-continental climate, with cold winters and hot summers. Annual rainfall, 36 inches; annual snowfall, 31 inches. January average daily low, 18 degrees; high, 33. Through winter, average 134 days at or below freezing, 10 days below zero. July: low, 63; high, 84. Average 14 days at 90 or above.

Economic base: Farming, manufacturing, county-seat retail and governmental services. Huffy Bicycle Company is largest employer in town. Other big payrolls: Reynolds & Reynolds, business forms; L. J. Minor, frozen soups, sauces, gravies. Countywide, 54 firms employ 4,600 people, making manufacturing the largest job sector. Wholesale/retail trade is next, 2,800; then government, 2,000; services, 1,600. Mercer County usually places 1st or 2nd statewide in agricultural receipts—$148 million in 1987. 1,500 farms average 184 acres. Major commodities are corn, soybeans, wheat, oats, milk, hogs.

Newspaper: *The Daily Standard*, 123 E. Market Street, Celina, OH 45822. 419-586-2371. Daily, Monday through Saturday. Joe Lersky, editor. $80 a year.

TV, radio: 1 AM, 2 FM stations locally. Fort Wayne, Dayton TV can be received off-air; NPR from Lima. Cable carries PBS, network TV from Columbus, Toledo.

Health care: Mercer County Joint Township Community Hospital, 93 beds. 19 physicians, 10 dentists in local practice.

Schools: 3 elementary (K–5), 1 junior high (6–8). Celina Senior High School enrolls 680, sends 65–70% to higher education—40% to 4-year college. Recent composite ACT, 22.

Educational level: 8.3% of Mercer County residents have 16 or more years of formal education; state average, 13.7%. Per capita expenditure for public education, $466; state average, $445.

Library: Celina Public Library, 72,400 volumes.

Recreation: 4 city parks, year-round program of organized sports including Little League, soccer, men's and women's baseball leagues. Municipal swimming pool. Swimming, boating, fishing, camping in and around Grand Lake St. Marys. Lakeside Players, community theater group. Auglaize-Mercer Family Y, with indoor pool, courts, fitness programs. Private racquet club with 9-hole golf course; 2 public 18-hole courses. Bowling alley, 5-screen movie theater. Sunday night concerts in summertime around the gazebo in lakeside park.

3 BR, 2 BA house: $50,000 to $80,000.

Cost of electricity: $.07 per kilowatt hour.

Cost of natural gas: $.52 per therm.

Sales tax: 6%.

State income tax: .743% to 6.9%.

Churches: 27. Denominations: Apostolic, Assemblies of God, Baptist, Christian Science, Church of God, Community, Congregational, Friends, Jehovah's Witnesses, Lutheran, Missionary, Nazarene, Roman Catholic, Southern Baptist, United Brethren, United Methodist, Wesleyan Gospel.

They say it's quite a parade—certainly the best in northwestern Ohio. It's always on Saturday night of Lake Festival weekend, the last weekend in July. The parade is so popular that local residents begin staking their curbside claims to viewing space as early as Thursday morning. By Friday night, Main Street and a little bit of Logan are pretty well lined with empty lawn chairs in anticipation of the big spectacle the next evening. Bands, floats, beauty queens, local celebrities—it takes at least an hour and a half for Celina to pass in review.

What residents say ...

Mary Jean Grandlienard, receptionist, Chamber of Commerce; farmer: "I've lived here all my life, and that's a long time. . . . We have an excellent courthouse, which is a tourist attraction because it is all marble inside, terrific acoustics, a skylight of colored glass. We take our guests through there. . . . Our main street is well taken care of. We do not have empty places. It looks busy and thriving, and it is. . . . Celina is laid out very much in squares. Easy to get around. The side streets are wide, with lots of trees. . . . Agriculture is the biggest revenue-maker in Mercer County. It's going to account for a lot of our town's being strong. We have dairy, beef, hogs, chickens, grain farming. Turkeys are becoming a large element. . . . During the early 1980s, when farming went to pieces, enough people were diversified that when one [commodity] went down the other was strong enough to carry them. That's significant. . . . We have grain and hogs. Relatively small, 300 acres."

Nancy Barta, Welcome Wagon representative: "We moved up here from Worthington, Ohio, when my husband accepted a position with Huffy, the largest manufacturer of bicycles in the United States . . . right here in Celina, Ohio! . . . There simply are no absolutes about people who are moving here. People move back after receiving their education elsewhere . . . because this is a nice place to rear a family . . . because of job opportunities. . . . Celina is small enough to make things happen for the better. It is a controllable number."

Joe Lersky, editor, **The Daily Standard:** "We're still an independently owned operation, highly unusual in this world of chain papers. We're the last paper in North

America to go offset. The owner was convinced that Linotypes were the way of the world. . . . We're a very liberal paper in a very conservative community. I think our editorial positions are not embraced by the multitudes. We've been at swords-point many times. . . . The most recent example was rural homelessness. Local social service agencies were dickering for property to establish a shelter for the homeless. They did obtain state money. Of course, we had editorials very strongly in favor. But neighbors objected. . . . It isn't the kind of situation where you go down the street and see bag-ladies and panhandlers. But people have problems everywhere. Normally working people are rendered jobless, plus transients coming in. . . . I'm from the East . . . New York City. I came here maybe 30 years ago when I answered an ad in *Editor & Publisher*. The ad said, 'Are you underworked and overpaid? Come to Celina and we'll correct both of those problems for you.' . . . I applied, and met my wife here."

Doug Temple, president and CEO, Mercer Savings Bank: "I was born and went through school in Celina. I taught school six years, coached junior high basketball. But I got out of coaching and went into banking here in Celina, moved away to Findlay, Ohio, was in the banking business there for a few years, from there to Philadelphia, Ohio . . . then eventually an opportunity arose in Celina. Probably one of the main reasons we came back is the school system. The quality of teachers is excellent. . . . The school system right at the present is suffering with growth problems, and it's been unsuccessful in getting a bond levy passed. But I'm currently active on the steering committee to get that recti-

fied, mostly a dollars-and-cents question. . . . We have mainly a German background in the Celina area. I think the work ethic that's been taught here is a lot better than you get elsewhere. That's why I think the Huffy's and others have located here. We would have trouble if another large employer moved here. I don't think we would have the work force."

Rich Stein, curriculum director, Celina Senior High School: "We're fairly rich for a small school. The state requires 45 [courses]. We usually have more than twice that available. We have an AP [Advanced Placement] English course, AP government, AP biology, calculus. We also treat one course as AP art. We have second-year chemistry and physics, a wide spectrum of offerings. The only inherent danger is it takes good counseling and guidance. . . . One of the more interesting courses is marine biology, given as half-credit during winter months. It culminates with a trip to Andros Island, gathering specimens. . . . Another thing strong about our schools is they have a lot of field-trip enrichment. The Shakespeare Club goes to the Shakespeare festival in Stratford. German students take our exchange students from Germany to Chicago, students in voice and drama go to New York for plays, our eighth grade goes to Washington, sixth grade to an outdoor week at Yellow Springs. The band plays at Disney World every four years."

Phil Hawkey, city engineering staff: "City parks are very well-developed and quite extensive for a community our size but used almost entirely for organized team sports . . . real active Little League . . . the Grand Lake Mariners, a summer league for college men, kinda like a minor league pro team, they play at Eastview Park, a very nice beautiful field . . . a very good women's fast-pitch softball team, the Celina Suns . . . big soccer tournament each fall. One of the few pieces of noncompetitive park space that gets a lot of use is the bike path between Celina and Coldwater, five miles. . . . The ethnic makeup of the community is primarily German Catholic south of the lake and south of Celina. In the northern part of the county, I imagine it would be more Protestant. There is very little ethnic diversity . . . far more Asians than any other minority group. They tend to be professionals. . . . The schools are tremendously overcrowded. In the elementary school my daughter goes to, 11 classes are held in modular, temporary classrooms. . . . What people don't realize is we need to build a major school building every generation in a growing town like this. Now my generation needs to build one for our kids." ■

Cleveland, MS 38732

Location: 110 miles south of Memphis, 317 miles north of New Orleans, 19 miles east of the Mississippi River, in northwestern Mississippi.

Population: 15,384 (1990).

Growth rate: 5% since 1986.

Per capita income: $7,384 (1985), 99% of state average ($7,483).

Geography/climate: Mississippi - Delta, utterly flat but very fertile. Short, cold winter with January low averaging 32, high, 55. 50 days at freezing or below, 2–3 inches of snow. Humid much of the year. July daily highs averaging 91, lows 70. Long, hot summers with 75 days at 90 or above. Annual rainfall, 49 inches.

Economic base: Good balance between agriculture, industry. Educational services very strong. Farms cover 80% of county. Rice, soybeans are major crops, with diversification into catfish farming, milo. Large payrolls: Bolivar County Schools, 1,185 employees; Baxter Health Care, hospital supplies, 960; Douglas & Lomason, automotive trim, 680; Delta State University, 521; Bolivar County Hospital, 375; Duo-fast, nails and staples, 325; Ampco-Alabama Metal, 240; Color Tile, 174; Cives Steel, fabricated structural steel, 150.

Newspaper: *The Bolivar Commercial*, 821 N. Chrisman, Cleveland, MS 38732. 601-843-4241. Daily, Monday through Friday. Norman Van Liew, editor and publisher. $48 a year.

TV, radio: 1 local AM, 2 FM stations. Cable carries TV-network stations from Memphis,

Jackson, Greenwood, Greenville, and PBS. NPR received off-air from Greenwood.

Health care: Bolivar County Hospital, 199 beds. 29 physicians, 12 dentists in local practice.

Schools: 5 elementary (K–6) including 1 magnet school, 2 junior high (7–8). Under court order, Cleveland has 2 high schools (9–12). Students living on west side of railroad tracks attend Cleveland High School, mainly white, enrollment 650. Students living east of tracks attend East Side High School, mainly black, enrollment 595. About 75–85% of high school graduates go to college, majority to Delta State University, in town. Composite ACT runs in 17–18 range (state average, 15). Private schools: Bayou Academy (K–12), Presbyterian Day School (K–6). Delta State University enrolls 4,500.

Educational level: 14.1% of local residents have 16 or more years of formal education; state average, 12.3%. County per capita expenditure for public education, $407; state average, $333.

Library: Bolivar County Library System, 5 branches, 100,000 volumes.

Recreation: 12 city parks, 10 ball fields, skating rink, bowling alley, 4 swimming pools, country club, 25 tennis courts, 2 golf courses, auditorium-coliseum, 4 movie theaters, amateur theater. Museum of natural history, art center, planetarium at Delta State University. Delta Blues and Archaeological Museum at Clarksdale, 32 miles north. Great River Road State Park, 20 miles northwest.

3 BR, 2 BA house: $60,000 to $80,000.

Cost of electricity: $.08 per kilowatt hour.

Cost of natural gas: $.44 per therm.

Sales tax: 6%.

State income tax: 3% to 5%.

Churches: 40. Denominations: Apostolic, Assemblies of God, Baptist, Baptist-Independent, Baptist-Missionary, Church of Christ, Church of God, Church of God in Christ, Episcopal, Foursquare Gospel, Lutheran, Nazarene, Pentecostal, Presbyterian-American, Presbyterian-USA, Roman Catholic, Seventh-Day Adventist, United Methodist.

Synagogues: 1.

"**I**f you always thought the Mississippi Delta was nothing but sleepy, boring little towns, we invite you to visit us," says the promotional flyer for Cleveland and Bolivar County. Statistics support this assertion. While most smaller Mississippi places have barely held their population, or declined, Cleveland keeps growing at a sustainable pace—5 percent since 1986. As county seat and by far the biggest town, Cleveland once depended very heavily on traditional Delta agriculture for its well-being. And while you still pass cotton fields on the way to town, you also see industrial parks under heavy cultivation. But the largest industry is higher education—Delta State University is growing at a faster rate than any other state college or university. What's behind Cleveland's economic evolution? Charles Dean, a mover–shaker consulting engineer, thinks the catalyst is a place called Rosedale, a Mississippi River town 19 miles west that links Cleveland to the universe and is blossoming as the fastest-growing river port. On the other hand, maybe it's something more down home, like the Hot Wings they're producing at the new Brandywine plant.

What residents say ...

Lucy Janoush, human-resources manager, Brandywine Foods: "We deal with what we call the front half of the chicken, the breast with wings intact. The process is like a big kitchen. . . . All of our products are for the restaurant and food-service industry. . . . The work ethic here is very good . . . good attendance rate, low turnover. You would describe the labor force as dependable. They have pride in their work. They, too, are looking for a long-term relationship. . . . I was born here, lived here all but five years when I went to Washington to work for the congressman from this district. . . . Cleveland's growth has always been slow and steady. Now it's kind of booming. . . . It used to be in the small community you would see all your friends leave. There are pretty good employment opportunities. . . . Leadership has always been really good. . . . With the mechanization of agriculture, we started losing population because farm labor just wasn't needed. This community got real aggressive. . . . In a lot of other towns you had the agricultural mentality predominate and they looked at industry as a bad way to go. We didn't. . . . I have a first-grader. . . . I'm sure you've heard of white flight from the schools? We've never had that . . . 93 percent are in the public schools. . . . We're opening up a new mag-net school, with emphasis on computer, math, and science, speaking Spanish in first grade."

Norman Van Liew, editor and publisher, **The Bolivar Commercial:** "I came here in December 1972 and the paper went daily in February 1973. That was sort of a condi-tion of my coming. We've enjoyed very good growth. Starting at about 4,000 weekly, circulation dipped to about 2,500 when we converted to daily and scared me half to death. But we've come back to about 7,000. . . . Cleveland through all the racial-strife years has had good rapport. . . . You've got to attribute a lot of that to the leadership. . . . Things weren't done lopsided. . . . If they did something for one side of town they did it for the other . . . al-ways been open to meetings, not just trying to drive things down people's throats. . . . Industrially, it's just amazing what is hap-pening here. . . . One person who probably stands out as the mover is Charles Dean. He had the vision for the slack-water port."

Charles Dean, consultant civil engineer: "Rosedale was an old river steamboat town, 19 miles from here, near the confluence of the Arkansas and Mississippi rivers, what we would call a Mark Twain town. The river changed its course and left Rosedale on a cutoff. There was nothing there, zero, and of course the area was going

downhill. . . . Bolivar County organized a port authority. . . . We ended up with a slack-water channel three miles long but also filled 300 acres as industrial sites. We've got a public port terminal with a $3 million dock. . . . Went into operation in 1978 and it has just bloomed. The Rose-dale port is probably the fastest-growing port in tonnage on the Mississippi River system. . . . Duo-Fast ships most of their raw steel wire into the Port of Rosedale. They are on their third expansion of the plant in Cleveland. That's a direct result of the port. . . . We've started running out of land because it was so successful."

Martin King, mayor: "We are surrounded by rice fields. They have to flood the fields and make the rice come above the water-line to sunshine. This is ideal breeding grounds for mosquitoes, and they are pesky devils. It used to be about eight o'clock at night in the summertime you couldn't be outside at all. You had to stay inside to keep from getting bitten. . . . We have quite a mosquito-control program. We patterned it after a program in Stuttgart, Arkansas. . . . This is the second year and it's beginning to pay off. The quality of life has improved greatly. . . . We are most for-tunate in having Delta State University and 4,500 students. We consider the university our prime industry. . . . The city and Delta State pool our resources and bring in cul-tural events that can be enjoyed by both. We have a good gown–town relationship. . . . I went into office July 1, 1969. I had an opponent the first time. The second time it was just token, and I haven't had an opponent since then. I'm trying to decide whether they think they get a sucker in there and don't let him out." ■

Crawfordsville, IN 47933

Location: 49 miles northwest of Indianapolis, 132 miles south-southeast of Chicago, in west central Indiana.

Population: 13,584 (1990).

Growth rate: 2% since 1980.

Per capita income: $9,727 (1985), 97% of state average ($9,978).

Geography/climate: Basically flat, farmland. Continental climate: moderately cold winters; nice spring, warm to hot, often humid summers; pleasant, dry fall. Average temperatures: January: low, 19; high, 36. July: low, 65; high, 86. Average rainfall, 39 inches; snowfall, 17 inches.

Economic base: Diversified manufacturing, agriculture, retail, county-seat services. Large payrolls: R.R. Donnelley & Sons, commercial printer and binder, 2,600 employees; Raybestos, brake materials, 675; Hi-Tek Lighting, 700; Integrated Plastics Technologies, injection moldings, 297; Inland Container, corrugated boxes, 115; California Pellet Mill, mill parts, 100; Crawford Industries, plastic sheet products, 225; H.C. Industries, closures, 302; Crown Cork & Seal, closures, 190; Midstates Wire, 261; Sommer Metalcraft, wire products, 230. Crawfordsville Community Schools, 325; Culver Hospital, 250; Wabash College, 225. Montgomery County ranks among state's top producers of corn, soybeans, hogs.

Newspaper: *Journal Review*, 119 N. Green Street, Crawfordsville, IN 47933. 317-362-1200. Daily, Monday through Saturday. Gaildene Hamilton, editor. $87 a year.

TV, radio: 1 local AM, 1 FM station. Cable carries network TV, PBS from Indianapolis, Terre Haute. NPR from Indianapolis, West Lafayette.

Health care: Culver Hospital, 120 beds. 33 physicians, 13 dentists in local practice.

Schools: 6 elementary (K–5), 1 middle (6–8). Crawfordsville High School enrolls 600, sends 46% to 4-year college; 16% to 2-year, vocational. Composite SAT for 1990, 73 students: math, 526; verbal, 424. Wabash College enrolls 850.

Educational level: 10.9% of Montgomery County residents have 16 or more years of formal education; state average, 12.5%. Per capita expenditure for public education, $404; state average, $422.

Library: Crawfordsville Public Library, 100,000 volumes.

Recreation: Milligan Park, 40 acres, adjacent to 18-hole public golf course, 50-meter swimming pool with slide. 5 lighted softball diamonds used by about 100 youth and adult teams. Indoor and outdoor tennis courts. 2 regulation soccer fields, 2 downsize fields. Country club with 9-hole course. Bowling alley. Twin-screen movie theater; drive-in. Boys and Girls Club, for kids 6–18, had 1,107 members in 1990–91: ball teams, game rooms, crafts, tutoring, special events. 2 state parks, nature preserve, 360-acre lake within half-hour drive. 16 miles of canoeing on Sugar Creek.

3 BR, 2 BA house: $50,000 to $70,000.

Cost of electricity: $.05 to $.06 per kilowatt hour.

Cost of natural gas: $.45 per therm.

Sales tax: 5%.

State income tax: 3.4%.

Churches: 38 total. Denominations: Apostolic, Assemblies of God, American Baptist, General Baptist, Independent Baptist, Southern Baptist, Christian, Disciples of Christ, Church of the Nazarene, Church of Jesus Christ of Latter-day Saints, Episcopal, Full Gospel, Jehovah's Witnesses, Lutheran, Methodist, Nondenominational, Pentecostal, Presbyterian, Presbyterian USA, Roman Catholic, United Methodist.

"**O**ne of our great blessings is also one of our biggest headaches—the fact that Crawfordsville is on the intersection of four major highways," says long-time resident Dick Munro. "We're blessed with too much traffic!" A bypass is in the talking stage. They're also talking about building a new recreation center to replace an old building bursting at the seams. It would be sited next to the new $30 million high school, and the two would share ball fields, pool, courts, and other big-ticket items—a cooperative venture that has attracted interest from around the country.

A century ago, Crawfordsville attracted comment as "The Athens of Indiana." It was home to a small group of writers whose names have mostly faded—all but one: General Lew Wallace, soldier, statesman, artist, and author of the epic novel *Ben Hur*.

What residents say ...

Donald Thompson, retired librarian, Wabash College: "Lew Wallace is by far the best-known person Crawfordsville has ever produced. *Ben Hur* was published in November of 1880. Quite a bit of it was written here in his study, quite a bit while he was in Santa Fe, New Mexico, as the territorial governor between 1878 and '81. . . . His livelihood was based on the law, for which he did not care at all. He made a fortune on *Ben Hur*. I'm editing his letters for the Indiana Historical Society—3,500 letters."

Will H. Hays, Jr., lawyer, former mayor, writer: "I grew up in Sullivan, Indiana, a coal-mining town, went away to prep school in New York, then back to Wabash College, then to Yale Law School, then to Sullivan to practice law. . . . I was writing a book at night and on weekends, sent a few chapters to a friend in Hollywood, a producer and screenwriter. He liked them. 'I've just been assigned to Darryl Zanuck to write a screenplay. . . . Come out and write it with me,' he said. 'It will give you an opportunity to get away from the law and still make some money.' So I worked for Twentieth Century Fox. . . . I finished the book in California, *Dragon's Watch*, published by Doubleday in 1954, a novel laid in a small southwestern Indiana town. Doubleday said, 'We're going to introduce you as the newest Indiana author. But you're living in Beverly Hills and that doesn't quite jive.' So I talked to the president of Wabash College. He said, 'I hereby offer you a job as visiting instructor in creative writing for the year.' I was back in Indiana when the book came out. That made honest people of Doubleday. I came back to Crawfordsville, where my mother had been born. Crawfordsville has always been my second hometown. We've lived here from '55 on. . . . I'd inherited some money from my dad which enabled me to start writing again. . . . Some friends with whom I had worked in civic affairs said, 'Why don't you run for mayor? The town needs a full-time mayor.' . . . I campaigned going house to house. At that time there were 3,300 houses in Crawfordsville and I knocked on every door. My opponent said, 'What do you want a Hollywood playboy looking over our affairs?' I overcame that stigma, got elected, worked hard, and enjoyed it. . . . I never had an unlisted phone when I was mayor. My phone rang frequently. Everything from barking dogs to holes in the street to things like how do we put together a program to persuade industry to locate here. . . . The eight years I spent as mayor I would consider the most interesting and rewarding years of my life. . . . Crawfordsville is a small industrial town in the middle of a rich agricultural region with a distinguished small college in it, and it's difficult to get a better combination for quality of life. Add to that, 49 miles nonstop to Indianapolis. . . . My dad was away all the time I was growing up. Our acquaintance and love for each other developed through correspondence. He kept every letter I wrote to him. I began to edit them, interspersed with narrative by me. Right now this book is out in New York with an agent. It's a story of my dad and me, growing up in a little coal-mining town. I'm calling it, 'Come Home with Me Now,' from the line, 'Father, dear father, come home with me now.' "

Dick Munro, general manager, WCVL/ WIMC: "In a market this size you have to be a local radio station. You can't pay higher salaries or play better music than Indianapolis. But you can do things locally better. . . . We broadcast the police blotter daily, local sports teams, we have a swapshop program. This is an agricultural community so we have indepth farm programming. We carry IU and Purdue, we carry the Pacers and the Colts. . . . We keep fairly busy. We just had an accident here at 8:45 this morning. Somebody called us and tipped us off about it. I went up there and got the information, had it on the air within a half-hour of the incident. I doubt very much it will be on any other radio or TV station in the world. It's something that happened here. . . . The school district is building a new high school on the south edge of town, and they have indicated they would offer acreage to the parks department to build adjacent, so they could share facilities."

Rita Hamm, director of parks and recreation: "Wouldn't this be a great venture if we could get together? They are giving us three and a half acres for our community center. . . . We're an unusual community. We've had such a good, cooperative effort. For a small community we probably offer the widest variety of programs. . . . It's a big boost to the economy, as well. When you have 100 softball teams in your community, people are going to be buying equipment . . . uniforms, shirts. . . . We're a community of shift workers. We plan to have the new center open 6 A.M. to 1 A.M. so the fellows who work 3 to 11 can play their volleyball or swim when they get off work. . . . When you've been a farm community for years, there's a lot of pride. I think a lot of it comes from your older citizens. . . . We're trying to instill a little bit of this pride in our younger generation."

Gaildene Hamilton, editor, **Crawfordsville Journal-Review:** "I see it happen so often here. Say one of the farmers has a heart attack. They're in planting his crops, harvesting. No one has to go looking for them, they are just there. It is also a community that gives generously. The paper serves as clearinghouse for 'The Sunshine Fund.' We simply run a story every day. Every penny that comes in is used for the needy. Last year I think they took in $25,000 from Thanksgiving to Christmas, and that's quite a sum of money. The Sunshine Society at Crawfordsville High School. I've been at the paper 30 years, and it's been going on all that time." ■

Crossville, TN 38555

Location: 120 miles east of Nashville, 74 miles north of Chattanooga, 72 miles west of Knoxville, in east central Tennessee.

Population: 6,930 (1990).

Growth rate: 8% since 1980.

Per capita income: $7,415 (1985), 80% of state average ($9,290).

Geography/climate: Located on the Cumberland Plateau, elevation 1,980 feet. Rocky soil, not especially good for farming, but very pretty—surrounded by mountains. Average temperatures: January: high, 39; low, 21; July: high, 82; low, 64. Average snowfall, 12 inches; rainfall, 52 inches. Prevailing winds from southwest. Growing season, 180 days.

Economic base: Tourism, agriculture, retirement living, manufacturing. Large payrolls: Flowers Snack of Tennessee, cakes and rolls, 376 employees; Dennison Stationery Products, office supplies, 265; Crossville Rubber, floor mats, 270; General Processing, water heaters, 240; Crossville Ceramics, tile, 125; Homestead Manufacturing, ladies sportswear, 130; American Apparel Associates, ladies sportswear, 110; TAP Publishing, trade journals, 95. Seat of Cumberland County.

Newspapers: *Crossville Chronicle*, 310 S. Main Street, Crossville, TN 38555. 615–484–5145. Tuesday, Wednesday, Friday. Mike Moser, editor. $26 a year. *Cumberland Times*, Hwy. 27 N, P.O. Box 745, Crossville, TN 38557–0745. 615–484–7510. Weekly, Wednesday. Richard Davis, editor. $10 a year. (Same company owns both papers.)

TV, radio: 2 local AM stations, 1 FM station. 1 TV station. Cable carries TV networks from Knoxville and Chattanooga.

Health care: Cumberland Medical Center, 216 beds. 45 physicians, 14 dentists in local practice.

Schools: 1 elementary (K–5), 1 middle (6–9). Crossville High School enrolls 1,171 students, sends 40% of graduates to higher education. Composite ACT, 19–20. Crossville Elementary School received Governor's Award of Excellence as 1 of top 10 schools in state. Cumberland County Higher Education Center, junior college.

Educational level: 8.6% of Cumberland County residents have 16 or more years of formal education; state average, 12.6%. Per capita expenditure for public education, $307; state average, $301.

Library: Art Circle Public Library of Cumberland County, 19,500 volumes.

Recreation: 2 public parks in town. Immediate area has 3 private, 2 daily-fee golf courses; 2 country clubs, 8 swimming pools, 2-screen movie theater, bowling alley, 5 public camp grounds. Seasonal hunting for deer, turkey, boar at Catoosa Wildlife Management Reserve, 20 miles northeast. Cumberland Mountain Rustic State Park, 1,720 acres, 10 miles southeast.

3 BR, 2 BA house: $60,000 and up.

Cost of electricity: $.05 to $.06 per kilowatt hour.

Cost of natural gas: $.63 per therm.

Sales tax: 7.75%.

State income tax: 6%.

Churches: 44 total. Denominations: Assemblies of God, Baptist, Independent Baptist, Southern Baptist, Christian, Church of Christ, Church of God, Church of Jesus Christ of Latter-day Saints, Congregational, Episcopal, Evangelical Free, Full Gospel, Interdenominational, Jehovah's Witnesses, Lutheran, Methodist, United Methodist, Nazarene, Nondenominational, Presbyterian, Roman Catholic, Seventh-Day Adventist, United Church of Christ.

"**W**e seem to be a clearinghouse for people looking for a better place to live," laughs Jim Moser, editor of the Crossville Chronicle, founded in 1886. Moser has fielded a lot of these calls from inquiring reporters. Crossville was "discovered" in the 1980s as a very nice place to vacation or retire. Just out of town, for example, Fairfield Glade is a retirement home to some 5,000 people. For most of its history, however, Crossville was a hardscrabble place where stone cutters carved quartzite out of the Cumberland Plateau and farmers scratched crops out of so-so soil. Green beans are the number-one farm export. The principal import besides retirees is tourists, on their way to such places as Cumberland General Store, Homestead Museum, Ozone Falls, the Simonton Cheese House, or the place that first turned Crossville from a crossroads into a destination—Cumberland County Playhouse.

What residents say ...

Ann Crabtree, music director, Cumberland County Playhouse: "Even to this day I find it hard to believe the connection to Crossville. Jim's maternal grandmother was born here, and his great grandfather established the first newspaper here.... Jim's father was a writer and in theater in California. He was looking for a place to subsidize a family of seven children while he wrote a book. The plan was just to stay here a few months.... One of the local school principals heard that Mr. Crabtree was in town and asked him if he would write and produce a show for the children. He wrote his own music to the show *Pinocchio*, for the junior high.... It just caught the town on fire. They couldn't let it go. Several people came to [Paul Crabtree] and asked him, 'How do we keep you here?' 'You'd have to build a theater,' he said. A year and a half later this beautiful theater, the Cumberland County Playhouse, sat on the countryside. You have to understand, this was one of the least-populated and poorest parts of the state.... The first season was 1965.... We had lived in New Haven and New London for nine years before we moved here in 1976.... There are still not just hotbeds of liberal politics which I wish there were.... The Congregational Church is still pretty small. But it used to be a super-poor area. I used to be able to see the poverty.... We still have a huge number of takers for our Good Samaritan program.

But we have far more jobs. . . . The schools have improved drastically."

Jim Crabtree, producing director, Cumberland County Playhouse: "In 1963, we were kind of in the middle of nowhere. Crossville was the town people went through to get someplace else. . . . There was not much opportunity in the arts for people here. The idea was very appealing and exciting. Several of the leading families understood the potential that a theater could bring to this area. The Playhouse was born out of that energy, with my father as catalyst and providing direction. . . . Now, into a town of 6,500 the Playhouse draws 85,000 customers a year. . . . I have what very few people in my field have: a career in the arts and a small-town lifestyle. I also have the wonderful opportunity of creating new works about my own region. . . . We have a very strong commitment to original works rooted in the history and culture of rural America, in Tennessee and the Cumberland Mountains. . . . I'm an itinerant theater-person by birth and rearing. I grew up in New York, Florida, and California, never living in one place more than two or three years at a time. I've had the great pleasure of discovering what it means to have roots and a hometown."

Bill Startup, president, Cumberland County Bank: "I have been here five years. The thing that has most changed Crossville is the wealth that the retirement-aged people have brought to Crossville. They have turned this from your average rural town into a town with relatively high income per capita. We have seen a rather affluent population spring up that is very unique to a small town. . . . The four retirement communities greatly add to the quality of life and, well, you don't lay off Social Security and pension checks."

Mike Moser, editor, **Crossville Chronicle**: "Our newspaper sold in 1988 to a national chain, the same thing that is happening to the corner drugstore and the friendly bank. To survive, you've got to be connected to deep pockets. The sale has been good for us. We are owned by American Publishing, the same company that owns *The Jerusalem Post*. There have been no personnel changes. We've had people with the newspaper for 17 and 20 years. The bank that's been here 100 years sold two years before the newspaper. . . . Locally, I think people accept it as a thing of the times. . . . When I interviewed for this job I was considering Centerville, Iowa, and Crossville, Tennessee. I drove up from Alabama, about four hours. I drove up on this mountain, that's what they call it. I saw the beautiful ridges to the east. I spent a day here and realized when folks told you 'Good morning' they meant it. I went home . . . and on the front page of the *Birmingham News* was a story headlined, 'Farmers Riot on Courthouse Steps of Centerville, Iowa, Over Farm Foreclosures.' "

Shirley Duer, member, Tennessee House of Representatives: "It's a farming community and yet doesn't have the rich soil of East Tennessee. . . . I think because making a living was more difficult than in other areas, there's a bond between people here. . . . When I was elected I was the third woman out of 99 legislators. We now have 12 out of 99. Interestingly enough, this rural county is the only county in the state that has both a female in the House and the Senate. . . . I think it says a lot about the way of life here, that everybody, male and female, had to work hard and had to work side by side."

Maureen Hodges, principal, Crossville Elementary School: "It's the oldest school building in the county. What we lack in facilities we have in staff and program. . . . We were selected as one of the top 10 schools in Tennessee because of the excellence of our program. . . . We've worked on whole language . . . teaching reading by way of good literature. . . . Our children are mostly from low-income housing. We are an inner-city school, and we are right up there with the best. . . . I'm from Long Island, Oyster Bay. My husband is a native, born in Crossville. His grandfather built the famous Hotel Taylor, where they filmed *The Rise of Sergeant York*. Eleanor Roosevelt had lunch there when she came to dedicate the Homestead Project. . . . I'm here by choice . . . 26 years." ■

Culpeper, VA 22701

Location: 75 miles southwest of Washington, DC, 45 miles north of Charlottesville, in the north central Piedmont region of Virginia.

Population: 8,581 (1990).

Growth rate: 23% since 1980.

Per capita income: $10,961 (1985), 92% of state average ($11,894).

Geography/climate: Gently to heavily rolling hills. Town elevation, 430 feet. Weather moderated by Blue Ridge Mountains to the west, Chesapeake Bay to the east. Mild winters, warm and humid summers. Average temperatures: January: high, 44; low, 26; July: high, 87; low, 67. Average annual rainfall, 41 inches; snowfall, 19 inches. Westerly winds prevail.

Economic base: Diversified economy with strong manufacturing, trade, services, agricultural sectors. Major payrolls: ITT Teves Automotive, antilock brake systems, employs 375; Rochester Corporation, cable, wire rope, fiber optics, 325; SWIFT (Society for Worldwide International Financial Telecommunications), North American headquarters of Belgian-based financial telecommunications company, 160; Merillat Industries, kitchen cabinets, 200; Keller Manufacturing, furniture, 200. Culpeper is county seat, retail trading center.

Newspaper: *Culpeper Star-Exponent*, 122 W. Spencer Street, Culpeper, VA 22701. 703–825–0771. Monday through Saturday morning. David Smith, publisher. $86.40 a year. *Culpeper News*, 605 S. Main Street, Culpeper, VA 22701. 703–825–3232. Weekly,

Wednesday. Kathleen Hoffman, editor. $15 a year.

TV, radio: Local AM, FM stations. Cable carries network TV, PBS from Washington, Richmond, Charlottesville. NPR received off-air from Roanoke.

Health care: Culpeper Memorial Hospital, 96 beds. 41 physicians, 12 dentists in local practice.

Schools: 5 elementary (K–3, 4–6), 1 junior high (7–9). Culpeper High School (10–12) enrolls 1,026, sends 50% to college, 20% to trade/technical school. Average SATs: math, 461; verbal, 431.

Educational level: 11.4% of Culpeper County residents have 16 or more years of formal education; state average, 19.1%. Per capita expenditure for public education, $405; state average, $430.

Library: Culpeper Public Library, 34,000 volumes.

Recreation: 2 public parks totaling 105 acres: Commonwealth Park, a horse-showing facility; Yowell Meadow Park, with fitness trail, soccer field, tot lots, picnic grounds. Town amenities include 12 tennis courts, 3 swimming pools, 4 ball fields, roller-skating rink, bowling alley, 3 theaters. Rappahannock River forms northern county boundary, Rapidan River the southern boundary. 2 man-made watershed lakes in town. Entrances to Appalachian Trail and Skyline Drive of the Blue Ridge Mountains are 27 miles northwest of town, near The Pinnacle, 3,730-foot peak.

3 BR, 2 BA house: $105,000 to $150,000.

Cost of electricity: 18$.04 to $.07 per kilo-watt hour.

Cost of natural gas: $.53 per therm.

Sales tax: 4½%.

State income tax: 2% to 5.75%.

Churches: 36 total. Denominations: Baptist, Independent Baptist, Southern Baptist, Brethren, Christian, Church of Christ, Church of God, Church of Jesus Christ of Latter-day Saints, Episcopal, Holiness, Independent, Jehovah's Witnesses, Lutheran, Methodist, Nazarene, Nondenominational, Pentecostal, Pentecostal Holiness, Presbyterian, Roman Catholic, Seventh-Day Adventist.

Culpeper has the three essentials: location, location, and location. In addition to its attractive Piedmont setting and Victorian town center, Culpeper is prime real estate and inescapably under the influence of its big neighbor to the northeast, the Washington, DC, metropolitan area. Though they worry over sluggish growth now, town managers seem likely to inherit the far more difficult problem of preserving Culpeper's small-town qualities as the place grows. Nevertheless, Culpeper is determined to grow. Among other strategies: Culpeper may be designated a Foreign Trade Zone by the U.S. Department of Commerce.

What residents say ...

Jim Witherspoon, executive director, Culpeper Chamber of Commerce: "At this point, it is 99 percent certain we will become a Foreign Trade Zone.... It's a positive addition to your economic-development portfolio, and right now, economic development is extremely competitive. If a company is involved in international commerce, it can be that one plus when the company is making a decision.... Another focus is making sure you have an adequate inventory of sites.... You used to take a prospect out to a cornfield and say, 'Imagine your factory there.' It doesn't work that way anymore. The land needs to be properly zoned with the proper infrastructure. That's something you can't do after the

fact.... Communications are extremely important. The Federal Reserve has an underground facility ... adjacent to Culpeper. Because of their presence, and SWIFT's, we have an extremely sophisticated fiber-optics network. The fact we are 50 miles from Dulles International Airport, we hear frequently that is a big plus, and at the same time having the quality-of-life aspects."

Eric Johnson, owner, financial-services firm: "Roughly 23 percent commute to jobs in northern Virginia at major corporations and many federal agencies. Almost a like number commute to work in Culpeper, a market center for five rural counties.... Culpeper in the late '70s and early '80s became host to several large multinational companies. . . . We have attracted, somewhat serendipitously and somewhat due to the merits of Culpeper, diverse industry. . . . It has taken on an international flavor. Culpeper does remind Europeans of Europe . . . pretty locations, a green verdant look throughout the community, a nice true downtown. . . . Where are we going from here? This is where it gets a little worrisome. . . . Virginia is engaged in a fairly strong competition for companies relocating into America. . . . Folks trying to establish a beachhead in America find Culpeper interesting because of the link to DC but far enough away. The difficulty we're having in an economic slowdown is that incentives by other state legislatures are sometimes more significant than they are in Virginia. Virginia has done a good job with job training, access roadways . . . things that aren't necessarily a tax abatement. My point is that folks looking to move here have to weigh economic incentives into the equation. . . . We're finding ourselves in those competitions coming up second or third place. I believe as economic recovery continues, because of our proximity to Washington, DC, and reasonable costs, Culpeper will become very, very attractive again."

B.B. Mitchell, III, retired school-board employee: "Culpeper County hosted the Army of the Potomac during 1863–64. There were over 100,000 Union troops here. Our county was sort of a crossroads for Confederate and Federal forces between Washington and Richmond, and it has great historical significance. . . . The Battle of Brandy Station, on June 9, 1863, was the prelude to Gettysburg. Heretofore, Federal cavalry had not fared so well with the Confederates, but they held their own

at Brandy Station. . . . We are members of the 'dreaded preservationists,' if you will. We are trying to preserve some semblance of the battlefield here at Brandy, but we are under great pressure from the community and development and special interests to build a city in the northern part of the county. . . . In September 1990, the Board of Supervisors approved 1,500 acres of commercial and light-industrial zoning on the Brandy Station battlefield. . . . I've got 10 acres of land. I'm on the battlefield. . . . Several landowners, and I'm one of them, have sued the county because of their impropriety, we feel, in zoning that much commercial land to one developer and going against the recommendations of our Planning Commission who, by a vote of five to three, felt the developer had too many unknowns in his plans . . . water, transportation, environmental impact. . . . One of their selling points is the reverse trend in commuting. Now people in dc will commute to Brandy Station. . . . What makes our county attractive is the open space and beauty. . . . I don't think anybody is going to come here to see a parking lot next to a high-tech building. . . . We want to save . . . enough to interpret what happened here. . . . We realize development is inevitable and we welcome it. But at whose expense? Those who profit will be a very select, special interest group, not the people of Culpeper."

Patty Seiter, director, Culpeper Renaissance: "Culpeper just completed a public improvement project . . . infrastructure, the things under the street. . . . We had the old fluorescent light-poles. Main Street has a Victorian look, so we picked a Victorian-style pole to replace them. Especially at night, when you drive through, the new lights are just great. . . . Renaissance, as a nonprofit organization, sort of piggybacked on those improvements, fund-raising for benches, landscaping, and trash receptacles. . . . The whole Main Street philosophy is to treat downtown as a shopping destination and manage it the same way you would a shopping center. The strip centers can say they have a gazillion parking spaces and two anchors, one at either end. Downtown Culpeper is trying to achieve that by improving parking lots and making some sort of anchors, major stores, or the Courthouse area, thinking of downtown employees as assets to the shops, also improving the quality of customer service. . . . I'm a native. I moved away to go to college at Virginia Tech, in Blacksburg, a degree in history. Then I worked in Northern Virginia. Then I moved home because I got tired of city life, got a master's in public communication, and I started working with Renaissance. . . . Culpeper is right in line for development, which is kind of sad in a way but it also brings new influences to the area which are needed badly. It's a Southern town, and certain members of the community have tunnel-vision. . . . I don't want us to turn into another Manassas. Culpeper needs to maintain who it is, the ruralness, its proximity to Skyline Drive and a lot of neat places, well-kept secrets around the area . . . just the sort of hometown." ■

Danville, KY 40422

Location: 85 miles southeast of Louisville, 35 miles southwest of Lexington, in the Bluegrass region of central Kentucky.

Population: 14,500 (1990).

Growth rate: 9% since 1986.

Per capita income: $9,298 (1985), 8% higher than state average.

Geography/climate: Gently rolling hills, elevations varying between 900 and 1,000 feet. Temperate, 4-season continental climate. Average snowfall, 16 inches; rainfall, 45 inches. January low average, 25; high, 42, with 2 winter days below zero and 97 at or below freezing. July averages: high, 81; low, 59, with 16 days reaching into the 90s. 46 thunderstorm days annually. Fall weather typically clear and dry.

Economic base: Agriculture is the backbone: burley tobacco, livestock, grain, horses. Within 30-mile radius, the highest concentration of Angus cattle in the world. Diverse industrial base. Largest payrolls: American Greetings, 793 employees; R.R. Donnelley, printing, 700; Matsushita Floor Care, vacuum sweepers, 700; A.T.R. Wire & Cable, 690; McDowell Regional Medical Center, 430; Matthews Conveyors, 355; Thom McAn, 150. Retail trading center and seat of Boyle County.

Newspaper: *The Advocate-Messenger*, 330 S. Fourth Street, Danville, KY 40422. 606–236–2551. Daily. Mary Schurz, editor and publisher. $85 a year.

TV, radio: 2 local AM stations, 1 FM station. Cable carries network-TV stations from Louisville, Lexington. NPR received off-air from same cities.

Health care: McDowell Memorial Hospital, 177 beds. 44 physicians, 17 dentists in local practice.

Schools: 3 elementary schools (K–6); 1 junior high (7–8). Danville High School enrolls 580 students, send 66% to college. 1989–90 composite ACT score, 20.8. Also in town: Kentucky School for the Deaf, enrollment 320; Lindsey Wilson College, 2-year business school; Centre College, enrollment 900.

Educational level: 12.6% of Boyle County residents have 16 or more years of formal education; state average, 11.1%. Per capita expenditure for public education, $342, 8% higher than state.

Library: Boyle County Public Library, 60,000 volumes, including bookmobile.

Recreation: 3 large parks, 5 mini-parks, 9 playgrounds, 2 tennis courts, 3 baseball diamonds. 4 each softball, football, soccer fields. All within 20 miles: Herrington Lake, 3,600 acres; fishing, boating, camping, swimming. Old Fort Harrod State Park; outdoor dramas concern Daniel Boone, Abraham Lincoln. Pleasant Hill, restored Shaker village. Private recreational facilities include country club, golf course, 2 swimming pools, 4 movie theaters, bowling alley, roller-skating rink, racquetball court.

3 BR, 2 BA house: $60,000 to $110,000.

Cost of electricity: $.05 per kilowatt hour.

Cost of natural gas: $.43 per therm.

Sales tax: 6%.

State income tax: 2% to 6%.

Churches: 32. Denominations: AME, Assemblies of God, Baptist-Fundamental, Baptist-Independent, Baptist-Southern, Christian, Church of Christ, Church of God, Church of Jesus Christ of Latter-day Saints, Disciples of Christ, Episcopal, Independent Christian, Interdenominational, Jehovah's Witnesses, Lutheran, Nazarene, Pentecostal, Presbyterian, Salvation Army, United Methodist.

Besides Kentucky, there are Danvilles in 11 other states, including five neighbors of the Blue Grass State: Illinois, Indiana, Ohio, Virginia, and West Virginia. To avoid confusion with any other place, Danville in Kentucky would like to point out that certain things happened first here. The first post office established west of the Allegheny Mountains was opened in Danville, Kentucky, in 1792. The first major abdominal operation was performed here, on Christmas Day, 1809 (presumably on someone whose goose was not cooked). Centre College, founded in 1819, was among the first institutions of higher learning in the new West. The Kentucky School for the Deaf, first of its kind in the world, was established in 1823. And as every Kentucky school kid learns, Danville was the first capital of the state and site of the first nine constitutional conventions. But more to the point, Danville is home of the one and only—the Hub.

What residents say ...

Joseph Frankel, Hub Department Store: "It is a family-owned store. We're probably into the third generation of Frankels. It opened in 1904 and has been where it is since then, at the corner of Third and Main. We like to call Main Street 'The Heart of Danville.' We're a full-line department store, carry a broad spectrum of merchandise and price points. We have considerable staff for a store our size and a town this size. It's a very worn-out phrase, but our hallmark is service. That's what we're all about ... things like knowing a customer's pants-size, knowing they prefer navy over purple, and when a navy jacket comes in, letting them know. ... We have just one store. Many times we have contemplated expansion. But we like to have days with our families and don't like to be away running branch stores. We're independent retailers. In sheer size we're the largest store, but we're not the only anchor on Main Street. ... I think the attrition has leveled off. What is downtown are businesses that will survive and remain. I think there was a movement to the malls on the outskirts under the impression it might be more convenient and people would frequent them for convenience reasons. I think the downtown has tried to combat that a number of ways. They've tried to make it esthetically pleasing. Also, downtown has the services people want in a given area ... bakery, printing shop, re-

99

tailer, jewelry store. . . . The mix has deterred some of the exodus. The financial institutions and hospital downtown have kind of kept the Hub intact."

Cecil Dulin Wallace, farmer, horse-breeder:
"My family have been here since 1822 and I've lived here all my life. Farming and horses. We have thoroughbreds now. . . . The general roll of the land is quite conducive to livestock, cattle and horses, sheep and hogs. Then the crops have been hay, very predominantly tobacco, wheat and corn not as much anymore, and pasture. . . . I'd say the character of the town has been twofold since the very beginning. Farming and education. They started hand in glove. . . . Danville was fortunate when they laid it out in 1787. Very broad, wide streets, eight lanes, you'd almost say. It was well-thought-out. . . . This was a shopping hub before you could whip to Louisville in nothing flat. Three fine department stores, two particularly elegant. You couldn't do better in the cities. Joe's family very much has believed in the future of a downtown center of a town. It has been a key to holding downtown. A world of people come here from Louisville. . . . When the college was first founded it was just classrooms. All the students lived in private homes, and everybody kept an extra room for a college boy."

Richard Brown, retired professor of history:
"I taught at the State University of New York, in Buffalo. . . . Everybody who lives in Buffalo takes long spring vacations whenever spring comes. We grew up in southern Ohio, so we became familiar with central Kentucky. We like to go to the races and always thought we'd like to move to Lexington. But it has grown too big and expensive, so we started looking for small

towns. . . . Everyone from New York retires to Florida. We were determined we weren't going to retire there. We spent a winter in Roswell, New Mexico, gave that a try. But the verdant East is more attractive. . . . We've been very happy here. . . . You've got to get out and work at it. I joined the community theater. The second question people ask you is, 'What church do you go to?' Joining a church or going to church is significant. If one didn't go to church it would be difficult. . . . I joined the Presbyterian Church. . . . Centre College alumni, after careers elsewhere, come back to Danville. That is one source of retirees. The college is like a little cocoon. Even if you escape it, life in there seems very attractive."

Michael Adams, president, Centre College:
"I don't know if anyone has mentioned The Norton Center for the Arts . . . three theaters, the largest will seat 18 hundred . . . a magnificent facility, nothing like it on a small college campus, and we have a nice operating endowment. In the three years we've been here, the Bolshoi Ballet, Pinchas Zukerman, James Galway, the Pittsburgh Symphony, the Cleveland Symphony. . . . The cultural life here, frankly, is better and more accessible than it was in Los Angeles. . . . We were in Malibu. I was vice president at Pepperdine University. . . . That's my younger son on the answering machine. He's 11 and he's done very well moving. His older brother did harder. He was a blond-headed beach boy and it has taken some adjustment time for him. I think we would have a hard time getting them to move back now. . . . The school system is largely influenced by the presence of the college, and that makes it very strong. . . . Danville is probably the most progressive community in the state of

Kentucky. . . . I think this shows up in a number of ways. We have over 120 houses on the national registry, having been restored in the last 20 years. One of the best-planned industrial parks, with blue-chip tenants. Main Street looks like something out of a Norman Rockwell painting. . . . The school system is 23 percent minority, a number of poor blacks in Danville. . . . I think there is more of a security net or safety net in a small town than in a major city. The poor who are here still need more help than they are getting. The churches seem a little more sensitive to the problem than they do in a large city. . . . There is less insulation from the need. You go to school with these people. You see them on the streets. In Los Angeles, or in Chicago, which I know well, the neighborhoods are so divided ethnically that one is not as likely to come in contact with need as in a small town." ■

Devils Lake, ND 58301

Location: 400 miles northwest of Minneapolis, 181 miles northeast of Bismarck, in northeastern North Dakota.

Population: 7,782 (1990).

Growth rate: 5% since 1980.

Per capita income: $9,455 (1985), 98% of state average ($9,635).

Geography/climate: Flat, high plains, elevation 1,475 feet, largely treeless except for some woodsy areas around lake. Rugged climate. Average 55 days below zero, with stretches of 30 below zero; 35 inches of snow. Average temperatures: January: high, 14 above zero; low, 4 below. July: high, 83; low, 59. 15 or more days over 90 through summer. Annual rainfall, 15 inches.

Economic base: Retail, wholesale trade; government and health services, agriculture, tourism, manufacturing. Seat of Ramsey County. Service center for 60,000–70,000 people living within 50-mile radius, including Sioux Indian Reservation, south of town. County labor force of 4,530 includes: retail trade, 1,226 employees; wholesale trade, 263; health services, 625; social services, 307; government, 990; manufacturing, 156. Durum wheat, the pasta flour, is major regional crop. Noodles by Leonardo has a local plant. Summers Manufacturing, agricultural equipment.

Newspaper: *Devils Lake Daily Journal*, 516 Fourth Street, Devils Lake, ND 58301. 701–662–2127. Monday through Friday. Michael Bellmore, editor. $70 a year.

TV, radio: 1 AM, 2 FM stations. Local TV station carries ABC. Cable broadcasts NBC, CBS, PBS from Fargo, Grand Forks. NPR received off-air from Grand Forks.

Health care: Mercy Hospital, 110 beds. 14 physicians, 6 dentists in local practice.

Schools: 3 elementary (K–6), 1 junior high (7–9). Central High School (10–12) enrolls 402, sends 50% to college. St. Joseph's Elementary School (K–6) enrolls 167. University of North Dakota–Lake Region, a 2-year institution, enrolls 695. North Dakota School for the Deaf also is in Devils Lake.

Educational level: 13.1% of Ramsey County residents have 16 or more years of formal education; state average, 14.8%. Per capita expenditure for public education, $637; state average, $522.

Library: Carnegie Public Library, 26,500 volumes.

Recreation: Devils Lake, largest natural body of water in North Dakota, has 300 miles of shoreline, covers 55,000 acres. Lake and perimeter area attract vacationers from Upper Midwest. Northern pike, walleye, white bass, perch abound. Migratory waterfowl cross area in Central Flyway. Goose, duck, white-tailed-deer hunting. Boating, skiing, curling, ice-skating, swimming, camping. 55 miles of groomed snowmobile trails. 9-hole golf course. Nature walks, birdwatching at Sully's Hill National Game Preserve, south of town. 4 state parks located around lake. 2 city parks include Winter Sports Arena, softball diamonds, tennis courts, swimming pool, exercise trail, ice-skating rink.

3 BR, 2 BA house: $50,000.

Cost of electricity: $.06 per kilowatt hour.

Cost of natural gas: $.54 per therm.

Sales tax: 6%.

State income tax: 2.67% to 12%.

Churches: 18. Denominations: Baptist, Church of God, Church of Jesus Christ of Latter-day Saints, Episcopal, Evangelical, Jehovah's Witnesses, Lutheran (5), Presbyterian, Roman Catholic, United Methodist.

Devils Lake derives its name from a Native American word meaning "bad water." Local officials are frank to admit that their prime resource—the largest natural lake in arid North Dakota—is a worrisome asset. The lake is a closed basin fed only by runoff from surrounding lands. It needs a stabilizing, outside source to moderate the long-term ups and downs of cyclical drought. The Lake Preservation Coalition, a four-county group, hopes a long-proposed, 17-mile canal link to the Missouri River system may be the answer. Delegations fly off to Washington periodically.

What residents say . . .

Chaun Foughty, former commodore, Devils Lake Yacht Club: "Back around the turn of the century the lake was even higher than it is now and there was quite a tourist trade. In fact, Devils Lake was one of the sites of the Chautauqua. The Devils Lake Yacht Club was established in 1903. It was active until the lake deteriorated, probably in the '20s. Then in the early '70s the lake started coming up again. . . . We're quite active, eight or 10 sailboat races a year. Most of the boats are offshores, between 22 and 26 feet. . . . This year we've had ample rain supply. . . . What is needed is a wet fall so that the ground freezes up, then ample snowpack in the drainage system. If that happens, in the spring we'll have a big snow runoff."

Kyle Blanchfield, resort owner: "It's a family resort now going into our fourth season, built and created on land where my mother grew up as a kid. . . . I was born and raised here. I'm a single person but this is a family business. My parents work here also. . . . We're on West Creel Bay, five miles out of town. We have a real neat, cozy little restaurant lounge, full-service cabins, boat rental, fish-house rental, real nice store and bait shop. . . . North Dakota is a pretty treeless area but we're very wooded. Just to clear the trees was an incredible task. We took as few as we could because trees are so precious in this part of the world. . . . We're doing all right, up to full strength. We get people from all over the country but the majority from the Upper Midwest, Wisconsin, Minnesota, Iowa. . . . Fishing is really our bread and butter, especially in winter time. Most people picture the resort business open first of May to Labor Day. this part of the world offers us a lot of natural resources. We have summer. We go into fall hunting season. We're in the . . . largest fall staging areas for snow and blue geese. . . . The lake freezes up the first of December and then our ice fishing picks up, carries us through the second week of March. We're famous for our two-pound perch. It's a trophy-class-size fish. . . . Normally most perch are small. It's what a lot of kids catch first."

Rick LaFleur, co-owner, amusement business: "I.F. LaFleur & Son, Inc. The son is actually my father. My brother and I hold the company. . . . Juke boxes, dart games, pool tables, video games. . . . We go from Sidney, Montana, all the way to the Minnesota border, and the northern two-thirds of North Dakota. We do everything from ma-and-pa cafes to local sales meetings. . . . The video games have been wanting a little because of the home entertainment systems. Pinball machines are enjoying a romance with the customers, coming back strongly. CD juke boxes, up to 2,000 selections, have been a very good plus. But primarily we have dart leagues and pool leagues. I'd say per capita there are more dart players in Devils Lake, North Dakota, than any other part of the country. We have approximately 2,500 registered players in 45 different leagues. . . . It's one of the most social games you'll find. We even have a grandmas' league, 15 or 20 ladies get together twice a week. . . . In our leagues, teams have to be made up of guys and gals. We're looking for the social benefits of having everybody together. Teams play a home-and-away schedule, and that creates a lot of camaraderie. We take care of all the stats. The bar owner mails them in and we compile them. I have one person full-time running the computer. . . . In darts, there isn't any defense. When you go up to throw at the line, it isn't anybody but you and the board. Seldom I've heard of a

fight, far different from pool. A pool player is in direct competition with his opponent. A good amount of the ability to win is how you leave your opponent, which can often leave him upset."

Penny Knudson, owner, Western store: "Devils Lake is the beginning of the Old West. A lot of people coming through from the East want to get a hat before they go on west. In 1977, when we started, there were only two western stores in the state, in Bismarck and Dickinson. Other than that, people did a lot of catalog-buying. We felt there was a need and Devils Lake was a good central location. . . . We were fortunate to get in at the beginning of the cowboy craze. . . . We have a loyal clientele from the Sioux Indian Reservation. Devils Lake Sioux Manufacturing and Dakota Tribal Industries primarily make camouflage netting and helmets for the Army. The tribe owns both of them and are working on getting more of their people employed, trying to become self-sufficient. We're certainly supportive of that. They employ between 400 and 500. It really helps the Devils Lake economy. . . . We're hosting the state finals for the Roughrider Rodeo Association. It's always the third week of September. Everyone dresses Western for a couple of days. We probably draw between 5,000 and 6,000 people."

Guy De Sautel, supermarket owner: "Devils Lake is very hometown, small-town feeling. People are very trustworthy. You can take them for their word. . . . We rely heavily on tourism and agriculture. . . . The town is really prospering. New Wal-Mart, new K-Mart, new Leonardo's. Lots of new retail. New hotels. I think a big part of it is our location. We're a hub for medical, wholesale, retail. For any of those services you have to drive 90 miles east, 90 miles south, or 90 miles west. we're kind of out on the prairie all by ourselves. What's happening is you see a migration of the population to these centers. . . . Are you familiar with the forecast? North Dakota is supposed to be just eight cities in 10 years. Grand Forks, Devils Lake, Minot, and Williston along Highway 2. Then on the southern side, Fargo, Jamestown, Bismarck, and Dickinson. Small towns are dying and the people are moving to these eight cities. A lot of people think that's sad. America was built on the rural towns. It's unfortunate in some ways, but it's just reality. We just have to accept it." ■

Douglas, WY 82633

Location: 227 miles north of Denver, 447 miles northeast of Salt Lake City, on I-25 in east central Wyoming.

Population: 5,076 (1990).

Growth rate: 16% loss since 1980.

Per capita income: $9,555 (1985), 98% of state average ($9,782).

Geography/climate: Elevation 4,815 feet, on the Platte River in a setting of rolling hills, with 10,200-foot Laramie Peak dominating the southern horizon. Average temperatures: January, 23 degrees; July, 75. Chinooks temper the winter bite, which can include 15 days below zero. Elevation moderates summer highs—average 17 days above 90. Average annual rainfall, 6 inches; snowfall, 40 inches. Prevailing winds 11 mph from northwest.

Economic base: Ranching, mining, oil, tourism. Variable energy industry has taken Douglas through big ups and downs. Planners see recreation and retail as steadier sources of revenue for the long haul. Major payrolls: Powder River Coal, 350 employees; School District No. 1, 256; NERCO-Antelope Coal, 70; PLM, rail-car maintenance, 60; state–city government, 65; Phillips Petroleum, 38; Nutra-West, vitamins, 35. Douglas is seat of Converse County.

Newspaper: *The Douglas Budget*, Drawer 109, Douglas, WY 82633. 307–358–2965. Weekly, Wednesday. Robert Dorroh, editor. $25 a year.

TV, radio: 1 local AM, 1 FM station. Cable carries network TV from Casper, Denver.

Health care: Converse County Hospital, 44 beds. 4 physicians, 3 dentists in local practice.

Schools: 2 elementary (K–5). Middle school (6–8) won national honors in 1984 for excellence in educational approach. Douglas High School enrolls 523, sends 55% to college. 75% of students take ACT; mean composite scores 1985–90 were about 2 points higher than national average, school officials report. Eastern Wyoming College, 2-year institution, enrolls 350.

Educational level: 13.4% of Converse County residents have 16 or more years of formal education; state average, 17.2%. Per capita expenditure for public education, $1,012; state average, $851.

Library: Converse County Library, 90,000 volumes.

Recreation: Recreational Center attached to high school, adjacent to elementary school: 2 gyms with 6 basketball courts, 2 racquetball courts, indoor pool, weight room. 2 outdoor tennis courts, baseball diamond. All facilities open to the public free. Also in town: 6 lighted ball fields, outdoor pool, bowling alley, 18-hole golf course, 10 lighted tennis courts, 2 shooting ranges, movie theater, 4 parks. Converse County home to one of the largest concentrations of pronghorn antelope in America. Fishing, water sports at Glendo Reservoir and State Park, 23 miles southeast. Camping at Ayres Natural Bridge, 14 miles west.

3 BR, 2 BA house: $40,000 to $60,000.

Cost of electricity: $.05 per kilowatt hour.

Cost of natural gas: $.38 per therm.

Sales tax: 4%.

State income tax: None.

Churches: 16. Denominations: Baptist, In- dependent Baptist, Southern Baptist, Church of Christ, Church of Jesus Christ of Latter-day Saints, Episcopal, Lutheran, Roman Catholic, United Methodist, United Pentecostal.

Douglas is an "energy-impacted" town, government-speak meaning it pre- sides over an area that is rich with deposits of coal, uranium, and oil but un- able to control the mining of this great wealth. Other people do that, some of them continents away, and without a clue to the beautiful wide-open spaces of Converse County. When battalions of work crews arrived in Wyo- ming in the mid-1970s to extract its mineral wealth, Douglas boomed. Astounding amounts of new money flowed in, and local officials, taking the optimistic long view, invested in basic services to provide for a much larger permanent population. That was a smart move, for even though the most re- cent energy boom is now past and the population has shrunk, Douglas has rebuilt itself and paid the bill. No one knows when energy will boom again. Stalking those riches is like hunting for the legendary Jackalope, a bizarre cross between a jack rabbit and an antelope, first seen in Douglas some years ago but never sighted since.

What residents say . . .

Fred Schroeder, hospital administrator: "Orig- inally it was Douglas's plan to grow to 14, 15 thousand. We've got all new schools, new hospital, new airport, new courthouse, an updated water system. . . . So we have an excellent infrastructure. . . . The old air- port we turned into Douglas International Raceway, a mile-long drag strip where races are held every other weekend throughout the summer. I'm told it's the longest drag strip. It does get quite a lot of use and attracts people from about a four- or five-state area."

Barb Wisecup, Cub Scout leader, drag racer: "My lifelong dream was to drag race. My first race was in May of '88. I started out in my family car, an '83 Dodge 4 cylinder ES, just a regular family car. I did real good, won quite a few places in Powder Puff. That's just for women. Then in the summer of '89 I was driving a '73 Dodge Dart . . . 12.88 seconds from a stand- ing start to the end of a quarter mile, at 105 miles an hour."

Paula Rider, rancher: "We live at the base of some mountains about 12 and a half miles out of town. We have a dry creek, at least it's dry most of the time, just west of our house. We can see I-25 from the house. I grew up here. When I was a little girl, that 12 miles was a long way . . . we came home on the school bus and stayed home. . . . My parents live across the creek a half mile. . . . Antelope season ends tomorrow. A lot of hunters from both coasts come out and do the macho thing and hunt antelope. Dad had probably 20 or 25 hunters this year. We don't really guide them but keep them separated so they don't shoot each other. . . . Douglas was just a little cow town. Then the uranium mines opened up. They told us when they came here the mines would be open 15 years, and that's just about as long as it lasted, beginning about 1974–75. It was good for our community, that influx of people. I felt like we were kind of closed socially. A lot of nice people came and stayed."

Diane Harrop, co-owner, R-D Pharmacy & Books: "We own a drugstore and bookstore, tonics for the body and tonics for the mind. We operate the oldest continuing business in Converse County. There's been a drugstore at this location since 1889, and we've owned it since 1979. . . . then we bought the store. . . . After the [energy] boom, we realized we were doing things pretty much the same way as everyone else. There are three drugstores, and you can't make a living here with just a drugstore. One thing that did not exist in our community was a full-line bookstore. It takes 18,000 to 20,000 people to support a bookstore, so there's been a real good economic reason why there hasn't been one. . . . But the secret is creating your own niche. I've specialized in Western and regional titles, and children's books . . . . We're right on the edge of the Great Plains and the Rocky Mountains. People have chosen to live around here because they like the animals and plants. I have a lot of titles on that. This is the edge of frontier history

here. . . .I was the mayor of Douglas for a couple of years. During my term we embarked on a project that is coming to bloom right now. We've completely redone the historic retail street of town. A lot of money went into things you'll never see, like getting rid of old coal chutes. . . . We put in new sidewalks, textured at the corners. It looks like flagstone but it's concrete . . . a few ornamental light-posts. It's maybe the nicest street in southeast Wyoming, a whole community effort in our State Centennial Year. . . . We are the home of the Jackalope, as you may know, and we've had this Jackalope statue. It used to be in the highway median. Now it is downtown, in Centennial Jackalope Square, with picnic tables, nice plants and trees, restrooms. I've noticed for the first time this year the hunters are spending time walking around downtown. That's the whole idea I had in mind fixing up the downtown. . . . I think Douglas is doing well. I see a return to optimism. I think that's vital. . . . There was a kind of refusal to look ahead, to take a leap of faith on behalf of ourselves. That happens in small towns. 'If it ain't broke don't fix it.' In larger places, people know they have to keep moving or they will fall behind. In small towns, people fool themselves into thinking they can keep things just the same, and that isn't valid. There is no standing still. . . . I grew up in larger places . . . Emporia, Kansas. . . . I went to school in Lawrence, Kansas. . . . I lived in Boulder and taught outside of Kansas City. In none of those places was I really ever tempted to get involved to change things for the better. I felt swallowed up, simply because the world was so big. I've come to learn in this small place that I have a lot of abilities, that I have a lot to give." ■

Durango, CO 81302

Location: 332 miles southwest of Denver, 214 miles northwest of Santa Fe, in extreme southwestern Colorado near the "Four Corners" junction with New Mexico, Arizona, Utah.

Population: 12,430 (1990).

Growth rate: 6% since 1980.

Per capita income: $9,624 (1985), 80% of state average ($11,713).

Geography/climate: Elevation 6,512 feet, in the Animas River Valley. To the north, San Juan Mountain peaks rise to average 10,400 feet. South and west lies desert land. Generally dry and sunny with 4 seasons. Average temperatures: January: high, 39; low, 20. July: high, 88; low, 64. Snowfall averages 69 inches in town, over 300 inches at Purgatory-Durango Ski Resort, 25 miles north. Average annual rainfall, 19 inches.

Economic base: Tourism, government services, retirement living, light industry. Large payrolls: Fort Lewis College, 379 employees; 9-R School District, 460; Mercy Medical Center, 500; federal government, 360; La Plata County government, 253; state government, 271; Purgatory-Durango Ski Resort, 700; Tamarron Resort, 505; City of Durango, 165; City Market, 258.

Newspaper: *The Durango Herald*, 1275 Main Avenue, Durango, CO 81302. 303–247–3504. Monday through Friday afternoon, Sunday morning. Dan Partridge, managing editor. $107 a year.

TV, radio: 2 AM, 4 FM stations in town. Cable carries network TV, PBS from Denver, Albuquerque, Grand Junction. NPR from Ignacio.

Health care: Mercy Medical Center, 94 beds. 83 physicians, 25 dentists in local practice.

Schools: 10 elementary (K–5), 2 middle (6–8). Durango High School enrolls 1,134, sends 58% to college. 1990 average SAT scores: verbal, 505; math, 531. San Juan Basin Vo-Tech. Private schools: Calvary Baptist, New Life Academy (K–4), St. Columba Catholic (K–6), Seventh-Day Adventist (K–8). Fort Lewis College, 4-year liberal arts, enrolls 4,000.

Educational level: 22.1% of La Plata County residents have 16 or more years of formal education; state average, 23%. Per capita spending for public education, $483; state average, $523.

Library: Durango Public Library, 70,000 volumes.

Recreation: 22 city parks, 15 playgrounds, 2 golf courses, 2 movie theaters, 2 theatrical companies. Alpine skiing 25 miles north at Purgatory–Durango Resort, capacity 6,500. Mesa Verde National Park, 38 miles west. Vallecito Lake, 22 miles northeast, has campsites, boat docks, fishing. Big new sport is mountain biking. Durango was host to first unified World Mountain Bike Championships, in 1990.

3 BR, 2 BA house: 1990 averages: in town, $83,000; county, $99,000.

Cost of electricity: $.05 per kilowatt hour.

Cost of natural gas: $.43 per therm.

Sales tax: 7%.

State income tax: 5%.

Churches: 31. Denominations: Assemblies of God, Baptist, Southern Baptist, Bible, Christian, Christian Science, Church of Christ, Church of jesus Christ of Latter-day Saints, Episcopal, Jehovah's Witnesses, Joy Fellowship, Lutheran, Lutheran ELCA, free Methodist, United Methodist, Presbyterian, Reorganized LDS, Roman Catholic, Seventh-Day Adventist, Society of Friends, Universal Life, Unitarian Universalist.

During a brief layover in 1935, humorist Will Rogers observed that Durango is "out of the way and glad of it." You may catch some wistfulness when people quote that line today. Durango is no longer remote. They've built a 9,200-foot runway at Durango-La Plata County Airport, and four scheduled airlines buzz in nonstop from Denver, Albuquerque, and Phoenix.

The big summer draw is a slower but more interesting means of transportation—the Durango & Silverton Narrow Gauge Railroad. The D&SNG carries tourists 45 miles north to Silverton, one of the old mining towns that put Durango on the map a century ago. The big winter draw is skiing at Purgatory, where there's room enough for 6,500 visitors a day. The big topic of conversation among Durango residents is how to retain the charm of the Old West as growing numbers of people discover their attractive place. After an emotional battle in 1991, one symbol of the olden days—the county fairgrounds—fell to the pressure of rising real-estate values. in a related matter, voters narrowly defeated home rule. But the proponents said they'd try again. In their view, La Plata County has outgrown governance by a three-member board of commissioners.

What residents say ...

Anne Putnam, chairwoman, La Plata County Home Rule Charter Commission: "To do this kind of thing takes people who are willing to sacrifice a lot of time for political service. From my standpoint that makes it idealistic and exciting. When Americans get excited about an idea they put it on the ballot. We had to have 11 people willing to serve. Thirty-four people ran for 11 positions. Not all of them were in favor of home rule. Some wanted to squash it. . . . We worked all winter, had the public hearings. We followed the state law and have done what we should do. We had our special election and lost by 5 percent. . . . The city, the college, the hospital, the electric company, they all work with boards, whereas the county commissioners do not. They do not have a hired professional manager. They're kind of the ones using a different system from everybody else. It's not a personality issue, more the idea that home rule would be better for us."

Dan Officer, owner, pottery store; president, Save Our Fairgrounds Association: "The fairgrounds has been part of Durango's history even before Durango was formed. We have records dating back to 1887, when they had the first Colorado–New Mexico fair. The fairgrounds was the place where feuding factions met and settled their differences. . . . Its construction is of native materials . . . stone columns that rise 40 feet into the air, an architecture emblematic of the era. I think it is really like a monument to a culture long past. . . . The La Plata County Commissioners want to sell it. They have never offered a plan how it should be disposed of. On their own, they were involved in negotiations to sell the land for a Wal-Mart. That's when our group stepped in and got public opinion moving back and forth. . . . I know the sentiment of the public is to keep [the fairgrounds] in the public domain . . . but no public entity has the funds to pay what they want for it. . . . In any small town you have people get elected to office and seem to change personally, almost like a power-ego kind of problem. . . . That's where home rule comes in. It will guard against people building up turfs."

Will Williams, director, La Plata County Economic Development Council: "Our main focus is on attracting and recruiting small manufacturing companies. I think we've been real successful at doing that. Most of the companies are coming from southern California. Probably the most recent to relocate here is Yeti Cycles, maker of damn good mountain bikes. They moved here lock, stock, and barrel from Agoura Hills and brought some of their employees with them. They really fit the mold of what we're looking for, the 10-to-30-employee, nonpolluting, environmentally conscious companies. . . . Here's the stereotype: the couple comes through here from southern California to ride the train or visit Mesa Verde or go to a guest ranch. They probably drive in, probably stay a week. They say to themselves, 'That was a really neat little town. We've got a business here in southern California. I'm tired of the long drive. Why don't we move there?' Then we get a phone call. . . . What we're seeing now is a real common sight of towns riding a crest of a wave. First, tourism is up. Second, for the same reasons, we're getting a lot of retirees. Third, it's causing a housing crunch. So, we're growing in spurts. If there's housing available, we fill up. Right now, affordable housing is kind of at a standstill."

Duane Smith, professor of history, Fort Lewis College: "We could use some lower-cost housing. We're going like Aspen. Houses in town are just skyrocketing. My house we bought for $32,000 when it was built, in 1970. In 1991, houses around us are going for $120,000 to $140,000."

Sally Morrissey, columnist, **Durango Herald:** "It's a hard place to make a living. We don't urge people to come here unless they have a job. There's a saying, 'The easiest way to make a million dollars in Durango is to come with two.' . . . I came here in 1954. My husband brought cable television to Durango, the first in Colorado. We chose Durango because we wanted to raise our children in a small town. It's grown, and turned from a rural farming community to a tourist town. . . . There's an awful lot of old Victorian residences here. People are buying them and fixing them up. . . . I think the main thing people like about the town, it isn't an Aspen, Telluride, and Vail. It has enough warts in it that it still is a working town. . . . The Indians are more or less in Ignacio, the center of their reservation. They keep pretty much to themselves. . . . 30 years ago it was difficult for the Spanish people here. Now they are integrated into the town. They have become better educated. They just had service jobs before. Now there are [Spanish] professionals here. . . . Another very, very interesting thing, we have 85 doctors. That's why many retired people have moved here. . . . We also have a very big arts community. Painters, musicians, symphony orchestra, a lot of galleries. . . . The old-timers resent the newcomers coming in. . . . The gay–lesbian community up at the college smacks these old-timers right smack in the face." ∎

Easton, MD 21601

Location: 59 miles southeast of Baltimore, 69 miles east of Washington, DC, 117 miles south of Philadelphia, on the eastern shore of Maryland.

Population: 9,372 (1990).

Growth rate: 10% since 1986.

Per capita income: $10,378 (1985), 20% below state average ($12,976).

Geography/climate: Flat, tidewater country. Continental climate moderated by Chesapeake Bay, Atlantic Ocean. High humidity. Average 100 winter days at freezing or below, 20 inches of snow. July daily average high: 87 degrees, low, 67. 31 days into the 90s. Annual rainfall of 46 inches, tending to concentrate in late summer and early fall.

Economic base: Seafood industry—clams, oysters, crabbing—and farming remain active while tourism, recreation, leisure-living grow. Manufacturing accounts for 26% of employment. Larger payrolls: Black & Decker, Waverly Press, Allen Family Foods, Wildlife International.

Newspaper: *Star-Democrat & Sunday Star*, P.O. Box 600, Easton, MD 21601. 301–822–1500. Daily. $64 a year. Larry Effingham, publisher.

TV, radio: Local AM, FM stations. Cable carries network stations from Washington, Baltimore. NPR from Salisbury, Maryland.

Health care: Memorial Hospital at Easton, 216 beds. 60 physicians, 23 dentists in local practice.

Schools: 2 elementary (K–1, 2–5), 1 middle (6–8). Easton High School enrolls 826, sends 65–75% to college. Average SAT scores, 1988–89: verbal, 450; math, 511. Chesapeake College, 2-year institution, enrolls 2,500.

Educational level: 18.1% of Talbot County residents have 16 or more years of formal education; state average, 20.4%. Per capita expenditure for public education, $389; state average, $477.

Library: Talbot County Free Library, 100,000 volumes, 190,000 circulation.

Recreation: 600 miles of shoreline attract waterfowl, hunters, boaters, fishers to rich variety of water sports, tourist attractions. Talbot County YMCA has full-time staff of 6, corps of volunteers, offers uncommonly large program for small town. Facilities: gymnasium, pool, racquetball, tennis courts; skills training, youth and adult programs, trips. 3 18-hole golf courses in town: 1 public, 2 private. Bowling alley. 4 movie theaters. Ocean beaches 60 miles southeast.

3 BR, 2 BA house: $90,000 to $200,000. Average existing, $120,000; new, near school, $170,000.

Cost of electricity: $.09 per kilowatt hour.

Cost of natural gas: $.60 per therm.

Sales tax: 5%.

State income tax: 2% to 5%.

Churches: 25. Denominations: AME, Baptist, Brethren, Christian Science, Church of God, Episcopal, Independent, Lutheran, Methodist, Nazarene, Nondenominational, Presbyterian, Society of Friends, Roman Catholic, Unitarian, United Methodist, United Pentecostal, Wesleyan.

Synagogues: 1.

When the idea to restore the old Avalon Theatre came along, some residents of Easton frankly wondered why. The town already had two decent performing houses: the 100-seat Academy of the Arts and the 250-seat Historical Society, not to mention the 1,200-seat Talbot County Auditorium. Why resurrect a rundown movie theater? Mayor George Murphy had a ready answer. "I refer to the Avalon Theatre as part of my triangle," he told a writer for the *Star-Democrat*, the local newspaper. "The three sides are the Academy, the Historical Society, and the Avalon. They represent art, history, and music, and those things are very important to a community that wants to remain a civil and attractive place to work and live."

Built in 1921, the Avalon was the entertainment center of the local universe, showcase of silent movies and vaudeville, and upstairs, ballroom dancing. There were special attractions, like the imaginative play-by-play reenactment of the 1924 World Series: a Western Union operator set up shop in the theater and relayed the action to a man on the stage, who moved a ball around on a big backdrop of a baseball diamond. In a time when most people didn't even have radios, this was magic.

Though the magic faded, the Avalon survived 60 years. When it went dark in 1985, worn and water-stained, few people could imagine new life for the old house. But Mayor Murphy could, and with a big boost from developer Richard Edgar, the Avalon was reborn on March 11, 1990, with a new season of music and drama. They called it "A Return to Razzle Dazzle," right in the center of downtown.

What residents say ...

William "Doc" Hill, owner, Hill's Drug Stores—"Get Your Pills at Hills": "My father started it in 1928. He was a pharmacist. He passed away in 1957 and I've run it since. I also have two daughters who are pharmacists. Both have worked with me. My son is a dentist. He started the William Hill Manor, a retirement and life-care community of cottages, apartments, protective care. . . . We have three stores. The old store is downtown that my dad started, still the busiest prescription store. . . . Downtown has perpetuated itself. My business is better than ever. A merchant has to be pretty clever now to stay in business and match the pushes by the chain stores. In my business, it's 'We deliver.' We've got several thousand customers, and there's nothing we don't do to try to help. Something as insignificant as a tube of toothpaste we'll deliver, they know that. The big stores, they won't do that. . . . We have an old-time soda fountain in my downtown store. We still operate it, don't make a cent on it. But people come in for a cup of coffee and see their friends."

Polly Shannahan, president, Talbot County Historical Trust: "Easton was a planned town from the beginning. It was chosen as the courthouse town of Talbot County in roughly 1710. The first record that we can find was mention of the appointment of a sheriff in 1661. . . . We have the court-house square and the streets that radiate off that to the west and to the east. . . . The present courthouse was built in 1794 and was considered a possible seat of government for the Eastern Shore. As far back as 1925, the Garden Club was interested in making the courthouse green more attractive. Just two years ago, in consultation with the county commissioners, the club did an extensive replanting of the green. There have been interested people here for a long time."

Larry Effingham, editor, **Star-Democrat & Sunday Star:** "Probably the number-one issue is schools. This is a beautiful area. People out of Baltimore and Washington come down and retire in Easton. That's bad news for families with school-age children. These retirees fight to keep the limit on the tax cap. It's hard to fund the schools the way they should be. . . . We have one of the top public golf courses in the country, and the YMCA here is as good as any in the country. . . . We've lived here seven years, moved here from Corpus Christi, Texas. We've got two children. It's a beautiful place for kids to grow up."

Georgia Adler, director, Historical Society of Talbot County: "We need volunteers all the time . . . two in the morning and two in the afternoon for tours, the same for the museum shop, which is open every day. [The volunteer corps] is one of those things you have to revamp about every six months. In a small town people like change and there's always something going on. . . . You wouldn't have a strong organization without volunteers. If you had the staff do everything you wouldn't have the involvement. . . . Easton is a small town yet it's somewhat sophisticated. I do know people who work in Baltimore, Annapolis, and Washington, but it's not really a bedroom community. . . . There are still many large properties in Talbot County, but a lot of the big places have been sold off. Not that all the shoreland is going to get developed. Hopefully it will never lose its integrity as a wetland. . . . Because the land is low and the fact that in the early days most of the homes were built on the water because you traveled by water, you have a lot of the big plantation feeling."

David Rhodes, venture capitalist; president, Mid-Shore Center for the Performing Arts, Avalon Theatre: "I turn businesses in crisis around. That's what I do for private companies, but I'm doing this for the town, to restore the original assumptions about the Center's ability to repay long-term debt. People were somewhat exhausted from the [Avalon Theatre] building program. We've restructured the board of directors. . . . In the next two days we'll have a strategic planning session, the first time in this organization's history. . . . We saw this town as undiscovered when we moved here three years ago. We moved from Singapore, before that Tokyo, before that Manhattan.

We were looking for a place that represented traditional values, close to family, accessible to larger cities but clearly apart from them. . . . We restored a three-story Victorian house. My office is on the third floor. A lot of my business is involved in using the computer, phone, fax machine. The people I speak with during the day have no idea where I am. . . . You can fly in for meetings. We're an hour and a half from a train station and just about an hour from there into Penn Central. . . . I'm enjoying a life that does not include subways, smog, and the unpleasantries normally associated with work in the cities." ■

Elizabeth City, NC 27909

Location: 160 miles northeast of Raleigh, 60 miles south of Norfolk, Virginia, off Albemarle Sound in coastal North Carolina.

Population: 14,292 (1990).

Growth rate: 4% since 1980.

Per capita income: $7,507 (1985), 79% of state average ($9,517).

Geography/climate: Situated at the Narrows of the Pasquotank River, 12 nautical miles up from Albemarle Sound. Elevation 8 feet. Low, level land with Great Dismal Swamp to the north. Common track of hurricanes and tropical storms passes south of the area, continental storm systems generally pass to the north, favoring Elizabeth City with pleasant springs and falls, mild winters. Average temperatures: January: high, 49; low, 32. July: high, 87; low, 70. Summers are warm, humid, long, with average 30 days at 90 or above. Annual average rainfall, 40 inches; snowfall, 5 inches.

Economic base: Coast Guard base employs 500 military, 700 civilians; brings approximately 1,000 military in for training annually; largest influence on local economy. Other payrolls: Elizabeth City Cotton Mill, yarn, 111 employees; IXL Furniture, cabinets, 150; Davis Yachts, 80; Superior Brands, pet treats, 90; J.W. Jones, lumber, 92; Airship Industries, blimps, 50; Desco, electronic systems, 50; Hockmeyer Equipment, commercial mixers, 38; Pell Paper Box, 38. Elizabeth City is seat of Pasquotank County.

Newspaper: *The Advance*, 216 S. Poindexter Street, Elizabeth City, NC 27909.

919–335–0841. Monday through Friday, Sunday morning. Michael Goodman, editor. $105 a year.

TV, radio: 2 local AM, 3 FM stations. Cable carries PBS, network TV from Norfolk, Hampton, Greenville. NPR from Norfolk area.

Health care: Albemarle Medical Hospital, 206 beds. 40 physicians, 11 dentists in local practice.

Schools: 6 elementary (1–6), 1 junior high (7–8). Northeastern High School enrolls 1,400, sends 45% to 4-year colleges. Composite SAT for 1990–91, 780. Parochial school (K–12) enrolls 70; private nonparochial (K–12) enrolls 170. Other local institutions: College of the Albemarle, 2-year college; Elizabeth City State University, part of University of North Carolina system; Roanoke Bible College, 4-year liberal-arts institution.

Educational level: 10.7% of Pasquotank County residents have 16 or more years of formal education; state average, 13.2%. Per capita expenditure for public education, $373; state average, $390.

Library: Pasquotank-Camden Public Library, 48,000 volumes.

Recreation: 7 city parks. Swimming pool, 16 tennis courts, ball fields, golf course. YMCA, YWCA, country club. 3 movie theaters. Free public boat dock. Intracoastal Waterway connects Elizabeth City with entire East Coast, making sailing and boating very popular. Area includes 3 state parks, numerous wildlife refuges. Wright Brothers National Monument is 36 miles to southeast, near Kitty Hawk, on route to Cape Hatteras National Seashore.

3 BR, 2 BA house: $70,000 to $100,000.

Cost of electricity: $.07 to $.09 per kilowatt hour.

Cost of propane: $1 per gallon.

Sales tax: 6%.

State income tax: 6% to 7%.

Churches: 20. Denominations: AME, Assemblies of God, Baptist, Southern Baptist, Church of Christ, Episcopal, Evangelical, Methodist, Pentecostal, Presbyterian, Roman Catholic.

Synagogues: 1.

In nautical terms, Elizabeth City lies at 36° 17′ North, 76° 12′ West. But those sailing directions fail to capture the essence of the place. *Carolina Cruising* wrote this a few years ago:

"North Carolina's Albemarle Sound is one of those unspoiled cruising grounds that forms the stuff of local boating legend. Nobody visits the Sound and the rivers of the Albemarle without vowing to come back again as soon as possible. One reason is the feeling of a closeness with Colonial history. Another is the long stretches of open water and forested shoreline. But the main reason is the special friendliness of the people in the waterfront towns"—as witness the fellow buzzing down to the waterfront in a white golf cart, bearing a long-stem rose for each skipper and wine and cheese for dockside camaraderie.

What residents say ...

Fred Fearing, first of The Rose Buddies:
"It started on a September Sunday in 1983 when Mr. Joe Kramer and I came out of church. Seventeen boats were tied up at the Municipal Docks. I said to Joe, 'I've got a gallon of wine. You go get some chips and dips. We'll have a Thanksgiving party.' He said, 'How dumb can you be. Thanksgiving isn't for two months!' I said, 'We have these 17 visitors. Let's go show how much we appreciate them.' So we went down and greeted the boating public, and it was so rewarding with them and with us that we just decided every time we had as many as five new boats we would have a

wine and cheese party. . . . We've had as many as 38 at one time . . . from all over the world . . . five from New Zealand and Australia this past June, and always somebody coming in from England. The nickname Rose Buddies came about in 1985. Willard Scott, the weatherman on NBC, I don't know how he heard about us, but he was trying to put together a package about people doing something for other people. Anyway, he came and visited us, put his arm around Joe and me and told us, for doing such good things for people all around the world, we deserved something, too. And he gave us a beautiful golf cart, emblazoned, "The Rose Buddies." . . . We give our visitors survey forms if they would care to make some little comment, and now our local paper has been publishing those under the word, 'Boat Notes.' . . . You wouldn't believe what those Boat Notes do for local pride . . . makes you clean up your act and be nice! . . . I was a mailman for 34 and a half years. That was serving people and making friends. . . . Points of Light, that's something President Bush started. He wanted every county of the country recognized. I was selected from Pasquotank County, July 15, 1991. I'm an official ambassador of hospitality of the State of North Carolina. But the one I appreciate more than any other is Distinguished Alumnus of Louisburg College."

Charlotte Thomas, Rose Buddy: "We were living in Washington, DC, where my husband was in the Air Force. We came to Elizabeth City to visit a friend who had retired from government service. My husband fell in love with the idea of having his power boat in front of his house. . . . We came the next year with a group of six boats, pulled into the boat dock, and met Fred Fearing. . . . We moved here. We're on the Pasquotank River, three houses off the Dismal Swamp Canal. . . . We met Fred again, at church, and were delighted and honored to help [the Rose Buddies]. . . . The busy time is April and October when the boats come through, snow bunnies going south for the winter and north for the summer. Fred will have a party every day. Thank goodness it rains occasionally! . . . We had never lived in a small town before. It took a little bit of adjustment on my part . . . the fact that you must visit for awhile in stores before you tell them what

you want, whereas in Washington if you didn't get right to the point the clerk would walk away. . . . The school system is not what it was in Fairfax County, but there are not that many places in the country like Fairfax County. Now I teach math part-time in an adult education center at College of the Albemarle. Illiteracy in the area is very, very high. It was astounding to discover. . . . One [student] drives an 18-wheeler up and down the East Coast. . . . One had worked for the telephone company his whole life and could not read. To the company's credit, they allowed him time off to attend classes two years before he retired."

Randy Harrell, executive director, Industrial Development Commission: "The largest industry we have in town is the Coast Guard. As far as manufacturers, we were fortunate to attract a company out of Quincy, Massachusetts, Superior Brands, which manufactures dog treats. We landed another company from New Jersey, Hoffer Flow Controls. That has turned out to be a real nice industry for us. . . . Most people we attract from northern states will tell you [Elizabeth City] is the friendliest community they've ever been in. Here in North Carolina, when you walk down the aisle of the grocery store, everybody speaks to you. . . . Over the last two years we've sold just about every piece of property. We've bought 550 acres but it will probably be three years before the infrastructure is put in. . . . We'd like to see high-tech industry come in. Then we'd be in a better position to keep our young people. . . . Let it be known, if any industry is thinking to expand, please consider Elizabeth City. If we don't have what they need at this time, we will have it in the next five years."

Francis (Bud) Tardiff, captain, U.S. Coast Guard: "All the Coast Guard airplanes come here to be overhauled. That's the biggest part. Then, there's the Coast Guard Air Station. Then, there's the Training Command, a school system which trains all the aviation enlisted people, of which I'm commanding officer. Then, the Atlantic Strike Team. As far as the Department of Defense is concerned, it's not much. But as far as the Coast Guard is concerned, it's pretty big. The city and the Coast Guard have been very good friends for many years. . . . We plan on retiring here." ■

Elkhorn, WI 53121

Location: 45 miles southwest of Milwaukee, 75 miles northwest of Chicago, in southeastern Wisconsin.

Population: 5,337 (1990).

Growth rate: 14% since 1980.

Per capita income: $10,323 (1985), just above state average ($10,298).

Geography/climate: Rolling terrain of the southern Kettle Moraine country. Continental climate, influenced by storms that move in from the west, across upper Ohio Valley and Great Lakes, as well as high-pressure systems rolling down from Canada. Winters can be severe and long. January temperature averages: low, 8; high, 24. 20 days at zero or below, average through winter. Sunny summer. July averages: low, 60; high, 83. Average 15 summer days at 90 or above.

Economic base: Surrounded by agriculture—dairying, grain, poultry—but heavily dependent on manufacturing. Historic center of band-instrument factories, including Allied Music, 72 employees; Frank Holton, 100; Getzen, 75; LeBlanc Case. Other large payrolls: ECM Motor, sub-fractional electric motors, 375 employees; Elkhorn Webpress, printers, 250; Intertractor America, grouser shoes, 98; Mesa Industries, tables, 110; Mann Brothers Sand & Gravel, 250; General Wood Workers, musical and gun cases, 50; Hudapack, metal-treating, 47. Elkhorn is seat of Walworth County.

Newspaper: *The Elkhorn Independent*, 11 W. Walworth Street, Elkhorn, WI 53121. 414–723–2250. Weekly, Wednesday. Dick Riddle, editor. $28 a year.

TV, radio: Cable carries network TV, PBS from Milwaukee, Chicago. NPR received off-air from Wisconsin Public Radio.

Health care: Lakeland Hospital, 119 beds. 12 physicians, 6 dentists in local practice.

Schools: 2 elementary (K–5); 1 middle (6–8) enrolls 322. Elkhorn Area High School enrolls 550, sends 55–65% to college. Composite ACT, 1990, for students taking core courses: 22. 2 parochial elementary schools in town. Gateway Technical College, part of Wisconsin Vocational Technical and Adult Education System, has campus adjacent to industrial park.

Educational level: 15.3% of Walworth County residents have 16 or more years of formal education; state average, 14.8%. Per capita expenditure for public education, $467; state average, $476.

Library: Mathison Memorial Library, 25,000 volumes.

Recreation: 4 city parks, with swimming pool, ball fields, tennis courts. Site of "World's Largest County Fair." 7 miles from Lake Geneva, major resort town. Snowmobile, cross-country trails; 6 downhill slopes in immediate area.

3 BR, 2 BA house: $85,000 to $110,000.

Cost of electricity: $.06 per kilowatt hour.

Cost of natural gas: $.58 per therm.

Sales tax: 5½%.

State income tax: 4.9% to 6.93%.

Churches: 17. Denominations: Baptist, Christian Science, Church of Christ, Church of Jesus Christ of Latter-day Saints, Community, Congregational, Episcopal, Evangelical Free, Jehovah's Witnesses, Lutheran, Evangelical Lutheran, Roman Catholic, United Methodist.

In the entire country, there may be no more than 10 band-instrument manufacturers, and two of them are in Elkhorn. When it comes to tooting its own horn, this Wisconsin town has the genuine article—in volume. Doc Severinsen gets his horns from a local factory. So do hundreds of future trumpeters, including middle-schoolers where the mayor teaches.

What residents say . . .

Paul Ormson, mayor; sixth-grade science teacher: "Mayor is part-time, teaching full-time. I came here from Elroy, Wisconsin. The governor of Wisconsin, Tommy Thompson, also is from Elroy and we're friends. When he got involved in politics, I got involved. He became an assemblyman. I came down here to teach school. I helped him run for governor. He's in his second term now, and I'm going for my second. . . . Elkhorn is known as 'The Christmas Card Town.' We have a very quaint setting. Lots and lots of decorations in the Square. Years ago, an artist named Cecil Johnson did a series of Christmas portraits of our Square for *Ford Times*. Then *The March of Time* did a series on small towns and picked Elkhorn. We were famous for those two things at that time . . . Elkhorn also has a rich heritage in band instruments. . . . And so we've picked up on our musical heritage with the new theme, 'Living in Harmony.' We have a new emblem, with the 'O' in Elkhorn a brass horn. It's being introduced this year. . . . Elkhorn is growing tremendously. We are blessed with a crisscrossing of many major highways . . . the last four or five years a real boom in apartment building. . . . We're very diversified, not at all dependent on any one

of our industries. We have had companies go out with no noticeable effect. . . . The greatest reward I have [as mayor] is trying to help people. A lot of times government bodies either turn you off or can't help you. We always try to solve their problems."

Frank Eames, former newspaper-publisher: "The paper was in my family for about 90 years. I was the third generation, published it for about 35 years before selling it in 1986. . . . I think homeownership is important, to have ties with the community. There's a sensitivity towards readers that isn't present with absentee owners. Generally you know the people you're writing about, and that tempers the way you say things. . . . It's a tightrope but I think we walked it pretty carefully. One example that comes to mind, about 30 years ago the County Board determined the easiest way to build a new courthouse was to put it in front of the old one. This would have put the new building right up next to the sidewalk of a beautiful square filled with oak trees. I got a tree expert in to measure the circumference of all those oaks that were going to be destroyed. Some were over 300 years old. I put together a front-page editorial pointing out that there were vacant office buildings where the county could move temporarily while the new courthouse was built. The County Board reversed its tack. . . . Downtowns in small towns are hard-pressed everywhere. Ours has probably survived longer than others because of the courthouse. . . . Walworth County is generally termed a Republican County. All of the county officers are Republicans. Once in a while we have a Democrat run but with no hope of being elected. When it comes to state and national politics we don't always necessarily vote Republican. . . . I personally feel that most local officials should be appointed rather than elected in partisan elections. . . . Too often the sheriff becomes a personality contest, where the technology of that business is such that you're really better off appointing. . . . The major political parties love these local-office elections. It keeps the parties active in off-years. . . . We have traditionally struck a good balance between tourism, agriculture, and industry, the three-legged stool, as my father used to call it. A lot of Chicago people have maintained second homes up here, and now some are moving up permanently. . . . One of the nice things about life here is we're less than an hour from a big city. For instance, we have tickets to the Milwaukee Repertory Theater, just 45 minutes from my house to the parking lot."

Alice Morrissy, attorney, member of Walworth County Board of Supervisors: "I will have practiced law 50 years next year. In 1942 I was admitted to the bar. . . . I was appointed to fill my husband's position on the board when he died in 1979. . . . The board is faced with the dilemma of whether we should move our courts, but not the courthouse, out to the county complex to be adjacent to a new jail. The issue is that Elkhorn, being a small community, has had its entire business life . . . circled around the courthouse. Elkhorn has been the county seat since the Lord was here. This creates an economic worry to the people. If we move the court system, we will lose a lot of travel into the courthouse. Title companies, insurance people, and many of my lawyer friends have bought or built office buildings either on the square or close by. For the restaurants, I would suspect 60 to 75 percent of their gross income is in the courthouse. . . . People are concerned about moving prisoners from the jail into the city. I think video arraignment would take care of most of the traffic. It's the coming thing. . . . About half the county board wants to move out. . . . This courthouse is a very beautiful building . . . fieldstone modern. It got an architectural award when it was built."

Pete Kouzes, founder, The Lakeland Players: "The name of the theater was The Sprague. It went through a very glorious chapter in this community . . . vaudeville, movies, a real community venture. It closed and was vacant for many years. It was sold to a guy who tried to run triple-X movies, but he found he couldn't do that here in Elkhorn. It sold again, and we bought it out of the sheriff's sale. We put a new roof on it, a new heating system. We're attempting to remodel it to as near the kind of building it was. . . . We're right across the street from the courthouse. One of our purposes is to hold together the downtown square. . . . The community theater group just finished producing *Cinderella*. Eventually we hope to produce once again the first show we ever did in there, *The Unsinkable Molly Brown*, as a grand celebration of the restoration." ∎

Elko, NV 89801

Location: 235 miles west of Salt Lake City, 289 miles northeast of Reno, 240 miles south of Boise, in remote northeastern Nevada.

Population: 14,736 (1990).

Growth rate: 26% since 1986.

Per capita income: $10,950 (1985), 98% of state average ($11,200).

Geography/climate: High desert, elevation 5,060 feet. Mountain peaks reaching beyond 11,000 feet, interspersed with low, flat valleys. Very dry climate, annual precipitation typically 15 inches or less. But underground water so plentiful that it's unmetered—free. Some bitterly cold winter days plunge to 15 below zero. Pleasant summer but short: growing season barely 90 days. "It's a gambling state and gardening is a gamble here," says Mayor Jim Polkinghorne. "Don't put your garden in 'til the first of June."

Economic base: Cattle, gold mining, gambling. Countywide, the service industry, including casinos, hotels, restaurants, employs 5,930; retail trade, 2,990; government, 2,090; mining, 1,340; construction, 1,310.

Newspaper: *Elko Daily Free Press*, P.O. Box 1330, Elko, NV 89801. 702–738–3118. Monday through Saturday. $82 a year. Mel Steninger, editor and publisher.

TV, radio: 1 local AM, 2 FM stations. Cable carries TV networks from Boise, Reno. Local PBS station.

Health care: Elko General Hospital, 50 beds. 31 physicians, 8 dentists in local practice. Elko Mental Health Center provides out-patient service; 2 psychiatrists fly in from Reno twice a week.

Schools: 5 elementary (K–6), 1 junior high (7–8); Elko High School enrolls 1,550, sends 40% of graduates to college. 1990–91 composite ACT, 21.1. Also, Ruby Mountain Christian School (1–12); Seventh-Day Adventists' School; Ruby Mountain Human Resources Center, for pre-school children who are mentally or developmentally disabled, and adult vocational training. Northern Nevada Community College enrolls 3,000.

Educational level: 12.7% of Elko County residents have 16 or more years of formal education; state average, 14.4%. Per capita expenditure for public education, $535; state average, $446.

Library: Elko County Library, 80,000 volumes.

Recreation: 3 parks in town total 120 acres. 5 lighted baseball fields, 2 bowling alleys, 2 18-hole golf courses, 2 soccer fields, 10 tennis courts, swimming pool, rifle and pistol range, athletic club. County offers many outdoor pursuits, including hunting, horsemanship, heli-skiing, mineral exploration. Ruby Mountains area, 35 miles southeast, a pine-forested range with several small lakes, numerous trout streams. Ruby Dome, 11,300 feet. South Fork State Recreation Area, 20 miles southwest, boating, fishing, water-skiing, camping. Hotels, casinos offer extraordinary entertainment and dining for a small town.

3 BR, 2 BA house: $90,000. City housing stock includes 2,431 single family, 1,537 apartments, 1,518 mobile homes.

Cost of electricity: $.06 per kilowatt hour.

Cost of natural gas: $.48 per therm.

Sales tax: 5¾%.

State income tax: None.

Churches: 17. Denominations: Baptist, Baptist-American, Baptist-Independent, Baptist-Southern, Church of Jesus Christ of Latter-day Saints, Episcopal, Independent Bible, Jehovah's Witnesses, Lutheran, Methodist, Nazarene, Nondenominational, Presbyterian-USA, Seventh-Day Adventist, Roman Catholic, United Methodist.

Gold mining, gambling, cattle ranching—on paper, at least, Elko looks as if it could be a ripsnorting little piece of the Old West. And it has had its moments. The transcontinental railroad arrived in 1868, followed by eager young Basque immigrants from the Pyrenees—shepherds for the sheep ranches. They settled down and became solid citizens, a fact that is remembered each year during the National Basque Festival, celebrated on the Fourth of July weekend. Gambling arrived next, with Elko something of a pit stop for big rollers on their way to Reno and Vegas. But the big money didn't arrive until the 1980s, when enterprises with names like Newmont, Barrick, and Independence found they could make a profit extracting microscopic gold from huge deposits of ore in Elko and adjacent counties. Though this latest boom has now peaked, gold mining is viewed as steady employment for decades. If that forecast should be erroneous, some cowpoke will probably offer reflections during Elko's one-of-a-kind, annual Cowboy Poetry Gathering.

What residents say . . .

Maryann Glaser, trustee, Western Folklife Center: "It's always the last weekend in January. This year it will be a nine-day event . . . and hopefully not exhaust our performers. . . . The first year, which was 1985, we had an audience of 250. We believe it's grown to about 8,000. You can imagine what it does to the town. . . . There has always been cowboy poetry. The songs a lot of people are familiar with grew out of cowboy poetry. . . . Some folklorists met in Washington, DC, and decided this was a medium that hadn't been examined. It needed some focus. . . . We contacted folklorists in western states and asked them to find the best cowboy poets. They have to be engaged in ranching or working on ranches. They have to audition, on tape or in person. A few are selected from each state . . . probably 50 cowboys the first year, 150 last year. . . . We have brought them from Hawaii and Australia, and this year there's the beginning of a focus on Hispanic cowboys. . . . They mostly recite by memory. There are women, too. Most of them like to be referred to as cowboys. . . . We have several rooms in the convention center and follow various themes . . . 'A Good

Horse and a Poor Ride,' 'The Good, the Bad, and the Ugly.' . . . Some of them are tear-jerkers. Each room has a theme. This goes on from about 10 in the morning. . . . At night, they have the best from last year's, and semi-professional readings . . . and dance all night. I would quote one of the founders as saying 'It's like a family reunion, only everyone likes each other.' "

Jim Polkinghorne, mayor: "I took office on July 1 for a four-year term. I'm semi-retired but figured I had quite a bit of vim and vigor left. . . . My proposal was harmony, experience, and the fact I could commit a lot of time to it. . . . I managed the Petan ranch for 12 years, one of the larger ranches in the United States . . . close to three-quarter million acres. . . . I had been the manager of Elko County from 1968 to '75. . . . Our next number-one priority is the airport. We have a little over 6,000 boardings a month. Sky West serves us with planes that seat 30 people. They have to keep the schedule staggered so that no two come in at the same time or they are swamped out there."

Lorry Lipparelli, city manager: "The big hit came in '87, when we grew 21 percent. . . . In '88, about a 16-percent increase. We anticipate about 3 percent to 4 percent annual growth now. . . . We had to go into fast-track sewer expansion. Another immediate impact was traffic. . . . From start to finish we bonded, designed, and built a new, 4.5 million-dollar bridge over the Humboldt River in under two years. . . . There was a corresponding increase in crime . . . traffic citations, driving under the influence, vandalism, the justice court and municipal court stuff. . . . We have had substantial donations from all of

the mines to alleviate these problems, in one year, $1 million cash, and they drilled a couple of wells and paid the salary for a couple of new policemen. They felt responsible, and I think they responded admirably to help us. . . . There are differences of opinion. All this growth has changed our community. It will never be the same quiet, conservative, slowpoke town where everyone knows everybody. But you cannot stand still. You go forward or you go backward. I see this as a tremendous advantage. The new people put down roots, raise families, and have as much right to be here as I do. . . . I was born and grew up here . . . 45 years next month."

Don Dunn, rector, St. Paul's Episcopal Church: "I think that Elko, unlike many western communities, is a small town that has the flavor of a large city. What does this is the casino, the fast lane there, the glitter and that type of thing. . . . The casinos exist but they don't really exist for the older residents. Oh, occasionally people will go out and play the slots, but they are quite content to let others from out of town pay for the roads. . . . You mustn't leave out the houses of prostitution, probably eight of them. There again, for our local people, unless I'm being naive, they just exist. They are just there. . . . We have a high transient population. Three and a half years ago, out of desperate need, the churches founded FISH, Friends In Service Helping. Often I would have 15 to 20 transients at the door each day . . . people who came out here searching for a job. It's difficult to find a job if you are dirty and unshaven. . . . The county has had to get out of emergency aid except for medical services. Because of the expense, they're out of the business of sandwiches and motels. . . . The churches just had to come up with a solution. FISH is now running close to a budget of $60,000 a year. St. Paul's, for example, gives $6,000. . . . In all honesty, part of the response is self-preservation. It's bad for business to have unwashed transients coming in and bumming. . . . FISH has won the J. C. Penney Award for creative use of volunteers. It's supported by the casinos, also. . . . Elko is a very satisfying community to live in. On any given evening there are half a dozen worthwhile events to attend. We bring lots of concerts here. We have a very fine community concert symphony. Perhaps it is a self-defense mechanism, creating an alternative culture. . . . There is a good spirit in the community. There's a lot of pride." ■

Essex, CT 06426

Location: 35 miles east of New Haven, 20 miles west of New London, 6 miles upriver from Long Island Sound, on the west bank of the Connecticut River.

Population: 5,904 (1990).

Growth rate: 7% since 1986.

Per capita income: $17,593 (1985), 25% higher than state average ($14,090).

Geography/climate: Lower river valley approaching the Atlantic Ocean. Old town center is on a narrow peninsula jutting into the Connecticut River. Ocean moderates the weather. Averages: snowfall, 30 inches; rainfall, 40 inches; days below freezing, 80; days above 90, 15. Generally mild summer and fall.

Economic base: Residential, with a little light industry and extensive boating services: brokers, marinas, sail-makers, repairs, storage. Historic Essex Village, Griswold Inn, boutiques draw tourist traffic to Main Street.

Newspaper: No Essex newspaper. Paper primarily covering area is *Main Street News*, 444 Main Street, Deep River, CT 06417. 203–526–4357. Weekly. $16.50 a year. Edward Ziobron, editor.

TV, radio: Cable carries TV networks from Hartford, New Britain; PBS from Hartford and New York City. NPR received off-air from Hartford.

Health care: Nearest hospital is 258-bed Middlesex Hospital and Medical Center, in Middletown, 20 miles north. 38 physicians, 14 dentists in local practice. Many other medical facilities in area, including Yale New Haven Hospital, 30 miles west.

Schools: 1 elementary (K–6) enrolls 500; 1 junior high (7–8). Valley Regional High School enrolls 460, sends about 50% of graduates to college. Average SATs, 1991: math, 512; verbal, 475.

Educational level: 20.4% of Middlesex County residents have 16 or more years of formal education; state average, 20.7%. Per capita expenditure for public education, $487; state average, $477.

Libraries: Essex Public Library, 21,000 volumes, 45,000 annual circulation. Ivoryton Public Library, smaller, has main children's collection.

Recreation: Boating and water sports are prime attractions. Tennis courts and playground in park adjacent to Town Hall. Country club several miles downriver, at Old Lyme. 7 state parks within half-hour drive. Ivoryton Playhouse is site of theatrical debuts of Katharine Hepburn, 1931; Katharine Houghton, 1964; and Schuyler Grant, 1987.

3 BR, 2 BA house: In Ivoryton, $150,000 to $200,000. Old sea captains' houses in Essex are very pricey.

Cost of electricity: $.09 per kilowatt hour.

Cost of fuel oil: $.92 per gallon.

Sales tax: 8%.

State income tax: 1% to 14%.

Churches: 8. Denominations: Baptist, Congregational, Episcopal, Lutheran, Roman Catholic.

Essex is an old river town with a long history of doing business with the world. First settled in 1648, the town became a player in the West Indies circuit of rum, sugar, molasses, and tobacco. Shipbuilding began in 1733 and thrived. When a British raiding party torched 28 sailing vessels at Essex in the spring of 1814, the local newspaper called the $160,000 loss the nation's worst disaster during two years of war.

Two inland villages, Centerbrook and Ivoryton, became part of Essex in 1859. Ivoryton is where tusks were transformed into piano keys. Other industries flourished in the area, everything from pianos to bicycle spokes, with dairy farms in between.

Today, major industry is gone and there is not a cow in sight. Essex is "a residential community that likes to play with boats," says Plan Commission chairman Jack Milkofsky. Of major concern is preserving the small-town qualities of the past.

What residents say . . .

Donald Malcarne, visiting lecturer, Wesleyan University: "The kids all graduated from college and I went back to study contemporary American history, but I got mixed up with Dr. Peter Hall, the great god of Connecticut history. I'm a social historian, using primary documentation . . . probate records, land records, tax records, census reports, Bibles, diaries. Archeology is very primary. . . . In '87 and '88 we uncovered the oldest wharf in the United States, built in 1660. We found it with archival work . . . uncovered an enormous excavation but couldn't preserve it, so we packed it in sand and plastic and it's now a parking lot again. . . . Right now we're doing a study of the Falls River, working on both a foundry and a shipyard. We did archival work and discovered people had plum forgotten that there was a huge shipyard here. . . . They laid down 500 keels in 50 years. Essex became a very, very, very significant town. . . . Today it's a residential community with a great boating industry, I mean parking, servicing, launching boats. . . . Essex has succeeded in attracting a certain conservative clientele, New Yorkers who retire. . . . We get a lot of young people into town. The school population has been skyrocketing, so much so a new school had to be built. . . . We have no police department, no paid fire department, extraordinarily low taxes for the value of real estate. I suppose one would call it a community without too many problems."

Brenda Milkofsky, director, Connecticut River Museum: "When industry moved inland, many villages along the Connecticut River went into a time warp and sat there. Essex was a backwater. It was rediscovered in the late Teens and early '20s by sportsmen who came to Essex to hunt and sail. They did not build new houses but bought old houses and maintained them . . . preserved almost by accident. The town turned down a nomination as a federal historic district . . . felt it would increase tourism. . . . We seem to have lots of semi-professional people who commute a portion of the week. . . . It's very much a retirement community except that the retirees are getting younger and younger. . . . There's one elementary school. Most of the people who move into Essex Village do not have school-age children. We've been fortunate they do not vote down school issues."

Joanne Behrens, retired auto dealer, descendant of William Pratt, a founder of Essex:
"I ran an automobile agency for a long time. Buicks, Cadillacs, Jeeps. My father started it in 1895 as a bicycle shop. Then it became a subagency for cars. . . . His first car was a 1901 curved-dash Oldsmobile, with a tiller. . . . I'm probably one of the few people born in Essex who lives in the same house in which I was born. I'm 73. . . . Essex is a little Williamsburg at the moment. A great deal of wealth has come in. Business people, lawyers, writers, professors. . . . They've moved up from Greenwich, they crawl from the cities, up the coast. . . . I live in Essex proper. I can see the river from my front windows. . . . They don't want tourists but they're getting them. We're not a very big town. . . . We can't have any more restaurants on Main Street without new sewers. They're fighting very hard to keep it a town you can live in. People who come to Essex as buyers are much more protective of Essex than some of the natives."

Charles Doane, retired postmaster of Essex:
"Anytime after lunch until midnight, cars are bumper-to-bumper on both sides of [Main] street, and not one in 20 you recognize. Traffic is a problem, especially on the weekend."

Cheryl Banas, president, Essex Community Fund: "We've lived here about five years. . . . Moved here from New Hampshire and lived before that in St. Louis and Ohio. . . . I'm from a small town originally and knew the only way to find out what's happening is to get involved. . . . We raise approximately $45,000 to $50,000 a year through a mail campaign. It's not a grand scale . . . that little bit of extra money, for the Boy Scouts, and senior citizens: we pay for their cable TV. . . . Although statistically you think everybody in Essex has a lot of money, we have a soup cellar in town, at the Baptist Church. Essex people attend. . . . The schools are fabulous, especially the elementary school . . . fabulous parent support, standing room only for programs, volunteers. I think that's what makes the school great. . . . I'm sometimes in awe of the ability to go off and leave your door unlocked, to drop your child off downtown without worrying about his safety. You feel like you're living 20 years ago."

Joshua Y. Crowell, pastor, First Congregational Church: "I am also a firefighter, by the way. I am known in the trade as the MPO, the motor pump operator . . . and I do get some funny looks driving the truck in my bell sleeves. . . . Increasingly, I've discovered that firefighters tend to be blue-collar, and that is a wonderful thing because our church tends to be. . . . At any rate, I've listened to my colleagues ask, 'Will our kids be able to live in this town?' One of the other questions is will we be able to get volunteers. Unfortunately, a lot of folks who are upwardly mobile economically and socially are not as apt to volunteer for fire and ambulance jobs though they do their part in a host of other ways. . . . I may have to cruise down and talk to my friends in Fairfield County. They may know some things about recruiting volunteers. . . . Socially speaking, folks of more means live on the Essex end of things. Ivoryton tends to be blue-collar. Centerbrook is sort of in the middle. . . . I guess my concern is the ability of folks of varying social classes to know and accept each other. We work pretty hard at trying to bridge those gaps." ■

Fort Payne, AL 35967

Location: 57 miles south of Chattanooga, 96 miles northeast of Birmingham, just off I-59, in the Mountain Lakes region of northeastern Alabama.

Population: 11,838 (1990).

Growth rate: 1% since 1986.

Per capita income: $9,652 (1985), 10% higher than state average ($8,681).

Geography/climate: Elongated valley running north–south at about 900 feet, between Sand Mountain, on the east, and Lookout Mountain, on the west. Cold but tolerably short winter with occasional ice, snow. Average snowfall, 3.5 inches. Average temperatures: January: high, 50; low, 31. July: high, 87; low, 67. Freezing days, 63. Annual rainfall, 59.5 inches. Average 48 days at 90 or above. Long, pleasant summer season can stretch as far as mid-April to mid-October.

Economic base: Self-proclaimed "Sock Capital of the World." 60 hosiery mills employ 4,000 people, produce 65% of socks in U.S. Other large payrolls: EarthGrains, commercial bakery, 700; Westinghouse, electrical generating components, 250; Gametime, park and playground equipment, 250; Heil, refuse truck bodies, 300; King's Haven, manufactured housing, 175; Sola Electric, electrical parts, 225; Vulcraft, steel joists, 320. Seat of DeKalb County, retail center. Agricultural production: poultry, pork, grain sorghum, corn, Irish potatoes, wheat, soybeans.

Newspaper: *The Times-Journal*, 200 Eighth Street, S.E., Fort Payne, AL 35967. 205–845-2550. Daily, Tuesday through Saturday.

Gary Gengozian, editor and publisher. $46 a year.

TV, radio: Local AM, FM stations. Cable carries TV networks, PBS from Huntsville, Chattanooga.

Health care: Baptist Medical Center DeKalb, 134 beds. 30 physicians, 12 dentists in local practice.

Schools: 1 elementary (K–2) enrolling 588; 1 elementary (3–5) enrolling 654; 1 middle (6–8), 608. Fort Payne High School enrolls 714, sends 65%–70% to higher education. 1989–90 composite ACT, 20.2.

Educational level: 5.7% of DeKalb County residents have 16 or more years of formal education; state average, 12.2%. County per capita expenditure for public education, $300; state average, $324.

Library: DeKalb County Public Library, 82,000 volumes.

Recreation: 26-acre sports complex has lighted fields for soccer, baseball, softball, football. Municipal swimming pool is designed for state Olympic competition. 6 tennis courts, 2 golf courses, bowling alley, rollerskating rink. Cloudmount Ski & Golf Resort, 12 miles north, offers year-round skiing, with artificial snow in winter, on Astroturf and grass other seasons. DeSoto State Park, 8 miles northeast, offers swimming, fishing, camping, hiking, picnic grounds.

3 BR, 2 BA house: $50,000 to $85,000.

Cost of electricity: $.065 per kilowatt hour.

Cost of natural gas: $.61 per therm.

Sales tax: 8%.

State income tax: 2% to 5%.

Churches: 23 total. Denominations: Bap- tist (9), Baptist-Missionary, Church of Christ, Church of God, Episcopal, Holiness, Jeho- vah's Witnesses, Presbyterian (2), Roman Catholic, United Methodist (3).

Every town likes to brag a little about native sons who have found fame and fortune. Fort Payne is proud to nominate Randy Owen, Teddy Gentry, Jeff Cook, and Mark Herndon, better known as the country-music band Ala- bama. They first hit the top of the charts in 1980 with "Tennessee River" and have scored big ever since. Born and reared in the area, the four Ala- bama boys continue to live in Fort Payne and are considered very solid, and generous, citizens. They sponsor an annual fund-raiser for charities and ser- vice organizations, "June Jam," that has generated more than $2 million since its founding in 1982. Top country-music performers appear gratis at the day-long musical extravaganza, held on a large field next to the high school. The 1991 event attracted a crowd of 67,000. What does a small town do to follow an act like that? Newspaper editor Gary Gengozian found an an- swer, with a lot of help from another local institution: EarthGrains, the largest commercial bakery east of the Mississippi. For the town centennial, in 1989, Fort Payne baked itself a 35-by76-foot, 128,000-pound birthday cake. Guiness gulped—and declared a new world record.

What residents say . . .

Gary Gengozian, editor and publisher, Fort Payne **Times-Journal:** "I was sitting at the July 4th fireworks display in the high school stadium, right behind the EarthGrains plant, and I said to myself, 'We could build a cake right here on this football field that would set a record' . . . just something to hang our hat on. . . . We formed a team of 20 key people, engi- neers, structural people. The cake was made of about 12,000 small cakes, each three feet long and three inches deep, and assembled on four-by-eight sheets of plywood. . . . Guiness approved the design as long as we iced it all the way around. It took us about three days to assemble the cake, working around the clock. . . . Alabama was there to sing Happy Birthday. . . . We attracted international attention. It was on TV in France, Australia. It happened the week of the big earthquake in California. . . . Educa- tion is a major concern right now. We spend less per student on education in this state than any other state. We have the lowest property taxes in the country, and that's bad, not that it is a hot issue. . . . But we overcome those things. We have a good school system . . . people who teach who don't need to for the money, tremendous support of the school system by business."

133

Linda Smith, community education coordinator: "I coordinate the 'Adopt-a-School' program. We have 23 businesses in Fort Payne that participate. . . . We didn't have an up-to-date computer lab in the high school. Jerry Pendergrass, president of AmSouth Bank, got three other bank presidents involved. Through local business and industry they raised $40,000. That is a large sum of money. Fort Payne is notorious for that . . . good at coming to the aid of the schools. I think it's just the fact people are very attuned and want to be involved. We are just a close-knit town."

Ike Bledsoe, owner, McDonald's: "Folks come from outside the town to work in the mills. That gives the town a lot of its personality. We have a lot of unskilled labor here. . . . When the hosiery mills shut down one week in the summer and everybody takes vacation, my business drops about 25 percent. . . . We are largely a rural-type area. The country is very scenic, a lot of natural beauty. Sand Mountain is the salt-of-the-earth area. Lookout Mountain is where the most famous people in town, Alabama, grew up. Three of them still live on Lookout. . . . Every two years we try to legalize the sale of alcohol and every time the margin has increased against. To those of us who favor the sale it is not a moral issue, it's a tax issue. We're surrounded by counties where you can buy alcohol. That's where people go, and that's where the tax revenue goes."

Chris Wright, DeKalb County Public Library System: "Our usage in the past 10 years has gone up 3,000 percent. In the past year it has almost doubled. . . . I think people are bored with the flashy movies, the video games, the shopping. People are doing research on their own about the community, the planet. We try to provide all the research material we can. Our main goal is to let everyone know we are there for them. . . . Our current holdings are 82,000 volumes with various sundry videotapes. We are ranked 25th in the State of Alabama, measured by circulation and volumes, out of 298 libraries. . . . If anything happens to any family, known or unknown . . . if a child is hurt and the family cannot meet the medical bills, help is everywhere. . . . The South is generally that way. There were hard times back in the '30s. There are always hard times somewhere. People generally stick together."

Frank Hoguet, plant manager, Westinghouse; president, Rotary; former president, United Givers: "We manufacture high voltage electrical coils that go inside of generators in power companies. It's a mature business but has a lot of high technology. . . . Westinghouse did a survey to find good work ethics, and this was one of 13 sites selected. . . . Basically, I define that as people wanting to come to work and give a fair day's work for a fair day's wage, being dedicated. When you get to the larger, more mature cities, there are lots of bad habits . . . from poor management practices. What I call bad habits are people barely coming to work and punching the clock. They'll do what you tell them and that's all. A good work ethic, the guy says 'I've finished that chore. Give me something else to do.' . . . Fort Payne does not have a shopping mall and there is not an awful lot of culture. But we're close to a lot of major cities. We use the airports and shopping malls in Chattanooga, Huntsville; Rome, Georgia. So we have a nice variety of choice. You just need to get used to driving further. The interstates are almost always uncrowded." ■

Franklin, LA 70538

Location: On the Gulf of Mexico, 90 miles west of New Orleans, 42 miles southeast of Lafayette.

Population: 9,004 (1990).

Growth rate: 6% decline in 10 years.

Per capita income: $7,508 (1986), 85% of state average ($8,836).

Geography/climate: Bayous, lakes, marshes, bisected by canals and the Intracoastal Waterway. Flat—average elevation 7½ feet. Mild winters with 13 days of freezing or below; short springs; very hot and humid summers, with 60–70 days of 90 degrees or above. Annual rainfall, 57 inches. Frequent summer thunderstorms.

Economic base: Originally—and still—sugarcane, then oil, gas, and salt. Carbon black, an oil byproduct used to make tires, produced in abundance since the '50s. Fishing industry—shrimp, crawfish, crab—employs 500. New directions: tourism, port development. Franklin is the seat of St. Mary Parish.

Newspaper: *The Franklin Banner-Tribune,* 111 Wilson Street, Franklin, LA 70538. 318–828–3706. Daily, Monday through Friday. Paul Godfrey, managing editor. $25 a year.

TV, radio: Local AM, FM stations. Cable has 24 channels, provides New Orleans stations, networks, PBS. NPR from Baton Rouge, Lafayette.

Health care: Franklin Foundation Hospital, 82 beds. 17 physicians, 6 dentists in local practice.

Schools: 1 elementary (K–5), 1 middle (6–8). Franklin Senior High School enrolls 1,150. Test scores not available. Roman Catholic parochial schools serve K–12.

Educational level: 9.2% of St. Mary Parish residents have 16 or more years of formal education; state average, 13.9%. Per capita expenditure for public education, $529; state average, $452.

Library: Parish library has 5 branches, bookmobile, 304,000 volumes, 16,000 patrons.

Recreation: Mild winter weather makes water sport practically a year-round possibility: skiing, sailing, racing, canoeing. Freshwater and sea water fishing. Hunting for ducks, deer, rabbit, squirrel. City park with swimming pool, recreation program. Country club has 9-hole golf course. Seaplanes land on Bayou Teche, within 50 feet of the 8-story courthouse at Franklin.

3 BR, 2 BA house: $70,000 and up for a subdivision house; $190,000 on the water. Antebellum houses sell between low $200,000s and upper $500,000s.

Cost of electricity: $.04 to $.05 per kilowatt hour.

Cost of natural gas: $.53 to $.61 per therm.

Sales tax: 7½%.

State income tax: Graduated 2% to 6%.

Churches: Denominations: Assemblies of God, Baptist, Church of Christ, Episcopal, Lutheran, Methodist, Pentecostal, Presbyterian, Roman Catholic.

To get a picture of St. Mary Parish, the county of which Franklin is seat, consider that Tarzan made his movie debut swinging from local trees. That was in 1917, when vast sugarcane plantations covered the land. The oil and gas industry arrived in the 1950s, making life even sweeter along Bayou Teche.

Then Franklin and vicinity suffered a double whammy: first, the end of price supports for sugar; then, in 1983, the collapse of oil. Census figures reflect these ups and downs: a 6-percent increase in population between 1970 and 1980, followed by an identical decrease between 1980 and 1990. The oil industry and sugarcane remain important props to the local economy, but the objective is to stabilize by diversifying. St. Mary Parish already claims the titles "Shrimp Capital of the World" and "Carbon Black Capital of the World." Now it would like to become better known as an ocean port and tourist attraction. Franklin has been selected four times since 1958 as "The Cleanest City in Louisiana."

What residents say . . .

Jessie Morton, chairman, Tourist Commission: "Gorgeous antebellum homes is our main thing. We have the Bayou Teche. I live on the bayou. It's in my backyard. I'm downtown yet I'm in the country. . . . We get lots of little squirrels, ducks, armadillos, possums, and some of the neighbors have seen an alligator. I have not been that lucky. There's a couple have been in the bayou the last couple of years. I think the ducks have a problem with them every so often. . . . I'm president of the Republican Women's Club in Franklin. Most of our elected officials are Democrats. I have run for the City Council twice and lost by 14 votes twice. But I got close, I scared them. . . . Right now the Tourist Commission has a special project on Highway 90. We were given an old house, an old plantation house, if we could move it. It's moved. . . . We'll have a tourist information center right in the middle of a four-lane highway. It should be ideal, staffed by volunteers."

Roger Robinson, general manager, morning on-air personality, KFMV: "We have a little trivia game, mostly news, weather, birthdays, meet your neighbor. . . . We're the only local radio station. . . . I came here 34 years ago to start teaching and I've found it to be a very nice town. We have about six titles as the cleanest city in Louisiana. Our economy is not the greatest in the world. When the bottom fell out, a lot of people moved away. Parish-wide we lost 6,000 people, a lot of that from the Morgan City end, the eastern end, which is more oil-related. Our industries here in Franklin did not suffer that much. . . . We are Cajun country, yet we are not as Cajun as some of the other cities in the area. Franklin was more of an Anglo community. . . ."

Sam Jones, third-term mayor, candidate for governor: "A lot of my campaign has to do with being from a small town and basically rural area, the struggles and problems we've gone through, the oil bust, the feeling of not being heard in Baton Rouge. Louisiana is still basically a rural state. We have a few large cities but better than half of the people are in rural areas. We feel we need a fundamental restructuring, accentuating of rural towns. . . . My message is, sweep it clean, throw the rascals out. Let's start all over . . . with someone who's built his town. . . . We were the flagship Louisiana program for the National Main Street program. In 1983 when the bottom collapsed here, I instituted the program . . . to save the retail businesses already in town as opposed to going out and chasing the Japanese. It was a real saver for us . . . taught our businesses how to compete with Wal-Mart. The first rule is you don't compete. You specialize in other things. Second is deliver service. Third, pay attention to customers you've always had, keep them from leaving. People are creatures of habit. They will go to familiar places to shop. . . . You always find that tough times identify the grit people have, how good some of the businesspeople are. People really did well tightening their belts. . . . I am author of the pamphlet 'Southern Secrets: Undiscovered Treasures of the South.' It was a cooperative tourism effort of 20 towns in Louisiana of similar size. We each put up $2,500 and we advertised nationally, reaching an audience of 13 million. To date we've received 25,000 requests for our pamphlet. . . . It's usually Mom who makes the vacation decision, so we advertised in Ladies Home Journal, Redbook, USA Weekend. We particularly targeted the South and Midwest. We were looking for some fall travelers and retirees. . . . I'm 38. I was 28 when I was elected mayor the first time. Last year, over two candidates, I received 70 percent of the vote. The other thing you need to know about Franklin is it's a tremendously beautiful town. . . .

Hanging moss from oak trees over Main Street conjures up the mystical South."

Gary LaGrange, president, Port of West St. Mary: "I was born here, reared here, went to school here. My father owned a furniture store on Main Street and was a local political figure for many years. . . . Afternoons we'd get in the pick-up truck . . . drive out. . . . He and I would listen to the ball games. . . . He told me so many times, what we need is a port. . . . I graduated from Hanson Memorial High School, the parochial school, 14 in my graduating class. . . . Got my bachelor's in urban planning and master's in economic development at Southwest Louisiana, the Ragin' Cajuns. . . . Never dreamed I'd have an opportunity to practice that in Franklin. . . . The Port was created by the Louisiana legislature in 1975. I'm the first and only director they've had. This was a golden opportunity to build something and suffer the consequences, if any. The local community has invested about $3 million and we now have a $31 million port . . . the rest from federal and state grants. We've worked 14 years to develop this and I'm really proud of it. It's a shallow-draft port, for mini-ships and oceangoing barges. Where so many other states have gone great distances for markets, it occurred to us we've got Tampico and Merida only 490 nautical miles away. We're shipping . . . pineapple pickers, tractors, pick-up trucks, pipe, rail spurs, shovels, paper pulp. We're working on bringing molasses in from Honduras and Guatemala for the production of vinegar. . . . We're the only shallow-draft port on the Gulf Coast involved in international shipping on a scheduled basis. . . . We have basically two ships a month coming and going. We hope to have a lot more in the near future." ■

Franklin, NH 03235

Location: 17 miles north of Concord, 91 miles north of Boston, in south central New Hampshire.

Population: 8,304 (1990).

Growth rate: 5% since 1980.

Per capita income: $9,373 (1985), 80% of state average ($11,659).

Geography/climate: Elevation 400 feet. Scenic river valley, where Pemigewasset and Winnipesaukee rivers join to form the Merrimac. Long, snowy, cold winters. Average temperatures: January: high, 31; low, 9. July: high, 81; low, 55. Warm summer days, cool nights. Colorful, pleasant falls. Annual rainfall, 36 inches; snowfall, 65 inches. 11 days at 90 or above, annual average; 26 days at or below zero.

Economic base: Historic mill town that has replaced textile and garment industries with durable goods manufacturers. More than half of employed persons residing in city work in local industry. Larger payrolls: Webster Valve, plumbing and heating supplies; PolyClad, computer boards; Jarl Extrusions; Acme Staple.

Newspaper: *Franklin-Tilton Telegram*, 427 Central Street, Franklin, NH 03235. 603–934–6560. Weekly, Wednesday. Leigh Sharps, editor. $25 a year.

TV, radio: Local AM/FM station. Cable carries network TV, PBS from Manchester, Durham, Boston. NPR from Concord.

Health care: Franklin Hospital, 49 beds. 6 physicians, 4 dentists in local practice.

Schools: 2 elementary (K–5), 1 middle (6–8). Franklin High School enrolls 435 students, sends about 75% to college. $65,000 raised locally in 1991 for distribution as scholarships. SAT scores, "average."

Educational level: 19.8% of Merrimack County residents have 16 or more years of formal education; state average, 18.2%. Per capita expenditure for public education, $375; state average, $396.

Library: Franklin Library, a Carnegie library built in 1907, 30,000 volumes.

Recreation: Community center with full-court gymnasium, game room, meeting rooms. City parks include tennis, basketball courts, softball and youth-league baseball, ice-skating. City-owned 643-acre tract has downhill ski area, cross-country trails, snowmobile trails, hiking trails, skating pond, day camping site. Daniel Webster Birthplace, a 147-acre park, is located in Franklin. 1,900-acre federal tract provides cross-country skiing, fishing, hunting, hiking. Webster Lake, 612 acres, provides boating, swimming, fishing. Country club with 9-hole golf course; 9 other golf courses within 15 miles. 20 downhill ski areas within easy reach. Lake Winnipesaukee, New Hampshire's largest lake, 15 miles northeast.

3 BR, 2 BA house: $80,000 to $100,000.

Cost of electricity: $.10 per kilowatt hour.

Cost of natural gas: $.69 per therm.

Sales tax: None.

State income tax: None.

Churches: 9. Denominations: Baptist, Christian, Congregational, Episcopal, Greek Orthodox, Jehovah's Witnesses, Roman Catholic, Unitarian.

Lawyer and statesman Daniel Webster was born in Franklin. The city honors its most distinguished son with a bust, outside the Congregational Church; also, a bridge, a street, a 147-acre park, and a 612-acre lake are all named for Webster. A more practical memorial to Webster is the healthy industrial sector along the river—and the city's gritty determination to operate the city like a business.

What residents say . . .

Brenda Elias, mayor, real estate agency owner: "Like New Hampshire and New England in general, we've experienced a very severe economic downturn. Perhaps I saw it coming earlier than most because I'm in real estate. We see the effects of the economy sooner. This community had suffered from . . . a 50-percent increase in property taxes . . . tremendous bureaucratic expansion everywhere. . . . My top agenda item is to continue stabilization of the tax rate. This past year we had no increase whatsoever. Also, we produced better than a $750,000 budget surplus, without letting go any personnel . . . primarily concentrated on tightening our belt, taking an alternative medical plan which will save us money . . . four people doing the job that five were doing. . . . We have a 10-percent smaller workforce than we did three or four years ago. . . . We've also funded our capital reserve account for the first time in a couple of years, and we began a capital reserve for the schools, as well. . . . Most of the presidential candidates find their way to our door. I basically serve as host, giving local people an opportunity to come to my home and meet the candidates. . . . Tom Harkin came into town at a quarter to seven in the morning and worked with my municipal service crew all day, actually physically worked, without the media being around. I think that's a very good way to keep in touch. My personal criticism with most Washington politicians is they become very insulated, lose touch with what's happening. Bill Clinton has come to the city. He taught a class at the high school. Governor Wilder was here last week. He visited some of the seniors' homes. He and I had quite a lengthy meeting just one on one. Ralph Nader will be here Thursday."

*Leigh Sharps, editor, **Franklin-Tipton Telegram:*** "The big thing this year, instead of going into factories and kissing babies, I think they're going for the small-town connection. Senator Harkin actually had on jeans, a flannel shirt and a hard hat. He replaced a fire hydrant, down in a ditch. . . . That really went over big in our city. . . . The mayor, you can definitely say she has higher aspirations. She founded the Franklin Taxpayers Association. It was the first one in the state. A lot of other towns now have one. . . . A referendum ballot calling for a 3.5-percent cost-of-living cap passed overwhelmingly. She was swept into office. . . . We lost a public kindergarten, several elective programs at the high school. We cut back on city workers. But nobody was ever laid off. . . . In the end, they restored the kindergarten and several other programs. . . . Two years ago, the newspaper here folded after 170 years because of an absentee owner. We hadn't seen him for a year. Two local businessmen didn't want the city to be without a paper. We were publishing within a month of the demise of the old paper. Two major daily newspapers compete with us. We're the only weekly, we keep the small-town flavor. We like to call ourselves, 'Your Hometown Newspaper of Public Record' . . . all the news, City Council, schools, personal columns from each town, so you get who's visiting, whose dog is sick with the flu. We cover sports in depth. I think that has garnered us a faithful following because people like to keep track of what the kids are doing."

Doug Boyd, chief of police: "Franklin is the smallest city in the state, by population. The real difference is you don't have the town meeting. You have your City Council. . . . When the mills get out, Franklin is a busy place. It keeps our modest police department very busy. . . . We run approximately 7,000 to 8,000 calls for service a year. That's not bad for a community this size. . . . Speeders, DWIs . . . domestic problems, child abuse especially now with the times as they are. Franklin has its share of those things. This is not what you would classify as a very affluent community. Blue collar, 95-percent blue collar. But a lot of the people that live here, their families have lived here for years. They expect a lot of people, and it's kind of a rewarding place to work. One of the

things that has always impressed me is the amount of volunteerism. When times are tough, people really come out and support the community. . . . Brenda Elias, she's done a lot here. The community was somewhat divided earlier in her political tenure. I think a lot of people have come to realize she does a lot for this community."

Thelma Lemire, director, Community Action Program: "We provide many services, right now in full force with fuel assistance, though the money still has not been released. Always, the elderly and handicapped are the priority. We have a great percentage of elderly up here. . . . I feel the government should encourage the elderly to stay in their homes. They can only do this if they are given benefits. . . . New Hampshire is one of the most depressed states of the Union mainly because benefits are so low, whether for state welfare or fuel assistance. . . . We were hit with a lot of self-employed losing their homes . . . carpenters, plumbers, electricians, carpenters mainly because they're not building any homes. It's just like a domino effect. . . . I do get up on my pulpit because I'm such an advocate for the low income."

Randy Brough, director, Franklin Library: "Business has really boomed. In the two years I've been here the circulation has gone up 66 percent. The economy is one reason. People realize that things are free at the library. When a book costs $20 or $25, you can read it free here. We have videos. The new children's librarian is really good with the kids. . . . I may not be your best bet because I'm single. There's not really any night life in Franklin. No movie theater here. What attracted me was the director's position, and Franklin is close to my home, in Laconia. Franklin is a nice, friendly town." ■

Geneva, NY 14456

Location: 53 miles southwest of Syracuse, 46 miles southeast of Rochester, in the Finger Lakes region of western New York.

Population: 14,143 (1990).

Growth rate: 6% decline since 1980.

Per capita income: $9,048, 77% of state average ($11,765).

Geography/climate: Gently rolling terrain. Town spreads around northwest corner of Seneca Lake, a 35-mile-long, 600-foot-deep reminder of the Ice Age. Invigorating continental climate. Cloudy, cold winters. Average temperatures: January: high, 30; low, 16. July: high, 80; low, 61. Average 9 days at 0 degrees or below; 6 at 90 or above. Average rainfall, 33 inches; snowfall, 62 inches. Average 140 days clear, sunny.

Economic base: Heavily dependent on rich agricultural production in surrounding area, primarily fruits and vegetables; and on large institutional payrolls: New York State Agricultural Experiment Station, Hobart and William Smith Colleges, Geneva General Hospital.

Newspaper: *Finger Lakes Times*, 218 Genesee Street, Geneva, NY 14456. 315–789–3333. Monday through Saturday evening. George A. Park, Jr., publisher. $79.05 a year.

TV, radio: Local AM, FM stations. Cable carries network TV, PBS from Rochester, Syracuse, New York City. NPR from Rochester, Syracuse.

Health care: Geneva General Hospital, 174 beds. 68 physicians, 9 dentists in local practice.

Schools: 2 elementary (K–5), 1 middle (6–8). Geneva High School enrolls 768, sends 70% to college. St. Francis DeSales-St. Stephen's School enrolls 57 in pre-K, 294 in K–8. DeSales High School enrolls 195. Hobart College, 1,060 men. William Smith College, 700 women. Community College of the Finger Lakes, 600 students.

Educational level: 13.8% of Ontario/Seneca County residents have 16 or more years of formal education; state average, 17.9%. Per capita expenditure for public education, $593; state average, $558.

Library: Geneva Regional Library, 50,000 volumes.

Recreation: Chamber of Commerce Park provides fishing, boat launching, picnic sites. Seneca Lake State Park, in town, has swimming, fishing, picnicking, snowmobiling. Public 9-hole and 18-hole golf courses. Private country club with 9-hole golf course. Seneca Lake yields trout, brown trout, rainbow, northern pike, small- and large-mouth bass, landlock salmon, pickerel, smelt, pan fish. Hunting for waterfowl, deer, rabbit, pheasant at Montezuma Refuge, 9 miles east. 3-screen cinema; opera house.

3 BR, 2 BA house: $80,000 to $110,000.

Cost of electricity: $.08 per kilowatt hour.

Cost of natural gas: $.62 per therm.

Sales tax: 7%.

State income tax: 4% to 7.875%.

Churches: 17 total. Denominations: Assemblies of God, Baptist, Southern Baptist, Christian & Missionary Alliance, Church of God, Eastern Orthodox, Episcopal, Lutheran, Presbyterian, Roman Catholic, Salvation Army, United Methodist.

Synagogues: 1.

Geneva is a city of historic "firsts" in New York State, and, in some cases, the nation. The first woman to receive a medical degree in America, Elizabeth Blackwell, was graduated from Geneva College in 1849. According to a local history, Geneva was "the first settlement in western New York to have an official post office and postmaster, to have a public hotel with a competent landlord, to be incorporated as a village, to have a consecrated or dedicated church building, to receive a name other than an Indian name, to have a glass factory, to incorporate a charitable society, to have a church bell, to have a water company, to organize a Community Chest, to be served by a completed canal, to have a railroad company, to have a YMCA. . . ."

Part of the explanation for all this civic activity was location—Geneva was on the main line west. If you were bound for Ohio, you went through the town at the top of Seneca Lake. But the fertile lands surrounding the settlement also were a final destination for farm families. Ontario County soil is reputed to be almost as rich as the potato fields of Long Island.

Geneva also was the first community in western New York to establish a free public library. And as the current library director notes, Geneva has some contemporary distinctions, as well.

What residents say ...

Frank Queener, director, Geneva Free Library: "We've just completed a million-dollar fund-raising in the city, all private money, which is pretty good in a small town. We're making a 16,000-foot addition to our present building. It was built in 1834 and formerly was a Universalist Church. . . . Geneva is an interesting place. It's suburban in one sense, a city in another sense, with a large minority population. African Americans have been here since the 1820s or '30s. We have a Puerto Rican community. . . . Big-city problems, and it's rural at the same time. So we have a little bit of everything. . . . The Experimental Station attracts world specialists in apples and grapes. In my daughter's class, one of her best friends is an Egyptian kid who was brought up in Mexico. You just see all colors of the rainbow. . . . We have our problems . . . crack. . . . But we're the size it's manageable still. We have big-city problems but they're manageable. . . . I moved to Geneva from Buffalo when I was a teenager, went to high school here. After I got my library degree I worked in Grand

Rapids, came back here when this job opened up. Great getting back. . . . We believe in term limitations here as a practical matter. The Democrats swept in this year. But the Republicans swept in in '87. Every four years there's a sweep. There hasn't been a mayor reelected in this town since the 1960s."

Frank (Pinky) Cecere, Jr., owner, Pinky's restaurant and bar, mayor: "I'm probably the only one ever returned to office for a second term . . . I ran for mayor in '83 and won. . . . We were able to put together a firm plan for the lakefront development project. We accomplished our political platform in one year. Then I was beaten four years ago, quite badly. . . . I think because we had been tackling problems people wouldn't touch. . . . So we got walloped. That was in '87. Now, here it is four years later. I made a very strong comeback. . . . The [incumbent] mayor came in third against a bar owner who showed up at the forums with long hair and wearing a T-shirt that said 'The City Sucks.' With very little advertising he got over a thousand votes. So there's definitely an element of hard-core negativism that either won't believe or hasn't been given the confidence in city government."

George Park, Jr., publisher, **Finger Lakes Times:** "There is only one issue, the proposed lakefront development project, 60 acres of prime lakefront land contiguous to downtown, ready to be developed. . . . It's going to include a marina, obviously a city park . . . some condominiums, townhouses, hopefully some commercial and retail. It's going to kill two birds with one stone: an economic boon to the community and also help [reverse] a decaying downtown area. You would be in walking distance of down-

town. There's already state and federal grant money available, as soon as the city lines up a developer."

Merrill Roenke, administrator, Rose Hill Mansion: "The grandson of one of the owners . . . gave it to the Historical Society. We haven't had to take any grants, loans, anything. I did the restoration, so naturally I think it's great. It was in very bad shape. All the pillars had to be taken down and restored. There was a lot of decay. . . . Our benefactor said he'd like to have the city pay for the furnishings. So I proceeded to pester people. We're fortunate in Geneva . . . very, very fine Federal and Greek Revival houses built here between 1810 and 1850, and still standing. . . . Their descendants still living in the homes were willing to place their furniture in the mansion, where they could enjoy and see it. . . . The Historical Society maintains a fund for repair and restoration of the façades of architecturally significant buildings. We loan up to $15,000 for exterior work. Usually there are five or six projects going on."

Allan Kuusisto, president emeritus, Hobart and William Smith Colleges: "The colleges are the second biggest employer in town, and the students they bring are, by far, the biggest economic factor . . . a very attractive campus overlooking the lake, really one of Geneva's biggest selling points. Without the colleges, Geneva would be a fairly drab place. . . . It's surprising for [Geneva's] location in rural upstate New York, the ethnic diversity. Why it has a fairly large Hispanic and African-American population I don't quite know. But it does, and it has a large Italian population, and a surprisingly large Syrian group, so that it's an interesting admixture. . . . There are more Italian restaurants. You can get more pasta. . . . If you looked at Geneva in the 1930s or '40s, you would see blue collar, industrial workers, with an elite of professional, entrepreneurial types who lived along South Main Street, and you had a real sense of class difference. That's changed. Because industry has left, the population has gone down in each census. . . . That's why the city is so anxious about the lakefront. If it can become a center of growing Finger Lakes tourist industry, I think Geneva has a fairly bright future." ■

Georgetown, SC 29442

Location: 35 miles south of Myrtle Beach, 60 miles north of Charleston, 8 miles inland from the Atlantic Ocean, on U.S. 17 in the low country.

Population: 9,517 (1990).

Growth rate: 6% decline since 1980.

Per capita income: $7,902 (1985), 89% of state average ($8,890).

Geography/climate: Coastal flatlands ranging from sea level to about 20 feet elevation. 70% of county land area used for cultivation of predominantly softwood trees. Temperate climate, modified by the ocean. Mild winters; warm, windy, often stormy springs; long, hot, humid summers; very nice but short falls, with much sun and pleasant temperatures. Average temperatures: January: high, 59; low, 36. July: high, 89; low, 70. Annual rainfall, 50 inches. Trace of snow.

Economic base: Manufacturing, tourism, retailing, commercial fishing. Top 10 payrolls: Georgetown County School District, 1,468 employees; International Paper Company, 1,371; Oneita Industries, knit outerwear and underwear, 800; Georgetown Steel, 726; Georgetown Memorial Hospital, 528; Georgetown County Government, 500; Superior Manufacturing, electrical switches, plugs, 299; Santee Cooper Winyah Steam Generating Station, 223; Rappahannock Wire, nails, 190; 3-V Chemical, 164. Port of Georgetown moved a million tons of cargo for first time in 1990, from 74 ships, 256 barges. Georgetown is seat of Georgetown County.

Newspaper: *Georgetown Times*, 615 Front Street, Georgetown, SC 29442. 803–546–4148. Tuesday, Thursday, Saturday. $40 a year. Ralph Parkman, publisher.

TV, radio: Local AM station. Cable carries network TV, PBS from Charleston. NPR from Charleston.

Health care: Georgetown Memorial Hospital, 142 beds. 53 physicians, 18 dentists in local practice.

Schools: 3 elementary (K–5). 1 middle school (6–8) enrolls 1,200. Georgetown High School enrolls 1,200, sends about 35% of graduates to 4-year college. Student body about 50/50 black/white. Advanced-placement classes offered. 4 years of French. On SATs, county students as a whole score 361, verbal; 394, math. College-prep students score above national, state averages. St. Cyprian's, Catholic school (K–8), enrolls 93. Calvary Freewill Baptist School (K–12) enrolls 30. Horry-Georgetown Technical College enrolls 2,000. Coastal Carolina College, 2-year institution, enrolls 4,000.

Educational level: 11.1% of Georgetown County residents have 16 or more years of formal education; state average, 13.4%. Per capita expenditure for public education, $476; state average, $403.

Library: Georgetown Public Library, 60,000 volumes.

Recreation: 3 city parks. Recreation Center at East Bay Park offers youth basketball league, Dixie Youth baseball, girls' softball, slow-pitch league for adults, annual baseball camp, soccer, soccer camps, cheerleading camp, square-dancing, karate classes, tennis.

11 golf courses in area. Marinas. 4 rivers flow into Winyah Bay, at Georgetown; Waccamaw River is part of Intracoastal Waterway. Camping, swimming at Huntington Beach State Park, 18 miles up coast toward Myrtle Beach. Swamp Fox Players perform in refurbished Strand Theater, on Front Street, downtown.

3 BR, 2 BA house: $40,00 to $70,000.

Cost of electricity: $.08 per kilowatt hour.

Cost of natural gas: $.60 per therm.

Sales tax: 5%.

State income tax: 3% to 7%.

Churches: 59. Denominations: African Methodist Episcopal (13), Apostolic, Assemblies of God, Baptist (7), Free Will Baptist, Independent Baptist, Southern Baptist (10), Church of Christ, Church of God, Church of Jesus Christ of Latter-day Saints, Episcopal, Full Gospel, Jehovah's Witnesses, Lutheran, Methodist, Nazarene, Nondenominational, Pentecostal (6), Presbyterian, Roman Catholic.

The Sampit River has always been a friend and supporter of Georgetown, as a freeway for commercial- and pleasure-boat traffic. Only since 1988, however, have river and town had a deeper relationship. Harborwalk has brought them closer together. It's a 12-foot-wide, 1,000-foot long walkway, built along the riverbank, behind what used to be the back side of stores on Front Street, downtown. Harborwalk has created, in effect, a new "Front Street" directly on the water, providing an attractive new connection between the town and the river, just off the Intracoastal Waterway. That's important to the future. Though Georgetown proper lost 6 percent of its population during the past decade, Georgetown County grew by 9 percent. Forecasts for the area are as rosy as sunrise over the Atlantic—or, if you're facing west on Harborwalk, sunset behind the steel mill and paper plant. Georgetown is a working town with smokestack concerns. Preserving clean water and clean air is one.

What residents say . . .

Tom Rubillo, mayor: "The two main items on the agenda next couple of years are, number one, make Georgetown a drug-free zone. The town measures 3.1 miles east–west, 4.9 miles north–south . . . about 10,000 people in the community, about 32 police officers, a very high ratio as those sorts of things go. The police have been doing a very good job of arresting people who do drugs on the street. The problem we have . . . once these people are processed into the court system, things tend to back up. . . . We have two prosecutors for a county of 45,000. . . . Plea bargaining becomes an unpleasant necessity. To turn prosecution into a deterrent, you've got to make sure punishment is swift and certain . . . funding a prosecutor who is going to handle just drug cases in the town of Georgetown. . . . It's not because we're overridden with drugs, but we take it more seriously. We do have crack cocaine on the street, and we want it off. . . . The other [item] is we have a small extension campus of Coastal Carolina College. . . . They have a limited number of offerings. You can get about a year and a half, then you have to go to Conway, about 40 miles away. Quite a number of people can't afford to do that. We want to increase the offerings at the local campus, make it possible for students of limited means to get a college degree here in town. . . . I'm originally from Philadelphia. I came here to open a local legal aid office. I'm a country lawyer. . . . You practice law. You deal with the problems that come up."

J. Mitchell Sizemore, city manager: "I was manager in a small city, Fort Mill, for eight or nine years. I was attracted to Georgetown because of the potential. It has a wonderful environment and a rich, warm history. As a coastal city with a seaport it has a lot of appeal and charm. I could see through some community effort that it could be greatly enhanced, and we are realizing that. The city has been reinventing itself. . . . Right now we are underway with a $4 million downtown revitalization . . . putting utility lines underground, bringing back the antique light fixtures, making [Front] street more comfortable to pedestrians and vehicles, adding parking. . . . The schools are much improved. . . . We still have some room to go. It is, after all, the South."

Beulah White, teacher, author: "I think some of the schools are doing well. I think some have not made the transition into the '90s. Small towns are very slow to change. I

grew up in Georgetown. I went to school here and returned 10 years ago. I was really shocked that a lot of things I left were still the same. . . . I'm currently teaching a graduate course on storytelling in the classroom. The National Festival of Black Storytelling will be here in two weeks. We expect about 2,000 people in Georgetown County and Horry County. We're doing programs with children, senior citizens. . . . People are just beginning to realize the magnitude of this festival. We have never had a gathering of this nature. . . . As we enter the third millenium, people are reaching back. We are spiraling into the new century, holding on to things that are there. In the cauldron, you don't need anything but a good story, told playing checkers under the tree, in barber shops, among friends at parties."

Pat Doyle, town historian: "Georgetown is the third oldest town in South Carolina. We've been recently trying to prove, without success, that it was the first Spanish settlement in North America. . . . It was at one time famous for growing rice, supplying about half of the entire United States. . . . Georgetown was the first planned town. We still have our original lot numbers and street names. . . . Front, Broad, Highmarket, and of course King, Queen, Prince, Duke. . . . Trees are mostly live oaks. A lot of dogwood, shrubbery, mostly azaleas. The moss is coming back on the magnolias. . . . We suffered from [Hurricane] Hugo, a great deal of flooding. . . . I guess the most characteristic thing is the town clock, on the Sampit River at the foot of Screven Street."

Mason Daley: "Eight years ago we moved here from West Chester, Pennsylvania. Two things attracted us, the historic buildings and the availability of boating. . . . We initially had a 31-foot sailboat. We now have a power boat about the same size, which we use for coastal cruising. . . . Georgetown has more eighteenth- and nineteenth-century houses than any place I have ever visited. . . . It's not a flashy town by a long shot. I think it's amazing that it has four or five very good restaurants. We live in the oldest building in town, built in 1737. . . . It is the original Cleland House. Mary Cleland inherited the entire city of Georgetown from her father, John Perry. This [house] was her dowry." ■

Glenwood Springs, CO 81601

Location: 159 miles west of Denver, 91 miles east of Grand Junction, on the Western Slope of the Rocky Mountains.

Population: 6,561 (1990).

Growth rate: 22% since 1986.

Per capita income: $11,689 (1985), 99% of state average ($11,713).

Geography/climate: Alpine valley town, elevation 5,746 feet, where Roaring Fork River joins the Colorado. Winter low temperatures around 20 degrees, highs to 40, except for 10 or so days below zero. Snowfall from early December typically covers the ground until March, averaging 67 inches for the season. Spring daytime highs into the 60–70 range. Summer days average in the mid-80s with hot spells to mid-90s, cooling off to 50s at night. Low humidity. Average annual precipitation, 17 inches.

Economic base: Tourism, retail trade, services. 4-season tourist and resort business generates about 60% of local income. Glenwood Springs is seat of Garfield County.

Newspaper: *The Glenwood Post*, 2014 Grand Avenue, Glenwood Springs, CO 81602. 303–945–8515. Daily, Monday through Friday. Robert L. Krecklow, publisher. $63 a year.

TV, radio: Local AM, FM stations. Cable carries network TV from Denver, Grand Junction, PBS.

Health care: Valley View Hospital, 80 beds. 40 physicians, 12 dentists in local practice.

Schools: 1 elementary (K–4), 1 middle (5–8). Glenwood Springs High School enrolls 478 students, sends 50% to 4-year college, 15% to 2-year. Composite ACT score, 21.6. Also, St. Stephen's School, Catholic; Cornerstone Christian School (K–6); Glenwood Christian Academy (K–6); Yampah Mountain High School, alternative for potential dropouts. Community Mountain College, a 2-year institution, enrolls 240.

Educational level: 20.2% of Garfield County residents have 16 or more years of formal education; state average, 23%. Per capita expenditure for public education, $570; state average, $523.

Library: Garfield County Library, 22,000 volumes. 30,000-volume collection at Community Mountain College also open to local residents.

Recreation: 8 city parks with playgrounds; facilities for picnics, fishing, skateboarding, baseball, volleyball, horseshoes, basketball, tennis. Hot springs pool fed by geothermal water provides a good soak at 90 to 104 degrees, winter and summer. Larger of 2 pools measures 405 by 100 feet, ranks 4th largest among state attractions. Summer swim team for kids 5–18. Hiking, biking, walking, jogging trails. Inner-city system of bike trails under construction. 2 9-hole golf courses. "Gold Medal" trout fishing nearby. Rafting. White River National Forest surrounds area, provides 60-plus campgrounds, several hundred miles of backpack trails. Ski Sunlight, 15 minutes from town, has slopes for all skill levels. 2½-mile Ute Trail, longest run, rated beginning to intermediate in difficulty.

Cross-country trails. More skiing at nearby Vail, Aspen. Snowmobiling out of Sunlight on longest groomed trail in Colorado. 3 movie theaters. 4-concert music series each winter.

3 BR, 2 BA house: $115,000–$120,000, midmarket. Composite cost-of-living index for Glenwood Springs, 108.6, 8.6% above national average.

Cost of electricity: $.08 per kilowatt hour.

Cost of natural gas: $.43 per therm.

Sales tax: 3¾%.

State income tax: 5%.

Churches: 20. Denominations: Assemblies of God, Baptist, Baptist-General Conference, Baptist-Independent, Charismatic, Christian Science, Church of Jesus Christ of Latter-day Saints, Episcopal, Foursquare Gospel, Full Gospel, Jehovah's Witnesses, Lutheran ELCA, Lutheran-Missouri Synod, Mennonite, Nazarene, Presbyterian, Roman Catholic, Seventh-Day Adventist, United Methodist.

During a stretch of 1965, Glenwood Springs was in a friendly competition with the eastern Colorado town of Brush to see which one could send more calves to market each week. Both towns were big producers, and the honors bounced back and forth over the Rockies. But who won is now immaterial. The point, as Mayor Ted O'Leary says, is that Brush is still a nice cow town, while the old stockyards in Glenwood Springs have been replaced by a Holiday Inn. Twenty-four other hotels, motels, and lodges—and three bed-and-breakfasts—now do business with a year-round stream of visitors and vacationers.

With its fabulous hot springs pool, Glenwood wasn't destined to be a cow town. Ute Indians probably were the first to discover the place. They called it *Yampah*, meaning "big medicine," in appreciation of a nice long soak in the soothing mineral waters. Teddy Roosevelt and Annie Oakley took the waters during Glenwood's Victorian era. Today, other pilgrims arrive daily on the Amtrak train from east and west. For skiers, Glenwood is a more affordable alternative than Vail or Aspen. For permanent residents, Glenwood provides the necessities of ordinary living: the department store, supermarkets, car dealers, Wal-Mart, government offices, doctors, and dentists. Mayor O'Leary believes the population of 6,500 is perceived as much larger. "We tend to be a big small town," he says.

What residents say ...

Marcia Hadenfeldt, owner, Summit Canyon Mountaineering, member of City Council:
"We've lived 13 years in Glenwood Springs, originally from Boston ... lived in Fort Collins on the Eastern Slope for nine years. ... We own and operate a sporting goods store specializing in mountaineering and outdoor equipment, plus all the clothing to go with it. ... Glenwood Springs is recession-resistant: however, we are not recession-proof. It's like rainwear. Some is resistant, some waterproof. Because of our

location we are the service base for the western area, Aspen to Vail to Grand Junction, a good base for economics."

Stephanie Fattor, high school junior, receptionist: "To be frank, there really isn't a whole lot of things for high school–age people to do, no place for kids to congregate. We rely on Grand Avenue, the 7–11, Thayer Park basketball courts. . . . Usually every weekend kids are going up skiing and snowboarding. That's really popular here. It's cheaper than Aspen, $24 at Sunlight. . . . A lot of kids work at fast-food places . . . maids for the hotels. Some work for their parents or construction. . . . I want to go to college. My hopes are to go to Georgetown, but I may go to Boulder."

Ted O'Leary, mayor, real-estate broker: "It's really expensive to build in the mountains. Also we have very limited land area on which to build . . . two river valleys, the river bottoms, and that's that. We do have an affordable-housing problem. . . . We made the decision we were not going to become the housing authority. So we put an ordinance in place that said any developer who can qualify for regular HUD funding . . . will not be charged the usual development fees. The first people that came to us were the Denver Archdiocese of the Catholic Church. . . . The projects they've been running on the Eastern Slope are by any standard a model. . . . We'll have 50 to 55 units, mostly attached pods of four to five units each, with a play area and on-site day care. . . . Many people in the lower-income range drive 40 to 50 miles a day on crowded highways to work in destination resorts. . . . I'm really proud of the fact that Glenwood has an ordinance on the books. . . . Glenwood did the right thing about 10 years ago. We didn't have a clear vision of what we were going to be-

come. Citizens asked the question, 'What is our strength and what do we do best?' We have unique strength being 40 miles from Aspen, 50 miles from Vail, on I-70 in two major river valleys. How can we enhance that for our benefit? We began by passing a three-quarter-cent sales tax. . . ."

Molly Downs, Glenwood Springs Volunteer of the Year: "We passed the three-quarter-cent sales tax in order to start work on some of the amenities that the city needed but couldn't afford . . . sidewalk replacement, trees, lots of flower beds, bike paths. . . . We have a very low property-tax base . . . and older citizens on fixed incomes. To promote Glenwood without affecting the income of residents, we passed an accommodation tax of 1 percent on a motel room. . . . We do have homeless people, unfortunately. We have a marvelous group called Lift-Up, started during the oil shale bust when a dramatic number of people were without income. Cash contributions are used to help find or at least place people in a home temporarily. . . . Just last week [Lift-Up] had a plea in the newspaper. Their cupboards were getting bare. They were overwhelmed with the response. . . . The other major project that a lot of citizens have requested is a community center. We have two quite active theater groups and no place to perform other than the high school auditorium. . . . We would like to see a municipal or lap pool. . . . One of the most important things that strikes me living in a small town is the concern of residents for everyone. We were at the office one day when our daughter was bicycle riding. It had rained and the streets were slick. She fell and knocked herself out. Somebody picked her up and took her to the hospital . . . and then called us. That's the type of concern you have in a small town like Glenwood." ■

Grand Rapids, MN 55744

Location: 80 miles northwest of Duluth, 172 miles north of Minneapolis-St. Paul, 120 miles south of International Falls, in the lake region of northern Minnesota.

Population: 7,976 (1990).

Growth rate: 0.6%—42 people in 10 years.

Per capita income: $9,174 (1985), 69% of state average ($13,212).

Geography/climate: Flat or gently rolling glacial plateau surrounded by a thousand lakes. Headwaters of the Mississippi River. Rugged, four-season climate with some winter stretches of 35 degrees below zero. January average daily high of 20 degrees. Average 126 days between killing frosts, 40 inches of snow, 26 inches of rain. Cool summers. Average daily high of 81 in July.

Economic base: Manufacturing, government services, health care, tourism. Seat of Itasca County and meeting center for region. Largest employer: Blandin Paper Company, with union payroll of 1,100. Related logging and paper interests employ several hundred more. City and county government, 718; Itasca Memorial Hospital, 320; Arrowhead Promotion, mail order, 100. As many as 165 summer and winter resorts draw tourist dollars, enhance retail sales.

Newspaper: *The Grand Rapids Herald-Review*, 301 First Avenue, NW, Grand Rapids, MN 55744. 218–326–6623. Sunday and Wednesday. Charles Johnson, editor. $38 a year.

TV, radio: 1 local AM, 2 FM stations including NPR affiliate. Cable brings in TV networks, PBS from Duluth.

Health care: Itasca Memorial Hospital, 106 beds. 277 nursing-home beds in area. 46 physicians, 22 dentists in local practice.

Schools: 4 elementary (K–6), 1 junior high (7–9). Grand Rapids High School (10–12) enrolls 937, sends 50% of graduates to higher education, 29% to 4-year institutions. Recent composite ACT, 22.0. High school was the first in Minnesota to become a member of the International Baccalaureate Organization. Itasca Community College.

Educational level: 12.4% of Itasca County residents have 16 or more years of formal education; state average, 17.4%. Per capita expenditure for public education, $607; state average, $554.

Library: Grand Rapids Public Library has 47,000 volumes, 12,000 registered borrowers.

Recreation: Extraordinarily large concentration of lakes support rich variety of water sports summer and winter: boating, swimming, fishing, hunting. 720 acres of wilderness at Bass Lake Park, just out of town. Hiking, cross-country skiing, snowmobiling, 3-wheeling. 18-hole golf course in town. Central School, restored Romanesque Revivalist building, is cultural center in town: museum, shops, special events.

3 BR, 2 BA house: $40,000 to $80,000 depending on age, location.

Cost of electricity: $.05 per kilowatt hour.

Cost of natural gas: $.48 per therm.

Sales tax: 6½%, but does not apply to food, clothing.

State income tax: 6% to 8½%.

Churches: 30. Denominations: Assemblies of God, Baha'i, Baptist, Charismatic, Christian & Missionary Alliance, Church of God, Church of Jesus Christ of Latter-day Saints, Episcopal, Evangelical Free, Independent, Jehovah's Witnesses, Lutheran Evangelical, Lutheran Missouri Synod, Nazarene, Nondenominational, Pentecostal, Pentecostal United, Presbyterian USA, Roman Catholic, Seventh-Day Adventist, Unitarian Universalist, United Methodist.

Glaciers endowed Grand Rapids with a sparkling wealth of small lakes, and the town has taken steps to protect this legacy. "1000 Grand Lakes" is both a promotional theme and a registered trademark. Tourism is serious business here in north central Minnesota (call 800–472–6366 to receive full details). There used to be just one season—summer. The snowmobile is largely responsible for making Grand Rapids a winter tourist destination as well. Not everyone is happy to hear those snarly sleds in the wilderness, but it is the sound of revenue, after all.

Grand Rapids sprang to life as a logging and papermaking center, and the big Blandin Paper Co. has anchored the economy for decades. Though the company is now New Zealand-owned, its fabulous profits earlier in the century funded The Blandin Foundation, a perennial rich uncle to many local civic and social institutions. As a guide to the future, the town has Rapids 2000, its long-range plan. But as a guide to the past it has The Yellow Brick Road.

What residents say . . .

John Kelsch, executive director, Itasca County Historical Society and Judy Garland Museum: "The Yellow Brick Road was built in 1989 for the 50th anniversary of 'The Wizard of Oz.' It provides pedestrian access to Central School Heritage Center. . . . The bricks are concrete tile, shiny yellow, standard brick size. We sell personal engraved messages. . . . People put their family names on them. You have 16 characters per line, $50 for two lines, $55 for three lines. Part of it is a donation. Depending on your tax bracket you can write it off. We've sold 15 hundred bricks so far. It's what helps keep the July Garland Festival going. The last two years have been 'The Wizard of Oz.' We had the Grand Munchkin reunion, the largest gathering of original Munchkins. We had 13 of them here. . . . We've got a new festival this year, Jim Bailey and 'An Evening with Judy Garland.' He's an opera singer by training. 'The next best thing to Judy Garland.' That's what the Boston Herald called him. . . . It's a two-hour makeup. . . . We get people from Australia, England, California, all over. The museum is open year-round. We're seeing attendance at about

12,000 annually. That doesn't sound like a lot but it is for us. . . . The town has never really reconciled to the fact that a superstar was born here, I don't think. A lot of people were disappointed when Judy didn't come back in 1941, our 50th anniversary. I'm sure her production schedule made it impossible, but that's kind of a sore spot. . . . The last three years have really changed attitudes. The town understands now it's an important part of entertainment history. . . . For a town of only 8,000 in the city limits, there's probably more going on here than in any small town in the United States."

Craig Mattson, city administrator: "The city proper is 8,000. The community is 43,000 people who live on surrounding lakes and demand services from the City of Grand Rapids. The challenge facing Grand Rapids is to consider annexation so these people can help pay the tax bill, or find creative ways of financing . . . joint powers, trying to relieve some of the burden."

Beth C. Sundin, news editor, **Grand Rapids Herald-Review:** "I've been here since November 1987, straight from St. Cloud State University. . . . There are a lot of professional organizations centered around here, people employed by the county, a large hospital with a lot of physicians, a community college, the paper mill and their top management. It tends to draw people trying to get away from the metropolitan area. . . . A study by United Way basically states Grand Rapids is like a home in a sense. Some can be adapted to it. Most feel it's a friendly community though it is not easy to be a newcomer. People try to rope you in. There's a lot of civic activity. . . . Professionals like to grab you right away and pull you in. If you just came up to do your job,

it is hard to meld. What I see is a lack of professionals between the ages of 24 and 35. A lot of people come back after they've been someplace else. For those people who come in the between years, there is not a lot of social activity. Most of those are mill workers and a number of people on assistance . . . because of the services they can get in Itasca County . . . good housing for people on assistance, apartments easier to get. . . . There are plenty of churches if you're into churches, all the way from Catholic to Baha'i, you've got it all here. . . . The people that get overlooked have been here 50, 60, 70 years, the normal folk. A lot of professionals came in as [Grand Rapids] got better. It couldn't get better without a basic start by the people who worked the mill and owned the land in the first place."

Todd Driscoll, The Blandin Foundation: "It's a peppy place. It has a can-do spirit. One of the reasons you can be peppy . . . is a stable base of high-quality blue-collar jobs, three shifts a day, year in and year out. That provides stability. . . . You can't build a community on retail. Our employment is based on fiber. The paper company adds value. They take a low-value wood and convert it to a high-value product called No. 5 Coated Paper for printing magazines like *Time* and *Newsweek*. . . . Adding value in rural areas is the key to our future success. If we can take milk and make cheese, or corn and make syrup, that's the future. . . . It's a peppy town. We get people together. We have a lot of groups here . . . for every diversity of interest. I think it's part of the American way of getting things done. At the drop of the hat you can get an ad hoc task force. What the Russians would love to have, we have in spades. They're so fascinated by grassroots organization, they have come to The Blandin Foundation to copy our community organization. . . . Six Russians are coming here this fall to catch this American thing, rural organization. What is township government? What is a school board? How are they organized? What do people do when they volunteer to serve on a planning commission? But I think the spirit of this town is not unique to Grand Rapids. . . .

It's my prediction that as we bring the infrastructure to rural areas, we're going to find that more high-tech people can make a good living in these communities. They're going to be the next wave of homesteaders. . . . We can get the St. Paul Chamber Orchestra to come here and play, and we say 'Hallelujah!' Then we go back and cheer our local performers. That's what I mean by peppiness. As a foundation, we lubricate that process." ∎

Greencastle, IN 46135

Location: 40 miles southwest of Indianapolis, 160 miles south-southeast of Chicago, in west central Indiana.

Population: 8,984 (1990).

Growth rate: 6% since 1980.

Per capita income: $8,045 (1985), 81% of state average ($9,978).

Geography/climate: Elevation 835 feet. Rolling terrain in town, quite hilly on outskirts. Continental climate: moderately cold winters; pleasant spring commencing March; warm to hot, often humid summers; pleasant, dry fall. Average temperatures: January: high, 36; low, 19. July: high, 86; low, 65. Average rainfall, 39 inches; snowfall, 17 inches.

Economic base: Manufacturing, especially auto-industry suppliers; agriculture, especially corn, soybeans, hogs; limestone quarries; hardwood. DePauw University, 2,200 students and 600 employees, is single largest economic influence. Other large payrolls: Shenandoah Industries, auto door trim parts, 328; Wal-Mart, distribution center, 300; TechnoTrim, auto seat covers, 425; F.B. Distro, apparel, 150; Lone Star Industries, cement, 145; North American Capacitor, 125; Lobdell-Emery, metal stampings, 200; Happico, auto exterior parts, 125; Putnam County Hospital, 250; Heartland Automotive, auto interior parts, 100.

Newspaper: *The Banner-Graphic,* 100 N. Jackson Street, Greencastle, IN 46135. 317–653–5151. Daily, Monday through Saturday. Eric Bernsee, editor. $95 a year.

TV, radio: FM station in town. Cable carries network TV from Indianapolis, Terre Haute. PBS, NPR from Bloomington.

Health care: Putnam County Hospital, 85 beds. 21 physicians, 8 dentists in local practice.

Schools: 3 elementary (K–5), 1 middle (6–8). Greencastle High School enrolls 549, sends 65% to higher education. 1991 composite SAT scores: verbal, 400; math, 470. Latchkey Program at Methodist church serves any child K–6; school bus provides transportation. Area vocational school services junior, senior high school students. DePauw University.

Educational level: 12.1% of Putnam County residents have 16 or more years of formal education; state average, 12.5%. Per capita expenditure for public education, $403; state average, $422.

Library: Putnam County Library, 65,000 volumes.

Recreation: 2 public parks totaling 47 acres, with playgrounds, lighted tennis courts, softball fields, Olympic pool with waterslide, picnic grounds, band shell. Big Walnut Sport Park, 80 acres, when finished will include 10 baseball/softball fields, 9 soccer/football fields, BMX bicycle track, exercise trails, shelters. Recreational center at DePauw—pool, workout rooms, handball courts, gym—available for use by public for a fee. Two 9-hole golf courses, 1 public, 1 private. Bowling alley. Twin-screen cinema. 2 state parks within 25 miles provide hunting, fishing, camping. Admission minimal to

DePauw Performing Arts Series and free for programs at the Center for Contemporary Media.

3 BR, 2 BA house: $60,000 to $90,000.

Cost of electricity: $.05 to $.06 per kilowatt hour.

Cost of natural gas: $.45 per therm.

Sales tax: 5%.

State income tax: 3.4%.

Churches: 16 total. Denominations: Assemblies of God, Baptist, Christian, Disciples of Christ, Church of Christ, Church of God, Church of Jesus Christ of Latter-day Saints, Church of the Nazarene, Episcopal, Jehovah's Witnesses, Lutheran, Pentecostal, Presbyterian USA, Roman Catholic, United Methodist.

Mayor Mike Harmless flew to Washington in August 1991 to accept a coveted award on behalf of all the people back home. Greencastle had been named an All-America City. In the White House Rose Garden, President Bush congratulated the winning cities, with special reference to the little town in west central Indiana. Listen to the story of Greencastle, the president said, and "you'll share our unshakable optimism in the future of this great land."

Optimism had been especially important on November 11, 1986, the day IBM announced it would close the distribution center it had operated in Greencastle for three decades. At a stroke, 985 well-paying jobs were yanked from a town of only 8,403 residents—actually, 6,000 residents if you excluded DePauw students. Recounting this local earthquake, editor Eric Bernsee of the daily *Banner-Graphic* wrote, "Suddenly, community residents were faced with replacing 20 percent of the local tax base, more than 70 percent of the local industrial payroll, and some 40 percent of all local jobs." Today, Greencastle has more than recovered from its loss. It's a different place, and probably better.

What residents say . . .

Steve Jones, owner, Greencastle Wash & Fill: "People were forced to lose their jobs in 1987 who had been with IBM since graduating from high school. They had grown up here. Their families were here. They owned a car, had houses, had a good life, with no more than a high school education provided in Greencastle, Indiana, they had a darn good life. . . . I think, sadly for a lot of small towns, what they contribute to the national picture are a lot of real capable young people with small-town values that everyone seems to brag on. I mean, they certainly said that when Neil Armstrong walked on the moon. There's something about small-town background that seems to carry some weight. In communities that don't offer job opportunities, people leave and take those things with them. That's what small towns export. . . . We're going to need desperately another bowling alley, because as the community turns more blue-collar, and I hear this over and over again, bowling is the chosen recreation of the factories. They want their bowling teams and they want their softball leagues. I think we're going to see fewer bridge clubs and more softball teams. . . . I'm in Greencastle because my great, great, great grandfather came to Putnam County in 1822 with his wife, eight children, and 22 Negro slaves. He was an Abolitionist, from Kentucky. The Rev. Benjamin Jones was a Methodist minister. He also taught school and was a very respected citizen."

Kathy Jones, founder, Greencastle Civic League: "I think Greencastle was in transition even before IBM announced its plan to leave. A group of people between the ages of 30 and 50 saw that Greencastle needed to make some plans for its future. They liked what they saw here but also saw they couldn't do in a small town the things they were used to because of funding and government regulations. You had to plan ahead. . . . I think it's interesting the number of people our age, Baby Boomers, who have opted to live here. I think a small town gives a sense of grounding, opportunity to be involved, and old-fashioned values, honesty. . . . I worry about the children. We're not isolated. You have MTV right here, and the morals and values of the city can be right here."

Ellen Sedlack, director, Putnam County Library: "I think in a small town there's a better chance of human needs being met. Children can run free after school more than city children do. I think young people have a greater chance of having a real childhood . . . an honest childhood where they go through the appropriate stages and activities at the appropriate age, so they can step forward to a city and handle it all right. . . . I also want to talk about the sense of powerlessness that a city person can feel versus the sense of power that a small-town person can feel. You can change things in a small town. . . . Before the '70s we didn't have special education at either end for our children. We didn't have a Mental-Health Association. We didn't have Planned Parenthood. Mental-health needs and physical-health needs were not being met. They were met in the '70s, and I would say largely by DePauw wives. . . . I grew up in Chicago, went to Cleveland for my master's degree in library science, met Bob Sedlack, and he was offered a job at DePauw University. We've been here 28 years."

Clem C. Williams, Jr., emeritus professor of English, DePauw University: "Someone ought to get on the record the rather elementary point that when IBM closed up this was not seen as an unmitigated bad thing. Through the years, IBM had been keeping out other businesses simply because it had raised the standards so high that others would not come to town. What the closing did was open up immediately to four or five factories. It was actually one of the best things that happened to the town. . . . The chief problem with the town is most simply expressed as the town-gown one. I don't think in terms of town-gown tension although there is a lot of latent tension there that doesn't surface very often. . . . I think there's a tendency for [town] people to suppose that education and books, the whole culture of books, is something that's done as a specialization at the university, and the rest of us don't have to do that, and we are not very good at it. . . . There are all kinds of ways in which the university's presence here both contributes to the community and tends to exacerbate problems. . . . When I came here from 120th and Amsterdam Avenue [in New York City], my children were young. I visited here and it looked like the perfect place. I had never heard of Green-castle and I had barely heard of DePauw. . . . We thought this was an amazing place. We had a sense of it being very democratic. There seemed to be no class borders. Actually there were but we didn't see them. It seemed wonderfully free from some of the things that were obviously wrong with the cities. . . . Our national life is full of people who have come from small towns, and they are very important creators and bearers of the national culture. In the people who come from small towns there is a kind of preliminary simplicity. Life is simpler when you just have Green-castle High School to go to, when you have a simple diagram of things. . . . I think we all need some simplicity to navigate in this world." ∎

Greeneville, TN 37743

Location: 68 miles northeast of Knoxville, 60 miles northwest of Asheville, North Carolina, in extreme northeastern Tennessee.

Population: 14,097 (1990).

Growth rate: 5% decline since 1986.

Per capita income: $10,350 (1985), 10% higher than state average.

Geography/climate: Elevation 1,557 feet, in the Great Valley of East Tennessee. Sheltered by thickly forested mountains and ridges, reaching to 4,400 feet in the southwest. Moderately cold winters, warm to hot summers. Average temperatures: January: high, 46; low, 27. July: high, 86; low, 65. Average 13 days into 90s. Annual rainfall, 42 inches; snowfall, 11 inches. 45% sunshine in January; 75% in October.

Economic base: Manufacturing, dairying, tobacco, general farming, lumber. Seat of Greene County. Larger payrolls: Air Maze, filters, 125; Ball Zinc, main supplier of penny blanks to U.S. Mint, 260; DeJay, bug killers, 175; Delfasco, metal fabrication, 225; Doehler-Jarvis, automotive engine parts, 400; Franklin Furniture, 225; Greeneville Industries, defense contractor, 450; Hurd Lock, 850; Huyck Formex, paper machine components, 200; Meco, barbecue grills, folding furniture, 850; Pet, evaporated milk, food specialties, 250; Philips Consumer Electronics, 2,100; Plus Mark, gift wrap, 1,100; TRW Ross Gear, 340. County leads state in dairy production, beef cattle, burley tobacco.

Newspaper: *The Greeneville Sun,* 121 W. Summer St., Greeneville, TN 37743. 615–638–4181. Daily except Sunday. John M. Jones, Sr., publisher; John M. Jones, Jr., editor. $99 a year.

TV, radio: 3 local radio stations. Cable carries PBS, network TV from Bristol, Kingsport, Knoxville, Asheville. NPR from Johnson City.

Health care: Takoma Adventist Hospital, 115 beds. Laughlin Memorial Hospital, 177 beds. 70 physicians, 26 dentists in local practice.

Schools: 4 elementary (K–5), 1 middle (6–8). Greeneville-Greene County Center for Technology enrolls 700 high school students in vo-tech program. Greeneville High School enrolls 935, sends 52% of graduates to college. First Church of God Christian School (K–12), Greeneville Adventist Academy (1–10), Towering Oaks Christian School (K–6). Tusculum College, founded 1794, a 4-year liberal-arts institution, houses the Andrew Johnson Library and Museum, enrolls 850. Walters State Community College, 2-year program.

Educational level: 8.9% of Greene County residents have 16 or more years of formal education; state average, 12.6%. Per capita expenditure for public education, $305; state average, $301.

Library: Greeneville-Greene County Library, 34,000 volumes.

Recreation: 3 city parks, 3 neighborhood playgrounds, 2 swimming pools, 2 Little League fields. Babe Ruth and softball fields. 6 tennis courts, basketball court, picnic grounds. Davy Crockett State Park, 12 miles east, has 75 campsites, swimming pool, fishing. Kinser Park, 6 miles south, has 110 campsites along Nolichucky River, 9-hole golf course, tennis courts, ball diamonds, go-kart track, swimming, boat ramp, small carnival.

3 BR, 2 BA house: $60,000 to $90,000.

Cost of electricity: $.05 to $.06 per kilowatt hour.

Cost of natural gas: $.58 per therm.

Sales tax: 8%.

State income tax: 6%.

Churches: 28. Denominations: AME, Assemblies of God, Baptist (5), Free Will Baptist, Independent Baptist, Christian, Church of Christ, Church of God, Church of Jesus Christ of Latter-day Saints, Episcopal, Lutheran, Nazarene, Pentecostal, Presbyterian, Roman Catholic, Seventh-Day Adventist, United Methodist.

Greeneville is rich with early American history. Named for General Nathaniel Greene, a hero of the Revolutionary War, the town and county were created in 1783—not by the State of Tennessee but by North Carolina—and thereby hangs the tale of the Lost State of Franklin. In 1783, Tennessee had not yet been formed. Greeneville was part of the Western Lands of North Carolina. The following year, North Carolina ceded these lands to the federal government, but the feds refused the gift, leaving Greeneville and Greene County without protection from any larger government. In self-defense, the Westerners organized their own state, the State of Franklin, and Greeneville served as state capital for a period. But Franklinites could not agree on a constitution, and marauding Indians only made matters worse. By 1789, Franklin had ceased to exist and Greeneville was back under the wing of North Carolina.

Greeneville's most celebrated native son is Andrew Johnson, the 17th President of the United States. Johnson's home, tailor shop, and national monument are tourist attractions. Just out of town, Davy Crockett's birthplace is an equally big draw.

Considering the overall vitality of the area, Mayor G. Thomas Love is puzzled by Greeneville's apparent loss of some 700 people between 1980 and 1990. One theory is that Greenevillians have moved out to the "suburbs" just across the city boundary, in Greene County. At the request of these unincorporated areas, and as city service capacity expands, Greeneville is growing by annexation.

A 1991 forecast of economic growth for the Greater Tri-Cities region of northeast Tennessee and southwest Virginia, prepared by the Battelle Memorial Institute, describes Greeneville and Greene County as "relatively strong: in transportation, human resources, quality of life (primarily for its physical setting), energy and utilities, potential market and supply linkages, the state business climate, and comparative costs." Meanwhile, Greeneville, like so many small towns, is paying attention to its business district.

What residents say ...

Sarah Webster, alderman: "We've tried to redevelop our whole downtown area, and I think we've had a lot of success. Downtown has a totally different feeling and look. . . . Nothing had been done to destroy its architectural integrity, so we started without having to tear down to begin. There's not even a lot that needs to be peeled off. [Stores] have moved in and moved out, of course. This is sometimes looked at as a negative, but you have to realize the same thing happens in shopping centers. We're nowhere near full at the moment, but we're closer than we've been at many times. . . . We've been developing our tourism potential. Experts tell us we have the two things necessary to encourage tourism growth, the scenery and the historical aspect. We're lucky to have the [Andrew Johnson] historic site, and Davy Crockett was born in the county. We say we're the second oldest town in Tennessee. . . . We raised taxes last year for the first time in many, many years. Anticipating continuing the same services, we expect we'll have to pay more for them. It's not an easy thing for any board to do. No one likes a tax increase. I think the residents of Greeneville place a great deal of trust in their elected officials. I think the elected officials respond in a like manner. We expect to do what is best for the community. We explain everything that is done. . . . We feel we can communicate with anybody about anything, and the town residents feel the same way. We have very positive support from the media."

John M. Jones, Sr., publisher, **The Greeneville Sun:** "In my view, the community can't be any better than the paper.

The paper should be involved in leadership of the community, to address the issues. We have taken positions that were not the most popular but because we believed in them very strongly. . . . This paper has been one of the leaders in industrial recruitment. As a result of the diminishing role of tobacco in the future we have tried to get the county more diversified. . . . [Absentee ownership] affects a community very adversely. We've seen what happens when you have the Wal-Marts and K-Marts. Your locally owned stores begin to diminish. The same thing is true in banks. Same thing in newspapers. It does not bode well for the future when you lose local ownership. You can't expect the chain groups to have the same interest in the community as the little store on the corner. . . . Where do you get the funds to build the YMCAs? To support charitable causes? You can't get them from the big companies. We have a classic case right now in Greeneville, raising money for a college. A locally owned bank has already put up $250,000. The chain-owned banks haven't opened their yaps yet."

G. Thomas Love, mayor: "Disposal of solid waste. That's one of the most important things we are facing today. I went through two landfill sitings in the last 15 years and got both of them. But the third one we're facing in the next two years is going to be pretty important. . . . I've been mayor for 17 years. It is a full-time job but only pays $200 a month. I do spend about three-quarters of my time in the mayor's office. . . . We're proud of our little town. We've accomplished a lot, and I've enjoyed it." ■

Grinnell, IA 50112

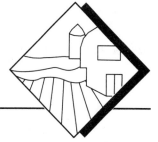

Location: 4 miles north of I-80, 60 miles east of Des Moines, in central Iowa.

Population: 8,902 (1990).

Growth rate: ⅓ of 1% (34 people) since 1980.

Per capita income: $10,410 (1986), 3% higher than state average ($10,096).

Geography/climate: Gently rolling mid-continent farmlands. 4 sharply etched seasons. On a few brittle, cold winter days temperatures may not rise above zero. Summer highs in the 90s. Precipitation averages 32 inches, snowfall 31 inches. Spring and fall each last about 6 weeks.

Economic base: Corn and soybeans anchor the agricultural economy. Big payrolls: DeLong Sportswear, maker of jackets and uniforms, 389 employees; Grinnell Mutual Reinsurance, 633; Grinnell College, 501; GTE Iowa Division, 431; Donaldson Co., mufflers, 240.

Newspaper: *Grinnell Herald-Register*, 813 5th Avenue, Grinnell, IA 50112. 515–236–3113. Monday, Thursday. A.J. Pinder, editor and publisher. $25 a year.

TV, radio: Local AM station. Direct reception from Cedar Rapids, Ames, Waterloo, Des Moines, including PBS and NPR. Cable service also available.

Health care: Grinnell General Hospital, 81 beds. 3 nursing homes. 22 physicians, 8 dentists in local practice.

Schools: 3 elementary (K–4); 1 middle (5–8); high school enrolls 480 students. 70% of high school students take ACT test; average score, 22.5. About 50% attend 4-year colleges; additional 20% to other higher education.

Educational level: 14.8% of Poweshiek County residents have 16 or more years of formal education; state average, 13.9%. Per capita expenditure for public education, $451; state average, $480.

Library: Stewart Library, built in 1901, has 43,000 volumes, 4,035 card holders. Grinnell College library also available for special use by town residents.

Recreation: 9 city parks; new swimming pool built 1989. 9-hole golf course in town, 18-hole course nearby. Swimming, fishing, boating at Rock Creek State Park, 9 miles west. Grinnell College facilities available to public for a fee include Olympic pool, indoor tennis and racquetball, weight-lifting, sauna.

3 BR, 2 BA house: $50,000 to $80,000. 4 BR, upper $70,000 average.

Cost of electricity: $.0553 per kilowatt hour.

Cost of natural gas: $.37 per therm.

Sales tax: 4%.

State income tax: Graduated 0.4% to 9.98%.

Churches: Assemblies of God, American Baptist, Independent Baptist, Christian, Christian & Missionary Alliance, Christian Science, Church of Christ, Episcopal, Lutheran, Lutheran-ELCA, Nazarene, Presbyterian USA, Roman Catholic, Society of Friends, United Church of Christ, United Methodist.

Al Pinder, editor and publisher of the *Grinnell Herald-Register*, describes the local economy as "a five-legged stool that gives a lot of solidity." The legs? "Agriculture all around, industrial base, educational base, retail, white-collar." While all these props are important, conversations about life in the central-Iowa town seem inevitably to begin and end with its celebrated college. Consistently ranked among the best small liberal arts institutions in the nation, Grinnell College draws students from around the world, transporting young adults with unfamiliar accents to Main Street, Iowa. This introduces an international flavor.

But so did Pinder's more-or-less one-man effort to bring in foreign journalists for a look around. It began one day nearly 30 years ago when the publisher of the largest newspaper in Taipei arrived in Grinnell during a two-month U.S. tour arranged by the State Department. Pinder and his spouse, Dorothy, thought their tribe of six young kids might learn something by sharing a meal with this man from the Far East. So they invited him and his interpreter to an honest Iowa supper of fried chicken, fresh tossed green salad, and homemade rolls. The guest was delighted, proclaiming through the interpreter, "This night is the most special one." Pinder asked why. "Because," the Taiwanese explained, "this is the first American home I have been inside of."

"Frankly, we were dumbstruck," Pinder recalled. "Here our State Department is trying to show him what America is like, and in two months had not opened a door to someone's home." Pinder began writing letters to state and other agencies. "We suggested that in small towns, people would take time to entertain guests, to show them where they work, where they play, where they worship. Through the use of home entertainment, the foreign guest could see just how people live, to learn their hopes, their fears, their plans for the future."

Thanks to many others in town who also have been willing to open their homes and lives to people from afar, Grinnell's fame has spread farther than one might expect of a pretty little town surrounded by corn and beans.

What residents say ...

William Deminoff, secretary of Grinnell College: "I'm a native of Pittsfield, Massachusetts. We came here in stages. . . . At Purdue University for five years . . . then to Grinnell, and it has turned out to be such a good job that we stayed. . . . As sec- retary I'm charged with finding a speaker of national renown every Thursday . . . for the old chapel hour, now given over to a distinguished lecture. We don't go for the celebrity types who charge a lot of money and give a canned speech. We go for people who can contribute something to the town . . . Molly Yard, president of NOW . . . Czeslow Milosz, the Polish writer and Nobel laureate. . . . Some years ago we had a study done of the economic impact of the college on the town. The impact is very great. Every dollar in payroll and purchases by the college probably generates three additional dollars, stimulating other businesses in town. . . . We have 1,270 students. That's optimum for us. . . . When we fill our residence halls, that's optimum. . . . There is a small dispute in town over whether we want to go to 15,000 or 20,000 population. I would like to top out at 12,000. You have a certain quality of life. . . . You go downtown, see tradespeople, your fellow citizens. . . . Everybody looks familiar. You may not know everybody's name but you are hello-ing everybody. You lose that kind of friendliness and neighborliness when you grow."

M.J. Zimmerman, self-employed: "I married my college sweetheart. He was a townie. He lived across the street from the college and worked at the Post Office to put himself through. We have lived here since then. . . . Grinnell is distinguished from other small towns in Iowa because it is a very international place. We're different because we're not very provincial. . . . We are a state in transition. Realistically, the days of the farm economy are gone. . . . Along with the fact we need more diversified small industry, we need the trust of the business community to be more adventurous. I want to temper that by saying retailing is in increasing difficulty. . . . On the main square downtown we have two consignment shops. Frankly, I don't think we need two. I believe the future of retailing is specialty. . . . I am in business for myself.

I sell Doncaster, very, very wonderful women's apparel. We do it by invitation only. People come to my home four times a year, like an old fashioned trunk showing that lasts a week. Our job is to help people plan their clothing. This appeals to the career women who are terribly, terribly busy."

Dan Agnew, senior vice president, Grinnell Mutual Reinsurance Company: "We have right at 700 employees, close to 600 in Grinnell. . . . Three or four carloads come in from Des Moines, but most of the work force is in Grinnell. . . . I was born and raised here in Poweshiek County. I started out as a teacher and coach in a town near here and have been active in sports all my life. . . . About eight years ago some friends and I started a junior high basketball tournament. We'll have about 32 teams in from all around."

Maynard Raffety, farmer: "I'm about five miles southeast of Grinnell . . . basically a corn and soybean farm. . . . I'm 62 years old. . . . I did milk cows for 24 years. Sold the cows. I'm responsible for about 600 acres . . . 200 corn, 200 soybeans, 70 acres alfalfa which I sell to the dehydrater and to some neighbors. . . . I was born and raised here, went through the first two years of college at Grinnell, then two years at Brown in Providence . . . just wanted to go away to school, normal kids get itchy feet. My dad farmed all his life, grandfather also, although both of them started out in school administration. . . . The future of farming in Iowa, well, we still have good soils out here. I think we'll still be feeding a good part of the world out of the State of Iowa for many years to come. . . . A lot of our kids, we educate them and export them out of Iowa." ◼

Harrison, AR 72602

Location: 139 miles northwest of Little Rock, 235 miles southeast of Kansas City, in northwestern Arkansas.

Population: 11,400 (1990).

Growth rate: 4% since 1986.

Per capita income: $9,010 (1985), 7% higher than state average ($8,389).

Geography/climate: Ozark Mountain town, elevation 1,150 feet. 4 seasons but generally free of extremes. 1 or 2 light snows, 45 to 60 days below freezing, generally in the 20s. Spring blooms in March. Summers warm and long, high averaging 93 in July. 42 inches of rain. Fall colors peak in mid-October and attract throngs of sightseers. ("I've been to Vermont once and I'll put us up against them any time," a native reports.)

Economic base: Agriculture, manufacturing, and tourism equally strong, plus retail and government services. Seat of Boone County. Significant beef-cattle operations in area, with poultry expanding. Major payrolls: McKesson Service Merchandising, 1,700 employees; Levi-Strauss, Tyson Foods, Flexsteel Industries, White-Rodgers, Duncan Industries. Claridge Products & Equipment, a home-grown company, makes classroom chalkboards, bulletin boards.

Newspaper: *Harrison Daily Times*, 111 W. Rush Avenue, Harrison, AR 72602. 501–741-2325. Daily, Monday through Friday. J.E. Dunlap, Jr., editor. $30 a year.

TV, radio: 2 AM, 2 FM stations. Cable brings in network TV from Little Rock and Springfield, Missouri.

Health care: North Arkansas Medical Center, 174 beds. 35 physicians, 16 dentists in local practice.

Schools: 4 elementary (K–5), 1 junior high (6–8). Harrison Senior High School enrolls 600, sends 60% of graduates to college. 1991 composite ACT, 20.1. 2 local institutions of higher learning: North Arkansas Community College, Twin Lakes Vocational Technical School.

Educational level: 9.8% of Boone County residents have 16 or more years of formal education; state average, 10.8%. County per capita expenditure for public education, $310; state average, $350.

Library: North Arkansas Regional Library is headquartered at Boone County Library, 40,000 volumes.

Recreation: 3 city parks, swimming pool, sports complex. 20,000-square-foot youth center completed in 1990. Bowling alley. 5 major lakes, 3 major rivers, including Buffalo National River, nearby. 18-hole golf course, health and racquet club in town. Dogpatch USA is 7 miles south; country music in Branson, 48 miles north.

3BR, 2 BA house: $45,000.

Cost of electricity: $.09 per kilowatt hour.

Cost of natural gas: $.39 per therm.

Sales tax: 6%.

State income tax: 1% to 7%.

Churches: 34. Denominations: Assemblies of God, Baptist, Baptist-American Baptist

Association, Baptist-Bible Fellowship, Baptist-Southern, Christian, Church of Christ, Church of the Nazarene, Episcopal, Full Gospel, Interdenominational, Jehovah's Witnesses, Lutheran, Methodist-United, Pentecostal, Presbyterian, Roman Catholic.

Hometown pride goes only so far, which is to explain why there are no parking meters on the streets of Harrison, Arkansas, a major world production center of parking meters. Traffic moves along without monetary incentives. And a lot of traffic, indeed, moves through this "Crossroads of the Ozarks." Scenic roads seem to lead in all directions. The beauty of the place must have been a factor in attracting the first settlers—rugged mountaineers from Tennessee, Kentucky, the Carolinas, Georgia, and Virginia. Poor but ambitious, they came looking for free or inexpensive land on which to settle. The descendants of these Anglo-Saxon pioneers are the old family names today. They are, on the whole, a conservative bunch who tend to "sit tight and watch things," as one native remarks. It is an outlook that produces, among other things, strong savings and loan associations. First Federal of Harrison is rated one of the soundest at midcontinent.

What residents say ...

J.E. Dunlap, Jr., publisher, **Harrison Daily Times:** "We are one of the seven out of 34 daily newspapers in Arkansas that is still home owned . . . me and my son and daughter. We're 115 years old. The city was chartered in March 1876 and the newspaper founded in October. . . . I write a daily column called "On the Inside," on page two . . . whatever comes to mind. . . . Some days it takes 15 minutes, some days two hours. . . . Today's was about a unique thing that happened today. A young man here was appointed to the National Transportation Safety Board, a local boy 42 years old, sworn in at Harrison, Arkansas. It so happened we had journalists from India and Pakistan visiting. I took them with me to the ceremony. The speaker remarked it was not often foreign journalists covered these events. . . . We're on the circuit for small-town America. We had some from Czechoslovakia a few months ago after they got their freedom. . . . I run a public record column every week, marriages, divorces, other legal matters. More than anything, they don't want their divorce in. . . . Everybody calls me. . . . 'Oh, does this have to be in the paper?' I say, 'My son was divorced two years ago and it was in the paper.' They say, 'I don't care, I just don't want my age in.' . . . This used to bother me but over the years I've learned to live with it. I've reached the age of 69 and been publisher for 46 years."

Jim Fram, executive vice president, Harrison Chamber of Commerce: "Our growth rate is caused by the diversity of the economy. No one sector controls. We have manufacturing, tourism, and agriculture, and they're all about equal. If I'm talking to industry, it's the dominant sector. If I talk to farmers, it's agriculture. Tourism, the same. And I'm pretty close to right. Retirees are another. It was an unknown two years ago and is becoming more important all the time. The fact [Harrison] doesn't look like a retirement center would appeal to the retiree who wants to move to small-town America."

Bob Hammerschmidt, owner, Coldwell Banker, real estate office: "I was born here, raised here, and lived around here all of my life. I was in the building material business before opening the real estate office. . . . The market is pretty good right now. We're getting a lot of people from the West Coast, I guess because of the cost of living out there. They can live here more economically. . . . Some have jobs they can bring with them. . . . One that comes to mind, a couple from Georgia came up here. He's a dental technician, his wife is a nurse. . . . Harrison is a trading center for seven or eight counties. We have excellent shopping facilities, a real nice mall and several strip centers, and of course the No. 2 Wal-Mart in the country. . . ."

Van Younes, attorney: "The community is a tremendous place to live in terms of raising a family, but it doesn't seem to enjoy as much progressive growth as towns on the more popular highways. A lot of work is going on now to develop an east–west corridor . . . a four-lane, major highway from Memphis to Tulsa. We have a north-to-south connection on U.S. 65. We're needing the east-to-west connection. . . . Settling in Harrison, one does give up a certain amount of income to enjoy the hills and family life. Harrison is in Boone County, which is a dry county, which makes us fairly unique. We have a high number per capita of various churches. We sometimes joke about it a little bit. I guess we're in what they refer to as The Bible Belt. . . . We're 30 minutes from Branson, Missouri, which has become the new Nashville area . . . stars like Johnny Cash and others. . . . What we find is that people who travel to enjoy the Branson area, some of them will stay with us, but so many don't find that there's any nightlife or entertainment for their vacation. But the people who stay here, the majority like the fact that it's a very low crime rate. We're kind of insulated here in the hills."

Kathryn Cavert, board member, The Theatre Company: "We produce one major musical a year. The selection for next year is to be voted on next month. We are considering "The King and I." It received the most votes in a survey of the audience. . . . Our last production was "My Fair Lady," before that, "The Sound of Music." We have found that when we try to do any type of straight play, we can't do it. The royalties are so incredibly high. . . . Just the general climate of the area lends itself to musicals. That's what people will come to see, especially if all their grandchildren are involved. We try to do small chamber productions throughout the year, but they are not profitable. . . . Is it quiet here? Extremely so. I moved here 15 years ago from northern California. I have one child and was pregnant at the time we moved. Our area was getting pretty much drug-ridden. We basically wanted a rural area, cheap land, and a low population. . . . It is a dry county. We are not teetotalers, and I'm sure there are drug problems here like everywhere. But I think not having liquor stores or bars makes the whole atmosphere of the town different. I don't want that to change." ∎

Hartselle, AL 35640

Location: 71 miles north of Birmingham, 13 miles south of Decatur, in north central Alabama.

Population: 10,795 (1990).

Growth rate: 10% since 1986.

Per capita income: $9,724 (1985), 12% higher than state average ($8,681).

Geography/climate: Elevation 573 feet. Flat to gently rolling terrain. Chilly, wet winters with 65 days at freezing or below, rare dip to zero, relieved by occasional surges of Gulf air. Spring arrives in early February. Long, hot, humid summer extends growing season to 214 days. Average rainfall, over 50 inches. Generally pleasant, dry fall for 2 months beginning about mid-October.

Economic base: Residential, with a few large industries, in farm country: broilers, eggs, cattle, hogs, milk, soybeans, cotton, vegetables. Major payrolls: Copeland Corporation, compressors, 530; Cerro Wire & Cable, 353; Baker Industries, wood and steel rods, 165; Young Door Company, 100.

Newspaper: *Hartselle Enquirer*, 407 W. Chestnut Street, Hartselle, AL 35640. 205-773-6566. Weekly, Thursday. C.P. Knight, editor. $16 a year.

TV, radio: Local AM station. Cable carries Huntsville TV stations for network coverage, PBS. NPR received off-air from Huntsville.

Health care: Hartselle Medical Center, 150 beds. 18 physicians, 4 dentists in local practice.

Schools: 2 elementary (K–5), 1 junior high (6–8). Hartselle High School enrolls 900, sends 60% to college. About 25% of graduates receive college academic scholarships. Recent composite ACT, 19.9. School system ranks in top 10 statewide as measured by the California Achievement Test and Stanford Achievement Test.

Educational level: 11.8% of Morgan County residents have 16 or more years of formal education; state average, 12.2%. Per capita expenditure for public education, $362; state average, $324.

Library: Hartselle Public Library, 25,000 volumes.

Recreation: Sparkman Civic Center (named for John Sparkman, a Hartselle boy and longtime member of the U.S. Senate), gymnasium, auditorium, meeting rooms, workout facilities; on an 80-acre park site with ball fields, swimming pool, tennis courts, racquetball courts. Bowling lanes in town. 3 public golf courses within 10-minute drive.

3 BR, 2 BA house: $69,000 to $85,000.

Cost of electricity: $.06 per kilowatt hour.

Cost of natural gas: $.65 per therm.

Sales tax: 3%.

State income tax: 2% to 5%.

Churches: 33. Denominations: Assemblies of God, Baptist, Southern Baptist, Christian, Church of God, Church of God of Prophecy, Church of the Nazarene, Episcopal, Jehovah's Witnesses, Methodist, Presbyterian, United Methodist, United Pentecostal.

Hartselle is very big on three things: schools, sports, and religion ("not necessarily in that order," one resident remarks). Concerning schools, Hartselle ranks fourth in the state measured by the overall performance on achievement tests. School superintendent Lee Hartsell, whose family founded the town 100 years ago (and spelled their name without the final *e*), says good schools depend on community support, a stable staff, and high expectations of students. And it doesn't hurt, in Hartselle's case, to have a high number of kids coming from families of aerospace engineers employed at the NASA base and Redstone Arsenal, in nearby Huntsville. Sports? The high school team won its second straight state baseball title in 1991 and is a perennial contender in football. Religion? There are 33 churches in town, a goodly number though not a record among towns included in this book.

What residents say . . .

Cliff Knight, editor, **Hartselle Enquirer:**
"Hartselle has benefited from North Alabama industrial growth the last 20 to 30 years. It has grown much faster than the average town its size. We're kind of a bedroom community. A lot of our people work in Huntsville and Decatur. . . . It's one and a half miles from the center of town to I-65. Commercial development has been slowed in that area because of lack of sewer access, but construction is in progress now. . . . The long-range plan is to build a service road connecting the two interstate access roads. . . . Hartselle is overshadowed somewhat by the city of Decatur, 10 miles north. It has the major commercial center and draws a lot of people. They spend money in Decatur. That means Hartselle schools, police department, fire department, recreational facilities . . . lose revenue. A town this size has to do something to hold trade. . . . The feeling is that we could possibly get some benefit from the interstate, quick on-and-off service establishments, motels, even discount centers, which are pretty big down here."

Ed Summers, writer of letters to the editor:
"In my last job I worked for the U.S. Army Missile Command at Redstone Arsenal, a civil service employee for 25 years. I was a program budget specialist, my last few years on a team that defended the missile command's budget. . . . Any time you go to Washington to do combat for money, that is interesting and exciting. . . . Hartselle has always tried to be a little bit better. We have asked and expected more of our kids, in sports, in academics. The kids know their parents and the community as a whole expect them to be a little bit better, and they respond to that challenge . . . I had a cousin, William Bradford Huie, who was editor of the American Mercury for a time. He told me once, somebody has got to be an SOB, look into things and tell folks they have got to be changed. I do a lot of that. I try to shake 'em up at City Hall. I don't write anything unless I research it. . . . I went in and talked to the mayor and each department head and to the employees. I asked them what they

were supposed to be doing and what they accomplished. That created a little disturbance, but somebody's got to do it. I presented my findings to all the civic clubs, had a slide presentation and made several recommendations. I wouldn't want to say it was because of my work but, for example, we now have one utility board where we used to have separate electric and water boards. . . . We are getting better. We're not perfect yet. Maybe I expect more than we're capable of doing, but I want to be No. 1 in everything. I am an eternal optimist."

E. M. Barnes, retired minister, Methodist Church: "If a person is passing through and is out of gas or needs food, they generally come to one of the churches. The minister determines need. They are sent to the police station, where they are given a coupon to take to a filling station for a tank of gas, or a coupon to a certain cafe, where they receive a meal for each person. . . . In any kind of charity work you're going to get hooked now and then. . . . The funds come from a free-will offering at the Fifth Sunday service. This has been going on for 10 years."

Gayle Strider, artist: "We came here with the space industry in 1960. We weren't really wild about Huntsville and for six months just looked at other communities. . . . Here was this little town that had not changed one bit since the turn of the century. We bought a newspaper and answered an ad that said, 'Farms for sale. Good, bad and ???' We checked out the farm and it was a ???, but we saw the house we now live in. It was owned first by a mule dealer, built in 1911. It was old and run-down, but we were young and ambitious. We immediately joined the church. The churches are very much the heart of Hartselle. They welcome strangers and were wonderful to us. That was one of the clues we should come here."

Paula Rigler, director, Hartselle Clean City Association: "I've only been here four years. My husband was transferred here. We chose Hartselle because of the school system. We had two teenage boys, and we were very concerned about placing them in the same atmosphere they had been in. . . . We got our realtor to set up a meeting with the school administration. We had our children's records with us. . . . We learned the SAT scores, the California test scores. . . . It was a very easy transition from a large school in Greenville, South Carolina, to a smaller setting. . . . Clean City is part of the Keep America Beautiful organization. We are responsible for environmental issues, beautification, and litter control. . . . We have adorned our main artery north and south, U.S. 31, with pear trees, some of the necessary funds earned through recycling. We also have a very strong educational program on litter control. I do a lot of speaking. . . . Near the Civic Center there is a large triangular piece of land at a stoplight. One of our major industries has agreed to take on a total relandscaping, crepe myrtle and low-growing shrubs. I'm hoping it will become the domino theory because we have two other target areas besides that one. . . . It just shows that the whole city pulls together. I'm very impressed by that quality."

Ferrell Rollins, author of* A Homey History of Hartselle: "Many small towns have had National Guard units, and for the size of the place probably sent more people into the commissioned and enlisted ranks. . . . Whenever our nation is threatened, the small town may not be able to furnish the technology, but it will be able to furnish the heart." ■

Hastings, MI 49058

Location: 35 miles southeast of Grand Rapids, 30 miles northeast of Kalamazoo, in southwestern Michigan.

Population: 6,549 (1990).

Growth rate: 1% since 1986.

Per capita income: $10,142 (1985), 93% of state average.

Geography/climate: Sometimes called "the only northern county in southern Michigan"—hilly, wooded countryside dotted with spring-fed lakes. Elevation 790 feet. Westerlies pick up moisture from Lake Michigan, 75 miles west, boosting the number of cloudy, wet days. But lake also moderates winter lows and summer highs. Average snowfall, 49 inches. 149 days below freezing, 8 days below zero. Average temperature: January: high, 30; low, 16. Average date of last frost, May 16. July: high, 84; low, 60. Moderate humidity. Annual rainfall 46 inches, heaviest in May.

Economic base: Tourism, manufacturing, residential. Bedroom town for commuters to Grand Rapids, Lansing, Battle Creek, Kalamazoo. Large local payrolls: Pennock Hospital, 486; Hastings Manufacturing Company, automotive parts, 465; Flex-Fab, hose and ducts, 300; Hastings Mutual Insurance, 260; Viking, car seals, sprinkler systems, 250; Barry County government, 195; E. W. Bliss, presses, 185; G&R Felpqusch, food products. Annual "Fiberfest" exposition attracts 10,000 people in August.

Newspaper: *The Hastings Banner*, 1952 N. Broadway, Hastings, MI 49058. 616-948-8051. Weekly, Thursday. David Young, editor. $14.50 a year.

TV, radio: Local AM/FM station. TV networks, PBS, NPR all can be received off-air from surrounding cities.

Health care: Pennock Hospital, 91 beds. 37 physicians, 10 dentists in local practice.

Schools: 3 elementary (K–6), 1 junior high (7–8). Hastings High School enrolls 950, sends 40% to college. Composite ACT, 1991: 20.7 ("lowest in five years").

Educational level: 10.4% of Barry County residents have 16 or more years of formal education; state average, 14.3%. Per capita expenditure for public education, $341; state average, $525.

Library: Hastings Public Library, 22,000 volumes.

Recreation: 5 city parks totaling 44 acres. 18-hole, 27-hole golf courses within city limits; 9-hole course, 4 miles west. Movie theater, bowling alley. Yankee Springs Recreation Area, 4,255 acres, 12 miles west. Gun Lake and many smaller lakes within 10–15 mile radius provide opportunities for hunting, fishing, swimming, boating, camping. Charlton Park, a 16-building historic village and museum, on Thornapple River.

3 BR, 2 BA house: $80,000.

Cost of electricity: $.07 per kilowatt hour.

Cost of natural gas: $.45 per therm.

Sales tax: 4%.

State income tax: 4.6%.

Churches: 24. Denominations: Anglican Catholic, Assemblies of God, Baptist, Bible, Brethren, Charismatic, Church of Christ, Church of God–Anderson, Indiana, Church of Jesus Christ of Latter-day Saints, Church of the Nazarene, Episcopal, Free Methodist, Jehovah's Witnesses, Lutheran, Nondenominational, Pentecostal, Presbyterian-USA, Seventh-Day Adventist, United Methodist, Wesleyan.

They buried a funeral home in Hastings, not a literal burial but it had the look of the real thing. The Wren mortuary on South Jefferson had reached the end of a 130-year existence and a new building was about to take its place. So the family, so to speak, gathered by the dying building to say good-bye. It was a good-sized crowd including the mayor and other dignitaries. The pastor who had led the most services there officiated, and they closed by tying a ribbon around the site. Then everyone drove in funeral procession to the magnificent new, Colonial-style establishment, where the senior Hastings pastor spoke the dedication remarks, commenting that enough concrete had been laid to cover three football fields. The parking lot, people agree, is phenomenal. And life goes on.

What residents say . . .

Mary Lou Gray, mayor: "This is my fourth year and I'm on the ballot unopposed for reelection. I was on the council for eight years, the first female to be elected to either. . . . These days the citizens of the community recognize that women should have a proportionate share of the responsibilities. At one time you would not have seen that in local government. The majority of the leadership in Barry County is female . . . prosecutor, county clerk, county coordinator, 50 percent of the City Council, those who run the medical facility . . . and I'm sure I'm not hitting them all. Two years ago WKZO-TV [Kalamazoo] did a close-up on small towns. Hastings was one of them. They recognized the female as the decisionmaker in this area, 'The Female Mafia,' they called us, in a kindly manner. But I couldn't help but wonder why it was necessary to explain why females can take dominant roles when it hasn't been necessary to explain the male Mafia. . . . We do a lot of joint city–county relationships, which I think is unique and a sign of the ability of people to work together. It's not a matter of turfism. We have joint police dispatch, jointly funded fire protection. The city and townships jointly subsidize ambulance service. . . . The mayor of this town never had a desk. Coming into office, I told the council I needed a spot to work. So they set up a table, put a piece of paper on it with a spot, Mary Lou's Spot. The first night I presided as mayor, this was a whole new experience for the men department heads. . . . They put a doily under my gavel."

Joe Rahn, director of economic development: "I answered an ad for the first full-time director of the County of Barry–City of Hastings Joint Economic Development Commission. That's what brought me to Hastings. . . . We did a survey and found we had lost more than 350 jobs in Barry County. . . . We have designed and funded an industrial incubator . . . in an old plant which dates back to the '40s, where they made bottling equipment for Pepsi and Coke. The state gave us $375,000 to purchase the property, the feds gave $300,000 to retrofit, and the city committed $125,000. It's divided into small spaces for entrepreneurial companies . . . several machine shops, sign companies, woodworking shops. . . . I heard an interesting statistic at the rededication of the courthouse. In 1884, when it was built, the county had 22,000 people. The new census says we just passed 50,000, so it is still rather secluded. . . . I'm president of Rahn Gun Works, an importer and manufacturer of high-quality firearms. We have designed the Rahn Series Rifle . . . working on one now for the Spanish Ambassador to South Africa. Our clientele is safari clubs."

Dorothy Conklin, owner, River Bend Travel Agency, president-elect of Chamber of Commerce: "We're a full-service agency. That means we do airline reservations, Amtrak, car rentals, hotels, that type of thing. I particularly put group tours together . . . whatever hits my fancy. I have done tours to China, to Europe. I've been to Russia. Hawaii and Alaska many times. . . . My motor coach tours are very popular. I do one to Washington, DC, and Williamsburg that's a 10-day tour . . . mostly seniors or people who don't want to worry about anything. I try to make their tours worry-free. The men as well as the women can sit back and relax and enjoy everything. Hastings is a very friendly city and county. We are the hub of the wheel of Kalamazoo, Grand Rapids, Lansing, Battle Creek. Because we are the hub, sometimes we get notoriety we prefer not to have . . . because we're the court system for Barry County. We like to hear on TV about all the plus, plus, plus of Hastings."

Mike Humphreys, owner, Miller Real Estate: "We perk along at a reasonable increase in values each year . . . four, five, six percent depending on the type of home and property. . . . People are generally looking for . . . more rural lifestyle, more room, more privacy, the peace and beauty. . . . People who move from Grand Rapids to Hastings proper . . . can save 25 percent on the purchase of a home."

David Young, editor, **Maple Valley News, The Hastings Banner**: "We publish *The Reminder* every Tuesday, a soft product like a shopper with a lot of feature stories, no real hard news. That's really the moneymaker. Then we publish *The Banner*, your classic county-seat weekly. . . . It's kind of a recreational area in lots of ways but also rural. The county's growing, though not as fast as you would think. . . . In Michigan, two cities are still growing, Grand Rapids and Kalamazoo, because they both have a tremendous quality of life. The northwest section of Barry County next to Grand Rapids is growing like a weed. . . . Hastings doesn't have an expressway, in other words, a pipeline to a major metropolitan area. . . . A lot of people will tell you they moved out here to get away from the city and now the city is coming to them. Hastings's biggest problem is it needs to accommodate more growth with new housing."

Sue Drummond, vice president, Fiberfest Ltd.: "This year we'll be at the Barry Expo Center on our new fairgrounds . . . two and a half days of seminars and a fiber arts show, 120 sales booths, nothing but natural fiber goods. Everything is handmade and one-of-a-kind. We'll have between 10,000 and 15,000 people from all over the country. In just one seminar last year, we had people from 30 states and Canada. There are beginning to be more of these festivals but we were one of the first to cater to all the fiber-producing animals . . . wool, mohair, angora, silk, llama, alpaca, any fiber that comes from an animal. . . . A lot of people are trying to get back to the land, and a very easy thing to do is get into the fiber business. . . . Much of the topography here lends itself to raising small animals, very rolly, hilly. . . . My husband and I started with angoras in 1979. . . . You could have 200 or 300 rabbits in a double garage." ■

Hendersonville, NC 28792

Location: 104 miles west of Charlotte, 23 miles south of Asheville, on a 2,200-foot-high mountain plateau in western North Carolina.

Population: 9,123 (1990).

Growth rate: 11% since 1986.

Per capita income: $8,312; state average, $9,517.

Geography/climate: An intermountain valley of rolling meadows protected from severe winter weather by the Great Smoky Mountains on the northwest. 4 distinct seasons—all mild, natives say. Average 9–12 inches of snow, 50 inches of rain, 8 90-degree days. More than half of winter nights dip below freezing, but daytime warm-up is dependable.

Economic base: Tourism, agriculture, manufacturing, retirement living, the arts. County seat of Henderson County, population 76,000. Manufacturers include outdoor lighting at General Electric plant employing 2,000, the largest payroll; rugs, paper products, women's and children's clothing, electric specialties, industrial ceramics. Henderson County is 7th largest apple-producing county in the U.S.

Newspaper: *Hendersonville Times-News*, 1717 Four Seasons Boulevard, Hendersonville, NC 28739. 704-692-0505. Daily. Joy Franklin, editor. $46 a year.

TV, radio: Cable brings in networks from Charlotte, Greenville, Spartanburg; PBS from Asheville, Greenville. NPR from Asheville.

Health care: Pardee Memorial Hospital, 222 beds. 70 physicians, 25 dentists in local practice.

Schools: 2 elementary (K–5); 1 middle (6–8). Composite SAT score at Hendersonville High School, 894. 49.5% of high school graduates seek higher education.

Educational level: 15.2% of Henderson County residents have 16 or more years of formal education; state average, 13.2%. Per capita expenditure for public education (Henderson County), $353; state average, $390.

Library: Henderson County Public Library has 122,000 books in 4 branches.

Recreation: 9 area parks provide ball fields, tennis courts, basketball, outdoor pool, playgrounds. YMCA has pool, gym, weight training/wellness center, Nautilus, tennis courts. 32-lane bowling alley 2 miles north of downtown. Hiking, camping, backpacking in Pisgah National Forest. Scenic roads and trails in Great Smoky Mountains. Blue Ridge Parkway is 12 miles north.

3 BR, 2 BA house: $70,000 to $100,000. Upscale housing ranges to $1 million in Henderson County, the 10th fastest growing in the state.

Cost of electricity: $.07 per kilowatt hour.

Cost of natural gas: $.50 per therm.

Sales tax: 5½%.

State income tax: 6%–7%.

Churches: 45. Denominations: Assemblies of God, Baptist (Independent, Southern), Christian & Missionary Alliance, Christian

Science, Church of Christ, Church of God, Church of Jesus Christ of Latter-day Saints, Episcopal, American Episcopal, Holiness, Independent, Jehovah's Witnesses, Lutheran, Nazarene, Nondenominational, Pentecostal, Presbyterian, Roman Catholic, Salvation Army, Seventh-Day Adventist, Unitarian Universalist, United Church of Christ, United Methodist, United Pentecostal, Unity, Wesleyan.

Synagogues: 1.

Thank you very much, but Hendersonville would prefer not to be included in another list of desirable places. People who have lived here a decade or more remember when the town first caught national attention, along with nearby Asheville and Brevard, through rave reviews in *Retirement Places Rated*, by David Savageau. That was 1983. Since then, Henderson County has become such a popular relocation site that the small-town charm of the county seat some days seems overwhelmed by sheer numbers of people wanting in. When traffic runs bumper-to-bumper on Four Seasons Boulevard, locals wonder whether success may have spoiled Hendersonville.

Not yet, according to informed observers, but it's going to be a close call. Hendersonville combines the best small-town qualities—thriving Main Street, attractive neighborhoods, good schools, broad economic base, ample health-care services, parks, and recreation—with cultural amenities that are uncommon in many much larger places. Nurtured by an enthusiastic, well-educated, and fairly affluent population of retirees, the arts flourish here. What other town this size has a symphony orchestra?

Hendersonville is surrounded by an adoring local population—and that's part of the problem. Housing developments have sprung up all around the town in county territory, close enough for easy access to services and pleasures but beyond the tax reach and direct management of the city. Finding a way to manage growth is number one on the agenda in Hendersonville—and the key to preserving its reputation as a nifty small town.

What residents say ...

Mary Jo Padgett, freelance writer: "I had worked for the *Atlanta Journal* and came to Hendersonville to become an associate editor at *The Mother Earth News*. . . . The major change we have experienced in our decade here is growth. Henderson County grew something like 17 percent. . . . My husband and I founded Environmental and Conservation Organization of Henderson County, ECO for short. . . . It is the typical struggle in small towns between economic growth and the impact of that growth on our environment. For example, there is a proposed thoroughfare plan that the Department of Transportation has helped create for us to ease congestion downtown by making a peripheral road around town. That's all fine, but rather than just focus on roads, let's look at a transportation management system . . . making sure lights are timed so traffic can actually move, increasing the number of sidewalks, more bike paths, park-n-ride on the outskirts and a neat little trolley to move people in and out of the city center. . . . The impact of the retirees has been positive and negative. The negative, an increase in traffic, housing costs, demand for sewage treatment and water. . . . The benefit, they do have free time and they generally have money. So by virtue of that, we have four viable theater groups here . . . a symphony orchestra since the 1960s. A town this size does not usually have its own full symphony orchestra. We have a very high caliber of artists in this community. . . . Many of these people have come from larger places. For them, this is a small town and it has the conveniences of a large place. . . . Growth is a given here. For me, controlled growth is the major issue."

Robert Campbell, former executive director, New York State School Music Association:
"We lived in Schenectady for 12 years and had a house on the coast of Maine. Four years ago I decided to give up the job of executive director, but I have remained editor of *School Music News*, so I'm editor of a New York magazine and living in North Carolina. All you need is the U.S. mail and the telephone. . . . The magazine was awarded a national prize as the outstanding state music journal. . . . I'm a choral man, not really an editor. My previous experience as editor was in the eighth grade. . . . In North Carolina I've also taken over the Hendersonville Choral Society. We have a big concert in December, then one in May, and generally fill the high school

auditorium. . . . I live about five miles outside the city, for two reasons: we've got a little land around the house, and we pay county taxes only. If we lived in the city we'd pay city and county. . . . Growth is a concern to us. I must admit the city fathers did not plan too well for it. They are now waking up to the fact and beginning to take steps to assure that cars don't overrun the population."

Donnie Parks, first black police chief of Hendersonville: "I'm honored to be in the position, but I don't think I draw much on the color factor. It does have its pros and cons in terms of being a black police chief of a southern town, but I think the people are saying it doesn't really matter the color of skin. . . . We want to form a coalition between the police and the community. . . . Community-oriented policing, a pro-active approach. . . . For example, if people call in to say they have dirty streets, we get in touch with the right people. The concept is total service, whether by us or another city agency. It's getting back to basics. We're growing just like a lot of other cities, but we don't want to grow to the point we don't know the people we are serving."

Maurice Beckett, retired chemist: "The growth has largely been people like myself from the North, though oddly a great many have been Floridians. For many years it has been customary for Floridians to come up here in the summer. Recently, because of the crowded conditions in Florida many of them have moved here permanently."

David Malpass, industrial arts teacher, consultant: "We've been very fortunate with our retirees. They are executive-level people. They bring their arts, their music, their zeal for community support, their expertise. . . . Before I came here I worked for the state board of education as a consultant. I have been in every high school in the State of North Carolina. . . . Hendersonville is one of probably only a handful of places in the country that doesn't have school busing. The city boundaries are such that children can go through the whole chain of schools and never have to get on a bus. The city school system is balanced racially proportional to the area, about 20 percent minority, primarily black, followed by Hispanic. Also a significant percentage of students from outside Hendersonville pay tuition to come here. I would match the curriculum at that school with any its size in the nation." ■

Houghton, MI 49931

Location: On the "thumb" of the Michigan Upper Peninsula, jutting into Lake Superior. 340 miles north of Milwaukee, 340 miles northeast of Minneapolis-St. Paul.

Population: 7,498 (1990).

Growth rate: 18 people since 1980.

Per capita income: $5,912 (1986), about half the state average.

Geography/climate: Geologists say rugged, rocky Keweenaw Peninsula is Precambrian, oldest land on earth. Lake Superior is weather controller, moderating winter lows to only 20 or so days below zero but dumping an average 210 inches of snow. Typically only 2 summer days above 90 degrees. 124-day growing season.

Economic base: Once the copper-mining center of the nation, Houghton County now depends on 2,000-person payroll of Michigan Technological University for the majority of dollars. Other major payrolls in Houghton, the county seat and retail trade center: Upper Peninsula Power Co., 589 employees; D&N Savings Bank, 404; Mead Lumber, 175. Winter snow sports attract tourists from throughout upper Midwest.

Newspaper: *Daily Mining Gazette*, 206 Shelden Avenue, Houghton, MI 49931. 902–482–1500. Daily except Sunday. Brian McMillan, publisher. $82 a year.

TV, radio: Local AM station; FM from Michigan Tech broadcasts NPR. Cable brings in all Detroit stations; ABC and NBC from Green Bay; PBS, CBS, and NPR from Marquette; CBC from Thunder Bay, Ontario. Also 2 French language radio stations.

Health care: Portage View Hospital, 93 beds. 41 physicians, 16 dentists in local practice.

Schools: 1 elementary (K–8). Houghton High School (9–12) enrolls 384. Composite ACT score, 22.6. 65% of high school graduates go to college, all but 4% to 4-year institutions.

Educational level: 14.4% of county residents have 16 or more years of formal education; state average, 14.3%. Per capita expenditure for public education, $347; state average, $525.

Library: 33,000 volumes in Portage Lake District Library. Residents of county area may order books by mail from published yearly catalogue. Library pays postage.

Recreation: 200 miles of groomed snowmobile trails link extended area, from tip of Keweenaw Peninsula to Wisconsin, Minnesota. Extensive cross-country network. Several state parks, major ski areas within a 2-hour drive. Improvements along Portage Lake waterfront have enhanced the recreational and tourist potential.

3 BR, 2 BA house: $35,000–$65,000 for older Victorians. Average county sale price, $35,000. A "real nice modern" house outside city recently sold for $61,000.

Cost of electricity: $.081 per kilowatt hour.

Cost of natural gas: $.43 per therm.

Sales tax: 4%.

State income tax: 4.6%.

Churches: 19. Denominations: Assemblies of God, Baptist, Southern Baptist, Christian, Church of Christ, Church of Jesus Christ of Latter-day Saints, Episcopal, Lutheran, Evangelical Lutheran, Missouri Synod Lutheran, Wisconsin Synod Lutheran, Nondenominational, Presbyterian, Roman Catholic, Salvation Army, Seventh-Day Adventist, Unitarian Universalist, United Church of Christ, United Methodist.

Synagogues: Temple Jacob, Hancock.

Snow! There's so much of it in Houghton that the bad jokes have become classics: "We have two seasons: winter's here and winter's coming." "We have two seasons: winter and bad sledding." "The four seasons are early winter, midwinter, late winter, and next winter." Houghtonites also pay respects to a snow god, Heikki Lunta, invoking his name when good snowfall is required for winter tourism and cursing his name when snow falls in April—and even May.

The record season was 1978–79, when snowfall totaled 390.4 inches—nearly 33 feet. Though Heikki Lunta may get the credit or blame, the real reason for all that snow is simple geography. As arctic air masses cross the comparatively warm water of Lake Superior, the air gathers moisture. Bumping into the Keweenaw Peninsula, this moisture falls as powdery snow.

Simple geology also endowed the peninsula with one of the largest copper-bearing deposits in the world, catapulting the Keweenaw to world attention a century ago. Houghton became rich and famous. But when the copper industry declined, it took human ingenuity to recreate the place.

What residents say ...

Jon Davis, executive director, Keweenaw Peninsula Chamber of Commerce, several-time winner of Press On Regardless: "The Press on Regardless is the oldest, meanest, longest car race in North America. It is run one car at a time, spaced generally one minute apart, generally at night through rather primitive backwoods roads. My term for it is the purest form of motor racing. Because of the rural road situation, the Upper Peninsula generally lends itself very nicely to this. . . . We won the Classic in 1981, when it was in Houghton. I was driving a Saab 99, two-door, four-cylinder engine. . . . We did seventh overall and won Production Class. That particular event was about 500 miles long. . . . We enjoy generally about 250 inches of snow every winter, but it is what I like to call 'user friendly' snow, very much the quality of Colorado. . . . It is white. . . . We depend on it for winter tourism. . . . I'm speaking to you now from a community with a residency of 12 people, my getaway from Houghton. . . . Lake Superior never freezes over. To my knowledge it only happened once. Lake Superior is our weather controller. It keeps us cool in the summer and

181

warm in the winter. . . . Our primary thrust is to try to generate more winter tourism. . . . We have not pursued cross-country as a winter sport. We have an intense effort now to connect the ski trails to the end of the Peninsula. . . . We feel we can be the cross-country mecca of the Midwest."

Bill Sottile, director, Upper Peninsula Laboratory, Michigan Department of Public Health: "Michigan Technological University adds a definite cosmopolitan atmosphere. Not only do you have professional staff but cultural events. Last year we went to more cultural events in one year than we did in eight years living in Chicago. . . . If the University were not here we would not have the quality of life. . . . The Houghton–Hancock area does have a real high unemployment rate. Mining is gone. We have lumber and associated industry. . . . Certainly our tourism is a 12-month industry. . . . Snowmobile corrals cover half the parking lots. They go directly from the center of Houghton to the trail, 50 yards away. . . . One of the things that has struck me about living here was not obvious at first. In Chicago there were impoverished areas. We would go through them every day. But in a suburban lifestyle, one became insulated from other people's problems. Here, if you want something to happen, you have to roll up your sleeves and make it happen. In this community, you are the community. You cannot insulate yourself, and I find I like that. It gives one a real sense of community, a sense of belonging. . . . One is responsible for everything. We're not going to have critical mass unless we share this with somebody else."

Margaret Sottile, spouse of Bill: "One of the things I particularly like is this is a low-crime area. The children can have more freedom. They can walk places. It's just a very different way of living. . . . And the tradespeople are very helpful, trusting, accommodating. I must tell you about the carpet. We were preparing to have a carpet laid . . . just as we were leaving for Chicago on vacation. So the carpet man said, 'Why don't you just give me the house key and I'll do it while you're gone.' So I left the key with him! . . . The plowing system here is wonderful. The roads are always clear. Children are out of school usually only one day during the winter. Everyone has one four-wheel-drive vehicle. If you can't go up a hill, you go around it."

Patricia Wood, psychiatric caseworker, friend of Margaret: "Margaret and I are setting up a drop-in center for mothers of infants and toddlers, one morning a week, the beginning of a family resource center we would like to develop for the church. . . . There are a lot of churches here for such a small community. People are very involved in church life, not in a righteous, holier-than-thou way, very much part of the community. . . . We came here about eight months ago from southern California. We were looking to leave California. We had placed a limit of 10 years living there. . . . We're both from Colorado. . . . We were investigating places to live where my husband could find a good university. He's a geologist. We found Houghton, and the beauty of the area is just staggering. . . . The university is very good for a scientist. . . . We wanted to live in a healthier place. Southern California is becoming so polluted, so crowded. . . . I think it takes a special sort of person to live here. Many people might feel isolated and remote. . . . There is a lot of poverty here, but people have their own homes. They take a lot of pride here making it on their own. . . . There are two communities, Tech and the local community. I haven't noticed any town–gown thing at all, no harassing of students by town kids. A lot of nationalities are brought in by Tech. The children get along fine. Except for the lack of black people here, there is a greater ethnic diversity than in Orange County."

Larry Lankton, professor of the history of technology, author: "The one that just came out is called, *Cradle to Grave: Life, Work and Death at the Lake Superior Copper Mines*, published by Oxford. It focuses on the industrial society that flourished around here until 1910 or so. Then I track the decline of this area as a mining center. . . . Most of the buildings still standing in town were built before 1910–15. It has a turn-of-the-century vista. . . . Streets around here are named for minerals and mining companies instead of trees and presidents, which is what you find in most mid-western towns. Another byproduct of mining: this is a very ethnically diverse area . . . at least 25 different ethnic groups in fairly substantial numbers. Of all of them, the Finns were the dominant group. You'll still find Cornish. There are Italians, Irish, Germans, French Canadian, Serbs. It doesn't strike you when you're downtown as a university-dominated town . . . not overrun by students. . . . You only wear two things here, heavy coats in winter and bug dope in summer. We're waiting for the snow to melt."

Olaf Rankinen, retired Lutheran minister: "Heikki Lunta. It means Henry Snow. There was a Hank Snow, a singer, you know. I think Heikki Lunta is a take-off by the local radio station comedians. Snow is needed here for certain events. They started this as a kind of joke. But Heikki Lunta is cursed when he makes appearances too late. We just had heavy ice and snowfall the last couple of days. We don't invoke his name now." ■

Jasper, IN 47547

Location: 122 miles southwest of Indianapolis, 55 miles northeast of Evansville, 79 miles west of Louisville, Kentucky, in southern Indiana.

Population: 10,030 (1990).

Growth rate: 9% since 1980.

Per capita income: $11,879 (1985), 19% higher than state average ($9,978).

Geography/climate: Gently rolling terrain, elevation 452 to 610 feet. Prevailing wind from south tempers winter extremes. January lows average 23 degrees; highs, 42. Cold fronts sweeping across the continent may push temperatures below zero a few days per season. Summers can be hot and humid. July: average low, 66; high, 90. Average rainfall, 43 inches; snowfall, trace to 20 inches.

Economic base: Agriculture; diversified manufacturing, dominated by furniture, lumber and wood products, food products. Large payrolls: Kimball International world headquarters, maker of office furniture, pianos, electronic organs, electronic components, business and home furnishings, 3,200 employees; Jasper Desk, 115; Aristokraft, kitchen cabinets, vanities, 1,200; Jasper Engines & Transmissions, 640; Jasper Rubber Products, 405; JOFCO, office furniture, 425; Memorial Hospital, 500. Jasper is retail center and seat of Dubois County, a national leader in production of turkeys.

Newspaper: *The Herald*, 216 E. Fourth, Jasper, IN 47546. 812-482-2424. Monday through Saturday. John Rumbach, editor. $86.10 a year.

TV, radio: 1 AM, 2 FM stations. Cable carries PBS, network TV from Evansville, Louisville; NPR from Evansville.

Health care: Memorial Hospital and Health Care Center, 131 beds. 57 physicians, 14 dentists in local practice.

Schools: 3 elementary (K–5); 1 middle (6–8). Jasper High School enrolls 815, sends 50% to 4-year college, consistently ranks 4th or 5th among all Indiana high schools in standard state test of educational performance. 2 Catholic parochial grade schools enroll 398. Vincennes University-Jasper Center enrolls 146 full time, 955 part time.

Educational level: 10.2% of Dubois County residents have 16 or more years of formal education; state average, 12.5%. Per capita expenditure for public education, $458; state average, $422.

Library: Jasper Public Library, 60,000 volumes.

Recreation: 17 parks totaling 224 acres. 205-acre public lake with shelter house and picnic grounds. Olympic-size pool with 65-foot water slide. 2 18-hole golf courses, 1 public, 1 private. 20 tennis courts, 2 volleyball courts, 6 baseball diamonds—all lighted. Basketball and horseshoe courts. Physical-fitness trail. Recreation department has 60-passenger bus and 16-passenger van available for group transportation. Bowling alley, roller-skating rink, 2 multiple-screen cinemas. Patoka Lake, 12 miles northeast, covers 8,800 acres and is site of state's largest park. Camping, boating, swimming, nature trails. Jasper Community Arts Commission, state's only tax-supported center for the performing arts, operates 675-seat Jasper Civic Auditorium, site of annual concert series.

3 BR, 2 BA house: $50,000 to $90,000.

Cost of electricity: $.04 per kilowatt hour.

Cost of natural gas: $.44 per therm.

Sales tax: 5%.

State income tax: 3.4%.

Churches: 15. Denominations: Assemblies of God, Baptist, Church of the Nazarene, Lutheran, Methodist, Pentecostal, Presbyterian, Roman Catholic, United Church of Christ.

A cathedral-size church is the first clue that something special is going on in Jasper, Indiana. Beginning in 1867, it took 13 years to raise stone on stone and top off St. Joseph's Church, at 1020 Kundek Street. The clock tower supporting the spire and cross marks time for a hard-working and prosperous German Catholic community. They came over from Baden at the urging of Father Joseph Kundek, who spent about 20 years spreading the faith and settling lands owned by the Bishop of Vincennes. Father Kundek was a busy man. He is credited with organizing 10 parishes, assisting the settlement of several communities, and laying the groundwork for the establishment of St. Meinrad Archabbey, one of the largest Catholic seminaries in the world. But the earliest settlers of Jasper were farmers, stone masons, cabinetmakers, and carpenters. Chances are, they'd feel right at home today.

What residents say . . .

John Fierst, history teacher, Jasper High School: "Jasper was settled first by the Cumberland Presbyterian Scotch-Irish. As the Germans came in, the Scotch-Irish were pushed into the background. Father Kundek, who was from Croatia, now part of Yugoslavia, founded the nearby town of Ferdinand, named after the emperor of Austria. Father Kundek started advertising in the Cincinnati paper and also overseas, trying to encourage people to come into this region. The cheapness of the land and the fact that Germans were already settling here . . . for a German that was quite an inducement. Around 1876 you get the beginning of wood manufacturing, and that remains very, very important. We're talking about walnut and white oak, very good quality white oak. . . . The building of St. Joseph's church started in 1867. First services were held in 1880, so it took a long time. The people who worked in it were named from the pulpit. Father Maute called their names from the pulpit, and they were supposed to work that week. The work was donated, and a lot of the materials were, too. . . . Strassenfest is the first week in August. They usually tap a keg on the Courthouse Square . . . German foods and culture, bands with German themes. It's a lot of fun. People from Jasper try to schedule their vacations so they are back for Strassenfest."

Claude Eckert, retired rural mail carrier:
"We have a German club here and were looking for something to do other than just have parties. So we adopted a sister city, Pfaffenweiler, in the southern part of Germany, because many of our relatives are from there. . . . The exchange program began in 1984. This year we sent about 20 over, and they sent about that many back. Pfaff depends on grapes. They make a dry wine, no sugar added, the sweetness comes from the grapes. When we make wine, we add two and a half pounds of sugar to the gallon and let that sit for a year. . . . They don't like our wine much. They are used to dry wine. We got used to theirs after we were over for a week or so."

Lillian Doane, former librarian: "I've always been a history buff. My husband's family published the *Jasper Courier* from 1858 to 1922. I have all the bound volumes in my basement. I am copying many topics and local news about Dubois County in the Civil War. The 27th Regiment, they called them the Iron Brigade because they never backed up. . . . You hear of farmers losing their land. Very few farmers have lost their land here because they know how to manage."

Jack Schneider, director of community affairs, Kimball International: "Back in 1949, a company called Midwest Manufacturing was on very shaky ground. A manufacturer had never failed in Jasper, so four local men led by Arnold S. Habig decided they would take controlling interest and get this company back on its feet. . . . The name was changed to Jasper Corporation

. . . radio cabinets, hi-fi cabinets, TV cabinets. . . . In 1959, Jasper Corporation acquired W. W. Kimball. . . . Pianos and organs were the principal business up to the early 1980s. . . . Office furniture gradually became our principal product. Of course, we still make pianos. We also make electronic assemblies, computer keyboards, antilock brake systems, home furniture. . . . The 'international' aspect comes from the fact we make the Bosendorfer piano in Vienna . . . two plants in England and one in Mexico. . . . We are a vertically integrated company, which we think has been the largest factor in our success over the years. . . . Obviously this is not a company town. While we are the largest manufacturer, there are a lot of other vibrant and strong companies. We want to do our share and participate with the others in whatever we can do for the community."

Vic Knies, member of City Council: "The secret is that people who own the businesses are actively involved in the management of them, and I feel that's very important. I could actually go to the chairman of the board of any of these companies and not have to leave town. I think that's a real good thing. These people have been putting it back into the business. I look at that as compounding interest. . . . I suppose we would have a labor shortage if it weren't for the depressed economic conditions of surrounding counties. Our population is 10,000 but in the daytime it possibly triples. We have traffic counts of 24,000 vehicles. For a city this size, that is a tremendous amount of traffic. But things do seem to move. We don't get into a gridlock situation. . . . I've been on the council for 20 years, and I'll be on it for another four." ■

Kalispell, MT 59901

Location: 226 miles northwest of Butte, 72 miles south of the Canadian border, in the Flathead Valley of northwestern Montana.

Population: 11,917 (1990).

Growth rate: 11% since 1980.

Per capita income: $10,358 (1985), 18% higher than state average ($8,781).

Geography/climate: Town situated 9 miles northwest of Flathead Lake, at 2,930-foot elevation. Range of 7,500-foot mountains to northeast blocks worst of cold Alberta air in winter. Average 191 freezing days; 17 days at 0 degrees or below. Long, gray winters. Average temperatures: January: high, 27; low, 11. Pleasant, dry summers. July: high, 81; low, 48. Annual rainfall, 16 inches; snowfall, 67 inches.

Economic base: Ranked by income, wood products industry generates 36%; aluminum smelting, 21%; other manufacturing, 7%. But most jobs are related to tourism, services, government. Large payrolls: School District 5, 590 employees; Kalispell Regional Hospital, 570; Fred Meyer Store, 250; Semi-Tool, computer-manufacturing equipment, 205; Northwestern Telephone, 175; K-Mart, 140; Outlaw Inn, 135; City of Kalispell, 130. Elsewhere in county: Plum Creek Timber, 850; Columbia Falls Aluminum, 714; Burlington Northern, 450; Flathead County, 389; Flathead National Forest, 300. Kalispell is county seat, regional retail center. 2 enclosed shopping malls.

Newspaper: *Daily Inter Lake*, 727 E. Idaho, Kalispell, MT 59901. 406-755-7000. Daily. Dan Black, managing editor. $90 a year.

TV, radio: 2 local AM, 2 FM stations. Local TV station is NBC affiliate. Cable carries other network TV from Missoula, Spokane, and Lethbridge, Alberta. PBS from Spokane. NPR from Missoula.

Health care: Kalispell Regional Medical Center, 100 beds. 87 physicians, 26 dentists in local practice.

Schools: 5 elementary (K–6); 1 intermediate (7); 1 junior high (8–9). Flathead High School (10–12) enrolls 1,450, graduates 91%–92%, sends 45% to higher education. Composite ACT, 22.6; SAT: math, 501; verbal 454. High school enrollment projected to reach 1,800–1,900 by year 2000. Laser School, public alternative high school, enrolls about 125. 7 private pre–K, elementary, secondary schools in area. Flathead Valley Community College enrolls 1,824.

Educational level: 15.4% of Flathead County residents have 16 or more years of formal education; state average, 17.5%. Per capita expenditure for public education, $504; state average, $570.

Library: Flathead County Library System, 200,000 volumes in 5 branches.

Recreation: 2 city parks, with lagoon, playgrounds, picnic areas, horseshoe pits, fitness track, swimming pool, ice-skating rink. 27-hole municipal golf course with views of Glacier National Park to 15-mile-long Flathead Lake. 3 other golf courses in area. Many options for outdoor pursuits at 4 national forests, 5 state recreation areas. Big Mountain ski area, 20 miles north. 4 bowling alleys, 2 cinemas. Resident orchestra and chorale. Concert series.

3 BR, 2 BA house: $75,000 to $80,000.

Cost of electricity: $.04 to $.05 per kilowatt hour.

Cost of natural gas: $.37 per therm.

Sales tax: None.

State income tax: 2% to 11%.

Churches: 52. Denominations: Assemblies of God, Anglican Catholic, Baptist, American Baptist, Independent Baptist, Missionary Baptist, Bible Fellowship, Christian Science, Church of Christ, Church of God, Church of Jesus Christ of Latter-day Saints, Episcopal, Four-Square Gospel, Fundamentalist, Jehovah's Witnesses, Lutheran, Mennonite, Methodist, Nazarene, Nondenominational, Pentecostal, Presbyterian, Roman Catholic, Seventh-Day Adventist.

U.S. highways 93 and 2 cross in the middle of Kalispell. 10 blocks directly south of that intersection stands a gorgeous turn-of-the-century structure, the Flathead County Courthouse, right in the middle of Main Street, and the street splits to go around it. This is a reminder, says Mayor Doug Rauthe, "of the need to slow down if you live here." That message might have seemed irrelevant a decade ago when Kalispell was more a Montana phenomenon than a national celebrity among small towns. But traffic has been picking up. "Growth is happening," Rauthe says. "We are no longer the undiscovered jewel."

What residents say . . .

Dan Black, managing editor, **Daily Inter Lake:** "I checked classified ads for rental units on the first weekend of October 1987 and compared that with this year's. Something like 57 houses were listed for rent, 25 apartments, unfurnished, and a like number of furnished. This year there is one house listed for rent, one apartment. Things are tight. . . . Real estate prices are up. I live 12 miles out of Kalispell, a 15-minute drive. In the last two years, appraisals are up 22 percent, probably borne out in real estate. . . . Traffic is a major issue. There is urgent need for a truck bypass. Summertime traffic has gotten worse. . . . The city has had a very good public–private cooperative spirit. Business has, for its own selfish reasons, been good at making sure the town is progressive. The worst thing the city does is build streets. Kalispell streets are not in good shape. Part of that is weather. The water system is up-to-date and more than adequate. We have a new sewer plant. . . . I think the school system is good. They probably have less administration than in most places. . . . This is an area far removed from urban problems. These are white Anglo-Saxon Protestant people who don't know anything about urban problems at all. Consequently, the schools don't have any of the real problems to overcome they do in other parts of the country. . . . Small towns are the repository of traditional American ideals of family and community. . . . A local Army Reserve unit shipped to the Desert Storm operation. The community reaction to that was almost Norman Rockwell, with the parades and public things in the park downtown, people dabbing at their eyes. Real Americana. At the same time there's a certain sophistication here because there's so much mobility in society. . . . I have people regularly applying for jobs wanting to leave *The Washington Post*, believe it or not. They're looking for the small-town ideal. I think they're chasing a dream and not reality."

Carol Santa, language arts coordinator:
"About seven years ago, the secondary teachers and I developed . . . a program to show students how to learn. That project now is in 33 states. [The publisher] became interested in our elementary program. They wanted to evolve a new way to teach students to read and write. Basically we've been writing a whole new K–6 reading curriculum . . . a cross-curricular approach to teaching language arts. . . . Typically what kids do is read short clips of things. In our program kids read whole books. . . . In sixth grade we teach the greenhouse effect. They read a whole book on the greenhouse effect. One book becomes the driver for getting into a whole theme. . . . We have wonderful teachers because they've had a lot of freedom to be professional. Bill Cooper is a perfect example, letting teachers decide and be in charge. We try to unleash them."

Bill Cooper, superintendent of schools:
"Five or six years ago, *Women's World* rated us one of the top 25 schools in the nation. That doesn't indicate we are one of the top 25, but for some reason we were brought to their attention. Our early use of computer technology in instruction may be a factor. . . . Our science and math students do extremely well. . . . What I'm most proud of, we've had a continual commitment from the community to support education, and we have a very dedicated teaching staff that really works hard."

Georgia Lomax, director, Flathead County Library System:
"We have an interesting community up here, a lot of writers and a lot of highly educated people. They are interested in all types of writing, from Harlequin romances to the more esoteric fiction. A lot of people are working on advanced degrees, doing research. . . . We have a pretty large research collection on Montana, a fairly extensive reference collection, a real variety of fiction types, and a very good nonfiction collection. . . . There is a lot of concern about so many people moving up here without jobs. . . . It's not a place where you can easily live off the land. We get a lot of people moving in who find they cannot support themselves. . . . We don't get paid up here what you do in other places. There is a lot of turnover. . . . We have a lot of what they call at-risk homelessness, extremely low-income people living on the verge. . . . Movie stars live here. Jim Nabors and Carol Burnett. Rumor is that Burt Reynolds has a place down on the lake. Tom Cruise can be seen in the K-Bar from time to time."

Doug Rauthe, owner, Rauthe's Art'n Frame; mayor of Kalispell:
"I've been in office exactly 13 months. . . . We needed someone trained and knowledgeable in managing a $10 million budget and staff of 125 to 150 people, depending on the season. I felt I could offer that. As an aeronautical engineer, the last part of my career I was coordinator between the government and nine

189

major contractors. Negotiating, interfacing, and compromise were the tools of my career. . . . I've told a number of people that Kalispell is not a company town. There is not one large industry. Tourism is big, timber industry is big, agriculture is still a major contributor. . . . We have the largest freshwater lake west of the Mississippi, bigger than Lake Tahoe and more pristine." ■

Lander, WY 82520

Location: 369 miles northwest of Denver, 181 miles southeast of Yellowstone National Park, in west central Wyoming.

Population: 7,023 (1990).

Growth rate: 23% loss since 1980.

Per capita income: $9,628 (1985), 98% of state average ($9,782).

Geography/climate: Elevation 5,357 feet, in a valley on the eastern slope of the Wind River Range of the Rocky Mountains. Sunny most of the time. Cool summers; snowy, cold winters. Average temperatures: January, 17 degrees; July, 70. Average annual rainfall, 15 inches; snowfall, 120 inches.

Economic base: Agriculture, state–federal agencies, tourism, retirement living. Major payrolls: Wyoming State Training School, 576 employees; Fremont County School District, 266; Fremont County Courthouse, 210; Lander Valley Regional Medical Center, 180; National Outdoor Leadership School, 54. Lander is the seat of Fremont County.

Newspaper: *Wyoming State Journal*, 188 N. Third Street, Lander, WY 82520. 307-332-2323. Monday, Wednesday. William Sniffin, editor and publisher. $25.50 a year.

TV, radio: Local AM, FM stations. Cable carries network TV from Denver, Casper, Riverton.

Health care: Lander Valley Medical Center, 107 beds. Psychiatric Institute of Wyoming, 48 beds. 33 physicians, 11 dentists in local practice.

Schools: 3 elementary (K–6), 1 junior high (7–8). Lander Valley High School enrolls 638. 43% of 1991 graduates went to 4-year college; 19% to 2-year; 5% to trade school. Composite ACT, 21.1.

Educational level: 16.3% of Fremont County residents have 16 or more years of formal education; state average, 17.2%. Per capita expenditure for public education, $895; state average, $851.

Library: Fremont County Public Library, 55,000 volumes.

Recreation: 12 city parks, recreation center. 3 baseball fields, 3 tennis courts, swimming pool, golf course, 4 soccer fields, 2 bike paths. Extensive year-round recreation program—leagues, lessons—for kids and adults. General area provides exceptional outdoor pursuits: hunting, fishing, camping, cross-country skiing, snowmobiling, mountain climbing. Lander is a gateway to Yellowstone National Park, Jackson Hole.

3 BR, 2 BA house: $55,000 to $70,000.

Cost of electricity: $.05 per kilowatt hour.

Cost of natural gas: $.40 per therm.

Sales tax: 3%.

State income tax: None.

Churches: 19 total. Denominations: Anglican, Assemblies of God, Baptist, American Baptist, Southern Baptist, Christian, Church of Christ, Episcopal, Evangelical Free, Lutheran (Missouri), Nazarene, Presbyterian, Roman Catholic, Seventh-Day Adventist, Society of Friends, United Methodist, United Pentecostal.

The Loop Road is a 60-mile round trip out of Lander, winding past a selection of the visual delights and natural wonders that make this part of Wyoming such a favorite with visitors. For example, eight miles out of town, at Sinks Canyon State Park, the Popo Agie River vanishes into a cavern, reappearing half a mile down the canyon in a trout-filled pool. Old Blue Ridge Fire Outlook, at 10,000 feet, brings distant mountain peaks into view. Loop Road passes mountain lakes and meadows; Atlantic City, an old mining town; Red Canyon, which really is; and back to Lander, where some residents work at the less visual but more farsighted challenge of preserving and building the local economy.

What residents say . . .

Linda Hewitt, community resource coordinator: "What I do is research and staff work for the mayor and council, and work on special projects. . . . I'm from Des Moines. We moved in May of '83 but we'd vacationed out here for 10 years. We just liked the quality of life in the Lander area . . . low crime, good schools, friendly people, you know who your neighbors are. Coming from a big city you appreciate those things. . . . Later in 1983, the Atlantic City Iron Ore Mine, a US Steel operation, closed and we lost 500 jobs. We were devastated. Our worst years were '85–'87. . . . Most businesses have stabilized and are doing OK. Our biggest employer base is the state. . . . Wyoming State Training School employs 650. Then we have the Game & Fish office, the Bureau of Land Management, our school district. The only really new business is Eagle Bronze Foundry. . . . Right now Lander has less than 75 houses for sale and essentially no rentals. In 1987 we had 400-plus houses on the market. We began a vigorous retirement recruitment campaign. We spent $10,000 and placed classified ads in the *Army–Navy Federal Times, Stars & Stripes, Ki-*wanis magazine, targeting people who had early retirement. We were quite successful, getting 25 to 30 couples. . . . Our biggest project is Main Street renovation. Highway 287 is our main street . . . lots of traffic through in the summertime. . . . We'll be doing new water and sewer pipes, colored and textured sidewalks, trees, benches. We're working with the business owners to improve their storefronts. Our theme is 'Turn of the Century'. . . . We're trying to get people to stay another night with us. . . . We're looking at ways our children can get back to Wyoming. We educate 'em and export 'em. As a mother, you think you want them close. Probably the most common comment I hear, we want some place for our kids to come back."

Tom Bell, editor, **Wind River Mountaineer:** "We're going into Volume 8. I kind of play it by ear. For instance, in the last issue I did a history of the South Pass, through which the Pony Express and the first continental stage lines ran. Just our luck, a company wants to put a pipeline through there. I thought people ought to be informed how much history has gone on at South Pass. . . . When the railroad pulled out of Lander in the 1970s, we were left high and dry. They even pulled up the tracks. But these things happen. My own thought is we need to maintain a very good educational base, which Lander has, and try to attract the type of industry that is compatible with great scenery. The tourist industry is gaining in importance. Dude ranches are kind of waning. People have their motor homes and pull their four-wheel drive behind them. . . . The county commissioners are trying to drum up interest in getting a low-level radioactive waste dump out there in the Gas Hills, where the uranium was taken. The governor has just acceded to a study, but it is getting mixed reaction, the old NIMBY effect."

Cathy Purves, environmental consultant: "I basically have a home office and work the whole state on various types of reclamation and planning, at old mines, mostly historical, that now come under the abandoned mine land programs, hundreds of sites. I go in and monitor them, evaluate them. I also work on pipelines, right now one that's coming across Wyoming north to southwest, the Altamont gas transmission line. It's going through some areas that are high controversy. I'm working on the vegetation reclamation plan, the environmental portion of it, making sure certain wildlife habitat isn't disturbed. . . . This is my fourth winter here. I see a big difference. I see a town learning to cope on its own without depending on one income, a very diverse population . . . a large number of state and federal employees in the environmental field. . . . The National Outdoor Leadership School headquarters is here. . . . You bring in for the most part college-educated people from all over the United States, fairly mid-30s, family oriented, and leaning

toward the conservative. . . . It's diverse. Blue-collar, white-collar. A strong retirement community, so we have a lot of people with wonderful pasts. It's a community that gets along well even though we have our basic squabbles. We are learning that progress without regard to the past may not be the best way. . . . I'm an Air Force brat, so I've lived all over the world. Lander reacts well to newcomers. The interaction, overall, is good. . . . I walk 10 minutes to go fishing . . . trout . . . brookies, brownies, rainbows. The Popo Agie is right at my back door."

Chavawn Woodall, publications manager, National Outdoor Leadership School: "Initially, there was not a great fondness between the town and this school. All the people from the outside were thought to be hippie types. Then a funny thing happened. Over the years NOLS has grown to where we are now one of the strongest economic factors that is not government-supplemented. There are still lingering prejudices. I think we have 259 paid employees between the Rocky Mountains branch school and headquarters. We occupy the old Noble Hotel, which was built in 1918. Students spend their first and last nights here. At the time it was built, the Noble was the jumping-off place to Yellowstone and the Tetons. . . . Our emphasis is on wilderness education, not on personal development per se. We stress expedition behavior. If you think about any big expedition, we can only succeed if all the people are working together. So the common goal is the expedition, not necessarily on making the summit. . . . City Park has very green grass, tall trees, and free camping. In the summertime a lot of cross-country bicyclists come through and spend the night." ∎

Lebanon, NH 03766

Location: 63 miles northwest of Concord, just east of the intersection of I-89 and I-91, on the Connecticut River boundary with Vermont.

Population: 12,183 (1990).

Growth rate: 9% since 1980.

Per capita income: $11,620 (1985), virtually the same as state average ($11,659).

Geography/climate: Elevation 607 feet. Gently rolling to hilly river-valley terrain. Invigorating continental climate. Long, snowy, sometimes very cold winters. Pleasant, sunny summers. Colorful falls. Average temperatures: January: high, 30; low, 8. July: high, 81; low, 53. Average annual rainfall, 45 inches; snowfall, 98 inches.

Economic base: Government, education, health care are the dominant sectors, with growing industrial base. Large payrolls: Split Ballbearing, 700 employees; Thermal Dynamics, plasma-welding and cutting equipment, 300; Dartmouth-Hitchcock Medical Center, 3,000; Veterans Administration Center and Hospital, Army Corps of Engineers Cold Regions Research and Engineering Laboratory, other federal employment, 1,500. Retail shopping center for the region.

Newspaper: *The Valley News*, P.O. Box 877, White River Junction, VT 05001. 603-298-8711. Daily, Monday through Saturday. Wilmott Lewis, publisher. $14.75 a month.

TV, radio: Local AM/FM station. Cable carries network TV, PBS from Boston, plus other northern New England stations. NPR received from Vermont Public Radio.

Health care: Dartmouth-Hitchcock Medical Center, 420 beds. Large population of physicians and other health-care professionals in area.

Schools: 4 elementary (K–6), 1 junior high (7–8). Lebanon High School enrolls 630, sends about 50% to 4-year college. 1991 average SAT scores: verbal, 437; math, 486 (69% of class taking test).

Educational level: 21.9% of Grafton County residents have 16 or more years of formal education; state average, 18.2%. Per capita expenditure for public education, $473; state average, $396.

Library: Lebanon Public Library, 44,000 volumes.

Recreation: Indoor recreation centered in new, $4 million annex to community building: pool, weight rooms, game rooms, gym. Hiking trails at 90-acre Goodwin Park. Skiing at municipally operated Storrs Hill Ski Area. Other ski areas nearby: Sonnenberg, Suicide Six, in Vermont; Whaleback, Mt. Sunapee, Dartmouth Skiway, in New Hampshire. Tennis courts in 2 locations; several ball fields.

3 BR, 2 BA house: $125,000 to $150,000.

Cost of electricity: $.10 per kilowatt hour.

Cost of fuel oil: $.90 per gallon.

Sales tax: None.

State income tax: None.

Churches: Baptists, Christian Science, Congregational, Lutheran, Methodist, Roman Catholic. Most other major denominations represented in nearby communities.

Synagogue: In Hanover, 5 miles north.

Look at a map of New Hampshire and Vermont side-by-side and you will see why Lebanon is doing well. It is situated where two major interstate highways cross—I-91, the north–south route running parallel to the Connecticut River, which forms the state line, and I-89, the link between northwest Vermont and Canada, and southeast New Hampshire and the Boston area. These trade routes form a big *X* across the two-state region, and Lebanon is at the center. But that has been true for some time. Centuries before the interstate system, Lebanon exploited the exceptional advantage of being located where the Mascoma River joins the Connecticut. For mill power, the town harnessed the Mascoma. For transport, Lebanon loaded its wares aboard vessels on the Connecticut. And for posterity, it kept copious records.

What residents say . . .

Robert Leavitt, city historian: "Technically, I was born in the next town, but I've lived all my life here in Lebanon. I'm retired now. I took over my grandfather's trade to take care of him. I was an upholsterer in my active years. . . . Being city historian keeps me busy collating . . . simply collecting things, newspapers, chronological listings. We keep them in an underground vault. . . . My grandfather started the thing in a way. He filled the house I lived in from the time I was a teenager. When I inherited the house I founded the Historical Society almost in self-defense. . . . There has been such a great interest in genealogical information ever since *Roots* came out. . . . Of course, all New England towns in the Upper Valley were agricultural and were founded as a result of soldiers coming down from the French and Indian Wars. They saw these great fields of grass and decided what a nice place for a farm. . . . The chartering of the town is dated July 4, 1761. Twice that date becomes important in Lebanon's history. The

Association Test was sent out by the rebel government at the time of the Revolutionary War. All the males of adult age were to sign, signifying they would fight against the Crown. In Lebanon, the Association Test was signed July 4, earlier than the Declaration of Independence. Every male in Lebanon signed it, without exception. Many of the towns around us had Tories, who sided with England. . . . Lebanon was agricultural. Then it became an industrial community. We were the first to make commercial brick, for sale. We had a machine industry very early. Recently I was shown the orders from the British government. They bought from Lebanon the machine to make the Enfield rifle. . . . The machine industry petered out and we had a woodworking industry, manufacturing 'house finish' as it was called, all kinds of things including furniture for living rooms. One factory had 600 men. Woodworking lasted until the first major fire. In 1887, all the industrial area of Lebanon burned. . . . Woodworking was succeeded by textiles, three large woolen

mills, that lasted through the Depression. . . .
Our largest industry now is Split Ballbearing
Corporation. Lebanon has gone full circle,
back to the machine industry."

Jean Mansell, librarian: "We have been
here since 1966, and Lebanon has
changed. It's become a prettier town. The
dirt is gone. The tannery is gone . . .
turned into low-income housing and made
very attractive. The Green is really pretty.
The library's at one end of it. . . . We have
a Carnegie, built in 1909. We've added on,
doubled the size."

Karen Wadsworth, state representative, former mayor: "In 1982, a group of people
thought we should go back to being a
town. They wanted a town council so they
could have a direct vote on the budget. . . .
We wanted to retain the council-manager
form of government. There were a lot of
neighborhood coffees, forums, and debates.
We ended up winning two to one on retention of the form of government. I think
that put a lot of controversy to rest. Those
of us who weren't born here never knew
how widespread the feeling was, but people
said the city-manager form of government
was correct for our community. . . . Right
now the master plan is being rewritten . . .
by community volunteer groups, working
on various sections of the plan. . . . About a
year and a half ago this community was
chosen to participate in . . . New Hampshire in the 21st Century, again, a broad
cross-section of people meeting to talk
about what is good about the community
and what should be changed. . . . This community seems to do that quite a bit. I think
it's the kind of place where people can
come in and feel they are able to contribute. I ran for City Council after living here
only two and a half years. A year later I
was mayor. I remember telling people, if I
can do that, anybody can . . . I'm a state
representative. The City of Lebanon is my
district and I'm in my fourth term. . . . I
think people in New Hampshire are used
to meeting [presidential] candidates. They
expect it. There is a lot of, almost, competition among people in certain communities
to get a candidate to come to their town
hall or senior center. In 1987, I had
George Bush as the sitting vice president,
right here in my home. It was so exciting
my parents came up from New York. . . .
This is something you can do in New
Hampshire that you probably can't do in
many places, the opportunity to talk directly with the candidates, sometimes one
on one. It's a very special thing. . . . Something else that happens here, a personal
story. We have a green, a park, in the center of town. In 1980, I wondered why it
wasn't decorated for the holidays. It used
to be done by the merchants association. I
asked if we could get some money in the
budget. We couldn't. I decided we should
do it, anyway, and we invited everyone to
come put together a community Christmas
on the first Sunday in December. It was
the most marvelous thing. All kinds of people were there, bringing greens and baked
cookies. . . . We lit a big tree on the bandstand and decorated it with homemade ornaments. The whole point is, it was a
community thing, done by
everybody. . . ." ■

Lewisburg, PA 17837

Location: 165 miles northwest of Philadelphia, 70 miles north of Harrisburg, in the central Susquehanna Valley of Pennsylvania.

Population: 5,768 (1990).

Growth rate: 7% since 1980.

Per capita income: $8,255 (1985), 80% of state average ($10,288).

Geography/climate: River valley, elevation 460 feet, with Appalachian Mountains to the northwest, Shamokin Mountain, Montour Ridge to the southeast. Changeable weather, a mixture of drier continental and more humid eastern seaboard. Annual rainfall, 36 inches; snowfall, 35 inches. Average temperatures: January: high, 35; low, 20, with average 1 day below zero. July: high, 86, with 20 days into the 90s; low, 63. Though humid and quite cloudy, nice summers and falls.

Economic base: Major local employers are Bucknell University (900 employees, $31 million payroll), North Eastern United States Penitentiary, Pennsylvania House Furniture, International Paper, Moore Business Forms. Seat of Union County. Bedroom town for people employed elsewhere in Valley, including Geisinger Clinic, at Danville, 20 miles east. Several sizeable dairy farms in county.

Newspaper: *Lewisburg Daily Journal*, 27 S. Fifth Street, Lewisburg, PA 17837. 717-523-1268. Mornings, Monday through Friday. Virginia Thompkins, editor. $94 a year.

TV, radio: 2 local FM, 1 AM station. Cable carries network TV, PBS from Harrisburg,

Scranton, Lancaster, New York City. NPR from Harrisburg.

Health care: Evangelical Community Hospital, 155 beds. 41 physicians, 14 dentists in local practice.

Schools: 3 elementary (2 K–5, 1 K–2), 1 middle (6–8). Lewisburg Area High School enrolls 468, sends 65% to 2- or 4-year college. 82% of high school graduates took the SAT in 1991. Composite scores: math, 500; verbal, 452. 4 high school seniors received National Merit Letters of Commendation; 1 was a semi-finalist in National Merit Scholarship program for 1990–91.

Educational level: 14.3% of Union County residents have 16 or more years of formal education; state average, 13.6%. Per capita expenditure for public education, $612; state average, $421.

Library: Public Library for Union County, 42,000 volumes.

Recreation: 4 public recreation areas total 67 acres, include swimming pool, tennis courts, soccer field, playgrounds, fitness trail, 2 Little League, 2 softball diamonds. Bowling alley, movie theater, 2 daily-fee golf courses. Trout fishing on White Deer, Buffalo, Penns creeks, all in Union County. Rabbit, pheasant, deer hunting in rural areas. R. B. Winter State Park, west of town, provides swimming, picnic areas, hiking, camping, fishing. A dozen other state parks within an hour's drive north and west.

3 BR, 2 BA house: South side, near Bucknell, some as high as $200,000 to $300,000. North side lower but rising. 1 house needing rehabilitation bought at $28,000, resold at $111,000.

Cost of electricity: $.065 per kilowatt hour.

Cost of natural gas: $.55 per therm.

Sales tax: 6%.

State income tax: 2.1%.

Churches: 23. Denominations: Assemblies of God, Baptist, Independent Baptist, Reformed Baptist, Brethren, Christian & Missionary Alliance, Church of Christ in Christian Union, Episcopal, Foursquare Gospel, Independent Bible, Lutheran, Evangelical Lutheran, Mennonite, Nondenominational, Pentecostal, Presbyterian, Roman Catholic, Unitarian-Universalist, United Church of Christ, United Methodist.

"Statistics are very dull," declares Nada Gray, the borough manager of Lewisburg. In a follow-up letter, after providing many statistics about her town, Mrs. Gray offered a few select comments:

"We have two museums: Packwood House and Slifer House, as well as an active county historical society that researches and publishes folk traditions and crafts in the area. Two of our three major employers are stable: Bucknell and the penitentiary. Pennsylvania House is cyclical.

"We have two supermarkets: Weis and Acme, and a new Wal-Mart, a possible threat. Our downtown is attractive and active. Our real-estate market is soft on $200,000 and higher, but improving. We are conservative, Republican, but friendly.

"Bucknell University is a cultural asset. Our relationship is cooperative rather than antagonistic. Music groups abound. We are the county seat for Union, one of the smallest counties in Pennsylvania. We have a lot of lawyers. The hottest issue in town is a proposal for a new high school. The community is polarized."

What residents say ...

Paula Fantaski, school superintendent: "I came here from suburban Pittsburgh, a very large district. I had spent several summers in workshops at Bucknell and fell in love with the area. When the opening came up, I applied. . . . In the last two years, 141 students came into the district. Those students represented 15 countries and 21 states. . . . Only two were foreign exchange. The rest were coming here because of employment in industry, the penitentiary, the medical center, and Bucknell. . . . We knew we had a more diverse population than any other town in the area. The point I was trying to make is we were not educating purely for Pennsylvania. Our student population is becoming more diverse in terms of minority groups, gifted students, students with disabilities, students of color. We are a fortunate school district having that kind of influx. . . . I can best characterize the community by describing the homecoming parade. The first car contained the police chief, followed by the Lewisburg band, followed by the football team and cheerleaders, followed by parents of the football players . . . the fathers dressed like cheerleaders and the mothers like football players. Then, floats for the ninth, 10th and 11th grades. This year for the first time an alumni float. . . . There's a great sense of community that people feel here. . . . Could I share something else with you? Last year, we had a student who played football and he also played in the band. So, in his football uniform at half time, he took his trumpet and marched with the band. I like that, I really do."

Barry Maxwell, vice president for administration, Bucknell University: "250 to 300 students live in rental units in the community. They occasionally cause some difficulty because of their lifestyle and radios and stereo sets, the typical kind of neighborhood problems late at night and on weekends. But by and large it is not a terrible problem. The community has been fairly tolerant, and students respect the rights of others. . . . Another very much more positive intersection . . . is the kinds of civic and community activities our students become involved in . . . assisting elderly residents, working on clean-up projects along roads, streets, and streams. . . . The Town–Gown Committee gets together three or four times a year to explore potential problem areas before they become significant . . . good, open, frank communication. It's a good town–gown setting compared to an awful lot of other situations."

William Stein, florist: "My father started this business in 1926 with two greenhouses and a flower shop on Market Street, two blocks away. He sold it to me in 1965. I built three more greenhouses and have a total of five. . . . We just had a hail storm the size of baseballs . . . . 2,000 panes of glass broken! . . . The local economy is pretty good. Several years ago when something similar to this recession happened, Lewisburg did not seem to be affected. I think it's just because people enjoy shopping here. It's an attractive place to shop."

D. Anne McClure: "There are other nice small towns in the area. This just happens to be the nicest! Part of it is its natural geographic location, surrounded by mountains. . . . One thing could be because of some of the things that haven't happened. No major highway goes through our town. The main highways bypassed us. . . . No malls, no shopping centers. They are off down the road. . . . Basically the town has kept its personality, structure, and character. . . . Possibly, too, because the main streets were laid out being nice, wide streets, with room for trees and traffic without being overpopulated. . . . Many new owners have restored the downtown district. In the last 10 years there seems to have been a definite feeling of appreciation for the structures that are there. . . . Some homes go back to the early 1800s, pretty much Federal and Victorian architecture. It's not a town with elegant, stately mansions, just handsome homes with big trees along the streets. . . . Bucknell University is a particularly beautiful school. Being a college town, it has to be one of the nice ones. I live on the corner at the end of University Avenue, with a Civil War monument in the triangle across the street . . . fraternity row on each side, so we don't have a very quiet street, students coming and going. . . . The fact it is a college town has kept income flowing into the business district. . . . People are willing to make their community better, always a feeling that when you can, you should do your part. . . . I'm 60 years old and have spent half my life here. Among our close friends, I can name half a dozen who went off into the world and came back. I see the younger ones coming back now, just like we did. There's an opportunity to make a living and it's a good place to live." ■

Lincoln City, OR 97367

Location: 92 miles southwest of Portland, 132 miles northwest of Eugene, on the Oregon coast.

Population: 5,892 (1990).

Growth rate: 7% since 1980.

Per capita income: $8,929 (1985), 90% of state average ($9,925).

Geography/climate: Sandy Pacific shoreline, backed up by Coast Range Mountains. 12 miles directly east, Stott Mountain peaks at 3,128 feet. Marine climate, controlled by warm, moist, ocean air. Moderate year-round temperatures. Average summer temperatures range from breezy 60–70 degrees on ocean front to 80–90 a few miles inland. Winter daytime average, 50 degrees, dropping to 37 at night. Light winter rains mixed with sunny days, occasional winter storms. Annual rainfall, 72 inches; snowfall, trace.

Economic base: Tourism, small business, retirees. 1 out of 3 jobs is tourist-related. Top 5 payrolls are North Lincoln Hospital, school district, Quality Factory Village, Inn at Spanish Head/Shilo Inn, city government.

Newspaper: *News Guard*, 930 S.E. Highway 101, Lincoln City, OR 97367. 503-994-2178. Weekly, Wednesday. Jim Moore, editor. $20 a year.

TV, radio: Cable carries network TV, PBS from Portland, Eugene. NPR received off-air.

Health care: North Lincoln Hospital, 49 beds. 20 physicians, 7 dentists in local practice.

Schools: 3 elementary (K–2, 3–5, K–5), 1 middle (6–8). Taft High School enrolls 526, sends 35% to 4-year college. SAT scores, "above the national average." Seventh-Day Adventist School (1–8).

Educational level: 14.4% of Lincoln County residents have 16 or more years of formal education; state average, 17.9%. Per capita expenditure for public education, $567; state average, $577.

Library: Driftwood Library, 23,000 catalogued items, 10,000 paperbacks. Outreach program for the homebound.

Recreation: 13 developed park sites, 25 acres undeveloped park land. 21,000-square-foot community center built 1980 has 25-meter pool, children's pool, meeting rooms, senior center, kitchen available to public. City has agreement with school district for joint use of gyms, ball fields. 7½ miles of public beach invites kite-flying in self-proclaimed "Kite Capital of the World"; storm-watching during winter months; beach-combing, especially after storms. Surfing, windsurfing, sailing on the ocean and Devil's Lake, 3-mile-long lake on city's eastern side. 4 golf courses in area, community theater, cinema.

3 BR, 2 BA house: $80,000 for 1,600 feet, no view; $200,000 to $300,000+ for ocean front, lake front.

Cost of electricity: $.04 to $.05 per kilowatt hour.

Cost of natural gas: $.57 per therm.

Sales tax: None.

State income tax: 5% to 9%.

Churches: 23. Denominations: Assemblies of God, Baptist, Christian, Christian Science, Church of Christ, Church of Jesus Christ of Latter-day Saints, Community, Congregational, Episcopal, Evangelical, Faith, Jehovah's Witnesses, Lutheran, Nazarene, Presbyterian, Roman Catholic, Seventh-Day Adventist, Shambhala, Universal Life.

They joke about the wind in Lincoln City. The only time it quits blowing is during a kite festival, of which there are many, because the wind is so reliable. They also joked when promoters built Quality City, a discount factory outlet—50 stores, name brands, big savings. It was the biggest thing to hit town in some time. People will come from all around to shop, the builders said. "We thought they were crazy," recalls Andy Andrews, an Air Force retiree. "It's amazing—it's become quite the thing."

Lincoln City should not be surprised by amazing things, however. Two stoplights up from Quality City is a much older attraction, the world's shortest river, a 220-foot waterway named simply D River, connecting Devils Lake and the Pacific Ocean. The Wayside at D River is reported to have more visitors than any other Oregon state park, a distinction that is likely to remain intact now that the factory outlets are just down Highway 101.

What residents say ...

Hal Hazelrigg, director of marketing, North Lincoln Hospital: "One of the most basic problems is to let people know that despite the fact we have only 49 beds and are a small hospital that we have up-to-date, first-class equipment and staff. . . . We lived in Houston, San Francisco, New York and Chicago, then we moved to Oregon ostensibly to retire. It would never have occurred to me in a million years to go to the local boondocks hospital for real health care. Unfortunately, we've had several opportunities to discover how untrue that was. . . . We have the latest version of the CAT scan, the latest in mammography, an all-new intensive-care unit, an entirely new surgical suite. The hospital is computerized from stem to stern. Our lab can do at least 90% of any procedure. People don't realize all that. . . . We are a taxpayer-supported hospital, a hospital district. . . . You move out to the boondocks and think [physicians] are either beginners or a bunch of retreads come out here just prior to retirement. Again, that isn't the case in Lincoln and a lot of other Oregon communities where people love the lifestyle. . . . Our intensive-care nurse chief came to us from a 900-bed teaching hospital in Orlando. She and her husband have four little kids. . . . One of our biggest difficulties recruiting male physicians is that there are so few cultural events to keep their wives happy. There's not a lot of social activity here in an urban sense and they get bored to tears."

Harvey Smith, director of sales, resort hotel; community-theater member: "Theatre West of Lincoln City is about 17 years old, strictly nonprofit, volunteer community theater started by a group called The University Women, who thought maybe the arts could benefit with live theater. We have our own theater, on U.S. Highway 101. It's a very small, intimate place, 78 seats. . . . We have a paid artistic director . . . six or seven productions a year, playing three to four weeks each. . . . All our money comes from gate receipts, selling to predominantly sold-out houses. . . . We choose good plays, recently *A Woman in Mind*."

Dave Juenke, former newspaper owner, community-service volunteer: "We were in the San Fernando Valley and decided we wanted a more personal lifestyle in relationship with our neighbors. . . . We came here in 1967. . . . The character of the community has remained pretty much constant. One of the important elements most of us enjoy is the fact there are no socioeconomic strata. We are a very homogeneous community with shared interests, whether it is the former chairman of the board or a retired dockworker. . . . We do have a certain amount of forest industry here although in recent years, timber cutting has fallen off. Most of the new employment relates to tourism. It is possible for a young family to enjoy a modest income and reasonably comfortable way of life, but it is also true that the hotel and restaurant industry tends to be among the lower paying. . . . We have entrepreneurs and retirees who do reasonably well. I suppose if one were to check the bank deposits and individual wealth, we could probably rank quite high. . . . Margaret and I [owned] the newspaper for 15 years. . . . Community

newspapers in Oregon tend to be the principal sources of communication for the community. . . . Fortunately, we've had strong leadership in the city, controversial but strong. Most major decisions in the community are very actively debated and often caused to be put to the vote. But once a decision is reached there tends to be [agreement]. . . . Small weeklies are quite strong on letters to the editor. Our paper in particular has an absolute plethora of letters on a weekly basis that are very helpful to define community issues. I think in my case, my intent with editorials was to encourage people to consider the issues rather than express a point of view."

Noel Walker, motel owner, City Council member: "We've only been here six years and I've gotten involved in everything. Originally we're from Richland, Washington . . . spent eight years in Montana as a soil conservationist. I guess I was a little tired of working with farmers and ranchers in an area where there wasn't much culture. We weren't very happy there. We discovered we're basically coastal-type people. . . . We found an abandoned motel on Devil's Lake and decided to try and resurrect it . . . Blue Heron Landing . . . it had been closed down for about 3 years. So it had no goodwill. Also the lake was going sour . . . filling with weeds. But one of the reasons I bought it was they had a plan to restore the lake. Half the people I met here the first year said they were going to buy the place, too. . . . My wife and I are the staff, and my 10-year-old son is starting to help out. . . . Lincoln City is a wonderful place in every way except for making a living. For a young family, unless they're professionals, doctors, lawyers, etc., they're not likely to make much. . . . Oregon schools are not the greatest because of the way they're funded, through property taxes. Measure 5 cuts back drastically on the amount you can charge. . . . We're talking about a two-thirds cut. I know the governor is pushing for relief. . . . We just passed a referendum for a new city hall, taking over an existing structure that will house city government, a new library, various county and state agencies, Oregon Coast Community College. . . . We're building a new skateboard park. We've had a 13-hole golf course for some years. The Japanese bought it and are going to finish it to 18." ■

Littleton, NH 03561

Location: On I-93, halfway between Boston and Montreal, across the river 10 miles from St. Johnsbury, Vermont, in northern New Hampshire.

Population: 5,827 (1990).

Growth rate: 2% since 1986.

Per capita income: $8,936 (1985), 23% below state average $11,659.

Geography/climate: Rolling Connecticut River valley, nestled against the White Mountains at elevation 822 feet. 24 miles west of 6,288-foot Mt. Washington, highest point in New Hampshire. Vigorous northern–New England climate with cold, snowy winters though somewhat protected from northeast winds by mountain range. Average 53 inches of snow, 160 freezing days, 20 days around zero. Average temperatures: January: high, 26; low, 8. Pleasant summers, low humidity. July: high, 82; low, 60, but with 6 days at 90 or above. Average rainfall, 33 inches.

Economic base: Retail trade, tourism and recreation, manufacturing. Shopping center serving half a dozen smaller nearby towns. Larger payrolls: Littleton Stamp & Coin; Harrison Publishing; Norton Pike, abrasives and sharpening stones; Tender Corporation, maker of "After Bite" insect repellent. Industrial park houses 6 businesses employing 450. Cluster of woodworking enterprises in area. Samuel C. Moore Dam, a hydroelectric station on Connecticut River, is a boon to local tax base.

Newspaper: *The Littleton Courier*, P.O. Box 230, Littleton, NH 03561. 603-444-3927. Weekly, Wednesday. Olivia Garfield, editor. $20.25 a year.

TV, radio: Local AM, FM stations. Cable carries network TV from Burlington, Vermont; and Portland, Maine.

Health care: Littleton Regional Hospital, 54 beds. 16 physicians, 7 dentists in local practice.

Schools: 1 elementary (K–5); 1 middle (6–8). Littleton High School, which shares a building with middle school, enrolls 300, sends 40%–45% to higher education. Of the 20%–25% who attend 4-year college, recent composite SAT scores are: math, 560; verbal, "close to 500." Also in town, White Mountain School, a college-prep, co-ed, boarding and day school operated by Episcopal Church (9–12).

Educational level: 21.9% of Grafton County residents have 16 or more years of formal education; state average, 18.2%. Per capita expenditure for public education, $473; state average, $396.

Library: Littleton Public Library, 38,000 books, 4,699 card holders. 1990 circulation, 68,000.

Recreation: 2 city parks with lighted ball fields, swimming pool, tennis courts, skating rink. Fishing, swimming, boating, picnicking at Moore Dam Lake, Partridge Lake. Recreation department sponsors summer camp, Little League, men's and women's softball leagues. Snowmobile races in January; trout tournament, hydroplane regatta in June. Within an hour's drive of 10 major ski areas, including Bretton Woods, Cannon Mountain, Monteau, Loon Mountain, Waterville. Appalachian Trail winds through Franconia Notch State Park, 15 miles south. Numerous summertime music and arts festivals in area. Movie theater in town.

3 BR, 2 BA house: $95,000 to $130,000.

Cost of electricity: $.07 per kilowatt hour.

Cost of propane heating fuel: About $1 per gallon for 2,000-square-foot house.

Sales tax: None.

State income tax: None.

Churches: 10. Denominations: Assemblies of God, Baha'i, Baptist, Bible, Christian, Christian Science, Congregational, Episcopal, Roman Catholic, United Methodist.

At the 1991 town meeting in Littleton, New Hampshire, residents once again exercised their cherished right of self-determination. They approved an amended budget of $3,336,483, including, among many other items, a $20,000 contribution to Littleton Regional Hospital for the expansion project; $60,000 for a recycling center on Mt. Eustis; $65,000 to close the landfill; and $119,048 for a new fire truck. And they accepted a gift of land from Hitchiner Manufacturing for development as a hockey rink. Oh, the pleasures of local decision-making!

Now if only they could make the federal Safe Drinking Water Act go away. Littleton takes great pride in its water, piped in by gravity from a lake on Mt. Garfield, in the Presidential Range. "We have some of the best water in the country, but the federal government is putting us out of business," says insurance broker Bruce Hadlock. "They're telling us we can't use surface water. To obtain a new source of water, we've got to spend millions." Sounds like a hot topic for a future town meeting.

What residents say . . .

David Harris, utility company worker; member, Board of Selectmen: "This is my sixth year. I am chairman of the board this year. . . . My parents grew up in Littleton. I grew up here, was in the service, and came back. . . . I think the satisfaction is seeing the town operate as a town. I have an ear to the older generation. . . . People say, 'Dave, I remember your mom and dad.' I think it makes everybody's job easier if people feel they have someone they can talk to

and trust. My biggest reward is having someone call me with a problem . . . being able to help. . . . What you do for one you must do for all. . . . I would say this takes 10 to 12 hours a week. . . . We get $1,400 a year. Several days a year we are requested to be in Concord. Because we work at regular jobs, we take a vacation day or a day without pay."

Frances Heald, retired social worker, recipient of the Paul Harris Non-Rotarian Award for Community Service: "I was born and brought up here, went to high school here, then on to college . . . bachelor of arts from Tufts University, bachelor of science from Simmons College School of Social Work, and a master's from the Harvard School of Public Health. . . . I worked in family service, child-care placing, day-care licensing. . . . I have always maintained a summer home here and moved back 20 years ago, when I retired. . . . We're getting very much used to having a town manager. We used to find fault and get rid of him. Now our only losing them is to better salaries and jobs. They've learned to work together as a team. Town management is big business now. . . . My father was a lawyer here back in 1919 when local men were coming out of World War I. Instead of building a monument . . . he was able to assemble a group of 100 men and women to purchase the Eastman home on Main Street for Littleton Community Center, as a memorial. . . . Thousands of people have used it. . . . This community has always been blessed with people who were willing to give. What is lacking is leadership. No one wants to be president of anything. The young women are all working. . . . Littleton is growing slowly. It seems the population changes with various events. When they put in the Moore Dam on the Connecticut River, that brought us a whole new group of people. The development of tourism and winter sports brought a new group. . . . Physicians are attracted because we have a well-equipped hospital and draw on a sizeable North Country radius, and I think they like the relaxed living in the country. Here the doctors come in a pickup truck. If you don't own a pickup truck, you're out."

Jack Colby, newspaper columnist: "I was ed-itor of the newspaper for 40 years, retired eight years ago. I still write a column. It's called "Mountain Musing" . . . a take-off on "mountain music." I started it in 1940 and it's certainly one of the oldest continuous columns in the country. . . . It's miscellany, whatever comes to mind. . . . I give people a lot of credit they can't get any other way, something that would not make a full-blown story in the news columns. I knock it out in a couple of hours on an IBM type-writer. I have stuck with IBM though people tell me I should have a word processor. This works as fast as my brain does, and I can spell well enough I don't need a machine. . . . We are growing slowly, but that is not all bad. If we are providing employment, that is the important thing. More people simply add to the cost of doing business and providing services. It isn't always necessary to have rapid growth if you are providing for people. . . . There are no burning questions except in education, efforts to keep the budget down. We have been fortunate not to get embroiled in political situations."

Richard Hill, veterinarian, New Hampshire State Representative, president of Littleton Historical Society: "We've had many young fellows go out and do well. We had a young fellow named Richard Gale went up to the major leagues. He's now with the Red Sox organization, pitching coach at the Pawtucket club of the Boston Red Sox. Then we had a boy who came to town at 16 years old and worked his way up to governor, Hugh Gallen. He was replaced by John Sununu. We also had Robert C. Hill, quite active in the State Department, ambassador to five countries. His last post was Argentina. Carl A. Hill became dean of the business school at Dartmouth, Tuck School.

We've done very well in the education of our children. It was a small town of close-knit families for a long time. We've had an injection of new blood in the last 10 to 15 years.... You know how it is in a historical society: the other fellow was sick and they asked me to serve.... One of the interesting things, we have an old horse cemetery where a man buried three of his horses. He had no children. Each horse has his own stone. It's rather unique and we're going to get it back into shape. That horse cemetery caused Interstate 93 to detour. We're trying to refurbish it so we can say, 'There's a man who thought so much of his animals that he made a special place for them, and the federal government has to go around it.' " ■

Marion, IL 62959

Location: 315 miles south of Chicago, 58 miles northwest of Paducah, Kentucky, in extreme southern Illinois.

Population: 14,545 (1990).

Growth rate: 4% since 1980.

Per capita income: $9,539 (1985), 84% of state average ($11,302).

Geography/climate: Level to rolling terrain, just north of Shawnee National Forest and within northeastern reaches of Ozark country. Continental subtropic weather: prevailing winds from the Gulf temper winter lows; contribute to hot, humid summers. Average temperatures: January: high, 41; low, 24. July: high, 89; low, 67. Seasonal average 40 days at 90 degrees or above; 103 days at freezing or below. Average rainfall, 47 inches; snowfall, 10 inches. Accumulation rare.

Economic base: Regional service and retail center, manufacturing, mining. Fruit, grain, livestock farming. Larger payrolls: Blue Cross/Blue Shield regional center, 550 employees; Olin Corporation, small-caliber ammunition, 400; Marion Memorial Hospital, 405; Marion Federal Prison, 340; GTE, telecommunications, 300; Marion Pepsi-Cola, 250; Amax, bituminous coal, 150; Diagraph Industries, stenciling machines, 125; Birmington Bolt, mine-roof bolts, 60. Marion is seat of Williamson County.

Newspaper: *Marion Daily Republican*, 111–115 Franklin Avenue, Marion, IL 62959. 618-993-2626. Daily, Monday through Saturday. Mike Vandorn, editor. $56.50 a year.

TV, radio: 2 local AM stations, 1 FM, 1 TV. Cable carries network TV from Paducah, St. Louis. PBS, NPR from Carbondale.

Health care: Marion Memorial Hospital, 103 beds. 37 physicians, 16 dentists in local practice.

Schools: 5 elementary (K–6), 1 junior high (7–8). Marion High School enrolls 1,156, sends about 70% to higher education. Recent composite ACT scores in 18–19 range.

Educational level: 10.5% of Williamson County residents have 16 or more years of formal education; state average, 16.2%. Per capita expenditure for public education, $394; state average, $442.

Library: Marion Carnegie Library, 54,000 volumes.

Recreation: 6 public parks totaling 90 acres. Swimming pool, 5 tennis courts, 5 basketball courts/softball diamonds, batting cages. 3 public golf courses, 2 country clubs. Crab Orchard Lake and National Wildlife Refuge, 44,000 acres, abuts city on southwest corner, serves as winter home of 90,000 ducks, 100,000 Canada geese. Numerous other nearby lakes and state parks offer hunting, fishing, boating, camping, hiking. Shawnee National Forest spans nearly entire width of state below Marion, attracts 2 million visitors a year to varied outdoor pursuits, sightseeing in scenic Shawnee Hills. 4-screen cinema, roller-skating rink, bowling alley, Civic Center in town with road shows.

3 BR, 2 BA house: $75,000 to $80,000.

Cost of electricity: $.06 per kilowatt hour.

Cost of natural gas: $.41 per therm.

Sales tax: 6.25%.

State income tax: 3%.

Churches: 40. Denominations: Advent Christian, Apostolic, Assemblies of God, Baptist, General Baptist, Southern Baptist, Christian, Christian Science, Church of Christ, Church of God, Church of Jesus Christ of Latter-day Saints, Episcopal, Full Gospel, Interdenominational, Jehovah's Witnesses, Lutheran-Missouri Synod, Nazarene, Nondenominational, Pentecostal, Presbyterian, Roman Catholic, Seventh-Day Adventist, United Church of Christ.

When you live in tornado country, you figure the odds and assume survival. And what goes for natural disasters serves pretty well on a personal level. In the 1972 All-Star game, for example, when Pete Rose plowed into Marion's own Ray Fosse as the Indians' catcher tried to block home plate, Fosse was hit so hard it dislocated the rest of his season as a major leaguer. But the Marion folks were so proud of their native son they named a public park in his honor. "He's still working for Oakland as a broadcaster," says Fosse's old friend Dick Stotlar. "He was back home last Thanksgiving." Pete Rose also has spent time in Marion—as an inmate of the federal penitentiary just south of town.

What residents say . . .

Dorain Fletcher, director of planning and economic development: "I was with the Chamber of Commerce here for a year and they fired me, the only time that's ever happened! It's an old coal-mining area. The community is clannish and to a certain extent afraid of expansion unless 'we' have an interest in it. . . . I work directly for the mayor. I answer to the Council. . . . We have a very unusual mayor. He has completed six terms and been reelected by three-fourths majorities. When he was first elected the community was so far into debt the police had to pay cash at the service station. We are now one of only two communities in Illinois that does not levy a personal property tax. The mayor put the city in the black, where it remains. Basically he tightened the belt and cut corners. . . . The Illinois Centre, that's my pride and joy . . . 110 small stores, four anchor stores: Dillard's, Phar-Mor, Sears, Target . . . 3,000 new jobs. . . . It has not been our personality that has attracted all this. Hogwash! It's the [I-57] interstate, our location, and demographics. . . . The county has a very real nickname, 'Bloody Williamson.' Where we live, there's a woods behind us. According to the history, they took these strikebreakers out of the mine, walked them in there, stripped them, beat them, and finally shot them. . . . That was back in the 'twenties and 'thirties. . . . We have a very huge underground mine that opened here in 1983. They have about 1,400 employees. A nonunion mine. All of the management personnel are required to live in the City of Marion. . . . That's because the City of Harrisburg is such a strong coal-mine union town. . . . I'm retired military and married my childhood sweetheart. . . . My wife was the proverbial girl across the street although it took us 30 years to get together. . . . Her first husband had died. I just happened to see the obituary. I proposed and within five minutes she accepted. We were engaged once before. Sometimes you do get a second chance!"

Robert Butler, mayor: "You have to create a climate that is going to be conducive to business, but you also have to create the impression that you have created the climate. We try to expedite the processing of applications for permits. We try to telescope these things down. . . . We get on a fast track and push things through. We keep red tape to a minimum. . . . One of the things I undertook was to expand the corporate limits of the city. We had various businesses on the periphery. They were receiving city services but not contributing. We embarked on an aggressive annexation campaign. Today our corporate limits are twice as large as when I took office. . . . We found the 1 percent sales tax was doing quite well for the city and we could whittle away at the property tax. . . . I know it's contrary to the general principle of government that you spend all the money you get. We could have kept the property tax, under the time-honored guise of improving city services. . . . Right now we are heavily engaged in an effort to get a permit from the Corps of Engineers to build a 1,200-acre lake to supply the city's water needs. This has been very controversial, not in

Marion but from the plethora of do-gooders we have floating around. Environmentalists. Conservationists. Fish and wild-life people. They all have some objection to the lake, none of which we feel are justified. . . . For our size community I don't think you could beat the quality of life anywhere. One example . . . the Orpheum Theater built about 1920. By 1970, TV had pretty well wiped out the theater business. We bought it for $11,000. It cost $160,000 to renovate. People thought 'Butler has flipped his cart. He's nuts!' It has been a tremendous success. We've had Robert Merrill, Julie Harris, Ernest Borgnine. A year ago, Mickey Rooney and Donald O'Connor. Doc Severinsen has been here. The Southern Illinois Beauty Pageant is held there. . . . Mud-wrestling had the shortest career."

Laurel Toussant, nurse, Sierra Club member: "For a long time the city fathers and citizens have realized we need a new water source. Now the city wants to dam a free-flowing stream named Sugar Creek. It's 11 miles from the city. What makes Sugar Creek special is a series of riffle and pool complexes. It's real pretty, home to a couple of state threatened and endangered species. By the city's own estimates they could hook onto Rend Lake cheaper. But Mayor Butler and the head of the Rend Lake water district can't stand each other. . . . We have tried to say the lake is being built for lack of cooperation among communities. . . . We've had a lot of gorgeous canyons down here. Granted, they weren't the Colorado River. But they're gone . . . turned into lakes."

John Sanders, attorney: "Some people think the mayor is a little brash. He's abrasive, kind of like Daley and mayors of big-

211

ger cities. . . . I did my U. of I. paper on 'Bloody Williamson.' . . . Now it's almost a badge of honor. It distinguishes us from other communities."

Ron Emery, real-estate salesman, twice mayoral candidate: "I got annihilated, lost 7 to 1. . . . Marion, like most small towns, has its 5 to 10 percent that basically run the community. I fall in the other 95 percent. I was happy that I ran. The issues were the need for honesty and openness in government. Marion is two basic towns. Your working people just going about their lives, the other people who maintain and use the system for their own gain. . . . We're proud of being Southern Illinoisans. We have a history of being very antagonistic with one another . . . rivalries between cities that have gone on for generations. . . . But there is a push now, and I believe it's working, a trend toward trying to heal all those rivalries and work together. . . . Marion has so much potential. We could be a world-class small community. Good location, good schools, good parks. Highway systems all intersect here. We could just be a fantastic community." ■

Marshall, MN 56258

Location: 150 miles southwest of Minneapolis-St. Paul, 88 miles northeast of Sioux Falls, South Dakota, in southwestern Minnesota.

Population: 12,023 (1990).

Growth rate: 9% since 1986.

Per capita income: $9,818 (1985), 74% of state average ($13,212).

Geography/climate: Flat to gently rolling terrain. Demanding weather, with winter and summer extremes. January average low temperatures several degrees below zero. Seasonal snowfall, 35 inches. Without snow cover, frost penetrates 3 to 4 feet. Short but pleasant spring arrives mid-April. Torrid midsummers, with 19 days into the 90s. Frequent thunderstorms, occasional tornadoes. Lovely falls. Average rainfall, 25 inches. Windy.

Economic base: Food processing, agriculture (corn, soybeans), industry. Large payrolls: Schwan's Sales Enterprises, ice cream and other foods, 850 employees; Southwest State University, 360; Heartland Food Company, turkeys, 350; Weiner Memorial Medical Center, 350; Marshall Public Schools, 246; HyVee Foods, 220; BH Electronics, 150; Schott Corporation, transformers, 134; Minnesota Corn Processors, ethanol, corn syrup, starch, 125. Marshall is seat of Lyon County.

Newspaper: *Marshall Independent*, 508 W. Main Street, Marshall, MN 56258. 507-537-1551. Daily, Monday through Saturday. Jim Tate, editor. $55.20 a year.

TV, radio: 2 FM, 1 AM station. Cable carries TV networks from Twin Cities, Mankato, and Sioux Falls. Cable also carries NPR from Worthington, Minnesota; Brookings, South Dakota.

Health care: Weiner Memorial Medical Center, 62 beds, plus 76-bed nursing home. 40 physicians, 11 dentists in local practice.

Schools: 3 elementary (K–6); 1 junior high (7–8). Marshall High School enrolls 750, sends 60% to college. ACT composite score consistently ranks above state, and state is consistently above national, the school reports. 3 parochial schools (K–8): Holy Redeemer (Roman Catholic), Marshall Area Christian School, Samuel Lutheran School. Southwest State University enrolls about 3,000 students in 2-year and 4-year programs.

Educational level: 12.4% of Lyon County residents have 16 or more years of formal education; state average, 17.4%. $493 per capita expenditure for public education; state average, $554.

Library: Marshall Lyon County Library, 156,000 volumes. Library-card holders may also use Southwest State University Library, 150,000 volumes and 700 periodicals.

Recreation: 5 city parks, 16 tennis courts, swimming pool, band shell. Soccer, baseball, softball, basketball, volleyball fields. Legion Field Stadium voted "Municipal Field of the Year." Indoor and outdoor ice rinks. Camden State Park, 10 miles southwest, a 1,500-acre river valley with forests, spring-fed lake, campgrounds, naturalist programs. Boating, fishing at Lake Shetek State Park, 33 miles southeast. 3-screen movie theater, bowling alley in town.

3 BR, 2 BA house: $58,000 to $62,000.

Cost of electricity: $.04 per kilowatt hour.

Cost of natural gas: $.50 per therm.

Sales tax: 6.5% (does not apply to food or clothing).

State income tax: 5% to 8.5%.

Churches: 18. Denominations: Assemblies of God, Baptist, Church of Christ, Church of Jesus Christ of Latter-day Saints, Episcopal, Evangelical Free, Evangelical Lutheran-Wisconsin Synod, Grace Life, Lutheran-ELCA, Lutheran-Missouri Synod, Lutheran, Roman Catholic, Thresholds of Faith, Albright United Methodist, Wesley United Methodist, United Presbyterian.

Chicago may have the reputation as the Windy City, but Marshall, Minnesota, has Wind—a certifiable year-round average of 16.5 miles per hour of wind on Buffalo Ridge, just out of town. Chicago has a wimpy 10.4 mph by comparison. Wind permeates Marshall culture. The Community Theater is named Four Winds. Parents know, as one said, "when winter comes, you listen to school closings. If any district is closed, it ends up being ours because of the wind."

Dan Juhl, a rural Minnesota native but newcomer in town, has big plans for the Marshall wind. He's cultivating a wind farm up on Buffalo Ridge, planting rows of utility-grade wind turbines, a colony of fantastic pinwheels on this highest point in Minnesota. If Juhl's calculations are correct, Marshall may soon be exporting electric power—besides corn syrup, Schwan's ice cream, and Ed Evans paintings.

What residents say . . .

Ed Evans, artist, professor of art at Southwest State University: "I just got back from Paris, where I have an exhibition at the Gallery Efte. . . . One-person shows in Brussels, Cannes, Lucerne, Tokyo. . . . One thing just kind of leads to another. . . . Living in a small town, it seems all the more exciting when I do visit the cities. . . . My home is St. Cloud. I've been here since 1969. I'd never been to this town before. There's a brightness of light and a feeling of space. I was amazed how big the sky is here, probably more like South Dakota than Minnesota. . . . Friends trying to fig- ure out why I live here, after coming here they know why. It's a very good place for an artist to work. An artist friend in New York says it's so difficult there, so much energy it just seeps under the doors. Here it's kind of quiet and doesn't take much to be motivated to work."

Margaret Bosshardt, director, Marshall Lyon County Library: "Out of our building we circulated nearly 200,000 items last year. Including the bookmobile, almost 300,000. . . . I think we're one of the busiest libraries of our size in Minnesota. . . . It may be because we're a state university town. I just think we provide the materials people want. We have a very helpful and willing staff, which attracts people. There has been some frustration because we have not passed two bond issues to improve schools, and I think that has increased some of our usage. Also, Marshall is a regional shopping center, so we attract people that way. I worked this morning. We had people in from Wabasso, about 30 miles, and from Hendricks, about 45 miles."

Vi Mayer, executive vice president, Chamber of Commerce: "We're in the middle of nowhere. Small towns in some areas are six, seven, eight miles away. Out here they're 20 to 30 miles. . . . Schwan kind of owns the town. This is where they make the ice cream that goes throughout the nation. . . . But it's also corporate headquarters. You have those people who are the movers and shakers of the company. . . . What you end up with is a good base, a good employer . . . in the 900 range. They're a private concern and don't like to give out their exact numbers."

John Feda, mayor: "We have lots of people with two incomes, and retired people. For them it is no problem to buy $75,000 to $125,000 houses. We also have people working in manufacturing at six dollars an hour. Both husband and wife working, that's $25,000. They have a tough time finding affordable housing."

Jane Christiansen, musician, teacher: "We have lived here 10 years. My husband grew up 10 miles away. I grew up in a small town in Iowa. He is an attorney. I am first a mother and homemaker. Now I have several part-time jobs. I'm minister of music at the Lutheran Church, adjunct faculty at Southwest University teaching voice, and also doing some substitute teaching in the

public schools. . . . We just had weekend visitors who live in Washington. He works for Dan Quayle. They were commenting it was noticeable to them that children have a much greater sense of self-identity because the family is stronger, church influence is stronger. Even ethnic backgrounds . . . Norwegian, Belgian, Irish. . . . Your heritage, it's talked about here. . . . Twenty-five years ago it made a big difference where you went to church. If you were Catholic you didn't go to a Protestant attorney. It influenced the people you dated, even your friends in school, and it was very much discussed. Now, it isn't an issue anywhere. Society has changed. . . . Church organizations as a whole have made an effort. We now have a citywide ecumenical service at Thanksgiving. We have it in the large Catholic church."

Rick Jueneman, anesthetist, former member of school board: "We have just changed to a split elementary system. In one building we'll have grades one and two. In another, grades three and four. In another, grades five and six. It's a new concept for Marshall. We feel we can make better use of our facilities, balancing out classroom size. . . . Actually, this will be our first year of it. We had a school-bond referendum fail. Because of that it was either a matter of doing this or cutting the budget. It will mean busing. . . . I have always been involved in some kind of community service. Having children in school, this just seemed a nice place to go to. I served one three-year term. I enjoyed it but we went through a real period of turmoil in our town. We had to make a lot of adjustments in budgets. I felt my kids took some abuse for decisions made by their father. In that aspect, I don't miss being on the board. . . . I think anybody owes a community some service." ▪

Martinsburg, WV 25401

Location: 79 miles northwest of Washington, DC, 85 miles west of Baltimore, 190 miles southwest of Philadelphia, in the Eastern Panhandle of West Virginia.

Population: 14,073 (1990).

Growth rate: 7% since 1980.

Per capita income: $8,783 (1985), 7% above state average ($8,141).

Geography/climate: 457 feet elevation. Hilly, forested terrain in county. Warm, humid summers; tolerably cold winters; long and pleasant springs and falls. Average temperatures: January: high, 41; low, 24. July: high, 87; low, 62. Average rainfall, 39 inches; snowfall, 26 inches.

Economic base: Manufacturing and tourism, blending with health care, electronics, services, retail trade. Martinsburg is seat of Berkeley County. Large payrolls: Veterans Administration Hospital, 1,239 employees; Berkeley County Schools, 1,213; Corning, glassware, 728; City Hospital, 680; General Motors, parts distribution, 674; Internal Revenue Service National Computer Center, 650; Knouse Foods, 350; Arcata Graphics, printing, 350; West Virginia Air National Guard, 270; *The Journal*, newspaper, 235; AT&T, consumer products, 216; Capitol Cement, 215; Handy & Harman, control cables, 194; Aker Plastics, shower stalls, spas, tubs, 175.

Newspaper: *The Journal*, 207 W. King Street, Martinsburg, WV 25401. 304-263-8931. Daily. Page Burdette, editor. $82.20 a year.

TV, radio: 1 FM, 2 AM stations. Local TV station. Cable carries PBS, network TV from Washington, Baltimore. NPR station in town.

Health care: City Hospital, 260 beds. 70 physicians, 16 dentists in local practice.

Schools: 5 elementary (K–5); 2 middle (6–8). Martinsburg High School enrolls 1,100 students, sends 48% to post-secondary training. Composite ACT score, 19.4. Other schools: Vocational–Technical Center; St. Joseph's Catholic School (K–8); Martinsburg Christian Academy (pre-K–12); Rocky Noll Seventh-Day Adventist Elementary; Faith Christian Academy (pre-K–10).

Educational level: 10.6% of Berkeley County residents have 16 or more years of formal education; state average, 10.4%. Per capita expenditure for public education, $459; state average, $454.

Library: Martinsburg–Berkeley County Public Library, 115,000 volumes.

Recreation: 3 city parks equipped with 2 pools, water slide, tennis courts, playgrounds, picnic areas, miniature golf, volleyball courts. 1 private, 3 daily-fee golf courses. 2 bowling alleys, 7-screen cinema. Concert series, chamber orchestra. 5 country clubs in area.

3 BR, 2 BA house: Wide choice, ranging from $70,000 to $150,000. Median price, 1991, $107,050.

Cost of electricity: $.06 per kilowatt hour.

Cost of natural gas: $.53 per therm.

Sales tax: 6%.

State income tax: 3% to 6.5%.

Churches: 42. Denominations: Assemblies of God, Baptist (8), Bible, Christian, Church of Christ, Church of Jesus Christ of Latter-day Saints, Church of the Brethren, Community, Episcopal, Jehovah's Witnesses, Lutheran, Nazarene, Presbyterian, Reformed, Roman Catholic, Salvation Army, Seventh-Day Adventist, United Methodist (6).

Imagine a plumpish bird taking flight, flying to the right. The outline approximates the shape of West Virginia, and the beak is composed of three counties, including Berkeley, whose seat is Martinsburg. Residents of the area use this simile to describe not only location but prospects. Martinsburg feels the gravitational pull of Washington, DC, Baltimore, and the Northeast. With some pleasure, Martinsburgers point out that they are closer to the state capitals of Virginia, Maryland, Pennsylvania, New Jersey, and Delaware, than to their own, Charleston, which might as well be in another solar system.

What residents say . . .

Tony Senecal, mayor: "We are geographically situated so that people are going to develop here in spite of anything we do rather than because of anything we do. We're going to run into all the small-town problems, gridlock traffic and the need for storm sewers, all the things that sleepy little towns have to address. Unfortunately, the state does not allow us at this point to charge any impact fees or tax our own citizens. There is a county tax, but a very small portion comes to the town. We pay most of our bills through fees, fines, and a business and operations tax, based on the gross . . . you can lose $100,000 in this town and still owe us money! Also because of our location we have had a drug problem. We are just outside the Washington–Baltimore corridor. . . . At one time we were listed with Miami, Boston, Chicago, San Francisco. . . . We have addressed the problem. For a small town, you're looking at a police force that by the end of June '92 will be 39 members. . . . We have some bums on the street, like everybody has. At one time I wanted them to buy a license to do business on the streets of Martinsburg. The media got ahold of it and I became a national hero and a local crackpot at the same time. The vote was six to four against. . . . Martinsburg now has its own TV station. One of the newscasters wanted my reaction to the vote but it was scheduled to come up too late for his show. I said, 'Come into my office and we'll film it both ways!' . . . We're going kicking and screaming into the 21st century."

Jay Sam Meek, superintendent, Berkeley County Public Schools: "We grew by 240 students this past school year. That's a little frightening given that growth occurred during a period of economic slowdown. I think this school system is poised for major growth in the very near future. We're trying to plan for that growth. . . . Martinsburg High School is presently undergoing a $7.7 million renovation and expansion. The building dates to 1926. It sits on about 40 acres sort of in the middle of town. It was my feeling, after working with members of the community, that they would rather keep the character of the existing facility. . . . That campus also houses a middle school. . . . We're trying to make Martinsburg a flagship operation, bringing the school up to date and including all the modern technology . . . completely wired for computers, a new library that, I think, will be a focal point for the school . . . designed with natural lighting, all new lavatories . . . outfitted with foreign-language labs. . . . The old school had a huge smokestack. That smokestack will stay . . . serve as a walk-through art gallery. . . . In fact, it is not a bond issue but funding from the state . . . not repayable. We received the grant primarily because a group of individuals took the initiative to propose this renovation . . . in a highly competitive process. This is the first time state moneys have been used to renovate rather than build new. . . . I think one of the real strengths of the region is the tri-county vocational center. There is good linkage between the center and the business community. We're frequently asked to train their employees. Arcata Graphics, maybe one of the largest printing companies in the U.S., recently moved to Berkeley County and asked the school system to become involved. We also have trained employees of the IRS National Computer Center. I've only been here four years. One of the things that makes this community distinctive is the posi-

tive interaction . . . the school–business connection is second to none."

Rick Wachtel, owner, radio station WRNR; member of City Council; board member, Eastern West Virginia Regional Airport: "News is our biggest forte. We've been named the top small-market news and sports station in West Virginia by the AP in 1989 and 1990. And our competition, they do a good job in news and sports, also. . . . I have very little turnover. People like living here. Most all of my employees are local people who started with us on a part-time basis and have become full-time. . . . We're on the main line of the CSX railroad. We've had rail-commuter operations going on for decades. I heard a figure, nearly 8,000 people commuting daily out of Berkeley and Jefferson counties. I think that's the primary reason we're growing. Secondarily, a lot of really good, blue-chip industries located here because geographically it's a place they wanted to be. We can reach a market of 80 million people overnight by surface transportation. . . . We're not suffering from overcrowding yet. Taxes on the whole are dramatically less than in Virginia or Maryland. A home here in Berkeley County requires about 25 percent of the property taxes of a similar home there. . . . This is my 20th year on the City Council. . . . We have our law-enforcement difficulties. We do have problems with kids, primarily minority kids who hang out in certain areas of town. . . . We're probably one of the very few small towns with an economic development fund in excess of $1 million. . . . Our airport is the largest in the state, in terms of land mass, larger than National Airport. . . . In terms of pure physical facilities, extremely modern. No regularly scheduled commercial air service at this time. Operations are going up 11 to 12 percent each year. The airport authority has one 240-acre parcel, with the goal of developing a state-of-the-art industrial park. The biggest problem we have is funding. . . . Air Force One and Two do all their proficiency here, touch and go. Literally, this airport can handle almost any aircraft in the world and has, except the Concorde. The airport is going to be a major factor in this area." ■

McPherson, KS 67460

Location: 55 miles northwest of Wichita at intersection of I-135 and U.S. 56. 230 miles southwest of Kansas City, 450 miles east of Denver.

Population: 12,422 (1990).

Growth rate: 5% since 1980.

Per capita income: $10,681 (1985), virtually the same as state average ($10,684).

Geography/climate: Flatlands of the Great Plains, relieved by a few gentle slopes. 4 seasons, with summer the most intense. Typically more than 60 days over 90 degrees. Annual rainfall, 31 inches. Annual snowfall, 16 inches. Temperatures will dip below freezing 114 days, below 0 two days, on average.

Economic base: 50 manufacturing plants include 10 Fortune 500 companies. Large payrolls: National Cooperative Refinery Association, oil and gas refinery, 469 employees; Sterling Drug, pharmaceuticals, 387; Manville Sales Corp., fiberglass insulation, 363; CertainTeed Corp., plastic pipe, windows, siding, 256; Farmers Alliance, insurance, 226; Farmland Industries, agricultural supplies, 161. Central College, 2-year institution affiliated with the Free Methodist Church, enrolls 248; McPherson College, 4-year, Church of the Brethren affiliate, enrolls 462.

Newspapers: *McPherson Daily Sentinel*, 301 S. Main Street, McPherson, KS 67460. 316-241-2422. Tom Throne, editor. Evenings except Sundays. $55.50 a year.

TV, radio: Cable system brings in PBS, networks from Wichita. NPR also from Wichita.

Health care: Memorial Hospital, 70 beds. 17 physicians and 8 dentists in local practice.

Schools: 3 elementary (K–5); 1 middle (6–8). High school enrolls about 670 students with average class size of 14. Composite ACT score at McPherson High School (1989-90), 22.8. 40% of graduates go to 4-year colleges, 15% to 2-year institutions.

Educational level: 15.6% of McPherson County residents have 16 or more years of formal education; state, 17%. Per capita expenditure for public education, $491; state average, $459.

Library: McPherson Public Library has about 50,000 volumes and 8,000 card holders. Librarian, a recent import from Denver, says downtown location across the street from historic courthouse helps keep library busy.

Recreation: 2 city parks with ball fields, pool, tennis courts, trails. YMCA has basketball, racquetball courts, whirlpool, weight room, swimming pool. Bowling alley, miniature golf, 18-hole golf course, 3-screen movie theater in town. Maxwell Game Preserve, 15 miles northeast. From November to March, only sport that counts is high school basketball.

3 BR, 2 BA house: Advertised from $40,000 to $80,000.

Cost of electricity: $.0445 per kilowatt hour.

Cost of natural gas: $.35 per therm.

Sales tax: 4.25%.

State income tax: 3.65% to 8.75%; higher rates apply to taxpayers deducting federal income tax.

Churches: Denominations: Baptist, Bible, Brethren, Christian, Christian Science, Congregational, Covenant, Episcopal, Free Methodist, Jehovah's Witnesses, Lutheran, Mennonite, Methodist, Nazarene, Presbyterian, Pentecostal, Roman Catholic, Seventh-Day Adventist.

The *Pher* in McPherson is pronounced "fur," not "fear." Officially speaking, there is no fear in this Kansas town, certainly no fear of larger places or big ideas. McPherson was barely on the map in 1872, when town fathers made a bid to become the state capital. They laid out a 160-acre "Capitol Hill" and spent $300 on an elaborate reception for state representatives. But Topeka was selected and McPherson went on to other things.

The largest celebration ever held was the dedication, on July 4, 1917, of a bronze likeness of General James Birdseye McPherson, for whom the town was named. Having fallen in the Battle of Atlanta, in 1864, the General was unable to attend, but he probably would have been impressed by the pageant, performed by a cast of 1,200 for a crowd of 40,000.

McPherson has a good sense of timing. It struck oil in the late 1920s, just in time to keep the local economy out of the Depression. After World War II, as farm consolidation began to create a surplus of farmers, McPherson had the foresight to develop an industrial base, well before many other towns caught the drift.

Today, in a bid to promote tourism, McPherson is developing its Scottish heritage. Never mind that the Scottish population is virtually nonexistent. The town already has a very respectable bagpipe band. Created originally for the high school production of "Brigadoon," the band of pipes and drums now appears in parades and pageants throughout the region, bringing a bit of the Scottish Highlands to the plains of Kansas.

What residents say ...

Xan Williams, member of the board, McPherson Scottish Society: "A small town north of us bloomed in the tourist business by taking advantage of its Swedish population. We thought, if people get off the interstate to go 15 miles north, they might come to McPherson if we have a gimmick. We are the only McPherson in the United States and we also have a very fine bagpipe band. . . . The first step was to form a society of possible Scots and others. . . . I am of German heritage and have lived in McPherson only seven years. . . . It's going very well. We've had several events. On the first weekend in May we'll be having a 'Scottish Sampler.' . . . We'll host our third annual School of Piping where we have an out-of-town instructor and solicit students from Chicago west. At the same time we'll have the Council of Clan McPherson to see if they can bring their clan gathering to McPherson in the near future. We have a store here selling Scottish goods ... and a sign out on the highway, 'Scottish Gifts.' "

Michael R. Henson, basketball coach, McPherson High School: "My older son, Steve, plays for the Milwaukee Bucks, a rookie this year.... He's getting some playing time.... He led the nation in free-throw shooting his sophomore year at Kansas State. The name Steve in Kansas means Steve Henson, the small-town boy who made good.... As you are aware, the two big schools are Kansas State and KU. Not a lot of kids from small towns get to play. My younger son, Brian, a senior, will go to Kansas State, in Manhattan. He's a guard. We're 20 and 1 so far this year. We were 24 and 0 last year and won the state championship. Year before, 21 and 3. This is our fourth trip in a row. Basketball has a long history in McPherson. It goes back to the old Olympics when AAU teams filled the rosters. We were represented by two teams sponsored by Globe Refiners, and they won. That sort of started the tradition of basketball here in McPherson. We get a lot of kids who are second- and third-generation players. It's the social happening here on Friday night."

Don Steffes, president, Bank IV: "I came here as manager of the Chamber of Commerce in 1960 and was with the Chamber until 1965 when I left for a couple of years.... One of the local bankers had liked what I was doing, and since he had no son as successor hired me to become

president of the dominant bank. It was an independent bank for 113 years, just sold last year.... Oil figured in the prosperity of McPherson in the late '20s and early '30s. We got oil when everybody else was going through hard times.... Our location is just superb, about an hour out of Wichita. If you're closer than that you're involved in all of their metropolitan problems. We are an hour's drive to the Wichita airport.... Executives just won't really drive much more than an hour to visit their branch plants. You've got to be close enough for the women to shop, close enough to the amenities.... We've had an excellent labor situation ... the agricultural Mennonite labor base with a very good work ethic. We were in a real good agricultural region but the technology was changing so fast we had to find jobs for these people being crowded off the farms. So we had the ready-made, technically able labor force.... We happen to own our own electric utility, the second largest public utility in Kansas. It's very profitable and superbly run. We provide electricity at a rate almost comparable to the Pacific Northwest. We get all the profits and it contributes to our municipal income base."

Jeannette Hess, freelance writer: "I've been doing some writing for the newspaper. I do our church newsletter. It keeps me into my word processor.... There are two ethnic groups. In the north part of the county, Swedes, mostly Lutherans. Kind of a dividing line at McPherson. South you have mostly German, Mennonite German extraction. They came here for religious freedom, and they brought with them hard red winter wheat, which is the mainstay of the agricultural economy. We're a nice mixture here in McPherson.... Every year in

May we have what's called All Schools Day. The schools are let out to recognize the eighth grade and high school graduates. The bagpipers are always in the parade, just a neat touch for McPherson."

Robert Wise, partner, Bremyer & Wise:
"We have a very general practice dealing with all the legal problems in small communities. There are eight of us lawyers here. Just as an incidental thing and to illustrate the opportunities people have in small communities, I'm presently serving as president of the Kansas State Bar Association. In that capacity I went to Moscow last year for a meeting in the Kremlin. Even though you're in a small town you can still go out in the world. . . . We're very proud of our industry. That came about because of the vision of farsighted people . . . more than three decades ago, long before most rural communities realized the tremendous need to diversify from the agricultural economy to manufacturing. I think our community was a decade ahead of most of its peers in recognizing that. But in addition, and I was not one of them so I can speak very objectively, we were able to pull together all the elements of the community and commit whatever resources were necessary to make appropriate concessions. And it may have been a unique time in the history of our town to be able to do that. . . . As we become special and enjoy a lot of success, perhaps we lose a sense of the need to sacrifice for growth." ∎

Middlebury, VT 05753

Location: 34 miles south of Burlington, 35 miles north of Rutland, 200 miles west of Boston, 265 miles north of New York City, in west central Vermont.

Population: 8,034 (1990).

Growth rate: 6% since 1980.

Per capita income: $8,762 (1985), 91% of state average ($9,619).

Geography/climate: Scenic New England village, elevation 366 feet, in the Champlain Valley, backed up to the east by Green Mountain peaks rising 3,000 to 4,000 feet. Typical northern New England weather—cold, sometimes intensely cold winters; pleasant summers; cool, colorful falls. Average temperatures: January: 18 degrees, with range of 8 to 26. July: 70, with range of 60 to 80. 5 or so 90-degree days during summer; average 28 days below zero through 5-month winter season. Average rainfall, 33 inches; snowfall, up to 80 inches.

Economic base: Agriculture, tourism, retirement living, retail, Middlebury College. Area is major producer of dairy products, apples. Nonretail companies with more than 25 employees: Breadloaf Construction, commercial builders; J. P. Carrara, cement products; C.P.C. of Vermont, molded plastic products; Kraft, Swiss cheese; Middlebury College, 900 employees; Porter Medical Center; Standard Register, business forms. Middlebury is the shire town, or seat, of Addison County.

Newspaper: *Addison County Independent,* Four Maple Street, Middlebury, VT 05753.

802-388-4944. Monday, Thursday. Angelo Lynn, editor and publisher. $21 a year.

TV, radio: Local FM station. Cable carries network TV from Burlington, Plattsburgh; Vermont PBS. NPR from Burlington, Rutland.

Health care: Porter Medical Center, 50 beds.

Schools: 1 elementary (K–5); 1 junior high (6–8). Middlebury Union High School enrolls 620, sends 50%–60% of graduates to 2- or 4-year colleges. SAT scores not made public—guidance staff report they are above state and national averages. Addison County Vocational Center, Community College also located in town. 3 private elementary–secondary schools. Middlebury College, regarded as one of the best small liberal-arts colleges in the nation, enrolls 2,000. Summer language school attracts 1,300. Middlebury's Bread Loaf campus, located in the Green Mountains, is home to the country's oldest and most famous writers' workshop. Town's public high school students are permitted to audit college courses at Middlebury, for high school credit.

Educational level: 20.5% of Addison County residents have 16 or more years of formal education; state average, 19%. Per capita expenditure for public education, $414; state average, $468.

Library: Ilsley Public Library, 35,000 volumes.

Recreation: 4 city parks, recreational department, swimming pool, hockey rink. Groomed cross-country trails, golf course at

Middlebury College available for public use. Camping, fishing, boating at state parks on Lake Champlain, Lake Dunmore. Several downhill-ski centers within hour's drive, including Sugarbush Valley. Numerous museums, historic sites, covered bridges. Sheldon Museum, State Craft Center, U. of Vermont Morgan Horse Farm, Vermont Folklife Center all in town.

3 BR, 2 BA house: $100,000 to $150,000.

Cost of electricity: $.07 per kilowatt hour.

Cost of propane: $1.18 a gallon.

Sales tax: 5%.

State income tax: 2.5% of modified federal income tax liability.

Churches: 14. Denominations: Baptist, Bible, Christian Assembly, Christian Science, Church of Jesus Christ of Latter-day Saints, Congregational, Episcopal, Islamic, Jehovah's Witnesses, Mennonite, Methodist, Nondenominational, Roman Catholic, Unitarian Universalist.

For solid commercial reasons, Middlebury residents sometimes describe their place as "the land of milk and honey." It is, after all, a big producer of dairy products and fruit. Add to that the scenic, cultural, and recreational riches of the area and you have the makings of a very attractive small town. Preserving the diversity and interesting complexity of Middlebury is an engaging topic. A tourist guide says: "Unlike other New England college towns that have sacrificed their roots to become postcards of themselves, Middlebury is as real as it is picturesque. Yet things do change. . . ."

What residents say . . .

Sally Reed, director, Ilsley Public Library: "I would say Middlebury is a place with two faces. There is a good deal of wealth in the area. On the other hand, the native population which is dependent primarily on agriculture is certainly not a wealthy population at all. Then, there is the very liberal and progressive side of Middlebury brought by people who come from away. That goes in contrast to the very conservative outlook of the native population and the farming community. And then, finally, a very high level of education. . . . I think the progressive, well educated Middlebury is the Middlebury people see at

first glance. . . . I have mixed feelings about it. People who have come primarily from away have the power and are able to articulate things well. I have seen the last vestiges of the old guard die and be replaced by these people who are making up a new power base [and] I have to agree with many of their values. But on the other hand, I think there is something lost . . . in the governance by the old guard . . . taking care of each other, taking care of yourself, sort of pulling-yourself-up-by-the-bootstraps philosophy, a desire to keep Middlebury the same as it always was, the desire for independent rights, property rights, for example. We are undergoing a lot of zoning changes and community-planning kinds of things. For the social good, quote–unquote, people are told what they can or cannot do with their property. In one significant way that has hurt the agricultural community. Their wealth is in their land, and their land is continually devalued. They have to use it as agricultural land. They cannot use it as revenue-generating, as they might have 100 years ago. . . . Some of those changes are occasioned by a desire to treat our environment well. . . . Here's a real interesting thing: Our public schools are union schools. All the surrounding towns pay for them, and therefore share in the governance. What has happened over the past couple of years, the surrounding community are the conservative, agricultural, nonwealthy, and since they have an equal vote in the schools, they have continued to campaign against adequate financing of the schools. Two years ago the high school budget went down four times, in Middlebury, of all places!"

Betty Wheeler, town manager: "We have a diverse community, with residential, commercial, agricultural, the college. We've got a good mix . . . we're concerned we will become a very affluent community and not have the mix of population. . . . Housing, that's something the town has been working on for a couple of years. We've been relatively successful at developing affordable housing. We just completed a 64-unit elderly housing project this last year, and a 32-unit affordable rental. . . . It takes innovative, private–public partnerships to make those things come off. . . . We have a concern with losing the less affluent members of our community."

Jim Ross, interim manager, Addison County Economic Development Corporation: "I'm a native Vermonter, went to Middlebury, graduated there, got my master's from Syracuse, served as an ensign and lieutenant j.g. in the Navy during the Korean War, came back and worked at Middlebury College for 35 years. I was business manager, meaning I did a little of everything. . . . The gal who ran our economic-development office took another position and I'm filling in while we interview. . . . Our main emphasis is trying to keep the industry we have. Surprisingly enough, a few of the smaller ones are expanding, which is very encouraging. The Marble Works, which was actually an old marble works, has been completely restored as shops, light industry, mostly retail. It has been a struggle trying to keep it filled, but it looks like it's turning around . . . just taken on three or four new tenants. . . . I think things are in pretty good shape. . . . They've asked industries why they are in and stay in Middlebury. Almost unanimously, it's because of the living conditions and the atmosphere. The main thing we sell is the atmosphere."

Angelo Lynn, editor and publisher, Addison County Independent: "With the decline of state and federal aid, a tremendous burden was placed upon the property-tax base. . . . What happened in Vermont in the mid-'70s to early '80s, home values rose tremendously. We had this New England boom. People came up to buy second homes. That drove the price of housing out of sight. You end up with elderly people who bought a home for $20,000 now worth $150,000, paying $4,000 to $5,000 in property taxes, and they can't afford it. . . . The other thing . . . Middlebury is the quintessential New England town, with the white steeple church at the end of the street, a very beautiful New England village. So you want to work hard to keep downtown vital, to keep the growth from going out to the highway. The town has renewed that struggle in the last five or six years. It was picked up again last fall with a town meeting that drew 150 to 200 people at an all-day seminar, to focus on the future of downtown, to hold the various units to-gether . . . Middlebury still has a chance. It doesn't have the strip development, at least not so bad it has ruined downtown. . . . Building the area's largest grocery store downtown doesn't sound all that exciting but does draw folks downtown . . . gives you a chance to walk around what was established as the village center 200 years ago. That's the charm of Middlebury, but you have to work very hard to keep it." ■

Monroe, WI 53566

Location: South central Wisconsin, 9 miles north of the Illinois state line. 35 miles south of Madison, 108 miles southwest of Milwaukee, 139 miles northwest of Chicago.

Population: 10,251 (1990).

Growth rate: 2% since 1980.

Per capita income: $12,135 (1985), 18% higher than state average ($10,298).

Geography/climate: Dairy-farm country with a gentle contour, punctuated by some hilly, rugged landscape. Continental climate, 4 distinct seasons. Typically long, hard winters with January average low of 8 degrees. Annual snowfall, 39 inches; rainfall, 34 inches, mostly between May and September. Thunderstorms on 45 days average. Pleasant spring and summer leading to colorful fall. Average 12 days over 90.

Economic base: Health care, cheese-making, diversified manufacturing. Swiss Colony, the mail-order food gift company, employs 350 year-round and five times as many during holiday rush. St. Clare Hospital, Monroe Clinic, Medical Center of Monroe employ 800. Other large payrolls: Advance Transformer, 600; Monroe School District, 350; Moore Business Forms and Dorman-Roth Foods, each 250.

Newspaper: *The Monroe Evening Times*, 1065 Fourth Avenue West, Monroe, WI 53566, 608-328-4202. Daily except Sunday. Judy Hyde, editor. $64 a year.

TV, radio: Local AM, FM stations. Madison, Rockford, Milwaukee, Chicago TV stations, including PBS, by cable. NPR from Madison.

Health care: St. Clare Hospital, operated by Sisters of St. Agnes, a Catholic order, 221 beds. 2 nursing homes with 337 beds, 2 clinics. 89 physicians, 13 dentists in local practice.

Schools: 3 elementary (K–6); 1 junior high (7–8); 1 senior high enrolling 800. Composite ACT score at Monroe Senior High School, 19.9. 45% of graduates go to 4-year college, 16%–18% to 2-year institutions.

Educational level: 10.9% of Green County residents have 16 or more years of formal education; state average, 14.8%. Per capita expenditure for public education, $486; state average, $476.

Library: Ludlow Memorial Library, 52,000 volumes, 147,000 annual circulation. Linked by computer to 12 other nearby libraries and U. of Wisconsin library at Madison.

Recreation: 5 city parks. Largest, Twining Park, covers 45 acres, includes band shell, various ball courts, fitness course, cross-country trails, hockey rink. Recreation Park has pool big enough for 974 people to swim at same time. Snowmobile trails start at town's edge. Annual hot-air balloon rally. 23-mile bike trail, 2 rivers suitable for canoeing, 3 state parks all within 25-minute drive.

3 BR, 2 BA house: $60,000 to $80,000. New houses, up to $130,000.

Cost of electricity: $.06 per kilowatt hour.

Cost of natural gas: $.54 per therm.

Sales tax: 5%.

State income tax: Graduated 3.4% to 7.9%.

Churches: 17. Denominations: Assemblies of God, Baptist, Church of Christ, Christian, Christian Scientist, Episcopal, Evangelical Free, Jehovah's Witnesses, Lutheran, Nazarene, Methodist, Presbyterian, Roman Catholic, United Church of Christ.

Say "Cheese!" and you've said much about Monroe. This is the Swiss cheese capital of the nation and the only place in America where limburger is produced. A German-style beer is made here, too. And if the local brew doesn't keep you fit, Monroe's clinics perhaps can help. This small Wisconsin town is reputed to be the largest health-care center between Chicago and the Mayo Clinics. It has an uncommonly large professional community.

Monroe Clinic, located just off the Square, draws its share of traffic into the center of Monroe and gets a lot of credit for keeping the old business district financially healthy. Green County Courthouse, a formidable brick and granite structure, is the focal point—and a symbol of the volunteer spirit common in many small towns. A few years ago, when the spire on the courthouse steeple fell apart from old age and there wasn't any public money to fix it, a local service club raised $50,000 to do the job.

Monroe's wish list includes a new library three times the size of the old Ludlow Memorial, and more classroom space to serve a growing school population.

What residents say . . .

Chuck Wellington, attorney: "My wife and I came up here 10 years ago with a six-month-old child. She's from Rochester, New York. I'm from Chicago. It's an exciting place to practice law . . . because it's a very people-oriented practice. We're an agricultural community and that tends to make the practice somewhat practical. Our emotions rise and fall with the agricultural community. That brings home the meaning of what you do. . . . A few years ago we brought a YMCA to town, built it from scratch. There have been very few YMCAs built in small towns over the last 10 years and made it. . . . We've got to preserve what we have here. That's an attitude hard to find these days. If there isn't involvement and caring, that attitude begins to disappear."

Chris Wellington, administrator, Blackhawk Technical College: "Chuck and I are both from big cities. We chose Monroe for the quality of life and the opportunity to raise a family in a small town. Chuck walks to work. I go a little further, a five-minute drive! . . . I think the process of improving a community means improving education.

You can never stand still, you've always got to be moving forward. In any small town, the tax base is a major concern. It's expensive to provide excellent education. . . . Monroe is very conservative though not to the point of not wanting to deal with reality. . . . There's a really strong work ethic. People work hard, save a lot of their money, not a lot of conspicuous consumption. We both grew up in fairly affluent homes in other states. Monroe is not a really showy, flashy community."

Ruth Barth, retired newspaper reporter: "We have a rather agreeable mix of professional services in an agricultural community and several fairly stable industries. . . . Back in the late 1930s, a couple of local physicians decided to form a clinic in Monroe. That was when clinics were not all that well established. After the war they got serious and expanded the clinic to as many as 45 doctors . . . serviced about a 75-mile area, basically because the cities hadn't expanded their hospitals. We're feeling the competition from the larger hospitals. . . . Right now we're sort of stagnating. We had our first slow growth in several decades. There was quite a burst of business development in the early '60s. We had labor, women basically, whom these industries looked for as a cheaper labor source. Part of the reason for the slowdown, all the other little towns drew their labor circles and our circles began to overlap. . . . We still have a downtown. We're not a ghost town, possibly because we didn't build a mall until 15 years after the big movement on the part of other communities, and by that time we realized these malls could be pretty devastating. . . . You don't have a large enough tax base to go around in a small town, and you have to go to the same people when you want money. A number of the things we have are run by volunteers."

Fran Thorpe, former mayor, owner of Thorpe Paint & Wallpaper: "I've lived here all my life. It's a nice clean city. Very low crime rate. Excellent police department. Kind of interesting for a city this size, we have an all-volunteer fire department. We have always been in the highest fire-insurance class because the department is so well trained. We now have a full-time chief, but the firemen are paid by the call. That helps keep our expenses down. . . . I was an alderman for four years and mayor for four years. While I was mayor we were involved in a $13 million wastewater treatment plant, a $2 million water project, airport expansion. I spent a lot of time down there, plus you don't make a lot of friends. You can't please everybody. The mayor is paid $6,800 a year including a $75-a-month expense account. There are also 10 aldermen, paid $1,800 a year. That's nothing for the number of hours they spend. It's getting harder and harder to get quality people to take these jobs."

Jack Kundert, president of Bank One Monroe: "We are affiliated with Bank One, headquartered in Columbus, Ohio. We had been an independent bank through 1986, called Commercial & Savings Bank, home-owned, then we affiliated with Marine Bank in Milwaukee, and two years later Bank One. It's a big bank holding company. But we're the same folks we were four or five years ago. We make our own loan decisions. . . . Monroe is only over the Illinois state line by five or six miles. People from Illinois like to buy their groceries in Monroe because we don't have any sales tax on food."

Bob Enterline, recruiter of physicians for Monroe Regional Medical Center: "Our mission basically is to bring another 46 physicians here over the next 48 months. We see over 200,000 patients a year at the clinic. . . . Frankly, we're surrounded by cows, corn, and cheese. But these are hardworking people who have been here for generations. We're selling quality of life, an excellent school system, a stable, prosperous economy, a regulatory climate favorable to the medical community . . . easy access to a city if we want to get there." ◼

Montrose, CO 81401

Location: 260 miles southwest of Denver on the Western Slope of the Continental Divide.

Population: 8,854 (1990).

Growth rate: 1½% increase (132 people) since 1980.

Per capita income: $10,215 (1985), 87% of state average ($11,713).

Geography/climate: Elevation 5,820 feet. Situated in center of Uncompahgre Valley: 14,000-foot San Juan Mountains to the south, 10,000-foot Uncompahgre Plateau to the west, Grand Mesa to the north, Black Canyon National Park to the east. Surrounding high mountains buffer harsh weather, lower wind velocity. Mild summers and winters. Semi-arid: low relative humidity, low average precipitation: 25 inches of snow, 9 inches of rain. 227 to 274 days of sunshine a year.

Economic base: Government provides 25% of jobs; commercial trade, 26%; services, 17%; manufacturing, 11%; agriculture, 2%. Major payrolls: Western Area Power Administration, Russel Stover Candies, Montrose Memorial Hospital. Montrose is the county seat.

Newspaper: *The Montrose Daily Press*, 535 S. First Street, Montrose, CO 81401. 303-249-3444. Daily, Monday through Friday. Richard E. Day, managing editor. $60 a year.

TV, radio: Local AM/FM station. 32 channels on cable including networks, PBS from Denver. NPR can be received off-air from Grand Junction.

Health care: Montrose Memorial Hospital, 75 beds. 38 physicians, 8 dentists in local practice.

Schools: 6 elementary (K–5); 1 middle (6–7); 1 junior high (8–9). Montrose High School enrolls 669 students. 52% of graduates go to college. Composite ACT, 21.7 ("statewide, we are just a tad above the average"). Also, 4 religious schools: Baptist, Seventh-Day Adventist, Interdenominational, Covenant Reformed.

Educational level: 13.8% of county residents have 16 or more years of formal education; state average, 23%. Per capita expenditure for public education, $536; state average, $523.

Library: Montrose Library District, 60,000 volumes.

Recreation: Exceptional variety of outdoor pursuits nearby. Black Canyon of the Gunnison River, 14 miles northeast. Telluride Ski Resort, 65 miles southwest. Grand Mesa, 50 miles north, supports large herds of deer, elk; 200 lakes. Ridgway State Recreation Area, 26 miles south, offers water sports, camping. In town: 60 acres of parks, 18-hole golf course, 10 tennis courts, Aquatic Center, 600-seat performing arts center, community theater group, symphony orchestra, Montrose Children's Museum, Ute Indian Museum.

3 BR, 2 BA house: $110,000 to $145,000.

Cost of electricity: $.07 to $.08 per kilowatt hour.

Cost of natural gas: $.46 per therm.

Sales tax: 6%.

State income tax: 5%.

Churches: 33. Denominations: Assemblies of God, Baptist, Christian, Christian Science, Church of Christ, Church of God, Church of Jesus Christ of Latter-day Saints, Community, Congregational, Covenant, Episcopal, Evangelical Free, Foursquare Gospel, Jehovah's Witnesses, Lutheran, Methodist, Nazarene, Pentecostal, Presbyterian, Reformed Presbyterian, Roman Catholic, Seventh-Day Adventist.

Montrose could be excused for being smug. On sunny days—the vast majority—this place seems to have it all: picture-postcard horizons, mild weather, pretty good mix of economic activity, diverse population interested in everything from symphony performances to tractor pulls.

So it was something of a reality check in 1991 when Colorado-Ute Electric Association, a big power company headquartered in Montrose, filed for bankruptcy, threatening a $5.8 million payroll and 170 upper-level, high-paying jobs. "Many of those individuals are already gone. We're facing a brain drain—exactly right," Mayor Tricia Dickinson commented at the time. "But we're confident things are going to turn out OK."

What residents say . . .

J. David Reed, attorney: "The Montrose School District has not been able to pass a bond issue since 1973, which is kind of inconsistent with general progress of the community overall. Early in January 1990, the Rotary Club said we believe school facility improvements are the number-one problem facing our community. A committee was appointed to assess why we had not been able to pass a bond issue. I was chairman. . . . We went to the school board and they gave us their blessing to conduct public hearings with various special-interest groups. We said we would assimilate all this information and put it into a report to the board. . . . What we found was very little feeling against the need for improvements. But we heard people saying they could not stand any more property taxes. . . . We suggested the city, the county, and the school district should meet and determine if the three of them could raise the $12 million needed to improve school facilities. We think what happened was a first in the nation. The city said it would increase the sales tax 1 percent and contribute $3 million to school district improvements. When completed, the 1 percent sales tax would go away. The county said it would do likewise, and came up with $3 million. The school district asked the voters to approve a $4 million bond issue. True—a property tax increase—but small enough that it's acceptable. The remaining $2 million will come from a state fund and be repaid from the district's capital reserve. The voters passed this proposition in excess of two to one."

Janet Sprouse, owner of The Typeshop: "I am a third-generation typographer. My grandparents met when they were both Linotype operators in Guthrie, Oklahoma. . . . I was a music major, taught music. . . . Never thought about typography until I moved here. I've been in business seven years. My husband is a geologist with the Bureau of Land Management. . . . I personally did not move here for small-town living. At first it was very difficult for me to adjust to the lack of fine dining, fine stores, fine cultural events. . . . I served three years on the Chamber. I've been active in the AAUW (American Association of University Women). I directed the church choir and played in the community orchestra. There are endless opportunities for you to do things, particularly things you might just be watching if you lived somewhere else, and that is very valuable. . . . I think it's amazing how much gets done in this town by volunteers. Of course, in cities people volunteer on symphony boards and things of that kind, but it is such a smaller percentage of people. . . . For me it is not preserving the quality of life as much as adding to the quality of life. For me the quality of life has gotten better as more people have come here who are interested in the types of cultural things I am. I think an enormous number come here hoping to find something to do, willing to take a lesser-paying job, less demanding intellectually. . . . Montrose is going to change somewhat because tourism south of us is increasing at a fairly rapid rate. People fly to Montrose and rent cars to drive to Telluride, 65 miles. Telluride is booming and Montrose has a lot of spillover . . . a great deal of employment for all the construction going on there. It has taken the place of mining."

Ken Gale, executive director, Chamber of Commerce: "We're working on the multiple use of public lands. We're concerned they're trying to eliminate uses other than recreation. 'Cattle Free by '93' . . . we hear that practically every day. Nobody will take credit, but it's environmental groups. . . . We're still an agricultural, rural community. 50 percent of our economic base is supported by agriculture. We want recreational use but we also want grazing cattle and sheep, we want mining to take place, and we want timber-cutting in certain places. They want our forests pristine . . . also the only way you can get back there is to walk. . . . We feel there is a middle of the road. . . . It's starting to create a stir in the area. The rancher and farmer have been a laid-back, independent sort. Now they are getting more vocal. We've been working with them on this issue a year and a half."

Dennis DeVor, attorney, banker: "Montrose is my hometown. I was gone for about 12 years and had the opportunity to return. My wife is originally from New Jersey. We really did some soul-searching and decided Montrose typified some of the values and lifestyle kinds of things we wanted. . . . Some of the trade-offs are economical. The opportunity to make a substantial amount of money in a small, Western Slope community like Montrose is not significant. . . . Our economy is well diversified . . . agriculture, small business, tourism. We have become a little bit of a regional base . . . the largest community in a six-county area."

Tricia Dickinson, mayor: "Montrose is a community of individuals who chose to live here and could live elsewhere. There is a strong sense of citizen ownership. . . . I used to live in Denver. We've lived in Montrose since 1971. My husband was the first boarded surgeon here. . . . There was a very vigorous growth period during the Seventies, an opportunity for educated professionals to move into smaller communities. We've seen that change in the Eighties. The thing that happened was the downsizing in agriculture, farm foreclosures, mining that bellied up. In the Nineties we are going to see an increase in active, vigorous retirees coming from Florida, the Midwest. . . . People can very easily conduct business and live anywhere they please . . . with the fax machine and the computer." ■

Moses Lake, WA 98837

Location: 176 miles east of Seattle, 109 miles west of Spokane, on I-90 in east central Washington.

Population: 11,235 (1990).

Growth rate: 3% since 1986.

Per capita income: $8,748 (1985), 81% of state average ($10,866).

Geography/climate: Flat, sagebrush desert where not irrigated, at 1,060-foot elevation. Average annual rainfall, 8 inches, peaking in fall; snowfall, 15 inches. Average temperatures: January: high, 34; low, 19 degrees. July: high, 87; low, 54. Average 28 days below freezing, 29 days above 90. Can peak above 100. Low relative humidity. Rainless periods of month to 6 weeks not uncommon at midsummer.

Economic base: Agriculture, industry, tourism. Moses Lake, though not the county seat, is regarded as commercial hub of Columbia River Basin in Grant County. Irrigation turns normally dry lands into farms producing wheat, alfalfa, corn, potatoes, beans, peas, asparagus, apples, soft fruits. Large payrolls: American Potato, 250 employees; Carnation Company, french fries and hash browns, 550; Sun-Spiced, fresh-pack potatoes, 110; Sundstrand Data Control, electronic components, 85; Willamette Industries, corrugated boxes, 83; public school district, 730; Big Bend College, 120; Samaritan Hospital, 225; Advanced Silicon Materials, 232. Port of Moses Lake has applied to become a Foreign Trade Zone.

Newspaper: *Columbia Basin Daily Herald*, 813 W. Third Avenue, Moses Lake, WA 98837. 509-765-4561. Daily, Monday through Friday. Ron Peterson, editor. $9 a month.

TV, radio: 3 AM, 3 FM stations. Cable carries TV networks, PBS from Spokane.

Health care: Samaritan Hospital, 50 beds. 30 physicians, 11 dentists in local practice.

Schools: 7 elementary (1–3, 4–6); 2 junior high (7–9). Moses Lake High School enrolls 1,000, sends 60% to college. SATs "average." Big Bend Community College, nationally recognized for commercial pilot program, enrolls 970 full time, 1,030 part time.

Educational level: 11.5% of Grant County residents have 16 or more years of formal education; state average, 19%. Per capita expenditure for public education, $608; state average, $498.

Library: Moses Lake Public Library, 50,000 volumes.

Recreation: Moses Lake has 120 miles of shoreline, covers 6,500 acres. 15 city parks fronting on lake provide boat-launching, beaches, campsites, playgrounds, ball fields. McCosh Park, downtown, has heated outdoor swimming pool, lighted tennis courts, basketball court, horseshoe pits, picnic tables, amphitheater. 280-acre sand dunes at south end of lake attract as many as 5,000 off-road vehicles on a peak weekend, state's largest ORV park. 1 private, 1 public 18-hole golf course; par-3 9-hole course. Ice-skating rink. Regional museum and art center. Petting zoo. 4-screen cinema. Hunters bag pheasant, duck in surrounding farmlands.

3 BR, 2 BA house: $50,000 to $70,000.

Cost of electricity: $.0163 per kilowatt hour.

Cost of natural gas: $.53 per therm.

Sales tax: 7.5%.

State income tax: None.

Churches: 24. Denominations: Assemblies of God, Baptist (Independent, Missionary, Southern), Christian, Christian & Missionary Alliance, Christian Science, Church of Christ, Church of Jesus Christ of Latter-day Saints, Episcopal, Foursquare Gospel, Lutheran (ELCA, Missouri Synod), Methodist (Evangelical, Free, United), Missionary, Nazarene, Presbyterian-USA, Roman Catholic, Seventh-Day Adventist.

Giving credit where credit is due, Moses Lake wishes to thank Mother Nature for providing one of its main assets—sunlight. The sun shines a lot on east central Washington. By contrast, western Washington, the populous Pacific Coast strip from Bellingham to Tacoma and environs, is often cloudy and wet, to the advantage of Moses Lake: "Lots of wet-side folks like to run away from home, and this is where they end up," says tourism director Spencer Grigg. He's biased, of course, but that's his job. Moses Lake was the first Washington city to create a tourism commission as part of city staff. The 747 you see making its final approach to Grant County Airport is not tourism, however, but a unique link with Japan.

What residents say . . .

Jim Anderson, administration, Japan Air Lines: "In the mid-1960s they decommissioned this Air Force base and made it into Grant County Airport. Japan Air Lines was looking for a place to train their pilots. They came here and rented a hangar in 1968, brought in a Convair 880 and a Boeing 727 to train on . . . a 747 in 1971. We train Monday through Saturday, sunup to sunset, 100 touch-and-go landings, around and around in circles, doing all the checkoffs. We're in a high plateau area and always stay below 5,000 feet. . . . It's a 13,500-foot runway, 300 feet wide, real easy to find in the air. At one time it was the longest runway west of the Mississippi. . . . We try to be a good neighbor. We take all the sixth graders up on a flight every year. We bring over 10 stewardesses from Japan especially for that occasion. It's a great day for us."

Rich Childress, owner, car dealership; chaperone, sister-city program: "In 1980, I think it was, the mayor got together with the publisher of the newspaper in Yonezawa, Japan. . . . Yonezawa and Moses Lake are very similar in make-up. Both are very agriculture-oriented. Both have had military bases that the government has abandoned and the local business community has redeveloped. . . . They came up with the idea to exchange adults. We did that for a year or two. Then we took Miss

Moses Lake to Yonezawa and they reciprocated. . . . Now we exchange five students, each living in the counterpart's house for a week. Japan Air Lines has taken an interest in the program over the years. . . . Sister-city programs in other towns are more or less ceremonial. This is truly a working, functioning way to bring two cultures together as best we can. The five students selected each year will come back with all kinds of stories etched in their brains forever."

Teri Looney, director, Adam East Museum & Art Center: "A man named Adam East, who had spent much of his life collecting Native American artifacts, deeded his collection to the museum. It was housed in a smaller building until 1989 when a citizen group got together and talked with city officials. An idea formed to move the museum to a prime downtown corner and create an art gallery and classroom, an activity room. . . . The city leases the building. It's at the corner of Third and Ash, a busy corner downtown. It's real great for us . . . gives us enough size to run a program. We try to have a variety of artists, from very realistic to totally abstract. We also have a shop where we sell art on consignment . . . adults and children's workshops. We have a good base of community support, a membership program, over 80 volunteers. This is a direct response by an open-minded City Council to the wishes of the community. . . . Because the Moses Lake City Council voted to fund both Adam East Art Center and the Centennial Amphitheater in the same year, they received the 1990 Governor's Arts Award. That is quite a coup. Not many cities have received that, and we're real proud."

Spencer Grigg, tourism and community events coordinator: "Centennial Amphithe-ater is on the lakefront. As you sit in the casual grass bowl and look toward the stage, the backdrop is the lake. This year we had two concert series, Thursday night and Saturday night. Thursday was a little smaller, up-and-coming-type people but nobody who'd really made a name. Saturday we had some national musicians . . . Glenn Yarborough . . . Ranch Romance, an all-female, country-western, acoustic swing, rock-a-billy group . . . the Platters. Saturdays we had no less than 2,000 people, lots of people with picnic baskets. . . . The most unique thing is, they're all absolutely free to members of the community and anybody else who wants to come down. . . . Bottom line, $526,000 to build the theater, paid 100 percent from the 2-percent motel tax. Essentially, tourists paid for that facility."

Henry Michael, administrator and CEO, Washington State Potato Commission: "I just got back from the Orient last Thursday, another market trip to the rim area. We started five years ago to develop the fresh potato market in Hong Kong and Singapore. That has turned out to be a very successful story. . . . First the hotels and restaurants, now Washington fresh potatoes are going into many of the teahouses of Hong Kong and retail trade. . . . Japan is our number-one buyer of french fries. . . . We're only about 200 miles from the Port of Seattle and Tacoma. . . . A container load of fresh potatoes, give or take, 20 days to market in Hong Kong or Singapore."

Greg Fitch, president, Big Bend Community College: "That was a trustee of the college at my door. He brought me some sweet corn, onions, potatoes, and I gave him some seaweed from Japan. . . . We serve primarily a three-county area, sparsely populated rural area. Five years ago our normal age [of students] was 31. Now it is just below 27. People are realizing they need some kind of formal training. . . . Our pilot-training program is unique in the state and we draw students from other states, as well. The program provides a student with an associate degree, with part of that training an aviation component . . .

ground school, private pilot's license up through multi-engine. . . . This is the old Larson Air Force Base, a B52, SAC base. . . . For one dollar we were able to buy a number of buildings . . . the NCO club, post exchange, theater, several hangars. . . . Our tarmac continues right into the Port of Moses Lake. . . . Over the past few years there has been quite a metamorphosis." ∎

Mount Airy, NC 27030

Location: 35 miles northwest of Winston-Salem, 10 miles south of the Virginia state line, in northwestern North Carolina.

Population: 7,156 (1990).

Growth rate: Holding steady—36 more people since 1986.

Per capita income: $8,916 (1985), 94% of state average ($9,517).

Geography/climate: Elevation 1,100 feet, surrounded by blue hills of Appalachia, with 2,400-foot Pilot Mountain to the southeast. Alleghany Mountain barrier to the north moderates winter weather. Average temperatures: January: 40. July: high, 87; low, 65. Up to 90 days freezing or below; none below zero. 25 days into the 90s. Annual snowfall, 11 inches; rainfall, 41 inches.

Economic base: Manufacturing, retail trade, farming. Shopping center of a five-county area. 109 factories in Surry County—two-thirds of these located in Mount Airy. Total county payroll about 15,000 employees. Dozen hosiery mills in town. Other major employers: Dixie Concrete Products, concrete blocks; Henredon, furniture; Insteel Industries, reinforcing wire; Leonard Aluminum Utility Buildings; North Carolina Foam, polyurethane; North Carolina Granite Corporation; Hamilton Beach/Proctor-Silex, toasters; Techform, thermoformed plastics.

Newspaper: *Mount Airy News*, 319 N. Renfro Street, Mount Airy, NC 27030. 919-786-4141. Daily, Monday through Friday, and Sunday. George W. Summerlin, publisher. $42 a year.

TV, radio: Local AM/FM stations. Cable carries network TV, PBS from Winston-Salem, Greensboro, Charlotte. NPR received off-air from Winston-Salem.

Health care: Northern Hospital of Surry County, 129 beds. 30 physicians, 14 dentists in local practice.

Schools: 2 elementary (K–6); 1 junior high (7–8). Mount Airy High School enrolls 530, sends 60% to some form of higher education; 40% to 4-year college. 1991 SAT scores (49.1% participation): math, 474; verbal, 430. Composite 904 was fourth highest in state.

Educational level: 6.3% of Surry County residents have 16 or more years of formal education; state average, 13.2%. Per capita expenditure for public education, $401; state average, $390.

Library: Mount Airy Public Library has 26,000 volumes, 6,000 average monthly circulation.

Recreation: 2 city parks provide outdoor swimming pool, 10 tennis courts, 4 soccer fields, 4 baseball fields. Reeves Community Center organizes basketball, racquetball, gymnastics, swimming, aerobics. 3 private golf courses. Community theater—the Andy Griffith Playhouse. Winter ski areas of Blue Ridge Mountains are about 2 hours west.

3 BR, 2 BA house: $90,000 to $140,000.

Cost of electricity: $.07 per kilowatt hour.

Cost of bottled gas: $.95 per gallon.

Sales tax: 6%.

State income tax: 6% to 7%.

Churches: 21. Denominations: Baha'i, Primitive Baptist, Church of the Brethren, Church of Christ, Church of God, Church of Jesus Christ of Latter-day Saints, Lutheran, Missionary Baptist, Moravian, Pentecostal Holiness, Presbyterian, Roman Catholic, Salvation Army, Southern Baptist, United Methodist, Wesleyan Methodist.

J ust east of Mount Airy, on state highway 103, is the world's largest open-faced quarry, a vast stony plain where they've been slicing out granite since 1775. Granite might be called the building material of choice in this town. The historic tour brochure notes, for example, that the Sam Hennis house at 215 East Lebanon Street, circa 1923, is "one of the best examples of the granite bungalow house form in Mount Airy." The First National Bank, at the corner of Main and Moore, was originally brick but got a granite veneer about 1910. Trinity Episcopal Church, at 472 North Main, is a granite copy of a chapel in Oxford, England. Mount Airy's fine white stone is mined mainly for export, however. The Wright Brothers National Memorial, at Kill Devil Hills, North Carolina, is made of Mount Airy granite.

But the most famous export of this small town is movie-and-TV actor Andy Griffith, who grew up at 711 Haymore Street and popped in and out of Main Street establishments like Snappy Lunch and Floyd's Barber Shop and other real places in the fictional town of Mayberry, setting of "The Andy Griffith Show." Mount Airy has made capital of Mayberry. There is a Mayberry Mall out on U.S. 52, north of town. Snappy Lunch is a tourist attraction. The second annual "Mayberry Days" was scheduled for early fall 1991 at the Andy Griffith Playhouse. But the hometown boy is pretty scarce.

What residents say . . .

Emily Taylor, commissioner-at-large: "This is my own personal opinion, that people were very sincere in honoring Andy. However, I'm rather disappointed that Andy hasn't found any time to spend in Mount Airy. Quite honestly, I think a lot of citizens have become disgruntled for that reason. . . . They named the Playhouse for him, but he didn't even bother to respond to come to the dedication. Some of our old buildings have become famous. Snappy Lunch is making a killing, so I hear. It's just a little hole in the wall. . . . If you are ever in Mount Airy, you must eat one of the famous pork-chop sandwiches. Everyone says they are delicious. . . . I'm a retired high school English teacher. . . . I just got the sudden urge I wanted to be more involved. I filed to run for commissioner-at-large. . . . I'm having a very good time talking to people I haven't seen in years, and parents of students I have taught. We have the salt-of-the-earth people, good hard-working people. . . . Incidentally, I am the only female who has ever served on our town board. There was too much complacency on the board before I got on. I am a very plain-spoken person and not the most tactful. I call the shots like I see them. No special-interest groups. I want fairness in government. Too much has been decided without consulting the city taxpayers.... For years and years, recreation was put on the back burner. Having taught teenagers I know the needs of these young people. The board has finally gotten six new tennis courts at the high school for use of the school and the citizens. We decided that was the most centrally located place."

Swanson Richards, president, Surry Community College: "I grew up on Highway 89 between Mount Airy and Galax, Virginia, on a farm, tobacco farming. A lot of small tobacco farms once were the source of family income in the area. They have gone by the way.... More and more people are having to look to industry to make a living. A lot of us grew up and had chores. We learned how to work. We contributed to the family income. We were assets to the family, and our parents looked at it as such. Now, with more and more two-parent employment, we find that the children become more ... a liability. They take from the family in terms of income, instead of contributing to it.... Not much can be done. Our youth are having to look away from home for employment. It separates and segregates the family more.... Surry Community College provides the community with an able work force to meet their employment needs, and industry and business provide us with tax support and gifts and assistance to students. It's a good marriage.... Lack of high school

completion is fairly high in the area ... and we are typical for the rural areas of the Appalachian Mountain region."

Barbara Summerlin, editor emeritus, **Mount Airy News:** "We have tried giving a year's free subscription to anyone who completes the literacy program at the college.... I think the role of the newspaper is pressing to educate the community ... the importance of knowing and voting properly.... I was born in Mount Airy. I'm a 10th generation of my family on four sides, maternal grandparents and paternal grandparents.... When I graduated from high school in 1952, I went into nurses' training in Charlotte. I came back to live here in the early '70s. It is almost a compelling feeling of belonging here.... Stories about my ancestors are written in a book by Hardin E. Taliaferro. He was born in 1812 and died in 1875, one of a group of Southern writers that included Augustus B. Longstreet, Johnson J. Hooper, Joseph G. Baldwin, George W. Harris. The book is called *The Humor of H. E. Taliaferro.* Accounts of my family in that book have given me a very strong feeling for the area they lived in.... When you start asking questions about how money is spent in a small town, it is difficult. Our paper began endorsing candidates at the local level. That can create problems. It is not easy. You are probably the most hated person in town."

Ruth Minick, town historian: "You don't pass through Mount Airy to go someplace else. People don't stop off for the heck of it. When you come to Mount Airy, you make a special trip.... It's supposed to be on the frontier but it isn't. Mount Airy has some very sophisticated and well informed people."

Susan Ashby, chair, Mount Airy Restoration Foundation: "Also, I chair the City of Mount Airy's Appearance Commission, and I have a seat on the Planning Board. The three sort of go together. . . . We have a National Historical District. I spent pretty much of the summer calling on neighbors to see if we might now ask the town to set up a local historic district. Certainly a local district has more protection over design on the front façades. . . . If you want to change your building structurally, you would ask a five-member board, and do it in harmony with your neighbors. . . . I know about every little house on every block. . . . What I do, I do out of pure love. I think we are the prettiest little town in North Carolina." ■

Mount Pleasant, TX 75455

Location: 117 miles east of Dallas, 100 miles northwest of Shreveport, at the intersection of I-30 and U.S. 271, in northeast Texas.

Population: 12,291 (1990).

Growth rate: 11.5% since 1980.

Per capita income: $9,214 (1985), 89% of state average ($10,373).

Geography/climate: Rolling hills with tall pine and hardwood trees. Average elevation, 415 feet. Generally temperate climate with mild winters. Lovely springs and falls. Hot, humid summers. Average temperatures: January: high, 56; low, 34. July: high, 94; low, 70. Average 94 days at 90 or above. Average rainfall, 46 inches; snowfall, 1.7 inches. Prevailing wind from southwest, 10 mph.

Economic base: One-fifth of labor force—2,000 people—employed by Pilgrim's Pride Corporation, a poultry processor. Lignite mining, petroleum, furniture manufacturing, cattle, and tourism are other major sectors. Larger payrolls include Mount Pleasant Independent School District; TU Electric, utility; Texas Utilities Mining Company, lignite; Titus County Memorial Hospital; Kwik-Way, wood doors; Mastercraft Industries, decorative wood items; Southwestern Electric Power, utility; H. B. Dinton, oil drilling. Mount Pleasant is seat of Titus County, retail and wholesale center.

Newspaper: *Mount Pleasant Daily Tribune*, 1705 Industrial, Mount Pleasant, TX 75455. 903-572-1705. Evenings, Sunday morning. Robert L. Palmer, editor and publisher. $50.18 a year.

TV, radio: Local AM station. Cable carries network TV, PBS from Dallas-Fort Worth, Tyler, Shreveport. NPR from Shreveport.

Health care: Titus County Memorial Hospital, 165 beds. 30 physicians, 13 dentists in local practice.

Schools: 4 elementary (K–5); 1 junior high (6–8). Mount Pleasant High School enrolls 1,162, sends 50% to college. Math–verbal average SAT score, 868. South Jefferson Christian Academy (K–3) enrolls 240. North Texas Community College, 2-year institution.

Educational level: 9.7% of Titus County residents have 16 or more years of formal education; state average, 16.9%. Per capita expenditure for public education, $426; state average, $441.

Library: Mount Pleasant Library, 42,290 volumes.

Recreation: 2 city parks equipped with playground, tennis courts, swimming pool, exercise trail, softball and baseball fields, basketball courts. 9-hole golf course at Mount Pleasant Country Club open to public. Lake Bob Sandlin State Recreation Area, 5 miles southwest, has boat launch, pier, camping sites, swimming, skiing. Monticello County Park provides access to Monticello, Bob Sandlin Lakes, both well-regarded for bass fishing. Also in town: miniature golf, skating rink, 4-screen cinema, bowling alley. Summer program for kids includes reading, Scouts, movies, swimming, basketball and baseball clinics, roller-skating, Bible school.

3 BR, 2 BA house: $70,000 to $135,000.

Cost of electricity: $.055 per kilowatt hour.

Cost of natural gas: $.40 per therm.

Sales tax: 7¾%.

State income tax: None.

Churches: 21. Denominations: Assemblies of God, Baptist, Baptist-Bible Fellowship, Southern Baptist (6), Church of Christ, Church of Jesus Christ of Latter-day Saints, Church of the Nazarene, Disciples of Christ, Episcopal, Full Gospel, Lutheran Missouri Synod, Presbyterian, Roman Catholic, United Methodist.

Because of its diverse employment base, Mount Pleasant fared well during the 1986–87 recession compared to other Texas communities. An economic analysis prepared by the state in 1990 pointed out that Titus County has added new jobs every year since 1983, and at a faster pace than the state average.

"Titus County has a colorful history especially during Prohibition days," the state report also notes in a curious little detour into the archives. "With 332 illegal stills seized during Prohibition, Titus County ranked second among all Texas counties and accounted for over 10 percent of all stills seized in Texas."

Though it may have placed only second in county distilling, the Mount Pleasant area is pleased to declare itself "Bass Capital of Texas." Four prime bass lakes just south of town produce trophy-size catch. The current record out of Lake Monticello is 14 pounds 1½ ounces, caught in 1980.

What residents say ...

Jerry Boatner, owner, Boatner's Furniture:
"I happen to be the immediate past mayor. I served eight years and I was on the Council for 16 years, so that's where I'm coming from. I have a home furnishings business.... I'm 47 years old, lived here virtually all my life. Went to Texas Tech, then to the University of Missouri for a journalism degree, then the Army. Came back here, where Dad had a business, and just seemed to stick. I chose to come back here because it is a very comfortable, pleasant place to live, everything its name says it is.... We have a trade area of 48 to 50 thousand people in a 25-mile radius. We are a fairly small county in physical size, which makes the adjacent counties somewhat look to Mount Pleasant as their main trading community. Plus we are somewhat isolated from larger metropolitan areas. Dallas is two hours, one hour to Texarkana.... Lignite coal is gold for us. It's our form of oil. Texas Utilities has a large strip-mining operation just to our west. They have taken a large part of the terrain, leveled it, scarred it, dug it. The good news is they are doing a beautiful job reclaiming the rolling hills to similar

topography. . . . We've had the coal-mining operation since the early '70s. . . . There's one other major employer, pretty much a home-grown industry. Pilgrim's Pride, Incorporated, poultry. Bo Pilgrim is a native of Camp County, immediately south of us. In the '60s he began growing birds and processing them. . . . We have an operation that employs more than 2,000 at the processing plant . . . even more work out in the surrounding counties for independent growers who buy their feed and chicks from Bo Pilgrim. They raise them and sell them back. . . . So, Texas Utilities gives you a higher end, largely unionized work force with a much more attractive pay scale, probably in the 20s to 30s for all workers. On the other end, $5-an-hour jobs. [Pilgrim's Pride] employs largely black and Hispanic workers. Recently Hispanics have surpassed blacks in total school enrollment. I would peg both at about 20 percent. Anglos, 60 percent."

David Anthony, superintendent of schools:
"We spend a great deal of time on college prep. . . . I guess our strong suit is science and mathematics. . . . On a statewide basis we've just received exemplary status for serving students in special education, mainstreaming them into academic areas everywhere possible instead of leaving them self-contained. We do a pretty good job of that. . . . Girls volleyball is a perennial power here. Boys baseball and football. We also have been the top-ranked drill team in the state . . . the Mount Pleasant Tiger Dolls . . . an exceptional group of 60 young ladies, very well trained . . . sophomore through 12th grade. Generally they'll make one major trip out of state every year. This year they were invited to New York to participate in the Desert Storm parade on July 4 in Man-

hattan . . . with several other drill teams from across the nation. . . . Sports is a focal point of Mount Pleasant. We have a lot of community support. . . . Usually a capacity crowd, couple of thousand show up. Baseball is really big here. We have a very active Dixie Youth summer league, a very active soccer program. Dixie Girls softball. . . . Four teams went to state or national playoffs. . . . Athletics is big in Texas, and we are certainly no exception in Mount Pleasant."

Bill Ratliff, consulting engineer; member Texas Senate: "I had never run for public office until '88, so I guess you'd say I'm a novice in politics. . . . I thought the person who was in there needed to come home. . . . As I began to run, I was shocked and amazed at the number of people who would simply ask me, 'Are you a lawyer?' . . . then express the opinion, 'I'll vote for whoever is not a lawyer.' . . . I think there is a real backlash against the legal community. There's a perceived conflict of interest, making the laws and then being the ones who interpret and enforce them and represent people . . . in particular a backlash against what used to be called the ambulance chaser, the personal-injury plaintiff's lawyer that is perceived as a leech on society. They benefit off other people's misfortune. I think it is fueled, in Texas at least, by a lot of television advertising by plaintiffs' lawyers. There is a real distaste for that. . . . People also believe, rightly or wrongly, that our litigious society is one of the problems of the American economy, one of the reasons we are lagging behind much of the world, because business and industry is so paranoid about liability. Industry spends an inordinate amount of money defending itself, and that is wasted motion, in effect. . . . I always knew there were few questions that had black and white answers. The more familiar you get with some of the problems facing state government and society, the more you realize everything is some shade of gray. I think that is a frustration trying to explain to constituents who tend to see things as black and white."

Jonice Crane, executive vice president, Guaranty Bank: "Mount Pleasant did not have a place for meetings that would accommodate many people. Everyone pulled together, everyone donated. We built a civic center without using any tax dollars. It's very, very nice, and it was paid for when it was completed." ■

Nevada, IA 50201

Location: 9 miles east of Ames, 40 miles north of Des Moines, in central Iowa.

Population: 6,009 (1990).

Growth rate: 2% since 1980.

Per capita income: $9,915 (1985), 98% of state average ($10,096).

Geography/climate: Flat to gently rolling prairie. Continental climate. Long, cold winters averaging 23 degrees but with 16 days at zero or below, 31 inches of snow. Hot, frequently humid summers with average 20 days in the 90s, 32 inches of rain.

Economic base: Seat of Story County, center of government services for agricultural area including city of Ames, population 47,000. Largest local employer is also largest private payroll in county: Donnelley Marketing, advertising mailer with 750–800 employees. 3 other printers in town plus half a dozen varied manufacturers. School district employs 170 people.

Newspaper: *Nevada Journal*, 1133 Sixth Street, Nevada, IA 50201. 515-382-2161. Weekly, Thursday. Marlys Thomas, editor. $32 a year.

TV, radio: All TV networks, PBS, NPR received off-air from Des Moines, Ames. Cable available.

Health care: Story County Hospital, 42 beds, with 80-bed long-term unit. 5 physicians, 5 dentists in local practice. Most medical specialties available in nearby Ames.

Schools: 1 elementary (K–4) enrolls 621; 1 middle (5–8) enrolls 422. Nevada Senior High School enrolls 400, sends 69% to college. Recent composite ACT, 22.1. Iowa State University is a 15-minute drive west.

Educational level: 33.9% of Story County residents have 16 or more years of formal education; state average, 13.9%. Per capita spending for public education, $367; state average, $480.

Library: Nevada Public Library, 32,000 volumes.

Recreation: Nevada Parks and Recreation Department operates 5 parks, with swimming pool, ball fields, tennis and basketball courts, playgrounds, picnic areas. Year-round recreation programs for children and adults include softball, baseball, soccer, swimming. 9-hole golf course in town; 2 other courses nearby. Camping at several sites within county. Movie theater in town.

3 BR, 2 BA house: $90,000 to $100,000.

Cost of electricity: $.08 to $.11 per kilowatt hour.

Cost of natural gas: $.55 per therm.

Sales tax: 6%.

State income tax: 0.4% to 9.98%.

Churches: 10. Denominations: Assemblies of God, Baptist, Disciples of Christ, Lutheran, Presbyterian, Reorganized Church of Jesus Christ of Latter-day Saints, Roman Catholic, Seventh-Day Adventist, United Methodist.

Nevada is pronounced with a long *A*: "Ne-VAY-dah." The town historical society says the town was named by a land commissioner who liked mountains and imagined the Sierra Nevada as a nice backdrop for flattish Iowa. Early residents improved the horizon by erecting fine houses. A number remain in good shape today, including the house where baseball-player-turned-evangelist Billy Sunday grew up.

With barely 6,000 people and only 10 miles from a university town that is eight times larger, Nevada might have lost its identity years ago. But as county seat, the small town remains the only place where certain official things can be done. That role, plus one very large home-grown industry, Donnelley Marketing, gives Nevada staying power.

What residents say . . .

Raymond Kassel, chairman, Nevada Economic Development Council: "About as many people commute out as commute in. Professional people commute out to Ames due to the university, federal government labs, and headquarters of the Iowa Department of Transportation. Commuting in are plant workers at Donnelley, the large direct-mail corporation. . . . Presently we're developing an industrial park for medium industry . . . warehousing, production of agricultural equipment . . . to the west of the community, and one for light industry on the east. . . . Central Iowa is the one part of Iowa that is growing. . . . Service industries are getting to be a big item. . . . Like many communities, we've revitalized ourselves. I think it happens because of the changing of the guard, a period when the community is very active."

Arlo Huse, vice president of production, Donnelley Marketing: "We are the largest private employer in the county, average about 750 to 800 employees. Our primary business is direct-mail advertising. We compile

the premier consumer mailing list in the country . . . 87 million nonduplicating households. We do a lot of major promotions for financial institutions, insurance companies, consumer products. The company was started here in 1917 as M&F Mailers, named for two men named Martin and Fowler. . . . Mailing lists began with automobile registrations. They started going down to the courthouse and copying registrations off onto envelopes. It just progressed from there, county to county and state to state. . . . Out of Nevada last year we mailed 250 million pieces and paid $37 million in postage. In receipts, Nevada is the next-to-the-largest post office in the state. Des Moines is a little larger."

Fred Samuelson, owner and operator of the Ben Franklin store: "I'm still real positive about business in the community although we have a lot fewer businesses than we did. We do have a beautification program in progress . . . streets, sidewalks, new lights . . . which we hope will rejuvenate downtown . . . 20 years ago we were a traditional variety store. Today about 50 percent is devoted to craft products, the other 50 percent to variety goods. You have to find your niche and promote that niche, provide the customers with what they're looking for. So far it has worked, sales have been good. . . . A change of weather every couple of weeks helps business, sets a new mood for the customer. . . . Nevada is right in the center of things, close to Iowa State University, 40 minutes from the airport at Des Moines, five minutes from Interstate 35. . . . I don't know who's moving in, but I'm 47 and they're younger than I am."

Francy Scudder, owner of Scudder's Department Store: "We've owned it since 1949 when my father purchased the business. But the store has been around at least a hundred years. At one time it had a women's side and a men's side, separated by a wall. Since then we've opened it up. Since we can't afford to be modern we take on character . . . racks for the ladies' wear . . . a little lady with a Vassarette girdle on . . . those wire drawstring things to shoot the money up to the cashier. . . . People come in from New York and find it wonderful. . . . I put in 40 to 50 hours a week, depending. The nice thing about business not being very good is I can be gone a little bit. . . . We're hoping it's the recession. We're hoping it's all the talk the commentators put out that scares people. People have been scared to spend money. We're about $10,000 down from last year, and last year was the worst we ever had. . . . We used to sell to a lot of teenagers and now we sell to very few. They want to go to the mall. . . . Nevada is an absolutely fantastic place. I've been married

three times and lived around the country. I came home to raise my kids in Nevada. In a small town they protect you. I'm not an eccentric in that sense, but we do have those people we take care of . . . people beginning to get Alzheimer's whose kids are far away. It's a caring, loving small town, and that's what small towns are all about."

Ken Shaw, superintendent of schools: "15 years ago we started an early kindergarten program, not 'pre-school' but children who for whatever reason are not ready to begin kindergarten. A few years ago we started Head Start for four-year-olds, held in our schools and run by federal grant money. . . . We've gotten into mentoring. Each year new teachers spend X number of hours with another teacher assigned to mentor them. . . . We have teachers willing to take classes and come back and teach other teachers. . . . There is so much research indicating that schools need to change. We probably do too much testing. Testing does not have a lot to do with learning. . . . We need to get away from the Carnegie Unit of Instruction [which says] you have to have X credits to graduate. . . . It is more meaningful if you base graduation on learning. . . . We're getting into assessments . . . observation, conferencing, portfolios, keeping track of students' writing progress from year to year. . . . Nevada has expectations of a very good work ethic. We have people willing to put in hours outside the school day. . . . We're now involved in the Alliance for Excellence, through Drake University, in Des Moines. It's a five-year program. . . . We're writing a case study for our district on what we can do to better reach our goals." ■

Newberry, SC 29108

Location: 40 miles northwest of Columbia, 60 miles southeast of Greenville, in the Piedmont region, north central South Carolina.

Population: 10,542 (1990).

Growth rate: 5% since 1986.

Per capita income: $8,554 (1985), 96% of state average ($8,890).

Geography/climate: Rolling terrain, heavily forested with pine. Long, hot summers; cool, sunny falls; mild winters. January average temperatures: low, 31; high, 55. July: low, 69; high, 91. Annual rainfall, 46 inches; heaviest in March, 5.5 inches. Trace of snow.

Economic base: Balance between agriculture, industry. Two-thirds of cash farm receipts derived from livestock, primarily cattle and calves; dairy products; poultry, chiefly turkeys; eggs. Textile industry is largest county employer. Big payrolls: American Fiber & Finishing, industrial fabric, 675 employees; Federal Paper Board, lumber and wood byproducts, 166; ISE America, eggs, poultry feed, 183; Louis Rich, fresh and frozen turkeys, 1,200; Packaging Corporation of America, corrugated containers, 108; Quality Stitching, athletic sportswear, 120; Shakespeare Products, antennas, 157; Thomas & Howard, wholesale food, 108; Thompson International, auto wheel covers, 241.

Newspaper: *The Observer Herald News*, 1716 Main Street, Newberry, SC 29108. 803-276-0625. Monday, Wednesday, Friday. Ollie Moye, editor. $21 a year.

TV, radio: Local AM station. TV can be received off-air. Cable carries PBS, network TV from Columbia, Greenville, Spartanburg, Charlotte. NPR from Columbia.

Health care: Newberry County Memorial Hospital, 102 beds. 33 physicians, 11 dentists in local practice.

Schools: 4 elementary (K–5); 1 junior high (6–8). Newberry High School enrolls 988, sends 55% to higher education. Composite ACT, 21. Newberry College, chartered in 1856, enrolls 700.

Educational level: 12.0% of Newberry County residents have 16 or more years of formal education; state average, 13.4%; per capita expenditure for public education, $357; state average, $403.

Library: Newberry-Saluda Regional Library, 73,300 volumes.

Recreation: 2 city parks. Facilities include baseball fields, tennis courts, swimming pool. Country club with 18-hole golf course. Movie theater, community-theater group. Lake Murray, 15–20 miles down the pike toward Columbia, is a popular place with Newberry residents. 520 miles of shoreline. Fishing, boating, swimming, golf. Camper, van hookups. Billy Dreher Island State Park, located on the lake, is popular campsite. Lake Greenwood, 20 miles west, offers variety of water sports. 3 principal rivers run through county: Saluda, Enoree, Broad. Sumter National Forest, 10 miles northeast, has extensive hunting preserve, large populations of squirrel, wild turkey, deer, rabbit. Popular with bow hunters.

3 BR, 2 BA house: $100,000 to $135,000.

Cost of electricity: $.07 per kilowatt hour.

Cost of natural gas: $.66 per therm.

Sales tax: 5%.

State income tax: 3% to 7%.

Churches: 56. Denominations: AME, Associated Reformed Presbyterian, Baptist (22), Independent Baptist, Christian, Church of Christ, Church of Jesus Christ of Latter-day Saints, Episcopal, Evangelical Lutheran, Holiness, Jehovah's Witnesses, Lutheran (10), Methodist, Nondenominational, Pentecostal Holiness, Presbyterian-American, Presbyterian USA, Roman Catholic, United Methodist.

"**Y**ou don't end up in Newberry by accident—you have to intend to go there," the Charlotte, North Carolina, *Observer* wrote in a sketch of the South Carolina town. Although Interstate 26 passes only a couple of miles northeast, "you just don't expect to find anything beyond the fields and foliage when you turn off to follow the signs into Newberry." But once into town, the newspaper continued, there are whole blocks of historic buildings dating from the early 1800s "and a populace who seem to enjoy talking to just about anybody."

What residents say . . .

Margaret Paysinger, retired teacher: "I taught in the public schools for 19 years and at Newberry College for 33 . . . English, both language and literature. Newberry is a Lutheran college . . . doing well when you consider the difficulties of smaller denominational colleges. We have some foreign students. Dr. Clem Chou has been influential in bringing Taiwanese students to the campus. . . . We have a very large group of black students at this point. We have been reaching out, trying to get minority students. . . . We're one of those old towns that has a square. Four buildings on the square are on the National Register. The old courthouse is now the Community Hall . . . an old opera house that we hope to raise enough money to turn back into an opera house. Right now it's the City Hall. . . . There is not a great deal to do for fun unless you like to play tennis or swim. . . . For fun you usually go to Columbia! . . . We have a group that likes to square dance, a group that clogs. . . . The Ritz Theater is now owned by the Community Players. The Ritz was considered the best of its kind in its day. Art deco. We have kept it in good repair. . . . I'll be manning the box office this afternoon, taking reservations for next week. We have a touring company coming in from Columbia. . . . *The Last of the Red Hot Lovers.* . . . Our big thing is musicals because of our association with the college. We have a children's show every summer. . . . Anything of Neil Simon's everybody loves, and the folks like mysteries. We have not chosen the straight drama for next year. We're looking for a director."

Bill Carter, orchid grower: "We were settled by three main groups, the Scotch-Irish, the Germans, and the Quakers, and they have left their heritage. The Quakers are gone except those who joined the Baptist and Methodist church. . . . Definitely a German influence here with the names. German was spoken some until the late 1820s. The Scotch-Irish were really Irish. A lot of the settlers came overland from Pennsylvania and Virginia. It was easier to get to the back country that way than coming by the coast. . . . I tell people we are in a very interesting country, rolling hills, granite-based, a hundred miles from the mountains and 130 from the ocean. Mild climate. Pleasantly wooded. The land is going back to pines now with the advent of pine-tree pulpwood. We are heavily wooded. The game has come back with the pine trees. Deer are a problem. . . . I live in a wonderful part of the world. The races have gotten along very well together. We have our heritage. We have tried to keep and are highly conscious of our past. . . . My cousin and I are orchid growers. We are known worldwide. Carter & Holmes Orchids, Inc. . . . We employ a good many people. We sell plants to New Zealand, Australia, Taiwan, Japan, South Africa, Italy, England, Canada. It sort of fills a niche."

Ollie Moye, editor, **Observer Herald News:** "I've been at the paper 34 years, added up all the bond issues proposed [during that time], they come up to little more than half the $25 million school-bond proposal. . . . We don't think it's going to be approved. The paper's against it . . . runaway costs in recent years. There's a lot of sentiment against it. Most of the property owners are adamant. . . . Quality education is not in buildings. It is in instruction and the people who conduct classes. I'm giving the newspaper's positions. . . . Also a big issue in the city and county has been local-option sales tax, a penny tax that's supposed to roll back property taxes. . . . But it doesn't affect school millage, and there is no guarantee that it will be rolled back. It was soundly defeated in the last election . . . just another

way they are going to get in our pocketbooks. . . . For many years our economy was deeply rooted in agriculture and textiles. . . . Textiles started having trouble in the South. So now we've got one textile plant [remaining] of four large ones that served the area. We're still heavily involved in agriculture. We're number one in the state in egg production and have been for many years. We're number two in dairy production. We vary from first to fifth in forest products. . . . We're a Knight-Ridder paper. We were twice a week until '83. Now Monday–Wednesday–Friday. We're one of the largest web commercial printers in the state. With the big bucks behind us, we've been able to expand this into one of the bigger small industries in the community."

Jane Ragland, co-founder, Newcomers' Club: "A lot of people who move to a small town in the South for the first time feel they are out of place. We didn't want them to feel that way. Newberry's slogan is 'The City of Friendly Folks'. . . . We formed that club in '61 and it's been going strong ever since. . . . It's for women, meets in the morning. This is something nice about a small town. People who live here in great big homes offer their homes for meetings. The women get to see a lot of other houses. . . . People are just hooked on genealogy here. They have a genealogy society . . . trace everybody's family. . . . That sense of family, I think it's passed on from generation to generation. My father was alive during the Civil War, though he didn't call it the Civil War. He told me things that happened way, way back, just fascinating to me. I grew up with a sense of history. . . . There's something really wonderful knowing the history of your family. People can excuse a lot of your faults if they know what your ancestors did." ■

Newport, OR 97365

Location: 133 miles southwest of Portland, 93 miles northwest of Eugene, on the central Oregon coast.

Population: 8,437 (1990).

Growth rate: 5% since 1986.

Per capita income: $9,577 (1985), 96% of state average ($9,925).

Geography/climate: Situated just west of the Coast Range at Yaquina Bay. Moderate coastal climate with mild winters, cool summers. December–March period can be dreary as Pacific Ocean moisture turns to clouds and rain onshore. January averages: high, 50; low, 39. July: high, 64; low, 51. August through October is sunniest stretch. Annual rainfall, 63 inches. Rare snowfall melts fast.

Economic base: Diverse, but changing. Historic timber industry down to about 15% of personal income countywide. Commercial fishing represents about 16% but is cyclical. Tourism, retirement living are big growth industries. Add in county-seat services, retail trade, large professional payroll at Oregon State University's Marine Science Center.

Newspaper: *Newport News-Times*, 831 N.E. Avery Street, Newport, OR 97365. 503-265-8571. Weekly, Wednesday. Mary Jo Parker, publisher. $19 a year.

TV, radio: 2 local, AM, FM stations. Cable carries network TV, PBS from Portland, Eugene. NPR received off-air.

Health care: Pacific Communities Hospital, 48 beds. 36 physicians, 16 dentists in local practice.

Schools: 2 elementary (K–5); 1 middle (6–8). Newport High School enrolls 544. 53% of graduates enroll in 4-year college, 22% in community college. SAT averages, class of 1991: verbal, 465; math, 525. Oregon Coast Community College Service District headquartered in Newport.

Educational level: 14.4% of Lincoln County residents have 16 or more years of formal education; state average, 17.9%. Per capita expenditure for public education, $567; state average, $577.

Library: Newport Public Library, 36,000 volumes.

Recreation: Large variety of outdoor activities along coastline and inland. Fishing, crabbing, clamming, boating, sailing, windsurfing, kite flying, scuba-diving, whale-watching, birding, bicycling. 29 state parks in vicinity. 600-slip public marina. New, $24 million Oregon Coast Aquarium. Visual arts center, 300-seat performing arts center, 2 amateur theater groups, 5 dance companies, movie theater, 5 daily-fee golf courses, YMCA with basketball court, swimming pool, fitness training. 6 public outdoor tennis courts.

3 BR, 2 BA house: $125,000 "when you can find them." Newer, with a view, $200,000 to $350,000.

Cost of electricity: $.04 to $.05 per kilowatt hour.

Cost of natural gas: $.57 per therm.

Sales tax: None.

State income tax: 5% to 9%.

Churches: 13. Denominations: Assemblies of God, Baptist, Christian, Church of Jesus Christ of Latter-day Saints, Episcopal, Four-square Gospel, Lutheran, Methodist, Presbyterian, Roman Catholic.

In the late 1970s, Newport determined to broaden its historic economic base of fisheries and forestry by becoming a destination resort. The strategy worked. Tourism has grown robust, even growing faster than many would like. The extraordinary natural beauty of Newport, combined with exceptional small-town amenities, has attracted short-term and long-term residents, creating an acute shortage of affordable housing. The current economic strategy is to pump new money into the fishing industry, with the goal of smoothing its cyclical ups and downs.

What residents say . . .

Don Lindly, county commissioner: "Tourism is growing 10 percent to 12 percent a year. Tourists are going to be here no matter what we do. Fisheries, on the other hand, is an industry that has gone through some difficult times. We really need to develop some value-added processing. It could be canning or frozen dinners, something to add value here rather than have it done someplace else. . . . There is an effort to develop auxiliary industries like ship repair and maintenance, for not only vessels out of this bay but in Alaska and elsewhere. . . . If you were to ask somebody on the street where people are moving from, they would say California. But if you look at housing permits, over 50 percent are coming from other places in the state. It's a nice place to retire. The physical environment is beautiful. . . . Folks living here in second homes also help pay for local services."

Jane Appling, director, Newport Public Library: "I was working in Albany, Oregon, down the valley, and moved here because of the job. . . . The library does have an outstanding reputation. . . . It's well-staffed. We have six full-timers right now, including two professionals. Our circulation last year was 144,000, one of the highest per capita in the state. For a small-town library I feel we have a lot of depth, quite a fine collection in the arts, literature, humanities in general. It's a quality collection. The community supports our budget. . . . One of our goals this year is to serve the pre-school age group, get them hooked on reading. . . . I'm sure you will hear that housing is very difficult to find. Part of the problem, especially with tourism growing, is we are creating a lot of lower-paying service jobs. It is really hard for these people to find affordable housing."

Mary Jo Parker, publisher, **The Newport News-Times:** "It is extremely difficult to get people to [move here to] work on the paper. Not everyone is willing to live with the climate we have. Housing is extremely expensive when you can find it. It's a very transitory area . . . people come and go a lot. . . . We already get close to half a million tourists a year. . . . I'm not anti-growth although our editorials have been labeled anti-growth. But growth for the sheer fact of making a buck is not appealing."

Laverne Weber, director, Hatfield Marine Science Center: "We have about 260 people work here, including 35 to 40 PhDs, sort of an unusual situation for a small town. A lot of these people are active in the community. I think our influence is pretty strong . . . annual budget of $15 million. . . . Probably most of us earn above the mean. . . . Oregon State University established the center primarily to provide two things: nearness to the ocean and running seawater in the labs. . . . I'm directly responsible to a vice president. I work with many colleges within the university. As a result, our activities are very diverse . . . geologists looking at sea-floor spreading . . . people looking at populations of fish . . . a fish-disease group . . . food science and technology. In addition we have a free public aquarium . . . 425,000 visitors a year."

Don Davis, city manager: "To me, that institution is the crown jewel in Newport's crown. The [Marine Science Center] adds a lot socially. It changes the demographic makeup of the community. These people want different things for their children than the loggers did 40 years ago. They have a totally different outlook on life. . . . Newport has been a growth-oriented community all these years. I don't think I've ever lost a bond election for the water system or sewer system. . . . We've built Jane Appling's library, the performing-arts center . . . the visual-arts center. What we tried to create was a strong base for the arts.

Newport has always been an artsy-craftsy town. . . . We're a government center, a research center, a retail trade center. And then we've had commercial products, fishing, and tourism . . . many little subgroups, none of them strong enough to beat up on the others. . . . We have controlled our destiny because we haven't waited around for handouts from Washington, DC."

R. Barry Fisher, owner, Yankee Fisheries: "Newport probably contributed more to new technology than any other port on the West Coast . . . an enormous contribution to the fishing industry from a relatively small handful of people. Unlike the typical blight that hits small towns . . . the best and brightest of every generation grow up and leave . . . a lot of very bright kids stayed home and became boat skippers. . . . I was a professor of fisheries at Oregon State. I quit the university in 1974. . . . We did very well in a small boat, had a brand new vessel constructed. An opportunity for a joint venture with the Russians came along in 1978. We took the 60-footer to Alaska and made nothing but money for 10 years. . . . Local fleets were making record landings and a large amount of money came back to the town. $29 million value at dockside in 1989, and another $12 to $13 million landed at other ports nearby. . . . Now the curve has flattened. We've reached the point of maximum harvest of the species. . . . But the critical element is overcapitalization . . . too many boats being built. . . . Newport also has an explosive growth in tourism, raising the argument, what are we doing pursuing tourism pell-mell? What kinds of jobs? You've brought in what are essentially part-time jobs that have to be supported by welfare or unemployment compensation in the off-season, a social cost that is underwritten by the rest of us. . . . On the surface, if you compare Newport to existence in most cities in the United States, we're pretty well-off. A lot of people would love to have our problems. The town has managed to build a very good network of the kind of amenities you would not expect a small, redneck town on the Oregon Coast to have. . . . We're good at putting on shows for the rest of the state. . . . It's a marvelous place to live if you can figure out how to make a living or have an income. . . . In summary of this place, it is just now beginning to recognize the less attractive elements of this kind of development, and to its credit is trying to face them sort of manfully." ■

Oxford, MS 38655

Location: 165 miles north of Jackson, 75 miles south of Memphis, in the hill country of northern Mississippi.

Population: 9,984 (1990).

Growth rate: 6% since 1986.

Per capita income: $9,222 (1985), 23% higher than state average ($7,483).

Geography/climate: Hilly, rolling land; average elevation, 500 feet. Short winters. January daily average low, 32 degrees; 57 days at freezing or below; high, 50; 5 inches of snow. Long summers, with hot, humid stretches. July averages: low, 72; high, 92; 66 days into the 90s. Annual precipitation, 52 inches.

Economic base: Manufacturing, retail and wholesale trade, agriculture, medical services, University of Mississippi. Cotton, hardwoods, clay, soybeans, beef cattle, hogs are prime commodities. Ole Miss, enrollment 10,500, is largest single employer. Other big payrolls: Whirlpool, gas ranges, 500; Emerson Electric, motors, 463; Georgia Pacific, particle board, 315; Oxford Wire & Cable, harnesses, 180; Denton Mills, apparel, 174; Outboard Marine, lawn-mower motors, 100. Oxford is the seat of Lafayette County. Besides downtown "Square," five shopping centers, enclosed mall.

Newspaper: *The Oxford Eagle*, 916 Jackson Avenue, Oxford, MS 38655. 601-234-4331. Daily, Monday through Friday. Jesse Phillips, publisher. $36 a year.

TV, radio: 1 AM, 4 FM stations, including NPR. Local TV-PBS transmitter. Cable carries network TV from Memphis, Tupelo.

Health care: Baptist Memorial Hospital-North Mississippi, 150 beds. 45 physicians, 16 dentists in local practice.

Schools: 2 elementary (K–2, 3–5); 1 junior high (6–8). Oxford High School enrolls 660, sends 80% to college, 1990 composite ACT, 23.1. Northwest Mississippi Junior College, Oxford Branch, enrolls 600. University of Mississippi. North Mississippi Retardation Center, 295 students on campus.

Educational level: 23.1% of Lafayette County residents have 16 or more years of formal education; state average, 12.3%. County per capita expenditure for public education, $278; state average, $333.

Library: Lafayette County and Oxford Public Library, 40,000 volumes. 1989–90 circulation, 119,000 items, highest in region.

Recreation: 4 public parks, lighted softball fields, 50-meter swimming pool. Little League, Kiddie League fields. Basketball courts, soccer fields. Activity Center: racquetball, weight room, volleyball, basketball, indoor tennis, gymnastics, stage. 56 public tennis courts in area. Public, 18-hole golf course; private club with 9-hole course. Ole Miss plays nationally ranked teams. Roller-skating, bowling, 4-screen cinema. University Theater has 8-show season. Local theater produces several plays each year. 4 state parks, including Sardis Reservoir, Holly Springs National Forest, within 20 miles: fishing, water-skiing, camping, hiking, hunting.

3 BR, 2 BA house: $70,000 to $90,000.

Cost of electricity: $.056 per kilowatt hour.

Cost of natural gas: $.52 per therm.

Sales tax: 6%.

State income tax: 3% to 5%.

Churches: 34. Denominations: Assemblies of God, Baptist, Baptist-Free Will, Baptist-Missionary, Church of Christ, Episcopal, Jehovah's Witnesses, Lutheran, Methodist, Methodist-Independent, United Methodist, Missionary-Baptist-ABA, Nazarene, Pentecostal, Presbyterian-American, Roman Catholic.

According to one account, Oxford was named for the English university town "in hopes that a similar university would evolve." Though it's not clear whether that original expectation has been met, what has evolved is a close and highly agreeable connection between a 10,000-enrollment university and a 10,000-population small town. To many residents, the University of Mississippi—Ole Miss—*is* Oxford.

To many visitors, Oxford is a charming town square with anchor tenants including The J. E. Neilson Company, considered the South's oldest department store; the 117-year-old Lafayette County Courthouse; and newer institutions like Square Books. "Oxford looks very prosperous and very beautiful," says local historian John Sabotka. "At night on the Square, it is a lovely place."

A literary giant once stalked the Square—William Faulkner, of course. They say you could have a perfectly normal conversation with Brother Bill one day, and the next day he'd seem out of reach. Those days, you may have been in the Square but he, presumably, was in Yoknapatawpha County.

What residents say . . .

John Sobotka, assistant to the dean, Law Center, University of Mississippi: "From what I've gathered in speaking to people who knew Faulkner, he was initially viewed as an eccentric. It wasn't until after his Nobel Prize that he was accepted by the locals as someone who was gifted. Even then, he was looked upon as an oddity. . . . Maybe Faulkner could have written similar material if he'd lived elsewhere in Mississippi or in some other state, but it's possi-

ble the people and surroundings in Oxford and Lafayette County were unique enough to provide him with what he needed to construct the framework for his stories . . . an intangible something that's special."

Jean Allen Young, retired home economist: "When I came here in 1948, Oxford was a very small town and the county was very underdeveloped. I came from the Delta, which was much more progressive than the hills. The roads were not all paved, and not all gravel, either. . . . I was more or less amazed at the lack of running water in rural homes. . . . I wrote my master's thesis on the uses of electricity in this county. The last electric lines were not installed until 1955. . . . Some people felt air conditioning was dangerous to the health, not just rural people but urban people. From my standpoint, I could sit down and concentrate on typewriting if I wasn't fighting the heat. . . . I'm a Presbyterian. I remember when they air-conditioned the church, and Neilson's department store. I don't know that it changed the church service all that much. . . . The quality of life in town is attracting executives from outlying towns. Some of them live here and work there. . . . We have one of the best book stores in the country."

Richard Howorth, proprietor, Square Books:
"Ever since I was a kid, there was speculation about why there wasn't a bookstore in Oxford, being the home of Faulkner and the University of Mississippi. . . . The American Booksellers Association at that time recommended not opening a bookstore in a town of less than 40,000 people. But because of Oxford's special population, my instinct was it would be fine here. . . . I worked at the Savile bookshop in Washington, DC, two years to get the experience to open my own store here. We've been open since 1979. Oxford has been very supportive. Our clientele is fractured in a number of ways . . . university students, university faculty, Oxford townspeople, and a surprising number of visitors that come to Oxford because of the university, and because it is not simply Faulkner's home town but Faulkner's work, depicted in this area. . . . We're very promotion-minded and have a lot of

writers come through on tours and do readings. . . . Peter Mathiessen, William Styron, Alex Haley, Allen Ginsberg. Eudora Welty has visited. . . . At least half a dozen published writers live here in Oxford. . . . Barry Hannah, Larry Brown, John Grisham, who's currently got the number two spot on the best-seller list. Ellen Douglas has taught creative writing at the university. . . . I graduated from the public schools here in Oxford. There is a great diversity of people. A large African-American population. Because of the university, children of faculty. Because the county is still a very, very rural place, a number of country folk in the city schools. And then you have the middle-class population. It's a good experience, something you don't have when you live in most suburbs, and most small towns. . . . Oxford is a very attractive town to most Mississippians. I may be geocentric about this, but people from Mississippi, in particular because of all the problems Mississippi has had . . . Mississippians have a loyalty and adoration about their state that people from other states do not have. . . . Aside from that, Mississippi is a beautiful state."

Louise Avent, civic leader: "I am a native Oxonian. With the exception of 14 months, I have lived here all my life. My husband and I had a family business that his father started in 1920, a dairy-processing plant. . . . I'm presently on the Tourism Council. . . . We have a 2 percent hotel–motel tax and 2 percent on prepared food and beverages. Part of the second fund is the 'baseball tax,' committed as Oxford's share of the new baseball stadium at Ole Miss. It's just a beautifully engineered place, a new landmark. . . . I'm also on the board of the Fellowship of Christian Athletes, an organization that works with athletes in junior high and high school. We feel that athletes are your role models. If you can influence athletes, that has an influence on many lives. . . . I'm a sports fanatic . . . just a spectator. We follow Ole Miss . . . tailgating in The Grove. . . . I'm fond of saying that we have the best of both worlds, the individualism and the relative security only found in a small town, and the cultural advantages found usually in a large city." ■

Page, AZ 86040

Location: 134 miles north of Flagstaff, 10 miles south of the Utah line, at Glen Canyon Dam and Lake Powell.

Population: 6,598 (1990).

Growth rate: 26% since 1980.

Per capita income: $11,847 (1985), 12% higher than state average ($10,561).

Geography/climate: Red rock, plateau country. Dry, high desert at 4,300 feet. Sunshine on 88% of days. Total annual precipitation, 6.28 inches. Daily average temperature November–February, 50; March–April, September–October, 74; May–August, 91.

Economic base: Navajo Generating Station, coal-fired electric plant, employs 720 people, largest single payroll. Tourism employs more in total, at various establishments, largest of which is Wahweap Lodge & Marina, 550. Public school system is 3rd largest employer in county. National Park Service employs significant number. Local industry: Boatel, houseboat fabricator; Yamamoto Bait, plastic worms (most shipped to Japan); Page Steel, fabricators.

Newspaper: *Lake Powell Chronicle*, Three Elm Street Mall, Page, AZ 86040-1716. 602-645-8888. Weekly, Wednesday. Ronald Rieb, publisher. $36 a year.

TV, radio: Local AM, FM stations. Cable brings in network TV, PBS from Phoenix. NPR cannot be received in area.

Health care: Page Hospital, 27 beds. 5 physicians, 5 dentists in local practice.

Schools: 2 elementary (K–5); 1 middle (6–8). Page High School enrolls 900, sends 57% to higher education. Recent composite ACT, 18.68.

Educational level: 23.2% of Coconino County residents (including Flagstaff) have 16 or more years of formal education; state average, 17.4%. Per capita expenditure on public education, $563; state average, $453.

Library: Page Library, 27,000 volumes, 4,850 registered borrowers.

Recreation: Water sports on Lake Powell very popular. Boating, off-road vehicles ("You can't drive down the street without seeing one or two toys in every driveway," says resident Will Hanneman). Grand Canyon is 2 hours south; Zion National Park (Utah), 3 hours west.

3 BR, 2 BA house: $70,000 to $150,000. Higher prices apply to property along Rim View Drive, overlooking Lake Powell from 300-foot-high mesa.

Cost of electricity: $.06 per kilowatt hour.

Cost of propane heating fuel: $1.42 per therm.

Sales tax: 6%.

State income tax: 3.8% to 7%.

Churches: 13. Denominations: Assemblies of God, Baptist, Church of Christ, Church of Jesus Christ of Latter-day Saints, Church of the Nazarene, Episcopal, Faith Bible Chapel, Jehovah's Witnesses, Lutheran, Methodist, Reorganized LDS Church, Roman Catholic, Southern Baptist.

Every town needs at least one historic building. In Page, Arizona, it is the one-story, stucco structure with bell tower on North Navajo known as the Babbitt Building, named for the same family as the Arizona governor who ran for president. But the interesting thing about this historic building is its age. Page is a page out of the old West. It is a frontier town, created in the desert wilderness by men and women with vision and stamina—except it wasn't even there 35 years ago. Page was settled in the mid-1950s by the Bureau of Land Management as a barracks base for workers building the Glen Canyon Dam. The Babbitt Building was erected about the same time that 200 or so concrete-block "Bureau homes" were built for workers. The homes now are privately owned residences. Meanwhile, the Babbitt Building has recently stood empty, waiting for a new retailing pioneer. Page may be a young place, but it's old enough to know those small-town downtown blues as new shopping centers spring up on the periphery.

The problem is complicated by geography, as city manager Curtis Schott explains. Page controls an area of about 17 square miles. But the original town and shopping center sits up on a mesa which Schott describes as a horseshoe shape, about four square miles in area. With land scarce on the mesa, new retailers are intercepting traffic down below, where motorists can opt to bypass the original town site entirely by staying on U.S. Highway 89. Downtown business owners are concerned.

What residents say . . .

Betty Jo Roundtree, general manager, Wahweap Lodge & Marina: "Wahweap is located about nine miles out of Page on Lake Powell. My family came out here in 1955. At that time it was desert. There was no roadway; they came out with a plow. . . . Prior to the dam being built, my family managed and ran a place at Marble Canyon, where the whitewater river trips started. They fed a lot of people . . . had a restaurant, service station, motel. In addition to that, my grandfather put an airplane propeller on a boat so he could take people upriver. At one point, a gentleman from the U.S. Geologic Survey was doing some scouting on the Colorado. My grand-father listened to the man talk about the possibility of a dam . . . this was in the early 1940s. My grandfather looked over a map and leased the land where he felt the water would come up. We used to stand up on the hill, and he used to point out where the water would fill the desert. . . . He's an old cowboy, he felt it in his bones. His name was Art Greene. . . . Today [Wahweap] is owned by ARA Leisure Services, but my family actually built it up. We have 350 beautiful rooms overlooking the lake . . . trailer village, 118 sites, a marina with about 700 slips and 175 buoys, 105 houseboats we rent. . . . We used to take six people every three days to Rainbow Bridge.

Now we take 600 people a day in 10 tour boats. . . . We have over three million visitors a year. I saw it from zero. . . . When you're in the business of helping people to have fun, that's a fun thing to do. I think you would find the people are friendly and happy here."

Rosie Hensley, owner, Page Fast Glass & Paint: "It was my father's idea. He wanted all of us kids to come back to Page. This business had been here since Page started, and with the original owner wanting to sell, my father saw the opportunity and called us all. None of us knew anything about glass. That was back in 1978. . . . We're on Vista, a real eyesore to Page for a long time, but in the last few years people have put a lot of energy into making it look better. It's the first main street to the left as you come into town. . . . I've been here since seventh grade. My father and mother were transferred here for work purposes. My mother was the license-plate lady in the motor-vehicle department. My father also worked for the state, at a checking station. . . . When we came here there was hardly anything, the beginning of the construction of the dam . . . a barracks for the men to live in. . . . The new Burger King just opened . . . Wal-Mart is here . . . a new optometrist . . . Radio Shack . . . a new clothing store, Corral West. . . . We're grateful for the opportunity to have Wal-Mart even though it does present problems with other businesses of the same sort. We may lose those businesses. In the long run it's going to help because if other businesses see Wal-Mart here, they will say we can be there, too. . . . We're also trying to get the off-road traffic that bypasses our city to see there is something up here. . . . There are two entrances

into Page, north and south. We're talking about big archways made of metal across both entrances and lighting them with neon."

Betsy Golob, real estate, president of Page-Lake Powell Main Street: "We have maybe a 10 percent [retail] vacancy in town and we don't want it to get worse. . . . We want to make our town more like Durango, a place to come to not just because of Lake Powell but because Page is a neat town."

Charles Brumback, plant manager, Navajo Generating Station: "A number of people were just kind of sitting around brainstorming about good ways to get civic organizations together for a worthy cause when a gentleman from the Park Service came up with the idea of a clean-up campaign. . . . Besides litter and trash, we've targeted junk automobiles around the countryside. We have some mesas around here and years ago, before people were smarter, they used to dispose of automobiles by pushing them off those cliffs. One year we retrieved some. . . . Clean-up day is called 'Page Attacks Trash.' It usually gets going about 7:30 or 8 in the morning. About 10:30 or 11 we start putting the barbecue lunch on. . . . It's grown considerably. This year . . . we're confident we had over 3,700 people participate. . . . Page, Arizona, was the 86th point of light identified by President Bush in his Thousand Points of Light."

Dan Dodds, superintendent of schools: "I guess I would describe Page as an oasis in the desert. I was totally astounded when I came to interview. Page enjoys facilities which are far beyond what I've seen in districts of 25,000 to 30,000 population. The student–teacher ratio is 25 to 1. There is one teacher's aide for every two teachers in kindergarten through third. . . . The community has been very supportive of a quality educational program. . . . We're not on the [Navajo] reservation. We border it. Yet our current enrollment is 57 percent Native American. Just a few years ago it was 70 percent Anglo. . . . What's happened is, because the Page schools offer such a good program, those Native American parents are just like any other . . . they're opting to send their kids to Page rather than the school on the reservation. . . . Of course, the Mormon church has a large influence on the quality of our students. Four out of our five top students are L.D.S. kids. . . . There are over 200 school districts in the state. We're in the 15th position overall in salaries. Athletically, this year we won seven regional awards. Page pretty much is seen as a progressive district in northern Arizona." ■

Penn Yan, NY 14527

Location: 56 miles southeast of Rochester, at the top of Keuka Lake, in the Finger Lakes region of western New York.

Population: 5,248 (1990).

Growth rate: Infinitesimal—6 people since 1980 Census.

Per capita income: $9,299 (1985), 27% below state average ($11,765).

Geography/climate: Gently rolling hills. Rigorous continental climate. Cloudy, cold winters with 135 freezing days, 10 below-0 days. January daily high averages 31; low, 16. Typical July range of 61–82 with 6 days at 90 or above. Annual rainfall, 36 inches; snowfall totals in the 90-inch range.

Economic base: Wine grape–growing in "the Rhineland of America." Dozen wineries include Glenora Wine Cellars, a Double Gold award-winner. Home to New York Wine & Grape Foundation. Dairying and diversified farming, tourism and resorts. Large payrolls: Soldiers and Sailors Memorial Hospital; Trans-Elco, ceramic engineers; Mercury Aircraft, aircraft components; Penn Yan Marine Manufacturing, boats; Birkett Mills, one of largest U.S. producers of buckwheat products; Coach & Equipment Corporation, small buses; Artistic Greetings; The Windmill, co-op farm and craft market.

Newspaper: *The Chronicle Express*, 138 Main Street, Penn Yan, NY 14527. 315-536-4422. Weekly, Wednesday. George M. Barnes, publisher. $19 a year.

TV, radio: Local AM station. Cable carries network-TV stations from Rochester, Syracuse; PBS. NPR received off-air from Rochester.

Health care: Soldiers and Sailors Memorial Hospital, 53 beds, plus 80-bed long-term care unit and 12-bed psychiatric unit. 23 physicians, 11 dentists in local practice.

Schools: 1 elementary (K–5); 1 middle (6–8). Penn Yan Academy (9–12) enrolls 800, sends 24% to 2-year college, 40% to 4 year. SAT average scores, '89-'90: verbal, 439; math, 502. ACT composite, 22.3. Keuka College, a 4-year college, enrolls 650, gives students off-campus "Field Period" to work at jobs that may become future careers.

Educational level: 8.6% of Yates County residents have 16 or more years of formal education; state average , 17.9%. Per capita expenditure for public education, $479; state average, $558.

Library: Penn Yan Public Library, 50,000 volumes. Residents also may use library at Keuka College.

Recreation: 3 parks with swimming, picnicking, playgrounds. Camping, boat-launching at Keuka Lake State Park, 6 miles south. Lighted tennis courts. Recreational leagues in soccer, basketball, baseball, volleyball, football. Driving range, 9-hole golf course at Lakeside Country Club. Pool, gym, sauna at Keuka College open during school year.

3 BR, 2 BA house: $60,000 to $90,000 in town. 3 times as much on choice waterfront.

Cost of electricity: $.02 per kilowatt hour (municipal utility).

Cost of natural gas: $.62 per therm.

Sales tax: 7%.

State income tax: 4% to 7.875%.

Churches: 13. Denominations: Baptist-American, Baptist-Community, Baptist-Conservative, Bible, Church of the Nazarene, Episcopal, Lutheran, Presbyterian, Roman Catholic, Society of Friends, Unitarian Universalist, United Methodist.

Penn Yan—that's short for Pennsylvania and Yankee—is the seat of Yates County, one of the prettiest parts of rural New York State. It is also a hard place to make a living. Penn Yan suffered a stunning loss of industrial jobs during the 1980s. Simultaneously, the drop in commodity prices threatened to bankrupt many farmers. When the price of ears of sweet corn plummeted to a dime a dozen, Ron Nissen, a lifelong resident of Penn Yan, figured it was time the town took control of its destiny, by taking advantage of what it was: a rustic, rural backwater with a wealth of local talent and willingness to work.

Nissen, a tire-company manager, called a brainstorming session of townspeople and farmers. The plan they settled on was an open marketplace to sell local produce, meats, crafts, and other products. To draw the crowds they needed, from 50 or more miles away, the marketplace had to be big, varied, attractive, and fun. They decided to call it The Windmill Farm and Craft Market.

Nissen and 12 other founders incorporated as Yates County Country Cooperative, and began to look for money. When their request to the state for $124,000 in start-up funds was turned down, they fell back on their own resources again, sold shares of stock in the community, and raised $55,000 initially. That was enough to buy the 26-acre site and some building materials, leaving nothing for labor. Enter a work force of 50 Mennonite men. Like an old-time barnraising, they got the frame and roof of two 60-by-100-foot buildings up in one day. Dozens of people driving by hopped out of their cars to lend a hand, their only reward a piece of lemon meringue pie. "We had a spread of food prepared by the Mennonites that would scare you to death," Nissen recalled.

The Windmill is open Saturdays only, May 1 to Christmas. It's doing well, recording more than $1 million in sales in 1989 and an estimated $1.5 million in 1990. But there is more to the story, as Nissen explains.

What residents say ...

Ron Nissen, tire-company manager: "Yesterday we had a downpour, an inch and a half of rain, and we had one of the biggest crowds ever, 12,000 people. . . . There's something about the Windmill that I can't put my finger on. . . . The vendors are so friendly and enjoying themselves that it radiates across the counters to the public.

267

There's no admission, no charge for parking. It's the old-fashioned country shopping. We have about anything you want to buy, from expensive Mennonite quilts to penny candy. . . . We're becoming the role model for New York State. Four other possible locations are looking at us. We were selected last year as one of the top 10 self-help rural group projects in the United States by the Department of Agriculture. . . . One of the surprising things about this project is all the new jobs. We have created about 115 full-time jobs. . . . We succeeded because of great planning, great sense of humor, no hidden agendas, and the women came to bat and did the job we asked of them. . . . Quality, quality, quality. Everything there has to be clean, spotless clean. The people have to be clean. Products have to be high quality. . . . As many brick walls as we hit in the development, I had this strange feeling it was time. I had no money. We'd been turned down by HUD. The banks turned me down. So I went to my friends, in hardware, construction, plumbing. Before I knew it we were $160,000 in debt with no collateral. They had great faith in us. . . . We strategically placed the Windmill exactly between Penn Yan and Dundee. It's not on a main highway . . . on a barren piece of land that no one wanted. One of the most important things that has happened, it's brought the two communities close together."

Peg Thompson, executive director, Chamber of Commerce: "We're one of the families that was drawn here by the type of community it is. We'd lived in Rochester. There are quite a few of us from there. . . . [Penn Yan] had that small-town quality, just enough different, but near enough to an urban area. . . . Some of the people who have always lived here don't understand what the pull is, but a woman raised here said to me, 'Every time I come back from a trip and start down the hill into town, my heart stops a little.' . . . The Mennonites started moving in eight to 10 years ago. Their land south of us in Lancaster County became very expensive. They have large families, there wasn't enough land, and other people were crowding in. So they started moving up here. I think there are 200 families here now. . . . At first there was some resentment because they were different, but actually they've improved the farms. They pull their own weight. When the cancer drive goes door-to-door, they give. They are very cordial. . . . I was standing near when a news reporter asked a Mennonite woman why they were helping build the Windmill. She seemed puzzled. 'Because they asked us to help,' she said."

Steve Marchionda, trucking-company owner; member, Yates County Tomorrow: "We ranked worst in the state in terms of lost manufacturing and private-sector jobs, 78 percent of our jobs gone over an eight-year period, the lion's share in the last four to five years. A bunch of them simply left the area. . . . Penn Yan Express, a winery, a woodworking company. You have to understand that New York is a very difficult state to do business in. . . . It's just the taxes that keep rolling back to us. . . . We tried to work with the legislature for almost two years and continued to run into roadblocks. They didn't have any practical business point of view. . . . So we put our heads down and went at it. We put together a little SWAT team. . . . When you have the chance to bring in a new business, you stand on your tiptoes and do everything you can to make sure they locate in your town. If anybody even sniffed at our area, we would contact them. . . . Artistic Greetings wanted to add to its data-entry staff. We found out about it and got them up here fast, on a Friday. We pulled out all the stops. Before they got back to their office in Elmira, we'd faxed them the answers to their questions. . . . They've been here one year this month. We got 43 new jobs to start, up to 100 today. We pulled that whole deal together in less than one month. . . . We do not rely on any government funding whatsoever. It allows us to remain independent and snag-free. . . . I would say absolutely we have turned the corner." ■

Petoskey, MI 49770

Location: 37 miles below the Straits of Mackinac, 260 miles northwest of Detroit, in the northwest corner of the Lower Peninsula of Michigan.

Population: 6,056 (1990).

Growth rate: 0.93% (56 people) since 1980.

Per capita income: $9,598 (1985), 88% of state average ($10,902).

Geography/climate: Scenic Lake Michigan shore town on Little Traverse Bay. Forested rolling hills. Snowbelt location brings average 121 inches a year, 32 inches of rain. January average temperatures: 15–28 degrees; July, 59–76. Long winters, mild summers, colorful falls.

Economic base: Seat of Emmet County and commercial base, service center of a multi-county area. Tourism a major economic force. 4-season vacation area. Large payrolls: Northern Michigan Hospitals, 1,233 employees; Burns Clinic, 560; Boyne USA, ski and golf resort, 600; Stafford's hotels, restaurants, 275. Numerous small plants produce wood products, fabricated metals, auto parts.

Newspaper: *Petoskey News-Review*, 319 State Street, Petoskey, MI 49770-0528. 616-347-2544. Daily, Monday through Friday. Ken Winter, editor. $113 a year.

TV, radio: 2 local AM, FM stations. Cable carries TV networks from Traverse City, Cadillac; PBS from Alpena. NPR received off-air.

Health care: Northern Michigan Hospitals, 299 beds. Burns Clinic Medical Center. 105 physicians, 23 dentists in local practice.

Schools: 4 elementary (K–5); 1 middle (6–8). Petoskey High School enrolls 705, sends 50% of graduates to college. Recent composite ACT score, 20.2. St. Francis Xavier (Catholic, K–8) enrolls 323. Montessori (preschool and K–6). Seventh-Day Adventist school (K–8). North Central Michigan College, a 2-year institution, enrolls 1,600.

Educational level: 17.6% of Emmet County residents have 16 or more years of formal education; state average, 14.3%. Per capita expenditure for public education, $486; state average, $525.

Library: Petoskey Public Library has 2 branches, 48,000 volumes.

Recreation: Winter–summer vacation mecca of the upper Midwest. Downhill skiing at half a dozen major sites, cross-country trails, 20 public golf courses; fishing in Walloon and Crooked lakes, Little Traverse Bay, for trout, bass, panfish, walleye, salmon, steelhead. 2 state parks within 15 miles. Morel-mushroom-hunting in May. Autumn color-watching in September–October.

3 BR, 2 BA house: $75,000 to $100,000.

Cost of electricity: $.07 per kilowatt hour.

Cost of natural gas: $.44 per therm (100 CCF).

Sales tax: 4%.

State income tax: 4.6%.

Churches: 22. Denominations: Assemblies of God, Baptist, Charismatic, Church of Christ, Church of Jesus Christ of Latter-day

Saints, Christian Science, Disciples of Christ, Episcopal, Interdenominational, Jehovah's Witnesses, Lutheran, Missionary, Nondenominational, Presbyterian, Roman Catholic,

Salvation Army, Seventh-Day Adventist, United Brethren in Christ, United Methodist.

Synagogues: 1.

Truth-in-advertising took a dive when Michigan tried to lure farmers after the Civil War. "Come to Northern Michigan!" the signs down South declared. "A climate like Kentucky. . . . Soil like Illinois!" Locals speculate that all the poor devils who took the bait probably died of frostbite before harvesting anything from the marginal soil. Winters around Petoskey can be more Arctic than Kentucky, but the place has enough year-round scenery and charm to serve as a second home to generations of families, especially from Detroit, Chicago, and other populous places at the lower end of the Great Lakes. Ernest Hemingway, who is reported to have spent 22 summers in the Petoskey area, pronounced it "priceless." At least that's the hype in a current flyer promoting summer vacation opportunities.

Long before tourism grew big, Petoskey was a head's-up place. In 1916, it became one of the first communities in the nation to adopt the council-manager form of government. Once a thriving railroad center, Petoskey now delivers goods and services to a growing resident population, including retirees, in addition to a large annual migration of skiers and cottagers.

What residents say . . .

Justin Rashid, owner, American Spoon Foods: "I grew up in Detroit and summered here from an early age, 12 miles east of Petoskey in a lost, forgotten lumber town called Wildwood. It's there I really bonded with this landscape and part of the country. I think if you talk to a lot of people you'd see that pattern. They started to come here to their parents' cottage . . . and spent the rest of their lives trying to figure out a way to get back. I moved back 14 years ago . . . opened a little roadside produce market. It did very well in the summer and bombed in the winter. One of my customers moved to New York to become a dancer. . . . At the River Cafe, underneath the Brooklyn Bridge, she met Larry Forgione, who was making his reputation as the quintessential American chef. She introduced Larry to me. I started sending him some wild mushrooms and fruits. . . . We both shared the fascination with wild foods . . . and we started this company, the finest fruit products in the world using Michigan fruits . . . one of the first companies to demonstrate you could make wonderful gourmet products from domestic produce. We're a decent-sized company for a small town. . . . We employ between 30 and 40 people and have 100,000 mail-order customers. Our stuff is sold in Macy's, Marshall Fields, fine food stores all over the country. . . . One hundred people go out and pick morel mushrooms for us. Morels that grow in the Midwest are much richer than the ones they get in the Northwest. . . . We sell them for $18 a dried ounce. It takes about 10 to 12 ounces of fresh to make one dried ounce. . . . I grew up in the inner city of Detroit. I dreamed as a kid of living in a town like Petoskey . . . a real old-fashioned downtown, built on a human scale, intimate, with a little jewel of a city park, perched on a hill overlooking Lake Michigan. . . . The one thing I miss about cities is not just the racial diversity but the cultural diversity that goes along with that of necessity. I grew up with a lot of black people. Petoskey is white, it's very white, except for a number of Ottawa Indians. . . . I grew up in an Arabic family, half Arabic, on the other side German. I miss ethnic food and the way we got together in extended families. . . . Petoskey as a very Christian town makes it very conservative. I sometimes wish it wasn't so. But on the other hand, the people here have a real sense of community. Very often in the city, because of diversity you have a lot of conflict. . . . Though I don't know people from as many different ethnic groups, I do know people in all social strata . . . from all kinds of occupations I would never know if I were living in a city. I like that. People in the city associate with their own . . . don't have a clear sense of where they fit into the picture. Small towns are comprehensible communities. My son knows people in every position. He has a better sense of the architecture of the local society. . . . My wife and I met at a repertory theater in downtown Detroit. We moved to New York. She was in off-Broadway, commercials, soap operas. I joined the Great Jones Repertory

Company. . . . We ended up doing "Agamemnon" at the Vivian Beaumont Theater . . . toured abroad. It's a good thing I wasn't more talented or I'd still be in New York or Los Angeles. I lasted three years in New York, then ran screaming to the country."

George Korthauer, city manager: "The city owns a big portion of the Lake Michigan waterfront, I would guess two-thirds of it, probably two miles. . . . Our charter was amended several years ago to require that any city-owned park lands could not be sold unless approved by vote of the people. There's a very strong concern in our community about maintaining the natural beauty that surrounds the area and the way that our little civilization coexists with those natural surroundings. We continue to pay very close attention to that balance. . . . I guess the big project for the next few years will be redevelopment of the central business district. The master plan has been approved. We want to maintain that solid central core. . . . We have capital improvements for the next five years totaling about $35 million, a rather ambitious program for a town our size. . . . The city does not rely heavily upon property taxes . . . only about 20 percent. By far our major revenue source is utilities. It's a business. We show profit and loss. Fortunately, we have shown profits for a long time. We are able to use moneys derived from utility operations to help our parks, the library . . . services provided not as a burden to the taxpayer."

Shawn Gray, general manager, Stafford's Perry Hotel: "The name Perry comes from a dentist, Dr. Norman Perry. He built the hotel in 1899 and ran it for 20 years. It's a brick structure, known for many years as the only fireproof hotel in Northern Michigan, one of 13 hotels in downtown Petoskey at that time and the only one that remains. . . . We are a National Historic spot. . . . We have 81 guest rooms, all with private bath. They range in price from $59 to $135, European plan. . . . We're just now getting into the high season, through Labor Day. We also do very well in color season. It varies with the weather but usually is the last weekend in September through the middle of October. Then we do very well with ski season,

Christmas through St. Patrick's. The two closest areas are Boyne Highlands and Nubs Knob. They're about seven to eight miles from Petoskey. . . . As you're coming up Route 131 from Cadillac, there's a little hill just south of town. As you come over the crest of that hill, you can see downtown, with the church steeple, the Burns Clinic, across the Bay to Harbor Springs. You can see the whole little place and all of a sudden realize why you live here. It's just a real neat area." ■

Pierre, SD 57501

Location: Dead center of South Dakota on the banks of the Missouri River, 32 miles north of I-90. 209 miles south of Bismarck; 395 miles southwest of Minneapolis; 523 miles northeast of Denver.

Population: 13,974 (1990).

Growth rate: 17% since 1980.

Per capita income: $10,867 (state average, $8,553).

Geography/climate: Rolling grasslands at mid-continent, subject to severe summers with stretches of 100-degree plus, subzero days in December, January. Average temperature in July, 91; January, 18. Spring can begin early as March but also much later and can be brief. Lots of sunshine, rare fog. Pleasant fall leading into hunting season. Weather suitable for flying all but 10 or so days a year.

Economic base: Government, agriculture, tourism. Pierre (pronounced "Peer") is state capital, employs 2,100 in state offices. Federal offices, St. Mary's Hospital, Pierre School District each employ 250–275. Retail center of central South Dakota, meeting center of the state, a recreational center of upper Midwest.

Newspaper: *The Capital Journal*, 333 W. Dakota, Pierre, SD 57501-0878. 605-224-7301. Daily. Dana Hess, editor. $60 a year.

TV, radio: 2 local AM, 4 FM stations, including NPR. Cable brings in 17 stations including HBO, PBS.

Health care: St. Mary's Hospital, 86 beds. Mary House, a 23-bed Medicare-certified sub-acute center. 4 clinics serviced by 19 physicians, 25 visiting specialists. 10 dentists in local practice.

Schools: 4 elementary (K–6); 1 junior high (7–8). Composite ACT at T. F. Riggs High School, 22.1, above national average and second highest in state. 60%–65% of high school graduates go on to 4-year colleges, 4% to 2-year institutions. Networked computer labs in all schools have become a model for the state.

Educational level: 26.1% of Hughes County residents have 16 or more years of formal education; state average, 14%. Per capita expenditure for public education (Hughes County), $424, same as state average.

Library: Pierre City Library, 43,000 volumes, 8,800 card holders. Residents also may use the South Dakota State Library, 173,000 volumes.

Recreation: 285 acres of city parks include tennis courts, baseball fields and lighted stadium, lighted football stadium, marina, ice-skating rink, swimming pool. 18-hole, 72-par municipal golf course 1 mile east of city. Oahe Dam turns the slow-flowing Missouri River into clear water Lake Oahe, stretching 231 miles northward to Bismarck. Known among fishermen as the "Walleye Capital of the World." Hunting, fishing, camping very popular. Springtime pari-mutuel horse-racing across river in Fort Pierre.

3 BR, 2 BA house: $50,000 to $60,000 existing to $90,000 new.

Cost of electricity: $.035 to $.037 per kilowatt hour from local hydroelectric plant.

Cost of propane: $.70 per gallon.

Sales tax: 4%.

State income tax: None.

Churches: 30. Denominations: Assemblies of God, Baptist, Church of Christ, Church of God of Prophecy, Church of Jesus Christ of Latter-day Saints, Community, Congregational, Episcopal, Foursquare Gospel, Jehovah's Witnesses, Lutheran, Mennonite, United Methodist, Nondenominational, Open Bible Standard, Pentecostal, Presbyterian USA, Reformed, Roman Catholic, Seventh-Day Adventist, United Church of Christ, United Methodist, Wesleyan.

Pierre is pronounced "Peer." That's the first thing you learn about this South Dakota town. Second, it's the second smallest state capital in the United States—only Montpelier, Vermont, is smaller. Because it is a capital and small, Pierre's demographics are extraordinary. State government jobs attract well educated workers, and Pierre is the second-best-educated small town of the 100 listed in this book: 26 percent of Hughes County residents have at least a 4-year college degree (only Nevada, Iowa, does better, with 33.9%). Because state capitals draw legislators, lobbyists, and interest groups, Pierre has more than 25 restaurants, 800 motel rooms, and a $3.4 million convention center built in 1987 on the waterfront.

Pierre was a cow town before it became a capital. In the land where buffalo used to roam, Fort Pierre on the Missouri River was an oasis. Nowadays, the buffalo are mostly fenced in, though some recently kicked up their heels as extras in "Dances With Wolves," filmed near Pierre. Development of the Oahe Dam has controlled flooding and transformed the muddy Mo into Lake Oahe, a 200-foot-deep, clear-water lake stretching 231 miles from Pierre to Bismarck, North Dakota. Lake Oahe ranks as one of the nation's best places to catch walleyed pike and bass. Fishing, boating, hunting, and camping are hugely popular pastimes.

The invisible line separating Central Time from Mountain Time runs right down the middle of the Missouri River at Pierre, creating an interesting little time warp. Folks who want to savor a certain moment can drive over the bridge to Fort Pierre, where the closing time at watering holes is an hour later. But elsewhere, people operate on pretty much the same time, which one immigrant from New Jersey happily explains is "15 years behind."

What residents say ...

Ron Neilan, real-estate broker: "I own my own firm, I'm 36 years old, and I've lived here all my life except for six years of college and grad school. . . . We're kind of like a training camp for the Minnesota Twins. Young people come here out of college, fine-tune their skills, and are recruited off to other states where they can make more money. Young attorneys and engineers come here and work for the state government for two or three years, then move on to bigger and better. We have a pretty good turnover of young people coming and going. Usually in a small town people come and stay. We lack some things . . . shopping and fine dining, but Pierre is very family-oriented. . . . People are very honest, very friendly. . . . The reason people live here predominantly is hunting and fishing. If you don't like that you may not like living here. A lot of the women are considered widows in the fall hunting season when they don't see their husbands. I don't know how many people own a boat in Pierre but it must be one of the highest per capita."

Bill Asbury, FBI agent: "We've been here about a year. My wife and I are both agents. She was stationed in New York assigned to Soviet counterintelligence. I worked organized crime, bank robberies, hijackings. We were pretty stressed out on the East Coast. We took a map of the United States and narrowed our interests down . . . hunting, fishing, camping . . . and put in for Minneapolis. A call came for Pierre, South Dakota, for two people. . . . We work nine Indian reservations, we're policemen. . . . This is quite a change for us. Our friends back East basically think we're on the edge of the world. We totally love it. . . . You've got to be mentally ready to live out here. The wind is constantly blowing. The winters are severe, the summers are severe. I don't think a guy from Brooklyn, New York, can come out here. But this is for me. I'm going to retire here."

Ellen Lee, executive director, Chamber of Commerce: "It's a shock, especially to peo- ple coming from the East, to discover that we've got a few trees here. We name each one of them and take care of them. Have you seen 'Dances With Wolves'? That will show you what I'm talking about. You can look for miles and see nothing on the horizon. It's pretty overwhelming. . . . Economic diversity, of course, is still an issue. Our major employer is the government. Almost everyone has someone in the family working in a state-government job. That is peachy keen and pretty stable, but when you depend on just one crop, one product, one service, you are pretty much at its mercy. . . . We do things by ourselves for ourselves. South Dakota has seven state universities but we had none. So we made our own school. . . . Capital University Center has no walls. We use the high school nights and weekends. It's giving everyone who wants an education the opportunity to get one. It's been studied as a model of an adult learning center. I don't know if this could have been started anyplace else. We wanted it and we did it."

Dianna Knox, school-board president, state employee: "I have a master's degree in counseling and work as prevention coordinator for the Division of Alcohol and Drug Abuse. I'm a real youth advocate. This is an opportunity for me to combine professional life with personal passion, increasing happy lifestyles for young people. . . . For the size of the community and state, there are a lot of options for young people. You can do very well in our schools. . . . We have a really strong music and art program that starts in about the fifth grade. . . . One of the most vital parts of our community is the community theater, the Pierre Players. It's been in existence about 23 years, an incredibly talented bunch of people. . . . You can be a big fish in a small pond in a hurry. For young people that is a real opportunity to get lifetime experiences. . . . This is a Republican town, and statewide very Republican. We're pretty much middle class, a preponderance of well educated, white-collar people. We're fairly conservative, fiscally and socially conservative, too much so to suit me. I'm a social liberal. . . . Something else you could say for Pierre.

This is a really beautiful place. I was born and raised here. This used to be thought of as a cow town. Sioux Falls was the mecca. Well, we have a saying here, 'Pierre Pride.' Every year we plant 12 miles of petunias along the boulevard. People take a lot of pride in their property. . . . Our climate is severe but we have six months when it's very pleasant. You have to have some oompah to live here." ■

Pikeville, KY 41501

Location: 139 miles southeast of Lexington, 100 miles south of Huntington, near the 3-state corner of Kentucky, Virginia, and West Virginia.

Population: 6,324 (1990).

Growth rate: 9% since 1986.

Per capita income: $9,211 (1985), 6.5% higher than state average ($8,614).

Geography/climate: Cumberland Mountains of Central Appalachia. Continental, temperate climate. Average 16 inches of snow, 2 days below zero, 100 below freezing. Average 41 inches of rain, 15 days over 90 degrees. Periods of high humidity spring, summer. Lovely fall.

Economic base: Coal-mining and related enterprises generate most industrial revenues—county is the top underground bituminous coal-producing county in the U.S. Government is main employer in service sector. Other large payrolls: Methodist Hospital of Kentucky, 700; Mountain Top Baking, cookie factory, 200; Pikeville College; Pikeville National Corporation, bank holding company. Tourism, conventions draw significant dollars. Pikeville is seat of Pike County, area retail center.

Newspaper: *Appalachian News Express*, P.O. Box 802, Pikeville, KY 41501. 606-437-4054. Monday, Wednesday, Friday. Terry Spears, editor. $37 a year.

TV, radio: Local AM, FM stations. Cable brings in Chicago, Atlanta, networks, PBS. NPR reception marginal.

Health care: Methodist Hospital of Kentucky, 221 beds. 75 physicians, 29 dentists in local practice.

Schools: 1 elementary (K–6). Pikeville High School (7–12) enrolls 620, sends 75%-80% of graduates to college. Recent composite ACT score, 21.6.

Educational level: 6.2% of Pike County residents have 16 or more years of formal education; state average, 11.1%. Per capita expenditure for public education, $353; state average, $314.

Library: Pikeville Public Library, 33,000 volumes.

Recreation: Bob Amos Park, in town, has miniature golf, horse-show ring, ball fields, tennis courts, basketball court, football field, picnicking, hiking. Scenic view of the Cut-Thru from an overlook. Fishing, boating, camping at Fishtrap Lake, 10 miles southeast. Breaks Interstate Park, 23 miles southeast on the Virginia border, offers camping, fishing, kayaking, whitewater rafting, nature trails, lodge. Pike County, center of Kentucky's mountain vacation area, embraces some of the most majestic scenery in the eastern US.

3 BR, 2 BA house: $70,000 to $80,000. Up a county creek or side road, $60,000s.

Cost of electricity: $.05 per kilowatt hour.

Cost of natural gas: $.52 per therm.

Sales tax: 6% (excluding medicine and food).

State income tax: 2% to 6%.

Churches: 14. Denominations: Assemblies

of God, Baptist, Southern Baptist, Christian, Church of Christ, Episcopal, Holiness, Lutheran-ELCA, Presbyterian, Roman Catholic, United Methodist.

Pikeville is a monument to a young man's dream and an old man's determination—the same man. He is William C. Hambley, Jr., a native, who observed while still in elementary school that the railroad running smack through the middle of Pikeville created an "other" side of the tracks, not to mention the soot it dragged in from coal-car loading operations at either end of town. Young Hambley resolved to improve his home environment.

Years passed. Hambley got a medical degree at Northwestern University, came back home to practice, got elected mayor, served 30 years, and left quite a mark on the community: a three-quarter-mile-long, 500-foot-deep channel blasted out of Peach Orchard Mountain. The Cut-Thru, as it is called, became a new route for the railroad tracks, a river, and four highways that converge at Pikeville. Dedicated in 1987, this immense engineering and earth-moving project took 14 years, $60 million, and extraordinary patience on the part of townspeople to complete. But when it was finished they had not only banished those divisive railroad tracks but solved a periodic river-flooding problem and created 240 acres of prime, buildable land on the old river bed.

Pikeville also is proud of its hillbilly heritage and sponsors an annual national gathering of the clans each spring, as the crocuses and jonquils bloom, and redbud and service dot the hillsides. It is a time to recall those two Pike County families whose names are legendary: the Hatfields and the McCoys.

What residents say . . .

Carrie Cinnamond, co-owner, Economy Drug Store: "Building the Cut-Thru meant suffering through a lot of dirt and filth and doing without for years. We looked at it and hoped one day it would be over. The idea of putting all your efforts into this one program! . . . We didn't have anything concrete happening so far as progress for the basic town. Everything Pikeville was doing was centering on this one thing, and only Mayor Hambley had the vision to see it. . . . Now that it's over, I have a great deal of hindsight and think why did I complain so much. . . . My house is built on land where the river used to be. . . . The business brought my husband and me to Pikeville. We have a 7,000-square-foot store in the first shopping center. It's 26 years old. . . . This little town serves a greater population than most little county seats. Retail trade has always been better than expected, even during a recession. . . . I guess because of the remoteness of our location, plus people wanting to shop at home. In

279

this part of Kentucky the people are really competitive. It's a matter of being close-knit.... As far as breaking into the old Pikeville society, it just doesn't happen to people like me.... I'm from Paintsville. I was accepted but still not one of them. Pikeville is loaded with people from other places.... We just lucked into Pikeville."

Bill Owens, president, Pikeville College: "The college was founded in 1889 by Presbyterians who realized there was a shortage of colleges and churches. Ninety-five percent of the students come from within 50 miles of Pikeville. They are non-traditional. The average age is 25 or 26 and three-fourths are female ... women who did not go to college or quit many years ago and have decided if they are going to improve the home situation they need a college degree. This tends to happen when the economy gets worse ... the women tend to move forward. Forty percent of our graduates are certified to teach. The nursing program and business program is large. Computer science is large. Our students come from this area and our graduates stay here.... People feel they need to rely on themselves. Many years ago, survival meant going outside for help. I have noticed a real spirit in this county of self-help.... That's what I like about Pikeville."

Sara George, co-owner of Printing by George: "I was editor of the newspaper. My husband was publisher. We decided this town needed a good commercial printing company that would concentrate on graphics, typography, and design. So we left the newspaper business.... This is coal-mining country. Up until the last couple of decades we were fairly isolated simply because we were in the mountains and

the road system was not as well developed as in other parts of the country. Not a lot of new people moved in.... Pikeville in comparison to other towns its size in Central Appalachia is much more cosmopolitan and sophisticated. At the same time, it is still a small town in the mountains.... Activities tend to center around church, school, children, and family.... When I was growing up in this area, it was an hour and a half to the nearest four-lane highway. Now I live on one.... We have been told for years that we are ignorant hillbillies. Many small towns being isolated in the mountains were slower to reap the benefits of federal programs and grant money. Pikeville was one of the first Model Cities. We've been the recipient of a lot of federal programs that have built everything from a day-care center that people come from Europe to inspect ... to a high-rise apartment building for the elderly and handicapped. Hopefully, we have been an inspiration to other towns in this part of the country."

Kitty Pauley, administrative assistant to the mayor: "I think Pikeville has a very liberal, tolerant view of many different lifestyles ... yet somehow maintains traditional values. A lot of that has to do with the churches and our college. It has been interracial ... we've had people from African cultures. I think any community with a college is a little more liberal. Being a church-related college may have something to do with it.... If people make an effort to become involved, I think they're rapidly accepted.... I don't think we knock on the doors of new people. We don't purposely ignore people, but we don't think of not knowing most people already."

Walter May, broadcaster, mayor: "For a city our size we have been able to attract some fairly good-size conventions. The Kentucky Broadcasters Association just met here, their first time out of Louisville and Lexington. I'm a member of the board of directors and they mostly came here as a favor to me. But they said it was the best convention they ever had. . . . I've been a broadcaster since the mid-1950s. I own two radio stations here in Pikeville. Used to own a group of stations. . . . We're the cleanest city in the State of Kentucky. We are obsessive about keeping our city clean. If we see litter in your yard, we'll go in and get it out." ∎

Plymouth, NH 03223

Location: 59 miles north of Manchester, 112 miles north of Boston, 200 miles south of Montreal, between the Lakes region and the White Mountains of north central New Hampshire.

Population: 5,811 (1990).

Growth rate: 12% since 1980.

Per capita income: $7,235 (1985), 62% of state average ($11,659).

Geography/climate: Elevation 514 feet. Scenic, heavily forested area, 5 miles west of Squam Lake, where *On Golden Pond* was filmed. Long, snowy, sometimes bitterly cold winters. January average temperature 15.6 degrees, with range of 8 to 30. Up to 90 inches of snow through season. July averages: low, 53; high, 81. Warm summer days, cool nights. Colorful, pleasant falls. Annual rainfall, 38 inches.

Economic base: Plymouth State College, 4,000 students and 450 employees, drives the economy. Other payrolls: Plymouth Manufacturing, paint paddles, 70 employees; Town of Plymouth, 72; Mountain Media, printers, 25; Sport Pillows, stuffed novelties, 16. Tenney Mountain Business District has the area's largest supermarket, auto dealers, specialty shops. Retail center for 7 surrounding towns.

Newspaper: *The Record Citizen*, 111 Main Street, Plymouth, NH 03264. 603-536-1311. Published weekly, Wednesday. Brian McCarthy, editor. $22 a year.

TV, radio: Local AM, FM stations. Cable carries network TV, PBS from Boston; Portland, Maine. NPR received in area—weakly.

Health care: Speare Memorial Hospital, 49 beds. 20 physicians, 5 dentists in local practice.

Schools: 1 elementary (K–8) enrolling 444. Plymouth Area High School enrolls 560, sends 41% to 4-year college, 12% to 2-year. SAT averages: verbal, 423; math, 469. Also in town: Holderness School (9–12), private boarding and day school enrolling 262. University of New Hampshire-Plymouth State College, 4,000 students.

Educational level: 21.9% of Grafton County residents have 16 or more years of formal education; state average, 18.2%. Per capita expenditure for public education, $473; state average, $396.

Library: Plymouth Public Library, 30,000 volumes.

Recreation: Cluster of nearby lakes provides setting for many outdoor pursuits. Largest is Lake Winnipesaukee, 12 miles southeast. Others: Newfound, Winnisquam, Squam, Ossipee. Many sites for camping, boating, swimming, fishing. White Mountain National Forest, immediately north of town, is major skiing destination, including Loon Mountain, Bretton Woods, Wildcat, Black Mountain. Hiking, hunting, cross-country skiing, snowmobiling. Plymouth has its own major ski area: Tenney Mountain. Parks & Recreation Department organizes year-round programs for all age groups.

3 BR, 2 BA house: $125,000.

Cost of electricity: $.10 per kilowatt hour.

Cost of propane: $1.85 per gallon.

Sales tax: None.

State income tax: None.

Church: Assemblies of God, Christian, Church of Jesus Christ of Latter-day Saints, Congregational, Methodist, Roman Catholic.

A number of college towns are represented in this book. Plymouth is one of those, and, along with Williamstown, Massachusetts, is one of the most heavily dependent on the college community. College students are counted as residents of the place where they are living when the federal census is taken. Thus, when the head counters counted Plymouth in April 1990, approximately 4,000 students at Plymouth State College were counted as residents of Plymouth, New Hampshire—outnumbering the 1,800 other, permanent residents by a significant margin. This might give a permanent resident an inferiority complex. However, Chris Northrop views the college population as an overall plus.

What residents say . . .

Chris Northrop, town administrator: "I'm the community planner. I administer the business of the Planning Board, the Zoning Board of Adjustments. Also, I review land-use permit applications for the Board of Selectmen, assisting people with applications for subdivisions. . . . We've been affected like everyone else [but] I think Plymouth has fared fairly well, and the major overriding factor is Plymouth State College, historically a big part of the community and increasingly becoming a bigger part. . . . It's getting to the point where the college is almost rivaling the town as to stature and influence. The college is by far the major employer and a very stable employer, not affected by fluctuations in defense, and that is good for the town. They are not losing a lot of faculty and staff. . . . We've really seen a marked decrease in construction, although two big churches have been built, the most recent Plymouth Assembly of God, and about three years ago, the Mormons. . . . One other aspect

that has been evident, an erosion of what small manufacturing base we've had. There were three manufacturers in town. Today only one exists . . . Plymouth Manufacturing, they make paint paddles, tongue depressors, and popsicle sticks. They're going through a miniature expansion."

Herschel Steen, project manager, Plymouth Manufacturing: "We're not General Motors by any means. We're a small company, about 70 employees. With expansion we'll be around 100. We manufacture die-cut wood products. . . . It's an old shoe machinery factory we bought and revamped. We're putting quite a bit of money into it now. . . . In paint paddles, we are probably one of the three biggest . . . in the area of three million a year . . . with major accounts like Sherwin Williams. This area of New England has a good supply of white birch. That's all we use. We buy from a 50-mile radius."

Dave Switzer, professor of history, Plymouth State; chairman, Plymouth Conservation

Commission: "Our biggest accomplishment this year, we negotiated a 'conservation easement' on 1,100 acres of land, which means the land stays in the hands of the owner; however, there are restrictions on how it can be used. No buildings, no signs, no utility lines. It's forest land. We have just finished a trail up Plymouth Mountain. Great views. On a clear day you can see all the way to Maine."

Gail Wiltse, guidance director, Plymouth Area High School: "It's amazing the cross-section. We have kids from Appalachia to children of college professors. . . . We have an honors program in the major areas, English, history. The only AP course we now have is calculus. Kids if they have a free period can take courses at Plymouth State at half tuition. Lots of them do it in the afternoon and evening. The college will give scholarships. . . . We've had a number of homeless, not living with any relative, living with friends . . . one boy living in his car. Our vice principal has taken a number of kids in. Teachers have. What's interesting is many of them are bright kids, definitely college-bound, who for whatever reason can't cope with the home situation and find themselves with no place to live. Certainly the kids view this school as their family. We are small enough that we do notice. . . . One of our secrets here, it's been a cooperative effort. We just sat down last Friday afternoon, and on a payday, no less, to talk about kids who had multiple failures here, and why, and what else we could do. Our failure rate is much better now than it was two years ago."

Susan Wei, college teacher; member, Pemi Valley Habitat for Humanity: "Habitat builds houses in partnership with low-income families and sells the houses to them at no profit. This enables people to own a house who could not own one. . . . The one qualification is that families have not been able to get a commercial loan from the FHA or a bank or any of the usual sources. Otherwise, it's a nondiscriminatory selection process based on need. Our latest one is going to be dedicated in a couple of weeks, a four-bedroom, walk-out ranch in Ashland, right next door to Plymouth, built for a family whose home burned down in January last year, and just shortly after that two of the children were in a very serious automobile accident. One is now confined to a wheelchair. The home is handicapped-accessible, built almost entirely by volunteers. The construction supervisor is one of the best in the area. He used to be a neighbor of this family. . . . The plumber was a volunteer. The electricians were volunteers. The heating and furnace man volunteered his time . . . as well as many, many volunteers on framing and Sheetrock. . . . I enjoy framing, Sheetrocking, and all kinds of small chores. I don't do finish carpentry. . . . The family participated like mad. They are supposed to put in 500 hours and also help on the next house, so they become not only receivers but also givers. This family has invested way over. . . . The house is costing them $18,000 because they got a great many contributions of materials. Normally our houses cost between $30,000, and $40,000. Our mortgages usually run about $150 a month. Our families are very low income. . . . Habitat owns the mortgage, so there is no bank involved. . . . So often we are asked to give money. In this case we're giving time and energy. You go home from a day of heavy labor. You're tired but it's a good feeling. It does a lot of community-building." ■

Poteau, OK 74953

Location: 130 miles southeast of Tulsa, 35 miles southwest of Fort Smith, Arkansas, in extreme east central Oklahoma.

Population: 7,210 (1990).

Growth rate: 2% since 1980.

Per capita income: $8,255 (1985), 85% of state average ($9,754).

Geography/climate: River valley north of Winding Stair Mountains and Ouachita National Forest. Generally mild climate with occasional extremes. Average daily temperatures: January: low, 28; high, 50. Annual snowfall, 5 inches. 80 freezing days. July averages: low, 70; high, 94. Hot summers: 65 days at 90 or above. Annual precipitation, 48 inches.

Economic base: Agriculture, with manufacturing, lumbering, and recreation supplementing farm incomes. Seat of LeFlore County, retail trading center. Large payrolls: Wortz Company, crackers and cookies, 275 employees; Arundale of Oklahoma, injection plastic molding, 130; Johnson Controls, control panels, 110; Burner Systems, gas tube burners, 85; Kenco Plastics, injection molding, 85. AES, new electric power plant 10 miles out of town, employs 105 workers. LeFlore County sits atop major reserves of coal and the Arkoma natural-gas basin.

Newspaper: *Poteau Daily News & Sun*, 804 N. Broadway, Poteau, OK 74953. 918-647-3188. Tuesday through Friday, Sunday. Robin Brown, editor. $8 a month.

TV, radio: 1 AM, 2 FM stations. Cable carries network TV from stations in Tulsa, Fort Smith. Local cable-TV station broadcasts community announcements, sports, public meetings.

Health care: Eastern Oklahoma Medical Center, 84 beds. 14 physicians, 7 dentists in local practice.

Schools: 1 elementary (K–5); 1 middle (6–8). Poteau High School enrolls 537 students, sends 65% of graduates to higher education. 27 juniors taking ACT in 1991 scored 20 or higher. Advanced-placement English, calculus. Gifted-talented program. Correspondence courses from U. of Oklahoma in subjects not offered at high school. School pays for qualifying seniors to take one concurrent course at Carl Albert State College, local 2-year institution.

Educational level: 8% of LeFlore County residents have 16 or more years of formal education; state average, 15.1%. County per capita expenditure for public education, $431; state average, $430.

Library: Buckley Public Library, 30,000 volumes. Circulation 92,000. Genealogy reference room. Center of adult literacy program for county.

Recreation: PARC (Poteau Area Recreational Complex) has 4 fields in cloverleaf design. Walking tracks, volleyball pits, batting cages planned. Twyman City Park, 20 acres. Lake, picnic area, swimming pool, playground. 3 soccer fields, 340 participants. Youth league football. Little League at lighted fields. Water sports at Lake Wister, 11 miles southwest. Talimena Drive, 29 miles south, rides Ouachita Mountain crests for 54 miles.

3 BR, 2 BA house: $45,000 to $75,000.

Cost of electricity: $.07 per kilowatt hour in summer; $.04 in winter.

Cost of natural gas: $.47 per therm.

Sales tax: 7½%.

State income tax: 0.5% to 10%.

Churches: 22. Denominations: Baptist (7), Baptist-Freewill, Baptist-Missionary, Baptist-Southern, Christian, Church of Christ, Church of Jesus Christ of Latter-day Saints, Disciples of Christ, Episcopal, Jehovah's Witnesses, Methodist-United, Nazarene, Pentecostal, Pentecostal Church of God, Presbyterian, Roman Catholic.

The best place from which to view Poteau, and much of LeFlore County, is the top of "the world's highest hill," a remarkable mound about a mile and a half west of town. It is called Canaval, and it measures exactly 1,999 feet above the official elevation outside Poteau's City Hall. That may sound like unnecessary detail. Not so, says Poteau, because 2,000 feet is the dividing line between hills and mountains.

Sen. Robert Kerr once had a house atop Canaval. Today, a paved road winds five miles to the public overlook, where the city owns a bit of land. Poteau has already grown to the base of its hill and expects to plant houses right up the side.

Some of the occupants may be modern-day Okies. In a new chapter to *The Grapes of Wrath*, Californians are moving to Oklahoma. "They are selling those $300,000 homes out there, coming back here and buying a comparable home for $75,000—with money left over to retire on or go into business," says Mayor Don Barnes. "I've only been mayor five months and I've opened up three new subdivisions."

What residents say . . .

Jay Wilmeth, developer: "I'm building a $165,000 house on Canaval right now. . . . We have people drive through here, no family ties whatsoever, buy a piece of property and move back, like a man from Ohio I ran into last week at McDonald's. . . . But it's amazing. They might not move back for five, 10 years."

Wally Burchett, publisher, **Poteau News & Sun:** "We were the first newspaper in the state to convert from nondaily to daily in more than a decade, in April 1990. Our newspaper is just a reflection of the community it serves. Fortunately, Poteau and LeFlore County have enjoyed some extremely positive economic trends. . . . I bought the paper with two other partners in January of this year. For a 34-year-old man, it sounds kind of hokey and clichéish, but it's the good old American dream-come-true of ownership. We've made capital improvements, the most dramatic, installation of a News-King six-unit press, a quarter-million-dollar investment. We think this press will take us into the next century. . . . Poteau is not totally dependent on one big 5,000-employee factory. . . . We've got poultry processing. Chicken consumption nationwide is going up. OK Foods has built a 17-million-dollar plant to process poultry. They employ 200 . . . compete against Tyson. But the real benefit to the community is they want to have an abundance of chickens within a small radius. They are encouraging the construction of new poultry houses in the area. They provide you the chickens and the feed and you take it from there. One poultry house will net a person about $15,000 to $17,000 a year. Raising broilers takes about two hours a day. Most people hold down another job. Those people buy new trucks, new homes."

F. L. Holton, Jr., businessman: "My grandfather came to the county the month of statehood, November 1907. He was a farmer. In 1915, my father started a country store in Cameron with $750. We moved to Poteau in 1926 and expanded into a department store. . . . We now have a True Value hardware, furniture store, bank, and feed mill. We had a supermarket but sold it. We had the Pontiac dealership for 31 years but sold it and have been involved in broilers since, the county program of chicken hatcheries . . . In 1940, LeFlore County had 45,000 people. In 1950, we had 29,000. That's when we started to work on the four-point Poteau Plan . . . pastures, pork, poultry, production, meaning factory jobs. We created about 900 new industrial jobs. Our cracker plant turns out a million and a half pounds a week for 150 private labels. . . . We think we're the buckle of the Bible Belt. That gives stability."

Don Barnes, mayor: "We're working very hard to get a bypass around our city. Our main thoroughfare, Broadway, has a traffic count of 25,000 cars a day. It's quite out of the ordinary. Poteau is the center hub for a population of about 50,000. . . . This is one of the first places Sam Walton put in a Wal-Mart. . . . I've been mayor for five months. . . . I had been for the last 20 years a radio announcer, in advertising and public relations. . . . My wife and I own a locally originated cable channel . . . two channels on local cable. One is public-service messages. On the other one we videotape things, basically home-type video cameras. We show our city council meetings. . . . Advertising time is sold. . . . I'm kind of a celebrity. Last summer I had articles in two national magazines telling people how to start a cable channel. It was the cover story in *Income Opportunities*. I produced a two-hour videotape telling people how to do this. It sold for $49.95."

Joe White, president, Carl Albert State College: "The community decided they wanted to attract the smartest and brightest students from this area. Being a two-year institution, we didn't have any campus housing. They decided the best thing was to construct a couple of dormitories to attract students and offer scholarships equal to a football scholarship at Oklahoma. . . . We have a half-million-dollar endowment fund, and two half-million-dollar dormitories paid entirely from private funds. . . . Our benefactor, Carl Albert, Rhodes scholar, Speaker of the US House 1968 to 1976, is 86 years old. . . . Last year for our speaker series we had former president Jimmy Carter visit. This year, former president Gerald Ford." ◾

Red Wing, MN 55066

Location: On the Mississippi River, 50 miles southeast of Minneapolis-St. Paul.

Population: 15,134 (1990).

Growth rate: 10% since 1980.

Per capita income: $10,936 (state average, $11,186).

Geography/climate: Bluffy contour along the Mississippi gives way to bottomlands and prairie. Rigorous climate—long and often severely cold winters with average 16 days below zero and 39 inches of snow; short spring and fall; warm summers with average 14 days in the 90s. Average annual precipitation, 27 inches.

Economic base: Red Wing Shoe Co. employs 900 people at 2 plants. Northern States Power Co., 2nd largest employer, 400. St. John's Regional Health Center, 320 employees. Other health services employ additional 450. Diversified manufacturing includes diplomas, transmission poles, rubber products, mechanical arms, robotics, kitchen cabinets.

Newspaper: *Red Wing Republican Eagle*, 433 W. Third St., Red Wing, MN 55066. 612-388-8235. Daily except Sunday. Jim Pumarlo, editor. 13-week subscription, $23.80.

TV, radio: 1 local AM, 1 FM station. All major networks, PBS, NPR from Twin Cities.

Health care: St. John's Regional Hospital, 84 beds, plus 15-bed chemical-dependency unit. 36 physicians, 16 dentists in local practice.

Schools: 5 elementary (K–5); 1 middle (6–8) enrolling 693; 1 high school enrolling 905. 65% of high school seniors seek higher education. Composite ACT score, 21.1. 1 Roman Catholic, 3 Lutheran elementary schools.

Educational level: 11.9% of Goodhue County residents have 16 or more years of formal education; state average, 17.4%. Per capita expenditure for public education, $616; state average, $554.

Library: 60,000 volumes.

Recreation: 2 golf courses, outdoor and indoor swimming pools, public tennis courts at 4 locations, 2 ski slopes within 9 miles, fishing for walleyes, crappies, northern, sunfish, and bass in the Mississippi and its backwaters. Abundant hunting on public lands nearby. Winter blahs dispelled by Shiver River Days, a January festival featuring triathlon of ice-skating, running, cross-country; mutt races starring youngsters and their dogs; softball in the snow; chili cooking.

3 BR, 2 BA house: $70s. New 4 BR, $85,000; next to country club, $99,000.

Cost of Electricity: $.06 per kilowatt hour.

Cost of Natural gas: $.51 per therm.

Sales tax: 6%.

State income tax: To $19,000 taxable income, 6%; over $19,000, 8%.

Churches: 23. Denominations: Assemblies of God, Baptist, Christian & Missionary Alliance, Church of Christ, Episcopal, Evangelical Covenant, Jehovah's Witnesses, Lutheran, United Methodist, Nondenominational, Pentecostal, Presbyterian USA, Roman Catholic, Seventh-Day Adventist.

They say that puffed rice was invented in Red Wing. In the Minnesota spirit of full disclosure, natives note that the discovery was probably accidental. A rare event. Little seems to have happened by accident in this well organized place that's not too big, not too small, and definitely not "small-town," according to natives.

Red Wing has been doing business for many years. Incorporated in 1857, a year before Minnesota became a state, by 1873 the Mississippi River town had become the largest primary wheat market in the world, with warehouse capacity of a million bushels. The pottery industry thrived for nearly a century. Its shoe factory has given work to generations of residents and plowed profits back into community improvements, in partnership with the city. Joint public–private ventures have restored old buildings to new life. Blending old and new is common: "We're kind of unusual in that we have both a nuclear plant and an Indian reservation," says newspaper editor Jim Pumarlo.

Public service has deep roots. The top local newspaper story in 1990 was a point of pride. Joanell Dyrstad, three-term mayor of Red Wing, won election as lieutenant governor of Minnesota.

What residents say . . .

Jean Chesley, director of the Goodhue County Historical Society: "Red Wing has such a strong and stable history to it. That's mainly because of the industries. We've been fortunate to have strong industry, skilled labor, and a large number of very generous people, philanthropists who helped to build the early things that are still with us. The Red Wing Shoe Co. is almost an institution in our town. . . . They make specialized shoes of all kinds but they're best known for their hiking shoes. . . . The company has been very, very instrumental in things that go on here. They have done a lot to restore old buildings— they restored the St. James Hotel."

Frank Chesley, consultant: "Two nuclear reactors within the city limits contribute to the high assessed value of the region, keep taxes low, and help with an outstanding school system. Being located about an hour from Minneapolis and St. Paul, you have the advantages of a metropolitan area. There is some commuting, of course. But we are just far enough away that we are not a bedroom community."

Dean Massett, city administrator: "We're growing at about one percent a year, and we think that's about right. If we were to grow much faster I think we would possibly tax our utility system. The electric utility represents about 70 percent of our tax base. That plus 10 leading industries totals about 85 percent. So residential taxes are rather reasonable. One of the things that makes us successful is public–private partnerships. The T.B. Sheldon auditorium is a good example. That historic theater was renovated at a cost of $3 million, half from private donations and the other half from a city bond issue. Being a native, I really appreciate this community, but I hear newcomers talk with pride. . . . It's a clean, safe community. We sweep our streets every other day!"

Gertrude Richardson, community leader: "I was on the auditorium board, a school board member for 16 years, active in women's clubs, very active with the American Cancer Society, the Red Cross, Girl Scouts, church, the Lutheran Church is finally getting into social problems. . . . Red Wing has a blend of natives with a tremendously loyal spirit and enough new people who have come here because of the wide opportunity to do things other than for pay. We're heavily, heavily endowed with people interested in the theater, and their interests and talents are put to work. One develops pride when one is part of an organization. . . . Another thing about this town, the people living in your area are not all one financial level. I always say my Red Wing friends are a lot more cosmopolitan than those who live in the suburbs of Red Wing."

Jane Donkers, former school-board chairman: "Has anyone told you about the Environmental Learning Center? It just celebrated its 20th anniversary. The ELC started when a couple of community people thought we should help our young people learn about their environment . . . if you know about it you will enjoy it. My children when they were in junior high were small physically, so football and basketball were not choices. But that was when the ELC was starting, through financial support of Red Wing Shoe. All my children participated, and two were later instructors. It has been the source of their developing many lifetime skills, as adults and now as parents."

Bruce Ause, director of the Environmental Learning Center: "We work with about 120 kids a year. Most start in the seventh grade. That age group is very vulnerable and also very enthusiastic. They like a challenge and things that are new. And they certainly like the outdoors . . . this fills a niche for kids who are not athletes . . . we're pretty strong into cross-country, winter camping . . . in the summertime quite a bit of kayaking, rock climbing, bike touring. In spring, making maple syrup, orienteering. . . . You have a general attrition. If you start with 40 seventh graders, by the 10th grade it is down to eight or nine kids from that group. And that's all right as far as we're concerned. We hope they learn to do a few things on their own and share with other people. . . . There's no membership fee. They are just expected to pay for their share of food and transportation." ■

Rexburg, ID 83440

Location: 28 miles northeast of Idaho Falls, 70 miles southwest of Wyoming-Montana-Idaho junction, on the Snake River Plain.

Population: 14,302 (1990).

Growth rate: 14% since 1986.

Per capita income: $5,733 (1985), 67% of state average ($8,567).

Geography/climate: High-country valley, elevation 4,850 feet, sitting atop the Upper Snake River Aquifer. Teton Mountains to the east, Targhee National Forest northeast, northwest. January average low temperature, 7 degrees. A week or 2 of 30-below not uncommon. Average annual snowfall 54 inches. Summer daytime temperatures: 80–90. Dry heat, low humidity. Rainfall averages 11 inches.

Economic base: Agriculture, especially the Idaho Burbank Russet potato, shipped nationwide. Large payrolls: Ricks College, 630 employees; Artco, wedding-invitation printer, 550; Madison School District, 500; Basic American Foods, 260; Madison Memorial Hospital, 220. Rexburg is the seat of Madison County.

Newspapers: *Rexburg Standard & Journal*, 23 S. 100 E., Rexburg, ID 83440. 208-356-5441. Weekly (Tuesday). Roger O. Porter, publisher and editor. $31 a year.

TV, radio: Local FM station is NPR affiliate. Cable brings in network TV, PBS, from Idaho Falls, Salt Lake City.

Health care: Madison Memorial Hospital, 50 beds. 20 physicians, 9 dentists in local practice.

Schools: 7 elementary (K–5); 1 central (6); 1 junior high (7–8). Madison High School enrolls 1,227, offers advanced placement classes, including English for college credit; sends about 70% of students to college. Recent composite ACT, 22. Many local graduates go to Ricks College, in town, which enrolls 7,500 students and is largest privately owned junior college in the nation.

Educational level: 18.7% of Madison County residents have 16 or more years of formal education; state average, 15.8%. Per capita expenditure for public education, $343; state average, $380.

Library: Madison Library District has 45,000 volumes, 14,400 registered borrowers.

Recreation: 3 city parks with ball fields, swimming pool, picnic shelters. Among more interesting possibilities an hour or 2 away: Yellowstone National Park, Grand Teton National Park, Jackson Hole, Kelly Canyon Ski Area, Targhee National Forest, Craters of the Moon.

3 BR, 2 BA house: $75,000 to $80,000.

Cost of electricity: $.06 to $.08 per kilowatt hour.

Cost of natural gas: $.41 to $.45 per therm.

Sales tax: 5%.

State income tax: Graduated 2% to 8.2%.

Churches: 92% of local population are members of the Mormon church—the Church of Jesus Christ of Latter-day Saints. Other denominations: Independent Baptist, Presbyterian, Roman Catholic.

Rexburg was founded in 1883 by a company of 600 Mormon homesteaders. The land was fertile and brought forth plenty of grain and hay, and within a few years the population had swelled to several thousand. The first potatoes were planted around the turn of the century. They also thrived in the warm days and cool nights. Today, potatoes anchor the economy—two whole pages of the classified phone book are devoted to potato-growing equipment and services. Rexburg sends spuds to the nation.

On the other side of the balance of trade, Rexburg has been cultivating sunbirds in Arizona and Texas and now attracts an annual migration of some 1,500 retirees—fugitives from summer heat seeking relief in an eastern Idaho town. The timing works out fine for Rexburg, which has a lot of rental housing available in summer when most Ricks College students have left town. "That's a real plus to our economy," says Mayor Nile Boyle, owner of a pharmacy. "Sunbirds don't have a lot of problems. They use Rexburg as a hub for shorter trips. And golf is pretty cheap here—a three-month pass for $120."

For a long time, events in Rexburg have been dated either before or after the catastrophic flood in 1976 when the Teton Dam burst and half the town was under water. But a new period began in 1986, the first year of a remarkable yearly gathering in Rexburg of folk dancers from all over the world.

What residents say . . .

Donna Benfield, chair, Idaho International Folk Dance Festival: "We just found out we got another $5,000! It's kinda like a dream. We put on a $100,000 event every year just by the seat of our pants. This year we decided to go to some of the major businesses . . . that was Valley Bank calling. If we include the volunteer money, it would go into two or three hundred thousand dollars. . . . Each year we bring in eight to 11 teams from foreign countries. They all come here to Rexburg, Idaho. . . . This year from the Soviet Union, China, India, Italy, Native Americans representing the U.S., Spain, Mexico. They all get here about the 24th of July . . . housed entirely by the community, all their food and lodg-ing taken care of. . . . We usually have close to 300 dancers, and easily 150 families that do the lodging every year. That's where the real connection is made. I had three Chinese stay with me, the following year three teenage boys from France, last year two Czech girls in their early twenties. This year I'm going to do China again. Though you don't speak their language, you do a lot of pantomiming and a lot of right-from-the-heart stuff. It's amazing how you can communicate . . . really fun trying to explain what a nerd is! . . . My husband and I are from Los Angeles. We picked Rexburg, Idaho, from a spot on the map. We had no friends, no relatives here. We gave up everything and moved here because we wanted to raise our kids in a good, clean, wholesome place . . . and we have loved every minute. . . . We did vacationing in the area and came here twice . . . parked in front of a local market and said, 'Let's just see what these people are like.' We liked what we saw, and said, 'Now we're going to vacation for two weeks and decide if we can really move here.' But it didn't take us that long. There's a phone booth on the highway at Sugar City, about five miles north of here. We called California and said we're moving. . . . We weren't [Mormons] then but we are now. We were just like everybody, kinda nothing, kinda Catholic from birth. . . . There's something special about Rexburg."

Louis Clements, director, Teton Flood Museum and Upper Snake River Historical Society: "We're having our 10th anniversary this year. It was pretty hard to put [the museum] together when all of our photos and most other things were lost in the flood. We went on an aggressive campaign to make sure people didn't throw things away because of the flood. . . . Rexburg is about 92 percent Mormon, and that does influence the community. I can give you a quote. I teach at the high school. My principal has said to me a couple of times, 'When I go to meetings of other schools our size, they want to talk about drug problems and alcohol problems. I want to talk about attendance.' The church does not believe in drinking or smoking. Oh, there is some, but it's not a major problem. . . . The church teaches, get as much education as possible. I think there is a much higher percentage of cultural events here compared to other towns. We have a fiddler tonight that traveled 300 miles to come over. Two nights ago we had a Western band. In

a couple of weeks, a Chautauqua. . . . We have a Catholic church and a Presbyterian church. The community is, well, tolerant. Religion doesn't seem to be an issue, although there's always someone. . . . We have a lawsuit now, the ACLU enjoining us from having prayer at the high school. . . . They are focusing on us now, whereas teams around us can have prayer before athletic events. . . . It's a minor issue."

Nile Boyle, mayor: "Our growth rate is about right. We're not anxious to grow any faster, steady growth rather than boom, bust . . . but fast enough to create more jobs. . . . One of our biggest exports out of here is our kids. . . . The hardest part about being mayor is zoning, where no matter what you do someone's mad. We are rewriting the zoning ordinance now, trying to cover everything in advance."

Gary Archibald, president, Archibald Insurance & Real Estate Agency: "We've had quite a little bit of growth, people moving into the area. We find a lot of people moving from the more populous states, California and even Utah. There are some jobs, particularly in skilled areas. The college requires some people, it seems to be the main draw. . . . If you can't find what you need in Rexburg, on a short shopping trip you can end up in Idaho Falls, 29 miles away. When people want to make a weekend of it they'll go to Salt Lake City, 240 miles, a four-hour drive. . . . If I look out to the east I can see the Tetons, about 60 miles away, some of the most beautiful mountains in the world. If I look to the west it's fairly flat. The soil came from two volcanoes, two dormant volcanoes, of course. The volcanic soil plus the warm days and cool nights . . . that's what makes the Idaho Russet." ■

Rockland, ME 04841

Location: 81 miles northeast of Portland, 63 miles southwest of Bangor, on a well-protected Atlantic Ocean harbor at the mouth of Penobscot Bay.

Population: 7,972 (1990).

Growth rate: Very slow—32 people since 1986.

Per capita income: $7,830 (1985), 87% of state average ($9,042).

Geography/climate: Rocky New England seacoast. Winters can be long and severe but are tempered by the ocean. Average 160 days at freezing or below. Up to 70 inches of snow, but it doesn't last long. "Spring makes it all worthwhile," says one native. Extremely pleasant summers with only 5 days on average into the 90s. Sunny, pleasant falls.

Economic base: Seat of Knox County, commercial and labor center of mid-coast Maine. 28% manufacturing, 25% retail, 25% service sector, the remainder mixed. Large payrolls: Penobscot Bay Medical Center, 600 employees; Crowe Rope, 350; Samoset Resort, 300; Hurricane Island Outward Bound, 200; FMC Marine Colloids, 186. Long known as "Lobster Capital of the World" and still exports tons. Commercial waterfront being redeveloped for leisure–vacation use. Home harbor of growing fleet of windjammers.

Newspaper: *The Courier-Gazette*, 1 Park Drive, Rockland, ME 04841. 207-594-4401. Tuesday, Thursday, Saturday. Raymond E. Gross, publisher. $60 a year.

TV, radio: Local AM, FM stations. TV networks, PBS, NPR received off-air from Portland, Bangor. Cable available.

Health care: Penobscot Bay Medical Center, 106 beds, all private. 55 physicians, 9 dentists in local practice.

Schools: 3 elementary (K–5); junior high (6–8) enrolls 336. Rockland District High School enrolls 550, sends 40% of graduates to 4-year college, about 20% to business schools, junior college. ACT not administered. No SAT information available. 3 private schools in area: Pen Bay, Riley, Calvary Family.

Educational level: 15.4% of Knox County residents have 16 or more years of formal education; state average, 14.4%. Per capita expenditure for public education, $403; state average, $398.

Library: Rockland Public Library, 39,500 volumes, 4,000 borrowers.

Recreation: As a popular tourist destination, Rockland offers variety. Boating, cruising, fishing, scuba-diving. Tennis, racquetball, golf. Picnicking, parks, hiking. Town recreation center. Schooner regatta in July, lobster festival in August, Olde Fashioned Days of Christmas in December.

3 BR, 2 BA house: Around $100,000.

Cost of electricity: $.10 per kilowatt hour.

Cost of heating oil: $.74 per gallon.

Sales tax: 5%.

State income tax: 2% to 8.5%.

Churches: 15. Denominations: Baptist, Christian Science, Church of God, Church of the Nazarene, Congregational, Episcopal, Living Waters, Lutheran, Pentecostal, Reorganized Church of Jesus Christ of Latter-day Saints, Roman Catholic, Salvation Army, United Methodist, Universalist.

Synagogues: 1.

Native Americans called the place Catawamteak, or "great landing place." Yankees named it Rockland, possibly for the abundance of limestone. An easily navigated deep-water harbor made it possible to ship this basic building material to many markets. When the commercial prospects for limestone faded in the early twentieth century, fishing took its place, and thrived. Rockland became a fish town of renown. As recently as 20 years ago, 20 percent of the labor force worked in the fishing industry. But then the catch began to fade away, partly due to natural forces but mainly due to international treaties that changed fishing boundaries. Today, fishing employs fewer than five percent, and Rockland is changing once again. The new place is growing more important as a tourist and recreation center. On Mondays of summer months, as the fleet of windjammers sets sail from Rockland Harbor with paying guests aboard, the town seems to have come nearly full circle, back to Catawamteak.

What residents say . . .

Cap deRochemont, president, C.R. deRochemont Real Estate: "Maine real estate slipped in value as little as 10 percent and as much as 30 percent. We have not turned the corner completely, but things are beginning to pick up. I have two closings set for tomorrow. If we could just encourage people not to watch the morning news programs. . . . We do seem to be the destination of a lot of people who have worked for their 25-year watch. Maine itself is probably a small town. . . . You have an opportunity to really know your fellow townsman for good or bad. There are fewer phonies in small towns than in large cities because it's pretty hard to fool someone where you are well known. . . . [Volunteering] over and over and over again, that's the price of admission to live in a small town. I think I'm pretty standard. I have served as president of the hospital, president of Rotary, president of the Chamber of Commerce . . . again not because of any unique talents on my part. The burden of responsibility of each of these positions is shared with a rather limited force of people. You're not one in a million. You're one in 79 hundred. Your opportunity for service is part of the price of living in the community, a chance to be part of it, not just a spectator. . . . I'm chairman of the marketing committee and a director of Camden National Bank, a truly local bank. We have about 42 percent of the local market . . . honored by *Money* magazine as one of the strongest and best-run banks in Maine . . . not so conservative that we don't participate in financing business. There are 13 directors, and since they come from all walks of life, not a great deal goes on that they do not have some personal knowledge of, probably a more accurate pulse. . . . Of course, the loan officer takes full credit. . . . I am living in the same house that has been in the family for 120 years. It may be heretical for a broker to say that. Turn that to a plus: One purchase should last 120 years. I live in a typical two-and-a-half story wooden home, converted about 60 years ago from a barn to a residence, with an office on the first floor. . . . This is world headquarters."

Clayton Fowlie, Jr., executive director, Chamber of Commerce: "We seem to be leaning more to service and retail for the mid-coast region. We've lost some manufacturing, most in fishing, probably 500 jobs lost in the last year and a half . . . eight percent unemployment right now. . . . We're very fortunate compared to many communities that have lost a mill. Even though we've lost fishing we have managed to survive. Tourism is going to play a bigger part. The commercial waterfront is being rediscovered as 'Rockland, The Schooner Capital of the World.' We have 11 that work out of the Rockland harbor . . . vacations, day cruises, as more windjammers have shifted here. It's been building for the last two or three years. . . . We try to get the message out across the country, mailings to the largest 200 newspapers, travel magazines and editors. We invite them to visit us, continuously bombard them with schooner news. We try to get as much free editorial as opposed to advertising. . . . I grew

up in Rockland. It's pretty neat to be the executive director of the Chamber of Commerce in your home town."

Jim Ash, managing partner, Samoset Resort: "Let me give you some numbers: 230 acres, located in two towns, Rockland and Rockport. 150 hotel rooms, 72 condominiums, townhouse–condo project with 31 homes. 18-hole championship golf course that has been called 'The Pebble Beach of the East.' . . . Last year we had just about 74,000 guests, not including time-share. Clearly the sports activities are one of the major draws. Just being on the coast of Maine, we get people from all over the world."

Christopher Crosman, director, Farnsworth Library and Art Museum: "I've been here three years and some-odd months, previously in Buffalo at the Albright-Knox Art Gallery. The museum opened in 1948. The way the collection was formed is a very unusual story. The fellow in charge, Robert Bellows, decided to try to put together an American collection at a time when nobody cared two cents for American painting. He was able to acquire some very nice things, a general American collection with a strong emphasis on Maine artists. We have probably the second largest collection of Wyeth . . . Andrew; N.C., the famous illustrator; Jamie, Andrew's son. . . . Sculpture and paintings of Louise Nevelson, raised in Rockland and probably one of the most important sculptors of the mid-twentieth century. . . . For a small museum, it's a very respectable collection. The local population supports [the museum] very well . . . at any given time, 100 businesses, over 200 volunteers, unusual for a museum this size. Our membership stands at around a thousand families. . . . Rockland is quite a mixed little town, traditionally a working town with an active seaport, but also a number of people coming up to this part of the coast for quality of life, retirees, the usual young professional types, a very open and friendly place. There seems to be a very strong sense of community. For example, they were having problems last year getting the annual lobster festival together. The people who had run it years and years were getting tired . . . other business leaders stepped in. . . . New Englanders keep pretty much to themselves but are more than willing to help out if people need it. There is a strong sense of privacy. The Wyeths live up here, but I have yet to figure out where. Nobody will reveal it . . . to protect their privacy." ■

Rolla, MO 65401

Location: 103 miles southwest of St. Louis, 61 miles southeast of Jefferson City, on the northern edge of the Missouri Ozarks.

Population: 14,090 (1990).

Growth rate: 6% since 1980.

Per capita income: $9,119 (1985), 89% of state average ($10,283).

Geography/climate: Rolling hills. Temperate, 4-season climate with relatively mild winters, hot and humid summers. Average rainfall, 37 inches; snowfall, 12 inches. January is driest month; May is wettest with average 4.7 inches of rain. January temperatures: low 23–high 40, with 2 or 3 days dipping below zero per season. July averages, low 70–high 86. Average 38 days at 90 or above.

Economic base: University of Missouri-Rolla is backbone of economy. UMR plus other educational institutions and public agencies, including U.S. Geodetic Survey and the Bureau of Mines, employ 3,400 people. Rolla is seat of Phelps County, retail trading center for population of 190,000 in adjacent counties. Large payrolls: Phelps County Regional Medical Center, 813; Schwitzer, automotive cooling fans, 116; Royal Canon USA, dog and cat foods, 104; Can-Tex, plastic pipe, 82.

Newspaper: *Rolla Daily News*, 101 W. Seventh Street, Rolla, MO 65401. 314-364-2468. Evenings Monday through Friday, Sunday morning. R. D. Hohenfeldt, editor. $102 a year.

TV, radio: 2 local AM, 4 FM stations, including NPR. Cable carries network TV, PBS from St. Louis. Also Springfield, Jefferson City stations.

Health care: Phelps County Regional Medical Center, 258 beds. 88 physicians, 14 dentists in local practice.

Schools: 3 elementary (K–4); 1 middle (5–7) enrolling 530; junior high (8–9) enrolling 600; vocational-technical school enrolling 513 secondary students, 291 adults. Rolla High School (10–12) enrolls 800, sends 65% to college. Composite ACT, 1990: 22. Composite SAT, 1989: verbal, 520; math, 580. 5 parochial schools enroll more than 350. B. W. Robinson State School, Rolla Cerebral Palsy School serve handicapped children from Phelps and surrounding counties. Gingerbread House, residential center for severely handicapped children. Park College School of Nursing has recently moved to Rolla.

Educational level: 14.9% of Phelps County residents have 16 or more years of formal education; state average, 13.9%. Per capita expenditure for public education, $337; state average, $378.

Library: Rolla Public Library, 25,000 volumes.

Recreation: 12 public parks, Olympic-size outdoor pool, lighted ball diamonds, 15 tennis courts, 2 small lakes stocked for fishing, daily-fee golf course, country club. Bowling alley, roller-skating rink, 3 movie theaters. Phelps County has more fishing streams than any other county in state. Lake of the Ozarks, 70 miles west, has diverse water sports.

3 BR, 2 BA house: Median price for existing house, $50,000. New construction ranges from $60,000 to $170,000.

Cost of electricity: $.05 per kilowatt hour.

Cost of propane heating fuel: $.96 per gallon.

Sales tax: 6.75%.

State income tax: 1.5% to 6%.

Churches: 34. Denominations: Apostolic Pentecostal, Assemblies of Yahweh, Assemblies of God, Baptist (7), Christian, Church of Christ, Church of Jesus Christ of Latter-day Saints, Church of the Nazarene, Episcopal, Full Gospel, Lutheran, Methodist, Non-denominational, Pentecostal, Presbyterian, Reorganized LDS, Roman Catholic, Seventh-Day Adventist, Society of Friends, Unitarian Universalist.

Every weekday morning, from 5:00 to 9:00, before city government officially gets started, Rolla is governed by "The Morning Mayors," radio personalities Bob McKune and Tom Colvin, on KTTR, at 1490 on the AM band. McKune introduced the idea to Rolla radio in 1968. Except for a short break after selling the station, McKune has presided continuously. Colvin took the oath of office in 1984. The Morning Mayors exchange news and views, support worthy causes, and end each show, in unison, with a Southwest-style goodbye: "Sa-we-dee-kop, y'all!"

What residents say ...

Bob McKune, "Morning Mayor" of Rolla: "What kinds of things make us mad? I would think unfairness to an underdog would get us uptight. The national media will get us uptight, particularly the national eastern media. . . . Not too many people realize there's a whole world on the west side of the Mississippi River. . . . We get a little uptight about the Congress. We're affected by taxes. We're also very much environment- and wildlife-conscious. We have a high amount of wildlife and try to take care of it. Yet someone who takes a turkey out of season to eat for his family probably isn't going to upset us. . . . We get pretty fired up about local politics. We still have a lot of politicians who walk the neighborhoods and knock on doors. We talk Democratic, we register Democratic, but we're voting Republican. . . . We're very much education-conscious, concerned about the quality of student we send out. . . . We, like many small towns, have trouble finding jobs for our kids suitable for a high quality of life. We're concerned when they go out. . . . When I came here in the later '60s, I had dinner one night in a one-room house with a dirt floor, yet the University of Missouri at Rolla has the state's first nuclear reactor. . . . In 1960, the census showed one out of four people had only an eighth-grade education. Yet today we have a triple-A school."

Kristi Creighton, sophomore, University of Missouri-Rolla: "I'm majoring in life sciences, a pre-med student. UMR is one of the best engineering schools in the nation. Chemical, mechanical, electrical. Also engineering management. Not many schools have a PhD program in management. There's a lot of smart people around here. Not a lot of nightlife, though. Students don't really like Rolla. But it's a good education and the faculty here is great. They go out of their way to help you. . . . Rolla is dependent upon UMR. The students bring in a lot of commerce. . . . St. Patrick's Day is a big celebration. St. Patrick is the patron saint of miners. We have a week-long celebration, a large parade. . . . That's probably the biggest time when UMR and Rolla interact. Rolla doesn't particularly like it. We're in the book of world records for the most alcohol consumed in a week. . . . We lived in Scotland when my father was in the Navy. We literally picked Rolla out of a book. It's close enough to a military base that we can get medical care. It is a college town, so there is some cultural life. Not a stagnating town where people just get old. Close enough to St. Louis so you can get there but it's not shoved down your throat. . . . They just opened the fine arts center at UMR to bring more arts to Rolla. They brought the Bolshoi Ballet in for the grand opening premier. I don't know how they got them. I was astounded. . . . Hey, we're not just a piddly little town. We can bring in the big names!"

***Roger Creighton, circulation manager, Rolla Daily News, *father of Kristi Creighton:* "I retired from the Navy after 23 years and wanted to get as far away from people and ocean as I could. Rolla had a nice downtown commercial area with a friendly atmosphere, low taxes and low prices for houses. The financial aspects were very positive. . . . With low cost also comes a sparsity of jobs. If you have an education and are not teaching, good jobs are about an hour and a half away. . . . We spent three years in Scotland. I had written to the United Farms real-estate company and told them I was looking for a small, midwestern town between 10 and 15 thousand. . . . They sent me everything. I took two weeks leave from the Navy. Rolla was the third one we looked at. I wanted a good school system to bring my kids up, a healthy environment that wasn't going to stagnate. The constant renewal of having students coming in makes the town stay young. . . . I said there's no more looking needed. I bought a 19-acre farm with a three-bedroom house and full basement for $65,000."

Leland Womack, retired teacher: "Lots of people live out on the farm. You farm and have cattle and a job somewhere. Bankers, lawyers, everybody enjoys being a farmer. We were eight miles out of town on a paved road. We had pasture for our cattle, made hay to feed them in the winter, taught the kids to paint and make fences. They had their horses and hunting. . . . We raised Angus cattle and for a long period we had hogs. Always produced our own hay. The boys learned to put it up and put it in the barn. Always had a big garden. We just kind of were self-sufficient. Liked it a lot."

Marilyn Stark, retired teacher: "We're new to Rolla. My husband was a principal in a west-St. Louis County school district and I was a teacher. We came to Rolla because we had observed the town for some 21 years passing through to our farm on the Big Piney River. My husband on trips began to look around for a house. Finally he found the one we are in now. It is 125 years old, a two-story farm house on seven and a half acres of land right in Rolla.... It wasn't for sale, but he looked up the owner's name and address and wrote her, saying hers was the only house that had appeal, and would she be interested in selling it? She wrote back that she wasn't interested in selling but liked what he had to say and would like to meet him. So we came to Rolla to meet Mrs. Richard. She is a bright, politically savvy widow. We struck up a friendship.... Two or three years later she asked if we were interested in buying.... She still lives in town.... During renovations they found a little board below the fireplace. Written on it in pencil was, 'In the year of our lord 1867, I, James C. Bradish, built this house for William Morse for the sum of $500 and lost money on it.'" ∎

St. Albans, VT 05478

Location: Northwestern corner of Vermont, just off the eastern shore of Lake Champlain. 30 miles north of Burlington, 62 miles south of Montreal.

Population: 7,339 (1990).

Growth rate: Under 1% since 1980.

Per capita income: $9,068 (state average, $9,619).

Geography/climate: Vigorous New England weather marked by long, cold winters averaging in the low 20s; pleasant, comparatively short summers averaging in the 70s but with rare days up to 90; cool falls. 79 inches of snow, 33 inches of rain on average. Varied, scenic landscape of lakeshore, rolling farmland, hills.

Economic base: Commercial center of Franklin County, leader in dairy production, maple syrup. Old railroad town being reborn with mix of industry: EverReady Battery Co.; Van Houten & Zoon, chocolates; Fonda Group, Inc., paper containers. State and federal office jobs employ about 400.

Newspaper: *St. Albans Messenger*, 281 N. Main St., St. Albans, VT 05478. 802-524-9771. Daily except Sunday. Emerson Lynn, editor and publisher. Year subscription, $104.

TV, radio: Local FM station. TV by cable, bringing in Burlington and Montreal.

Health care: Northwestern Medical Center, 73 beds including birthing center. 22 physicians, 13 dentists in local practice.

Schools: 3 elementary schools. High school, Bellows Free Academy (9–12), enrolls 910 students. Composite SAT scores: verbal, 431, math, 463. Half of high school graduates seek higher education, 36% to 4-year institutions.

Educational level: 9.4% of St. Albans residents have 16 or more years of formal education; state average, 19%. Per capita expenditure for public education (Franklin County), $464; state average, $468.

Library: Fletcher Free Library, 20,000 volumes.

Recreation: Smuggler's Notch, Jay Peak ski areas within 45 minutes; water sports, several state parks on Lake Champlain; hiking, hunting. Baseball and football fields, indoor tennis and hockey at city sports complex.

3 BR, 2 BA house: $70,000 to $100,000. Lakefront locations higher.

Cost of electricity: $.067 per kilowatt hour.

Cost of natural gas: $.63 per therm.

Sales tax: 4%.

State income tax: 2.5% of modified federal income tax liability.

Churches: Denominations: Assemblies of God, Baptist, Church of the Nazarene, Congregational, Episcopal, Presbyterian, Roman Catholic, United Methodist.

To produce one gallon of pure Vermont maple syrup, you plant a grove of sugar maples, wait about 40 years until they're ready to tap, painstakingly harvest 40 gallons of sap from your trees in the numbing cold of late winter, boil the liquid countless hours over a raging fire, and filter and pack the remaining sweet fluid according to strict state law. And if you actually had to do all that, what would you charge for a gallon?

With Grade A syrup going for $35 a gallon at the annual spring Maple Festival in St. Albans, sales patter becomes pure survival skill. But surviving is something St. Albans knows a lot about. This plucky old railroad town seemed doomed in the late '60s when the Central Vermont Railroad practically expired. Since then St. Albans has virtually remade the local economy with a mix of new jobs, new housing, and new community facilities, like the Collins-Perley Sports Complex.

What residents say . . .

John Kissane, local attorney, orchestrator of the sports-complex deal: "Steve Collins was a fine gentleman, a public-spirited kind of guy, very much interested in young people and athletics. He made his money in the oil business . . . gasoline stations and furnace oil. Steve had no children. Prior to his death he had gone over with me plans about what might be done with his money. All we had in St. Albans at that time was little old Coote Field, a swampy, miserable athletic field. Now, Bessie Perley had been an army nurse in World War I. She was interested in health and wellness. So my two friends decided they would do something but neither one knew the other had this interest. I drew up all the documents. Steve died before Bessie, and when Bessie died I was able to shop around and do something of some magnitude. The sports complex is 55 acres. It has five baseball fields, a magnificent football field, probably the finest in Vermont if not New England, a bigger hockey arena than the Boston Bruins, four indoor tennis courts. It was left by these two people for the use and benefit of Bellows Free Academy, and it's used all the time. I play tennis up there. . . . There's a tremendous sense of pride. . . . Everyone thought, what a magnificent thing. Of course, a couple of years later they thought they were entitled to it! But everyone agrees there isn't a better sports center in Vermont, and it didn't cost the taxpayers one dime."

Harry Moulton, director of guidance, Bellows Free Academy: "We're sometimes referred to as the hockey capital. Between 1973 and 1979 we won all the state championships in hockey. We won it again in 1982–83 and 1987–88. We've always been a contender. There's a very strong youth hockey program. . . . Our football team was state runner-up in its division. I'm a little prejudiced on that because my son's quarterback. Both our boys have gotten a good education. The older boy is a freshman at Potsdam, in New York, and doing well."

Steven Bourgeois, vice president and chief executive officer, Franklin Lamoille Bank: "Years ago we were dominated by the railroad . . . 2,500 employees all connected with the Central Vermont, which was headquartered here. But it started to dwindle . . . down to 1,000, then 700, probably today no more than 200, if that many. . . . We had an abundance of skilled employees with no place to work, the highest unemployment in the state, and it was a terrific problem. In 1969–70, the Legislature created a special fund, a target-area action program, and we were the pilot project, the model for the state. Since then our economic development commission has been very, very active. Our proximity to Canada was a tremendous asset. . . . We were ready for Canadian companies, and they were willing. Now our industrial parks are absolutely full. . . . What we have seen is that young people did not leave St. Albans. . . . The price of housing has outdistanced the growth in income. We could use 50 to 100 homes in the $70,000 to $100,000 range."

Mary Pat Larrabee, director, St. Albans Free Library: "I'd say fiction is our most popular item. Also history, anything World War II, the Civil War. We were fortunate to be one of the libraries that received a matching grant from the Macarthur Foundation. That allowed all these PBS videos to be brought to the library. Recently the VFW Post 758 gave us money to buy the Civil War series on PBS. That's been a real big hit. I'd say we are extremely well supported. A third or more of the people are registered in the library. We'd like to see that get up higher."

William Cioffi, city manager: "I'm a native of St. Albans. When we moved back here in the latter part of '72, the community

had bottomed out. Since then it has been a gradual rise . . . bringing in new and stable industry. We're seeing a lot of construction in the area and jobs coming in . . . the city itself is going to be hampered by its area, about a mile and a half square. It's relatively small, a case of making good use of our land. . . . I'm looking straight across the lake from a second floor window of my house. I can see the Adirondacks of New York State. On some nights you can see the lights of Montreal. . . . There are a lot of French here, people with family roots in Quebec . . . six or eight Italian families, six or eight Jewish families, and the rest of the community is Irish or French. When I grew up here, the tracks of the Central Vermont Railway divided the town. French lived on the west side, Irish Catholic on the east side. . . . We're all northern New Englanders, and if we can find a reason to complain, we do!"

Tim Soule, executive director, Franklin County Industrial Development Corporation: "Ben & Jerry's Ice Cream is considering St. Albans for a manufacturing plant, a big one by their standards. We are one of the last two sites. They've established a set of criteria including wastewater-treatment capacity, quality fresh water supply, quality work force. . . . We are positioned to take advantage of the benefits of a farm-agrarian work force and a strong work ethic. . . . My hometown is Fairfax, 12 miles away. . . . I was in the petroleum industry and traveled a lot. I have enjoyed living in Denver, London, Boise. . . . Vermont is a wonderful place to live in. . . . We have people who have a care and concern for one another."

Emerson Lynn, editor and co-publisher, St. Albans Messenger: "My wife is also co-publisher. . . . We came here in July 1981.

The paper was bankrupt. They had not made money in 42 years . . . and a lot of people didn't think it could be turned around. It took us three years. . . . Newspapers can be instrumental in the development of a community's attitude.

Vermonters are an extremely tolerant society, allowing you to exercise your own opinion. People don't take things personally . . . that's part of the dialogue . . . the debate is expected. Take a look at the letters to the editor . . . it's very lively, and the heart of the newspaper, I think. The newspaper is the one common denominator of a community. When you are that one common denominator, you've got a real job to do." ∎

St. Helens, OR 97051

Location: 31 miles northwest of Portland, 75 miles east of the Pacific Ocean, along the Columbia River in northwestern Oregon.

Population: 7,535 (1990).

Growth rate: 7% since 1980.

Per capita income: $8,587 (1985), 87% of state average ($9,925).

Geography/climate: Low mountains and hilly relief, elevation ranging from 20 feet along river to 2,500 feet. Coast Range on the west, Cascade Range on the east. Temperate maritime climate with dry, moderately warm summers; mild, wet winters. January daily average high, 44; low, 33. July high, 79; low, 55. Annually, 44 days below freezing, 10 days above 90. Annual precipitation, 60 inches. Rainy days average 152; cloudy days, 228.

Economic base: Forest products, agriculture, county-seat services. 80% of Columbia County is forested, the vast majority in commercial production. As timber production declines because of environmental mandates, St. Helens is becoming more a bedroom town for Portland. Large local payrolls including Armstrong World Industries, ceiling tiles; Boise Cascade, paper; Boise Cascade Veneer; Chevron Chemical, fertilizer; PSI, circuit boards; St. Helens School District; Multnomah Plywood; Letica, plastic buckets. Principal agricultural products, besides timber, are beef cattle, dairy products, berries, poultry.

Newspaper: *The Chronicle/Sentinel-Mist*, P.O. Box 1153, St. Helens, OR 97051. 503-397-0116. Wednesday and Saturday. Gregory Cohen, editor. $25 a year.

TV, radio: Local AM station. Cable available. Network TV, PBS, NPR can be received off-air from Portland.

Health care: Good Samaritan Medical Mall, clinic. 7 physicians, 10 dentists in local practice.

Schools: 5 elementary (K–5); 1 junior high (6–8). St. Helens Senior High School enrolls 725, sends 45% to college, including 20% to 4-year. Average SAT scores, 1991: verbal, 421; math, 461.

Educational level: 10% of Columbia County residents have 16 or more years of formal education; state average, 17.9%. County per capita expenditure for public education, $1,007; state average, $577.

Library: St. Helens Public Library, 17,000 volumes.

Recreation: 9 city parks, with swimming pool; soccer, football fields; tennis, basketball, racquetball courts. 9-hole golf course. Fishing, boating, hunting, swimming, sailing on and along the Columbia River and tributaries. Sand Island Marine Park and Dock, in Columbia River, offshore from the town center. 1 public, 5 private marinas. Sport, commercial fishing attract fishermen from wide area. Salmon, steelhead, trout, sturgeon most abundant. Deer, elk hunted in forested areas. Ducks, geese, pheasant abound in regulated hunting areas nearby.

3 BR, 2 BA house: $65,000 and up.

Cost of electricity: $.05 per kilowatt hour.

Cost of natural gas: $.57 per therm.

Sales tax: None.

State income tax: 5% to 9%.

Churches: 36. Denominations: Apostolic, Baptist (7), Bible, Bread of Life, Christian, Church of Christ, Church of Jesus Christ of Latter-day Saints, Community, Episcopal, Free Methodist, Jehovah's Witnesses, Lutheran, Reorganized LDS, Roman Catholic, United Methodist, Presbyterian.

The highway connecting St. Helens and Portland, U.S. 30, known locally as Columbia River Highway, was widened to four lanes a few years ago, bringing the small town a lot closer to advantages of the big city—and vice versa. When this news begins to dawn on more people, St. Helens figures it will be in for a period of faster growth—and possibly transformation into something more like a suburb. Though it is not officially within the Portland metropolitan area and retains a strong local identity, St. Helens lies in the only direction that Portland has not expanded.

Some people think the status quo is OK. "You see things eroding and wonder whether you can control it," says Rosaline Mallory, city recorder. "Though the crime rate is less than half the state average, crime seems much worse than 30 years ago."

What residents say . . .

Gregory Cohen, editor, **Chronicle/Sentinel-Mist:** "We're sort of in an interesting paradox. We are a small commercial timber and wood products–based economy but close enough to the metropolitan area as well as on the Columbia River. When the metropolitan area sneezes we tend to catch a cold. . . . We've suffered through the environmental issues over timber-harvesting. The spotted owl being declared an endangered species has already led to layoffs at some of the lumber mills. . . . We're finding more and more people moving into the area . . . work in Portland. They're coming out to our community to run away from crime and other problems. . . . Unlike our nearest neighbor, Scappoose, we're not even a semi-suburban area of Portland. We're still pretty much rural, larger tracts of land and a fair amount of timber and agricultural area. . . . Also, in Oregon we have the Land Conservation and Development Commission, a statewide land-use watchdog. Turning agricultural and forest lands into other uses is very difficult. That has a lot to do with the slowness of our growth. . . . The closure of the hospital . . . I think has caused a lot of introspection by the community. It's one of those subtle things. People are forced to take a look at what we as a small community can provide for ourselves and what we can share. . . . I think one of the pluses of a small community is that, despite problems, they always seem to find a way."

Helen White, former hospital board member: "The hospital was built by the Columbia Health District, which operated it for quite a few years. We sold it in 1984 to the Sisters of St. Joseph of Peace. They had an excellent proposal and did what they said they were going to do. But they didn't have a health plan that would keep the people here. It got down to one, two, or three patients a day. They had to have at least nine. We couldn't get the doctors. They preferred to go to the large city where all the equipment is and the interesting cases. . . . So the hospital closed in June 1990. Nobody believed it was actually going to happen. It was a resource that was always here. It just broke our hearts not to keep a viable hospital. But we're no different than anybody else. Small hospitals are having a terrible time. . . . It's frightening for the elderly and for families whose kids get sick on Friday afternoon or evening. . . . But we are hoping Good Samaritan, our closest hospital, is going to set up a clinic. It means longer hours, probably from eight in the morning, and some service Saturdays and Sundays. . . . As a whole, the community is very much aware of what needs to be done and do their best to get it done."

Rosaline Mallory, city recorder: "The city is more financially stable than many small communities. . . . Just good money management. We also enjoy a 2,600-acre watershed property that's programmed to be an unending [timber] resource. Because it is a water asset, all of the income goes to water-system improvements for the city. . . . We have had a very slow growth rate up to now. But in 1993 a major highway-widening project will go on through our city. The railroad runs right through the middle of town. We see those things as a future omen of development. A lot of people are looking at the community. It's a nice, neat little place only a little over an hour from the coast, an hour from Mt. Hood, 30 minutes from Portland. . . . The city owns Sand Island, right in the middle of the Columbia River. It's the only truly marine park in the state of Oregon, 36 acres, man-made in the '30s by the Corps [of Engineers] when they dredged the river. The city bought it and developed it. There are two large boat docks, and as of today, the Lady Washington, a $1.5 million replica of Robert Gray's ship, is docked here. Double-masted, it's fabulous. Gray discovered the Columbia, and 1992 is the bicentennial year-long celebration of the river."

Elmer Jensen, retired bank manager: "We're right on the banks of the Columbia River. We can see the Cascade Range from our front porch. . . . Mt. St. Helens, or what's left of it. . . . Mt. Rainier, Mt. Hood, and on a real clear January day, Mt. Jefferson, 100 miles southeast. . . . In the early days, this was hoped to be the center of shipping, the deep-water port on the river, whereas Portland is on the Willamette, a tributary of the Columbia. But capital was centered in Portland, and Portland won out."

Harvard Anderson, historian: "St. Helens was known as the payroll town. It had more payroll per population than any other town in Oregon. There was the paper mill, one big sawmill, the insulating board company, a big creamery. The broom-handle plant was the second largest in the world. We had a creosoting plant, a towing company. . . . I grew up in logging camps. In 1929 we heard of a machine shop for sale. 1929 was one bad time to buy a machine shop. The only reason we hung on to it . . . the bank went broke and gave us longer terms. We ran it right through the Depression, on into World War II, and did machine work for the Navy. . . . We built a 57-foot fishing boat. It was built for shrimp, but the shrimp market has gone to pot. . . . Steel hull, took us four years. I built it right here at my yard on the Columbia River. I took it to sea for six years, just to keep the license up. It hasn't been to sea for seven years now. 97 gross tons, 86 net. I've got $225,000 in it and I'm asking $75,000 direct to me. Its name is Pyramid." ∎

Shippensburg, PA 17257

Location: 130 miles west of Philadelphia, 180 miles southeast of Pittsburgh, in the Cumberland Valley of Pennsylvania.

Population: 5,331 (1990).

Growth rate: Very slow—increase of 21 people since 1986.

Per capita income: $9,946 (1985), 97% of state average ($10,288).

Geography/climate: Rolling terrain against a backdrop of low mountain ranges to the south and east. 4-season climate buffered by the Appalachians and coastal influence of the Atlantic. January average temperatures: low, 23; high, 41. July: low, 62; high, 87. Average annual rainfall, 40 inches; snowfall, 31 inches. 1st killing frost: 2nd week in October. Last killing frost: last week in April.

Economic base: Diversified manufacturing and agribusiness. Shippensburg University is biggest employer: 650 faculty and staff. Other large payrolls: Beistle Company, paper novelties, 380; Ingersoll-Rand Compaction Division, compactors, milling machines, 365; Richard Textiles, 314; Greif Companies, men's clothing, 220; SKF Industries, bearings, aerospace products, 161; Valley Baking Company, 91; Domestic Castings, ductile and grey iron, 90; Orweco Frocks, women's wear, 85; R&S Dress, 75. Letterkenny Army Depot in nearby Chambersburg employs 700.

Newspaper: *The Shippensburg News-Chronicle*, P.O. Box 100, RD 1, Shippensburg, PA 17257. 717-532-4101. Monday, Thursday. Kenneth Wolfrom, publisher. $26 a year.

TV, radio: Local AM station. NPR from Harrisburg. Cable carries network TV from Harrisburg, Lancaster, Hagerstown.

Health care: Carlisle Hospital, 21 miles northeast, 231 beds. Medical clinic in town. 7 dentists in local practice.

Schools: 2 elementary (K–6); 1 junior high (7–9). Shippensburg Senior High School (10–12) enrolls 615, sends about 53% to college. Average SAT scores: verbal, 418; math, 482. Shippensburg University enrolls 6,000.

Educational level: Shippensburg straddles 2 counties, Franklin and Cumberland. 14.6% of 2-county residents have 16 or more years of formal education; state average, 13.6%. 2 counties' per capita expenditure for public education, $452; state average, $421.

Library: Shippensburg Public Library, 38,304 volumes.

Recreation: Veterans Memorial Park has pool, baseball and softball diamonds, picnic grounds, tennis courts, children's playground. Dykeman Pond Wetland Park, refuge for waterfowl and fish. 2 country clubs, 5 public golf courses in immediate area. 3 state parks, 2 ski slopes within hour's drive. Appalachian Trail passes through Michaux State Forest, 7 miles southeast. Gettysburg National Military Park is 25 miles southeast. Numerous sites for hunting, fishing in 2-county area.

3 BR, 2 BA house: $55,000 to $90,000.

Cost of electricity: $.085 per kilowatt hour.

Cost of natural gas: $.49 per therm.

Sales tax: 6%.

State income tax: 2.1%.

Churches: 21. Denominations: Assemblies of God, Brethren in Christ, Church of God, Church of the Brethren, Episcopal, Lutheran, Nazarene, Presbyterian USA, United Brethren, United Brethren in Christ, United Church of Christ, United Methodist (6), Wesleyan.

For a small place, Shippensburg has an extraordinarily well-balanced blend of economic activities. Agriculture, of course. The town rests in the Cumberland Valley, rich with cornfields, apple orchards, and dairy farms. There is a diverse group of manufacturers, including a cluster of six in the apparel business. And Shippensburg has its 6,000-student university, which acts as a sort of stabilizer if the other big sectors go awry. *Business Week* inspected the town a few years ago and concluded that it was unaffected by recession—or prosperity. The Chamber of Commerce is a good deal more active than that assessment might suggest: Worried over several empty stores downtown, business leaders recently pulled together a novel care-package for new ventures.

What residents say ...

Allan Williams, executive director, Chamber of Commerce: "We ask the property-owners to offer very low interest rates for the first three to six months. The bank has dedicated a $100,000 loan pool at 6 percent. Then we're asking the utilities, the telephone company, and the borough itself to give some kind of relief on the basics. Perhaps we can get some carpenters to donate time to build shelves. . . . Whatever needs to be done to keep the cash flowing. . . . I retired from the field of industrial development. Then my wife and I started a bed-and-breakfast, Field & Pine Bed & Breakfast. We're about seven miles from Shippensburg. The house goes back 200 years . . . limestone walls, seven fireplaces, one big walk-in fireplace, 14 rooms. . . . My wife teaches home-ec at the local middle school and loves to cook. . . .

The Chamber started sending us guests, I went to one of the Chamber luncheons, and next thing you know, I'm the director. . . . We just brought in a very large manufacturer of cream cheese, Raskas, out of St. Louis. They wanted to be in an area where there was a good source of milk. . . . More important, they looked at the labor force. We're basically a farming community. As you know, most farmers have to supplement their living. We have a lot of Mennonite and Amish. When they are not farming, some of their sons and daughters can work in plants."

Mike Crabtree, proprietor, Cumbria Photo: "One employee, that's me. I've been in business three years. Actually, I'm an Englishman, I'm not from Shippensburg. A lot of business owners are not from Shippensburg. One of the reasons they come here is the university, and it's a nice town for children to live in. . . . It's not a very good business environment right now. Retailers haven't kept up with the changes in shopping habits. We're trying to attract specialty businesses. . . . A good example is my store. We're the type of business that tends to make it. Service-oriented businesses seem to do well."

William E. Naugle, III, co-owner, car dealership: "We sell new and used cars. Chrysler, Plymouth, Dodge. Family-owned, 43 years now. My brother and I are third generation. . . . Personally, I got in about six years ago. . . . Business could stand to be better. But compared with the rest of the market we are doing relatively well. The service department is extremely busy. . . . You can tell people are a lot more wary what they are spending their money on. They've all been doing their homework."

Jan Rose: "I've only lived here four years. I grew up in the Cumberland Valley, about 25 miles from here. My husband was in the Army 30 years. We decided to come back to this area because we think it has a lot going for it. . . . We were looking for a big old house, and this is the first one we found. It was built in 1798, a brick, two-story structure that has been added on to . . . sort of Victorian. . . . I've been very impressed how easy it is to become part of the community. . . . There is a core of old families that sort of consider themselves the establishment. But I have never found any difficulty getting along with these people. Socially, people are very friendly, very kind to us that way. . . . We also have a very good public library, right across the street from me. It's in a beautiful brick Georgian house."

Jane Trinklein, former librarian: "A banker in town built this in 1870. Then in the '30s it was remodeled extensively. It's not true Georgian. . . . Huge thick walls and next to the creek, sort of a town gathering-place for the coolness. . . . The library had been in several locations. Last one was in the railroad station which they were able to rent for $1 a year. But termites got it. They were hunting for a new place and contemplating building when this house came on the market. Mrs. Stewart offered to sell this to the library and soon afterwards gave the library $100,000. So whatever she got on the building went right back to the library. The Stewart family has been very generous to the library over the years."

William Burkhart, historian, author of seven books about the area: "The four things that had the greatest effect on our development were, number one, the coming of the Cumberland Valley Railroad in 1837. We were on that railroad line. Second, founding of Cumberland Valley State Normal School. Today, that's Shippensburg University. Third, building of the Pennsylvania Turnpike. It comes right near here. We benefited from that. And one more thing. When World War II started, the Army established an ordinance depot about 10 to 12 miles from Shippensburg. That thing paid good wages. They elevated the economy of this community tremendously. . . . These people in Shippensburg are a durable sort. If one thing doesn't work, they try another. That's their nature. . . . Anyone who comes here and starts to work in this community finds the people will [say], 'You're welcome here. We do the best we can to make it a good town. But if you don't like it, you can help make it better.' That's the spirit." ∎

Silver City, NM 88061

Location: 240 miles southwest of Albuquerque, 200 miles east of Tucson, in mountainous southwestern New Mexico.

Population: 10,683 (1990).

Growth rate: 8% since 1980.

Per capita income: $7,316 (1985), 83% of state average ($8,814).

Geography/climate: Foothills of the Pinos Altos Mountains. Mean elevation of Grant County, 6,000 feet, creates semi-arid continental climate. Topography ranges from flat semi-desert to mountain peaks over 10,000 feet. January average low, 24 degrees; high, 49. July average low, 59; high, 87. Rapid cooling after sundown on summer nights. Annual rainfall, 17 inches. Snow occurs several times a year but seldom stops travel. Average relative humidity, 31%. Sunny days, 83%.

Economic base: Copper mining, government services, tourism, retirement living. Agriculture centers on cattle ranching, apple growing. Mining employment is cyclical: recent loss of 500 jobs (out of 1,500 total) had ripple effects in local retail, services. Western New Mexico University employs 300 faculty and staff. Other large payrolls: U.S. Forest Service, Gila Regional Medical Center. Silver City is county seat.

Newspaper: *Press and Independent*, P.O. Box 740, Silver City, NM 88062. 505-388-1576. Daily, Monday through Saturday. Richard Peterson, editor. $50 a year.

TV, radio: 1 FM, 2 AM stations. Cable carries network TV from Albuquerque, El Paso.

Health care: Gila Regional Medical Center, 88 beds. 32 physicians, 10 dentists in local practice.

Schools: 4 elementary (K–5); 1 middle (6–8). Silver City High School enrolls 1,150, sends 65% to 4-year college. ACT scores for college-bound, "high 20s, lots of 27s to 29s." Western New Mexico University enrolls 1,800.

Educational level: 12.6% of Grant County residents have 16 or more years of formal education; state average, 17.6%. Per capita expenditure for public education, $637; state average, $564.

Library: Public Library, 40,000 volumes.

Recreation: 10 parks, 3 swimming pools, 16 tennis courts. Golf course, youth center, cinema. Gila National Forest provides numerous sites for hunting, fishing, camping. Within radius of 75 miles, at end of November, 7 species of game can be hunted: javelina, cougar, mule deer, turkey, bear, Barbary sheep, Persian ibex.

3 BR, 2 BA house: $75,000 to $110,000.

Cost of electricity: $.09 per kilowatt hour.

Cost of natural gas: $.30 per therm.

Sales tax: 6%.

State income tax: 1.8% to 8.5%.

Churches: Denominations: Apostolic, Assemblies of God, Baptist, Church of Christ, Church of Jesus Christ of Latter-day Saints, Episcopal, Jehovah's Witnesses, Lutheran, Methodist, Presbyterian, Roman Catholic.

Silver City sprang to life in the summer of 1870 as a tent city for thousands of miners, shortly after silver was discovered. One of the early residents was young Henry McCarty, who lived with his mother and stepfather in a log cabin at the corner of Broadway and Hudson. Arrested and jailed for stealing, Henry escaped jail at 15, said goodbye to Silver City, and began a short shoot-'em-up career as Billy the Kid. The home town paid little attention, preoccupied with replacing tents and huts with local brick. A history notes, "Architecturally, many of the buildings constructed in Silver City's early years reflected the extravagant optimism of the time and the conviction that the town would grow and prosper. Unlike a typical mining camp, Silver City was built to last. The boom years passed, but the people stayed."

Things haven't changed much. Copper mining has replaced silver mining. While there is enough ore to keep miners busy for decades, local employment depends heavily on the world market.

What residents say . . .

Bob Carson, bank marketing specialist:
"Studies by the University of New Mexico suggest there was no recession in New Mexico although there was an economic slowdown. . . . We consider ourselves kind of a shopping hub for southwest New Mexico. People like to come here to shop. Although we have only 11,000 in the city and 29,000 in the county, we project about a 55,000-person trade area. It's a good place for a retail business to locate. . . . I'm a native of New Mexico. I moved to Silver City nine years ago, having lived in the Taos area. We had been in 13 locations in 16 years. Rather than continue moving with two kids to raise, we decided to settle here . . . for the natural beauty, the climate, the terrain. You go from desert to high mountain pines in a 10-minute drive. . . . The community also offers a lot of warm-type feelings. We have lived in another mine community where there was a lot of movement of people. Here there are more roots. I attribute that to the university."

Steve May, director of public information, Western New Mexico University: "My uncle and his wife bought two of the major motels in the community in 1978 and built a rather large steakhouse and lounge. I was running their business in Carlsbad and came over here in 1979 to assist with this complex. . . . The economy was absolutely booming. Of course, it was an inflated economy. The price of copper was up. A thousand people were on payroll here as construction workers. You couldn't do anything wrong. From '79 to '81, business was tremendous. Then the mines shut down for an entire year. . . . I don't foresee a complete shutdown this time. One of the open pits has just played out. We'll lose 500 direct jobs, and the community will lose 500 more. They had been warning us and warning us, saying it was coming. Up until a few months ago the price of copper was OK. Unfortunately, it has dropped. . . . I do believe we're going to have to redirect our efforts away from the extractive industry as a source of our livelihood. I have been a big believer in that. At the university our goal is to add another thousand students by 1997. . . . I have always felt this university has been taken for granted. It will be 100 years old in 1993 and has seen very little growth until the last few years. It was established as a teaching school, but it lost its vision. We're lowest on the totem pole in state funding. We've had seven presidents in 10 years, a lot of upheaval. Under the new president, I came on board. We're concentrating now on turning out teachers and young business professionals. Let the bigs worry about research and engineering. Our students come mainly from southwestern New Mexico and southeastern Arizona. 57 percent female, 42 percent male. Average age, 27. 53 percent Anglo, 39.8 percent Hispanic, the remainder Native American. . . . Just in case you're interested, I'm a former mayor. I served from 1985 to '86. This town was incorporated before New Mexico was a state. We still operate under the Territory of New Mexico charter which requires the mayor to run every year. You barely have a grasp of what is going on and you're out campaigning again. We've tried to change [the charter] but the people turn it down. I guess they think it's easier to turn them out of office in a year's time than to tar and feather them."

Doris Wakeland, school-board president:
"Our district is really at the forefront of the state, and New Mexico is considered by all to be ahead of the field. We are leading the pack. . . . This movement is called 'Re: Learning.' . . . It encompasses nine principles of learning. One is that we are committed that all students will learn to use their minds well . . . that we will teach more about less, that teachers will become facilitators and coaches, and students will become workers and learn to take responsibility for their learning. . . . This has only been going on for two years. . . . We're now past the initial stage where all the teachers are saying it's just a fad that will never happen. In our seven schools we have five new principals. One of the things the proponents warn is that we can't change the monolith of educational bureaucracy. Let me tell you, we can. . . . Teachers are now working in groups. We are teaching on a thematic basis . . . big overall questions within which you can look at different aspects. . . . The kid can pick. Then he goes out and finds some answers. . . . In small-group learning, each one has a duty to teach the information back to the class. That way, you retain more of what you learn. . . . I'm from Chicago 'way back when. We moved to Albuquerque in '52. We picked this town to retire to. . . . As an outsider newcomer who wanted to be involved, I have not been frozen out. The mind-set of the old-timers is rather frontier. They didn't want to have a sign ordinance, anyone telling them what to do. At the same time, here we are restructuring the school and we're getting no flak whatsoever." ■

Smyrna, DE 19977

Location: 55 miles due east of Baltimore, 13 miles north of Dover on U.S. 13, at the upper end of the Delmarva Peninsula.

Population: 5,231 (1990).

Growth rate: 6% since 1986.

Per capita income: $8,535 (1985), 75% of state average ($11,375).

Geography/climate: Coastal flatlands. 4-season climate tempered by closeness to Atlantic Ocean. Annual rainfall, 40 inches; snowfall, 17 inches. 100 winter days below freezing but rarely any below zero. Summer weather influenced by Bermuda High, drawing warm, humid air from the South. Average days over 90, 31.

Economic base: Major local employer is Delaware Home & Hospital for the Chronically Ill. Principal area employers: Dover Air Force Base, state capital at Dover, industry in Wilmington. Surrounding county still predominantly agricultural: potatoes, strawberries, some wheat and corn, truck farms, nurseries. A few light industries in town.

Newspaper: *Smyrna/Clayton Sun-Times*, 25 W. Commerce Street, Smyrna, DE 19977. 302-653-2083. Weekly, Wednesday. Susan Biro, editor. $20 a year.

TV, radio: Baltimore, Philadelphia stations received off-air, including PBS, NPR. Cable available.

Health care: Kent General Hospital, at Dover, 13 miles south, 105 beds. 6 physicians, 2 dentists in local practice.

Schools: 1 kindergarten center (Pre-K; K); 3 elementary (1–4); 1 middle (5–7). Smyrna High School (8–12) enrolls 926, sends 40% to college. ACT not administered. Student team has been recognized at state and national levels in International Competition for Odyssey of the Mind.

Educational level: 12.6% of Kent County residents have 16 or more years of formal education; state average, 17.5%. Per capita expenditure for public education, $410; state average, $421.

Library: Smyrna Public Library, founded 1858, has 11,500 volumes, 3,300 card holders. Interlibrary loan connects local borrowers to holdings throughout state.

Recreation: Ball fields, picnic sites at Municipal Park; water sports at Lake Como, in town. Field-game hunting throughout area. Woodland Beach, on Delaware Bay, 8 miles east. Rehoboth, Dewey beaches, hour's drive south.

3 BR, 2 BA house: From $110,000. Recent average selling price, $130,000.

Cost of electricity: $.07 per kilowatt hour.

Cost of natural gas: $.54 per therm.

State sales tax: None.

State income tax: 3.2% to 7.7%.

Churches: 16. Denominations: AME, Baptist, Church of Christ, Church of God, Episcopal, Full Gospel, Lutheran, Methodist, Nazarene, Presbyterian, Roman Catholic, United Methodist, Wesleyan.

About 20 minutes below the Chesapeake & Delaware Canal, U.S. Highway 13, the big, north–south axis of Delaware, glances off the northeast side of Smyrna and rushes south toward Dover and lower towns of the Delmarva Peninsula. But you don't see much of Smyrna unless you turn off the four-laner, and some residents say that's why the town has retained its unique character.

Founded in 1768, Smyrna is older than the United States and one of the earliest trading centers in the Eastern Shore. It is a living gallery of American house-styles—pre-Revolutionary, Victorian, and contemporary. "Architecture is our crowning jewel," says Councilman Kenneth Brown. "South Street—I would put that Victorian streetscape up against any Victorian town anywhere. For the most part, property-owners are aware of what they have."

What residents say . . .

Bettielou Wagner, owner, Loving Care Nursery School: "My mother started the center 27 years ago, and three years ago I took over. . . . My mother's family has lived around this town since pre-1700s. . . . I live on Commerce Street, one of the two main streets downtown. My house probably was built 1760-ish. . . . The Town Charter was signed in this house. . . . George, I'm sure, didn't stop here. If he did, he didn't leave any record. . . . In 1812, our house became the First Bank of Smyrna. It functioned as a bank for 25 years. . . . We've brought it back to life . . . tried to maintain the historic character. I was fortunate my uncle was a master carpenter. He and my father did the fine work. . . . It's a nice quiet community. I think it needs a few light industries. The tax structure is reasonable."

George C. Wright, Jr., mayor: "There's a bridge that connects northern Delaware with southern Delaware. Once you cross that bridge, we're the next major city. We have all the resources necessary for growth. . . . You have heard of bedroom towns? That's what Smyrna was. We can no longer survive with that. The thing that's driving us is our stable work force, very stable and reliable. . . . Ten years ago when I became mayor, I opened negotiations with Kent General Hospital in Dover. They listened, and I am a very patient man. A medical center just got off the ground. . . . We've just annexed some land south of us for a shopping center and industrial park. . . . Minorities make up 21 percent of the total population. Mostly blacks, a very few Hispanics. I happen to be black."

Kenneth Brown, councilman: "Delaware is sort of unique. North of the canal is metropolitan and a fast life. . . . Below the canal, we're "Slower Delaware," and we love it. There's plenty to do here. Washington is two hours away. You can go to the playhouse in Wilmington, one hour away. We are three hours from New York. Thinking about it, I shouldn't tell you the virtues of

Smyrna at all! . . . Growth is inevitable, no doubt. But it should be an orderly growth. We have a comprehensive plan, but the Council has the right to amend zoning. We have a propensity to believe some entrepreneur who is going to put up these wonderful townhouses for old people. And we take agricultural lands and zone them for R-3. And then this entrepreneur moves on and sells it to somebody else. We're getting a lot of potentially very close housing. I know everybody has to live someplace . . . but to have houses tooth and jowl because a builder can make more money that way impacts the quality of life in Smyrna. . . . I guess I'm a very conservative member of Council."

George L. Caley, retired teacher and civil servant: "I'm the unofficial historian of the town. . . . I did a history of Smyrna, a history of the Methodist Church, and a book, *Footprints of the Past*, an account of some of the sites still in existence, the architectural features. . . . American Heritage called our Col. Allen McLane 'the unsung hero of the Revolution' . . . it was he who knew the British were going to get out of Philadelphia before anyone else did. Then we had in the War of 1812 Commodore Jacob Jones. . . . He had a medal struck for him in Congress. The first woman pediatrician in the State of Delaware was a native of Smyrna, Dr. Margaret Handy. She was a friend of Andrew Wyeth and a subject in some of his paintings."

The Rev. Frank Wismer, rector, St. Peter's Episcopal Church: "I was brought here to put things back in order. The parish had sort of dwindled off and the diocese had considered closing it. But the people decided to give themselves the opportunity to get things turned around by calling a full-time rector. . . . We've managed to grow by leaps and bounds. In a suburban area or a city, it takes a long time for the word to get out, because what you have is a lot of little communities based on where people work. In Smyrna, it doesn't take very long for word to get around. . . . Small-town America is always viewed as conservative, backward, resistant to change. There are some interesting stereotypes that I have not found to be true at all. . . . I am accepted as the resident theologian, one of the few times in my ministry when everybody in the congregation didn't know my job better than me. . . . I think it says they are willing to accept some leadership that involves them. . . . On December 27, my Reserve unit, the 401st Civil Affairs Company, was called to active duty in Desert Storm. . . . Generally when clergy go away attendance goes down. When I was gone, attendance went up slightly. Nobody wanted to let me down. . . . My fantasy about the town of Smyrna is that 500 years from now when everything has fallen down, it will be remembered as the place where there was a pig race once a year."

Nancy Finch, proprietor of Tully's Ale House, sponsor of the annual pig race: "This is our third year. One of the local farmers provides them for us . . . 12 pigs sponsored by different businesses and individuals. It's a straight course, about 40 feet. Whichever one can saunter across the line wins. The winner last year backed across. . . . We had about a thousand people attend. It's a benefit for the Smyrna Public Library. Last year we donated $3,000. . . . This year we are also having a softball game. The WDSD Dirt Divers versus the Run Amucs, spelled *a-m-u-c*. That's Gaelic for pig." ∎

Somerset, KY 42502

Location: 75 miles south of Lexington, 129 miles northwest of Knoxville, Tennessee, in south central Kentucky.

Population: 10,733 (1990).

Growth rate: 1% since 1980.

Per capita income: $8,315 (1985), 97% of state average ($8,614).

Geography/climate: Rolling terrain, elevation 975 feet, on the northeastern approach to Lake Cumberland, 8 miles south. January temperatures: low, 25; high, 42; seasonal snowfall, 12 inches; 2 zero-degree days, 97 freezing days. July temperatures: low, 66; high, 86; 16 90-degree days; annual precipitation, 47 inches. A continental, 4-season climate but without the worst extremes. September, October generally dry, clear, and quite pleasant.

Economic base: Manufacturing, tourism, health care, increasing number of retirees. Seat of Pulaski County, population, 49,489. Retail trading center of 5-county region. 43 stores, movie theaters, restaurants in enclosed mall. Large payrolls: Palm Beach Company, men's coats, 892; Humana Hospital/Lake Cumberland; Tecumseh Products Company, compressors, 647; Cumberland Wood & Chair Corporation, 350; Asahi Motor Wheel, 300; CR/PL, plumbing fixtures, 242; General Electric, pressed glassware, 237; Mid-State Automotive, 225; Kingsford Charcoal Company, briquets, 147; Somerset Refinery, gasoline, kerosene, diesel fuel, 100.

Newspaper: *The Somerset Commonwealth-Journal*, 110–112 E. Mt. Vernon Street, Somerset, KY 42501. 606-678-8191. Daily. Mark Conrad, editor. $101 a year.

TV, radio: 2 FM, 3 AM stations; local transmitter for Kentucky Educational TV, PBS. Cable carries network TV from Lexington.

Health care: Humana Hospital/Lake Cumberland, 244 beds. 70 physicians, 26 dentists in local practice.

Schools: 2 elementary (K–5); 1 junior high (6–8). Somerset High School enrolls 514, sends 76%-80% of graduates to college. Recent composite ACT, 20. City school system ranks 29th out of 180 districts in Kentucky. Essential Skills testing. Somerset Community College, enrollment 1,755, received US Department of Education award in 1989 for business-industry liaison program. Somerset State Vocational-Technical School enrolls 909.

Educational level: 7.1% of Pulaski County residents have 16 or more years of formal education; state average, 11.1%. County per capita spending for public education, $323; state average, $314.

Library: Pulaski County Public Library, 60,000 volumes.

Recreation: Lake Cumberland's 1,255 miles of shoreline are the big draw, for Somerset and surrounding area: boating, fishing, skiing, camping, canoeing. Pulaski County Park, 465 acres, has campsites, shelter houses, picnic sites, horse arena, rodeo arena, beach, boat-launching ramps. Summer Sport Park, 40-acre in-town: soccer, 2 baseball fields, driving range, community building. YMCA. 2 country clubs. 2 public golf courses. 2 public, 3 private swimming pools. 3 movie theaters, bowling alley.

3 BR, 2 BA house: $75,000 to $125,000.

Cost of electricity: $.05 per kilowatt hour.

Cost of natural gas: $.37 per therm.

Sales tax: 6%.

State income tax: 2% to 6%.

Churches: Denominations: Apostolic, Assemblies of God, Baptist, Christian, Church of the Bible Covenant, Church of Christ, Church of God of Prophecy, Church of Jesus Christ of Latter-day Saints, Episcopal, Interdenominational, Jehovah's Witnesses, Lutheran, Methodist, Nazarene, Pentecostal, Presbyterian, Roman Catholic, Seventh-Day Adventist.

In 1984, when the mall opened on the U.S. 27 bypass, many businesses abandoned downtown Somerset for the new location. "We were staring at tons of vacant buildings," recalls Bob Sams, president of the Downtown Development Corporation. On his block, his insurance office was the only occupied storefront for a time. If downtown was to be rescued, something had to be done right away. Something was: Local banks offered $1 million seed money at below-market rates. A development director was hired. Volunteers stepped forward. Renovations began, and now total $6 million. And vitality has returned. On Sams's block, there's a new china shop, crafts and gifts, a restaurant featuring nonfried food and live jazz. The old movie theater reopened. Today, the downtown vacancy rate is about 5 percent. Sams credits "progressive leadership."

What residents say . . .

Steve Fischer, owner, Goldenberg Furniture: "My wife's grandfather founded the business in 1904. We're third-generation. . . . I'm right on the corner across from the Square. Business is fine, especially in my business, large ticket. . . . Kentucky business is different from big-city. We don't sparkle but we don't have the dips. . . . I think we're the growth center for southeast Kentucky. . . . A small town is what you make it. To me it's an excellent place to raise a family. It's safer. People are much more honest. . . . About the schools, you have to understand, I grew up in western St. Louis. We had

things then that Kentucky is just getting into now. The basics of reading, writing, and arithmetic are excellent. My daughter went through the Somerset schools, was a National Merit finalist, received an academic scholarship, was a Rhodes nominee. It's possible to excel in any environment if you want to. The difference here is TLC. My graduating class was 650. My daughter's was 150. What she lacks in exposure, broadness of curriculum, and enhanced facilities they make up in personal attention. Parents are still involved in the educational process. . . . There's not enough for teenagers to do, organized activities à la youth center. Cruising the mall should not be entertainment. . . . If you're a night-life person you can go crazy. If you want some of the finer symphony things, you have to have a mind-set that it's OK to drive a couple of hours."

Lisa Blakley, president, Lake Cumberland Performing Arts Series: "We had 'Picnic with the Pops' last night. It was wonderful, the first year we've had the Pops, and it served as the kick-off to our season, a fund-raiser. We sold 38 tables of eight, $150 for a table. It was at Summer Sport Park. We were out in the open, the Lexington Philharmonic in their own tent. . . . The only problem was the weather. At least we made it 'til 8:30. They had to quit because the lightning was so bad. But I must say our community will not forget their first Pops. . . . In September we'll have 'Driving Miss Daisy,' by Mainstage out of St. Louis. October, The Fairfield Four, a gospel group. November, Lee Greenwood, a country-music star . . . January, local entertainment . . . March, 'A Tribute to the Beatles'. . . . April ends our season with the Marine Corps Field Band. A season ticket is $30 for an individual, $50 for a family. . . . That's the whole point: We're a low-income area and we want to bring in entertainment that adults and children would not see otherwise. We ask businesses to support half the cost."

Reed Hall, district manager, Kentucky Utilities: "We have a lake curling around us in every direction . . . one of the larger man-made lakes in the world. . . . We're becoming famous for the stripers, originally a salt-water species that has been bred to the white bass and generated great numbers of spawn . . . 30-, 40-, 50-pound fish."

Conley Manning, superintendent of schools: "School-based decision-making is starting this year . . . basically a council consisting of three teachers, two parents, and a principal. The principal is the chair. . . . They more or less have control over the school. We've employed a principal and a number of teachers through the council. I submit a list of names and they select from the list. . . . They decide curriculum issues, grading, scheduling, and eventually receive funds to use at their discretion. The intent is to bring more citizen input to decision-making. We view it here as very positive. . . . Another program that must be implemented by '92–'93 has the objective of decreasing the dropout rate by eliminating any stigmatizing of the student in primary school. . . . There are no grades. Students progress at their own rate. . . . Students may drop out physically at middle school, but they really drop out in kindergarten and first grade for lack of self-confidence. . . . A premise of all this is that all children can learn. It should be understood, but a lot of times teachers and administrators do not really believe that or teach to that principle. . . . Somerset's been fortunate. We have great tradition, a very strong faculty in all of our schools."

Bob Sams, owner, insurance agency: "Unionism has been a major part of life in Somerset. Our first big industry a century ago was railroad-repair shops. The word 'union' is not a negative per se here. . . . In the late '70s and early '80s, we had the reputation for a poor labor climate. One company had lots of difficulty. They employed a lot of part-time farmers who didn't want to relinquish farming. Came time to put crops in the ground, there would be wildcat strikes. That was real difficult for a company based in southern California to accept, so they packed up and went to Morristown, Tennessee. . . . We hired Fantus. They came down and told us we had a poor image, probably not correct, but a perception. . . . We put together a very successful labor–management team, plus we hired a fabulous director of industrial recruitment. He's been aided by the county payroll tax. . . . $750,000 a year goes to industrial recruitment. I think the situation is very positive today. Unionism is a nonissue." ■

Stephenville, TX 76401

Location: 62 miles southwest of Fort Worth, 100 miles southwest of Dallas, 207 miles north of San Antonio, in north central Texas.

Population: 13,502 (1990).

Growth rate: 12% since 1980.

Per capita income: $9,682 (1985), 93% of state average ($10,373).

Geography/climate: Rolling to hilly, partly wooded, partly prairie plains. County elevation ranges from 700 to 1,700 feet. Mixture of humid, subtropical and continental weather. Mild winters with occasional cold fronts slipping down from the Great Plains and Rockies. January temperature averages: low, 32; high, 56. July: low, 74; high, 92. Average 94 days over 90; 236 days between killing frosts. Average rainfall, 31 inches.

Economic base: Diversified. Agriculture the leader, contributing $190 million, of which $140 million is dairy production. Large manufacturing payrolls: Norton, coated abrasives, 385 employees; FMC Fluid Control Operation, pipe unions, 200; Fibergrate, gratings and fasteners, 135; Rayloc, auto parts, 111; Cason, clothing, 71. Tarleton State University faculty, staff payroll totals about 500. Stephenville is the seat of Erath County.

Newspaper: *Stephenville Empire-Tribune*, 110 S. Columbia, Stephenville, TX 76401. 817-965-3124. Daily. Jess Williams, editor. $96 a year.

TV, radio: Local AM/FM stations. Cable carries network TV, PBS from Dallas-Ft. Worth.

Health care: Harris Methodist Hospital, 98 beds. 27 physicians, 9 dentists in local practice.

Schools: 2 elementary (K–3); intermediate (4–6); 1 junior high (7–8). Stephenville High School enrolls 871, sends about 92% to college. Average SAT, 956. Vocational school on same campus as high school. Tarleton State University, fastest-growing.

Educational level: 14.8% of Erath County residents have 16 or more years of formal education; state average, 16.9%. Per capita expenditure on public education, $283; state average, $441.

Library: Stephenville Public Library, 27,000 volumes. Annual circulation, 64,000.

Recreation: 2 city parks. Downtown park of 111 acres has 6 ball fields, pool, recreation building, picnic areas, hike-bike trail, 14 tennis courts. Optimist JC Park, 18 acres, built atop old city dump. 2 golf courses—1 9, 1 18 holes. Indoor pool at university. Organized team sports beginning with 5-year-old teams. Baseball, softball, soccer, basketball, football. Classes, competition in gymnastics, twirling, dance, tumbling. Exercise and aerobics classes. Bowling, roller-skating, 6-screen cinema.

3 BR, 2 BA house: $60,000 to $90,000.

Cost of electricity: $.08 per kilowatt hour.

Cost of natural gas: $.50 per therm.

Sales tax: 6.25%.

State income tax: None.

Churches: About 50. Denominations: Assemblies of God, Baptist, Christian, Church of Christ, Church of God, Church of Jesus Christ of Latter-day Saints, Episcopal, Jehovah's Witnesses, Lutheran, Methodist, Nazarene, Presbyterian, Roman Catholic.

Stephenville, home of Tarleton State University and center of the Texas dairy industry, is far enough away from Fort Worth and Dallas to be insulated from city problems—but close enough to serve as a ready retreat for fugitives from teeming Metroplex. That's good for business at Bill and Paula Oxford's bed-and-breakfast establishment at 563 N. Graham. "The Oxford House," as it's called, was built by Bill's great-great-grandfather, W. J. Oxford, Sr., who founded a law practice in Stephenville in 1886. Bill is the fifth generation to carry on the Oxford Law Offices. Roots go deep in this Texas town.

What residents say . . .

Robert Hooper, attorney, candidate for the Texas Legislature: BA at Austin, MEd from Harvard University, MBA from Harvard, JD from Vermont Law School. Worked overseas in Europe, Middle East, South America as project administrator for Brown & Root, Fluor, major government clients. . . . My mother's great-grandfather moved to Erath County after the Civil War. My mother was born in Comanche County. My mother and father met in Dallas but lived a lot around here, retired back here in the '70s. This became my domicile, my tax home. When my mother passed away, I came back here and stayed on. . . . I'm in practice with my wife, and after January with my wife and sister. I've gone from sole practitioner to junior partner in a matter of months. . . . The environment is clean, there is a great deal of civic spirit and pride . . . for such a small town, such a tremendous diversity of people: university professors, business people, agriculture, and four world-champion cowboys. . . . I was watching something on the Discovery Channel about cows in Australia and they interviewed a cowboy, on this 100,000-square-mile ranch in Australia, from Stephenville, Texas! It's the cowboy capital of the world. To me, Stephenville is a microcosm of Texas because Texas has this cowboy heritage and is at the same time home of NASA and Rice University and a lot of economic power, and a very diverse constituency. You see that in a very small town. We have everybody from the far left to the far right, intellectuals to more traditional values. . . . There has only been one capital murder trial in the history of the county, a very low level of real violence, almost unheard of. I had one client in Comanche County who stole 12 vehicles in a single night. All 12 had their keys in them. . . . But you don't do the wrong thing or it will ruin you around here. . . . If someone starts putting on airs, it's a good way for them to get their head handed to them. . . . I don't really want to be a politician, I'm just disgusted by nothing coming out of the Legislature. I would just like to go down one or two terms to try to turn around some of the things I think are wrong. For instance, we have the second or third highest tax level in the country yet a $3 to $6 billion budget shortfall. Programs never die. There are probably 500 different boards of licensing. I think you can economize and build performance by eliminating dead programs and making others more efficient. Stephenville competes not only with other towns in Texas but with Japan. I don't think many legislatures have done nearly enough to enhance our ability to compete for jobs."

R.D. Lancaster, native, retired military: "I spent 39 years flying fighters in the Air Force and retired as a full colonel. While I was in the Pentagon, I was working on a Joint Staff paper concerning the Army's plan for a huge helicopter. . . . Since by law the Air Force had the mission of providing air support to the Army, it was my job to sell the concept of a specific airplane in place of their huge, expensive, vulnerable helicopter. . . . I did the study that resulted in the A-10 Thunderbolt 11, nicknamed 'Warthog.' It was a funny-looking airplane but it certainly had the capability. . . . I was Air Attaché to the American Embassy in Paris. I flew Ambassador Dillon's airplane, flew him around quite a bit. . . . I was born in the country, about six miles west, in a small area called Green's Creek. In those days our crops were primarily corn, cotton, and maize. . . . Now mostly hay. Erath County holds the title of Number One dairy county in the state."

Paula Oxford, Stephenville Study Club: "There is a plastic Holstein cow, a big huge thing, on our Square, signifying the industry. I think it was put there in the early '70s by the dairy wives, kind of a controversial thing. A few people don't like the cow on our Square. For the most part, I think it's well deserved."

Don Davis, city administrator: "I'm not one of those who is awed by the fact we have a plastic cow on the courthouse lawn. . . . There's a little story about our cowboy heritage. Several of the current [Professional Rodeo Circuit Association] live in Stephenville. About six of them in all, national qualifiers. Last year, during the national finals, the media kept referring to Stephenville, Texas. That's how we got the handle of 'Cowboy Capital,' actually through the news media. . . . We do have a ranching heritage here, but it's not like West Texas. There are some rolling hills, creeks, some terrain here. Also more vegetation than you typically expect, pecan trees, oaks, other shade trees in town."

Ronnie Isham, superintendent, Stephenville Parks & Recreation Department: "City Park is about 62 acres, and we just added 49 acres more. It's the downtown park, within a couple of blocks of the Square. The Bosque River runs through the middle of it. It's pretty nice. Within that park there are six ball fields, a swimming pool, a rec building, probably 50 picnic areas, about a mile and a half hike-and-bike trail, a travel-trailer camping area with full hookups, 12 horseshoe pits, four tennis courts, one section called Century Park, actually the focus of the park with a center gazebo. . . . We'll have about 800 playing baseball or softball, an adult softball program of about 60 teams, which is really amazing for a town our size. . . . All the adult programs are self-supporting. The youth programs are subsidized by the city. . . . We have an awful nice town. . . . In my profession it's just unheard of to have the type of program we do. Most cities our size do not even have a parks-and-rec department. . . . This year we're starting a 'Christmas in the Park' . . . local entertainment, church choirs, school choirs, arts-and-crafts booths, and, of course, the appearance of Santa Claus. We wouldn't be lucky enough to have it snow. It may be January before we get any." ■

Tahlequah, OK 74464

Location: 67 miles southeast of Tulsa, 65 miles northwest of Ft. Smith, Arkansas, in the Ozark plateau of eastern Oklahoma.

Population: 10,398 (1990).

Growth rate: 7% since 1980.

Per capita income: $7,201 (1985), 74% of state average ($9,754).

Geography/climate: Gently rolling terrain, heavily wooded. Elevation 873 feet. 4 seasons but generally free of extremes because of mid-continental position. January temperature averages: low, 26; high, 47. July: low, 70; high, 91. Average 42 inches of rain, 9 inches of snow, 343 flying days.

Economic base: Cherokee Nation largest employer, generating about 1,000 jobs in varied industries including defense contracting. Other large payrolls: Northeastern State University, 900; Greenleaf Nursery, 400; Mid-Western Nursery, 400; Tahlequah Public Schools, 360; W. W. Hastings Hospital, 320; City Hospital, 230; City of Tahlequah, 130. Tahlequah is county seat, center of popular tourist area.

Newspaper: *Tahlequah Daily Pictorial Press,* 106 W. Second Street, Tahlequah, OK 74464. 918-456-8833. Sunday, Tuesday through Friday. Kim Poindexter, editor. $72 a year.

TV, radio: Local AM, FM stations. Cable carries network TV from Tulsa, Ft. Smith. NPR from Fayetteville, Tulsa.

Health care: Tahlequah City Hospital, W. W. Hastings Indian Hospital. Total beds, 118. 80 physicians, 15 dentists in local practice.

Schools: 3 elementary (K–6); 1 middle (7–9). Tahlequah High School (10–12) enrolls 892, sends 45% of graduates to higher education. Average ACT, 1991: 20.4. Northeastern State University enrolls about 9,000.

Educational level: 17.8% of Cherokee County residents have 16 or more years of formal education; state average, 15.1%. Per capita expenditure for public education, $375; state average, $430.

Library: Tahlequah Public Library, 35,000 volumes.

Recreation: 2 city parks, located along Town Branch Creek, which flows through the center of town. Playgrounds, ball fields, pool, tennis and basketball courts. Elsewhere in town: roller-skating, bowling, waterslide, batting cages. 3 daily-fee golf courses. Riding stables. Drive-in theater. Illinois River, 2 miles east of downtown, popular for canoe-floating. Lake Tenkiller, 10 miles south: boating, swimming, fishing.

3 BR, 2 BA house: $50,000 to $100,000.

Cost of electricity: $.10 per kilowatt hour.

Cost of natural gas: $.43 per therm.

Churches: 21. Denominations: Assemblies of God, Baptist, Free Will Baptist, Indian Baptist, Bible, Christian, Church of Christ, Episcopal, Evangelical Free, Lutheran, Nazarene, Pentecostal Holiness, Presbyterian, Roman Catholic, United Methodist.

"**I**n the fall and winter of 1838–39, the Cherokees were driven from their homes and pushed along a dreary march westward. Of 16,000 who started that miserable journey, more than 4,000 died along the way from disease, hunger, and exposure. The march lasted nearly a year and ever after it was known as 'The Trail Where They Cried.' . . ." Thus begins the narration in *The Trail of Tears Drama* presented each summer at the Cherokee Heritage Center, just south of Tahlequah.

Tahlequah was the end of the "Trail of Tears" for a suffering band of Cherokees uprooted from their ancestral lands in Georgia. It became the new western capital of the civilized tribe from the eastern United States, 70 years before Oklahoma became a state. Compared to many other towns in mid-continent, Tahlequah has a deep sense of its position in national history. Native Americans represent 28 percent of Cherokee County population. Industries founded by the Cherokee Nation generate more than $50 million in annual revenues, one of the largest enterprises in eastern Oklahoma.

What residents say . . .

Jay Hannah, president, BancFirst: "I guess the uniqueness of our city is that we just celebrated our 150th anniversary. That ties directly to the fact we are the seat of the great and sovereign Cherokee Nation. I look out my window onto the Square and see the third capital building constructed by the Cherokee, where the tribal council voted to designate Tahlequah as its capital. We are steeped with heritage here, and that adds a very vivid stroke to our canvas. . . . Our local economy is good. We are not dependent upon one particular industry. Seventy-seven counties in the state of Oklahoma have oil or gas. Four counties have zero, and we are one of them."

Doris Hinds, Hinds Department Store: "The store was started in Arkansas in 1898. That store was washed away by a flood. They moved to Peggs, Oklahoma, and it was blown away by a tornado. Just one disaster after another. Then they opened a store in Hulbert. They expanded and opened an additional store in Wagoner, and another in Fort Gibson. All these are little towns surrounding Tahlequah. They moved to Tahlequah 69 years ago. It started out as a general merchandise store and sold farm equipment as well. Mr. Hinds went into politics. He became speaker of the Oklahoma House. That was in 1946, and he continued to manage the stores until Bill Hinds, Jr., joined the firm. He is the present owner and I am his wife. . . . We closed out the other stores in neighboring towns and decided we would do what we could to preserve small-town Tahlequah and main street. Wal-Mart came to town and our main street was moving. . . . Our city was filled with empty buildings. I kept a mini-department store but I started specializing. I opened a women's large-size specialty shop in one empty building, a children's shop in another empty building, a junior-size shop, a men's shop, and a ladies' specialty shop. The stores are all together . . . three of them are across the street. The idea was to keep our downtown together. I still maintain, the personality of a town is its main street. We were able to keep it alive. . . . I think we're doing better. . . . Another plus for this town, we're in the center of three major lakes, Tenkiller, Wagoner, Grand . . . makes this a paradise for tourists, yet we don't have a tourist air. Tahlequah still has the small-town flavor."

Robert Finch, library director: "I'm one person with three hats. I am the city librarian, the county librarian, and the branch manager of the Eastern Oklahoma Library System. We have a multi-county system. We share resources because libraries are so expensive these days. . . . We have pretty much a popular reading collection and a children's library. All libraries are a referral service. We try to keep track of the various hotlines. . . . We've had a library here since 1905. We began as a Carnegie Library sort of because this is the capital of the Cherokee Nation. . . . My great-grandfather, Sam Houston Mays, after he retired became the groundskeeper for this building. Various aunts, uncles, and my mom all helped with the grounds. My great-grandfather planted all the trees. . . . I've only been here six months. I'm a professional librarian. I have an MLS, a master's of library science. I was down in Houston and got tired of the rat race. There was a position here as branch manager, and I wanted to get into management."

Patty Skinner, chairman of the board, Tahlequah Lumber: "My dad started the business 43 years ago. Five family members are in it right now. We employ 65. Business is steady. Tahlequah doesn't notice recession or otherwise. We don't depend on an oil boom. . . . Tahlequah seems to be willing to do what's necessary when there's a need. We increased our school levy last year. . . . We lack industry. A lot of people drive to work in Muskogee, or in Tulsa, 65 miles."

Sally Ross, mayor: "I was city clerk for 20 years before being elected mayor. Our city is in relatively good shape. We have one of the best fire and police departments in the state. We have a very low crime rate, and we have a great quality of life . . . two good hospitals, an abundance of doctors, excellent medical facilities. We have approved funds for a new high school. We have a university here which is probably the best of its size in the nation. The university was established as a school for the youth of the Cherokee Nation back over 100 years ago. We have the largest Native American enrollment in the nation. . . . I think we have held to the traditions and heritage of our forefathers who came here 150 years ago. Even though we are very progressive, we are still holding on to the wonderful way of life of the past. . . . Right now we are getting ready for the Boare Heade Feaste, planned annually, similar to England. It is of the style that the old English had years ago. The costumes are just fantastic. People come from out of state . . . very good attendance, you have to get here ahead of time. It starts tonight." ■

Tifton, GA 31793

Location: On the I-75 expressway to Florida, 180 miles southeast of Atlanta, 233 miles northwest of Orlando. ·

Population: 14,215 (1990).

Growth rate: 3.4% since 1980.

Per capita income: $8,488 (1985), 83% of state average ($10,191).

Geography/climate: Flat to gently rolling coastal plains of south central Georgia accented by long-leaf pine, magnolia, live oak. Mild winters with 10–12 nights as low as 30 degrees, hot summers. Average annual rainfall, 47 inches.

Economic base: Rich agricultural area known for production of vegetable plants and grasses. Nonfarm employment: manufacturing, 28%; government, 25%; trade, 24%. Textiles and garment industries employ 2,300; Tifton Aluminum Co., 500; Union Camp Corp., 227. Other major employers include Abraham Baldwin College, Coastal Plain Experiment Stations, University of Georgia Rural Development Center.

Newspaper: *The Tifton Gazette,* 211 N. Tift Avenue, Tifton, GA 31793. 912-382-4321. Daily except Sunday. $72 a year.

TV, radio: 3 local AM stations, 3 FM stations, including an NPR member. TV by cable brings in Atlanta stations, networks, PBS.

Health care: Tift General Hospital, 168 beds. 50 physicians, 13 dentists in local practice.

Schools: 6 elementary schools (K–4); 2 middle (5–7); 1 junior high (8–9). Tift County High School enrolls 1,338, sends about 35% on to higher education, many to Abraham Baldwin, the local junior college. About 25% of graduates attend 4-year institutions. Average combined SAT score, 797.

Educational level: 11.5% of Tift County residents have 16 or more years of formal education; state average, 14.6%. Per capita expenditure for public education, $310; state average, $389.

Library: Tifton-Tift County Public Library has 60,000 books, 181 periodical titles. 15,674 registered borrowers.

Recreation: 9 city parks including swimming pool, tennis courts. Country club with 18-hole golf course; several other courses nearby. Summer water sports at Crystal Lake in nearby Irwinville. Reed Bingham State Park, 10 miles south.

3 BR, 2 BA house: $40,000 to $70,000.

Cost of electricity: $.045 per kilowatt hour.

Cost of gas: $.57 per therm.

Sales tax: 5%.

State income tax: Graduated 1% to 6%.

Churches: 45. Denominations: African Methodist Episcopal, Assemblies of God, Baptist, Baptist-Independent, Baptist-Southern, Charismatic, Church of Christ, Church of God, Church of Jesus Christ of Latter-day Saints, Episcopal, Holiness, Jehovah's Witnesses, Lutheran, Methodist-United, Nazarene, Presbyterian, Primitive Baptist, Roman Catholic.

Target Stores, the discount chain, was about to locate a new distribution center in northern Florida when Tifton, Georgia, decided this plum should be plucked by the Peach Tree State. As the story goes, Tifton activists took a map and drew lines connecting all the Target stores. The hub came within 10 miles of Tifton—reason enough to give the town a look. "Some of the competition had only one or two sites to show them, but when Target flew in here to see what we had to offer, we had six sites—and a helicopter waiting to show them around," recalls Homer Rankin, former owner of the town's daily newspaper. "To make a long story short, we landed it. We have that type of aggressive approach to opportunities."

What residents say . . .

Laura Tucker, executive director, Tifton-Tift County Clean Community Commission: "Keep America Beautiful awarded the title of 'The Cleanest Community in America' to Tifton. It's a marketing tool we use in trying to promote industrial growth and economic development. You can show a prospective new business what a wonderful industrial park you have. But what that prospect remembers is what he sees driving around, looking at the community. Since the inception of our program we've reduced litter 72 percent. . . . We've been recycling since 1978, the first governmentally owned recycling center in the State of Georgia. We were doing it before it became chic!"

Gloria Sulkowski, real-estate sales: "My husband had a job offer with Tifton Aluminum and we came down with that. He has since lost his job but we are very determined to stay in Tifton. Oh, gosh, it's just a great place to live. Normally when an outsider comes in you feel a little bit of resentment. Not here. Most of them just open up their arms to you. This is where I want my roots. I feel I belong here. It's strange for me, being a Northerner. I was born in Connecticut, lived in New Jersey most of my life. We had moved to North Carolina for about five years and just fell in love with the South. You see the difference in school, the respect children show, the 'ma'am,' the 'sir.' A lot of respect. Everything is family. I have three boys. My oldest is 16, one 13, one 10. At first I thought we were going to have a hard time moving. My oldest was in eighth grade when we moved and left a lot of friends. Now the boys say, 'We aren't going to move, are we?' My oldest son plays football for the high school. Football is real big here. Usually there are eight- to 10,000 people out for a game. When we play Valdosta and Worth County, usually 12 to 15,000. If you don't go to the football game on Friday night, nobody is going to talk to you the next day because you won't know what happened. . . . I'm involved in everything that's here, I believe. We're trying to restore the Tift Theater. It's an old movie house right on Main Street. I don't know how many years it was closed. . . . The real-estate market right now is a little bit slow, but it's starting to pick up. . . . The house we purchased when we came to Tifton three years ago would have sold for at least $300,000 or more in New Jersey. We paid $112,000."

Homer Rankin, former owner, **The Tifton Gazette:** "The founder of Tifton was Henry Harding Tift, known as Captain Tift. I don't know whether that's a Kentucky Colonel title. The Tift family came from Mystic, Connecticut. . . . He set up a lumber mill here. This whole area was covered with beautiful virgin pine. . . . Most of the timber was shipped down to Brunswick or Savannah and carried by schooner back up to Connecticut for shipbuilding. . . . I'm a native of New Orleans. . . . I was in California going to school, in my junior year, when two Southern boys showed up, James Caldwell from Lookout Mountain and Henry Harding Tift, III, grandson of the founder of Tifton. . . . He invited me to come spend the summer with him. I met the girl I would later marry, Lutrelle McLellan. I was 17 and she was 15. . . . I entered Tulane Law School. . . . She was a journalism graduate. Each summer she ran a little newspaper on St. Simon's Island. . . . We have been in Tifton since 1945. When the war was over, I and half a dozen other husbands were brought back home. . . . Back in 1914, this little old hick town in Georgia had enough interest in world affairs that the townspeople prevailed upon the local newspaper to publish every day, so that they might have daily news of the developments in Europe. They could see there was going to be a world war. . . . At the time we bought the newspaper in 1952 it was the smallest daily in the United States, four pages a day except Thursday

when we published six. Circulation was 2,933. When we sold in 1981, it was 10,300. We really had a first-class small-town newspaper. People told us they did not need to buy the Atlanta newspaper. . . ."

Steve Rigdon, physician, co-president, Tift County Foundation for Educational Excellence: "My family came here in 1830 and has been here ever since . . . mainly farmers, fought through the Civil War. A number of my ancestors were killed in the war. . . . We're related to a number of families in the community. . . . Being a native it was very important to me to come back to this town. I love it. I grew up with a view of the world that was very balanced. . . . I grew up thinking that no one was really better than anyone else, and no one particularly worse . . . a middle-class town where people were what they were. . . . I thought it was a valuable view of the world. . . . Education has always been very important to me and my family. I had a very good education here and I wanted to make sure my children did, too. Several of us got together and established this educational foundation. We go to private industry and raise tax-exempt money to buy extras for the schools . . . serve as an interest group that focuses public attention on the needs of the public school system . . . get together seed money to institute new programs. One thing we're proud of is we're the third place in the state to be named a Georgia Youth Science and Technology Center, established through our foundation and the local junior college . . . to upgrade science teaching in primary, middle, and junior high school. Apparently there is a big deficit in those areas. We sponsor a number of incentive grants for teachers . . . and monetary awards for teacher merit. . . . In the last year and a half we have raised a little over $200,000. For a community this size it really is a lot of money."

Bruce Greene, manager, Main Street Project: "In the early '80s, a local pioneer, Mr. Harold Harper, bought a couple of buildings in our downtown, very much to the surprise of the community. Downtown was suffering from neglect and decay, as so many downtowns were. He rehabbed them into apartments and offices, and it was very successful. The next project was to redo an old, 1930s department store into a new retail facility. A business out in our mall, J.J.'s Men's Store, moved back into downtown. . . . That really set the town to talking. . . . I interviewed for the job of Main Street Project manager in the spring of 1986 . . . really a Cinderella story since then . . . a manager who is knowledgeable of what needs to be done, and a town ready to do it. . . . We've done some very large projects, such as the 22,000-square-foot Cotton Warehouse right in the heart of downtown, turned into a wonderful array of gymnasium, karate studio, bakery, pizza restaurant, upper-end ladies store. What it did was change the attitude of people, that downtown didn't close at 5 p.m. . . . We have Florida money out on the Interstate, about 40,000 cars a day on the perimeter of town. It's almost like an aquifer of money . . . a 53-and-a-half-million-dollar industry there . . . hotels, motels, restaurants, retail trade . . . a corridor. . . . I think that Tifton is the small town America is looking for. When you experience it, you will see what I mean." ■

Ukiah, CA 95482

Location: 120 miles north of San Francisco, 30 miles inland from the Pacific Coast, on U.S. 101.

Population: 14,599 (1990).

Growth rate: 11% since 1986.

Per capita income: $9,327 (1985), 78% of state average ($11,885).

Geography/climate: Fertile, deep valley of the Russian River within the Coast Ranges, surrounded by vineyards, orchards, and oaks on the foothills. Rainfall averages 45 inches, mainly in December–February period. Winter temperatures seldom below mid-20s. Hot, dry summer days into the mid-90s cooled by afternoon sea breeze to 60s–70s.

Economic base: Lumber and wood products, grapes, pears, tourism, some manufacturing. Biggest payrolls: Masonite, Louisiana-Pacific, Carousel Carpet Mills, Retech, Inc. Principal wineries are Mendocino Vineyards, Fetzer Vineyards, McDowell Valley, Parducci Winery, Weibel Champagne. Ukiah is county seat.

Newspaper: *The Ukiah Daily Journal*, 590 S. School Street, Ukiah, CA 95482. 707-468-0123. Daily except Saturday. Jim Smith, editor. $10.50 a month.

TV, radio: 1 AM, 3 FM stations. Cable brings in San Francisco stations, networks, PBS.

Health care: Mendocino Community Hospital, 56 beds; Ukiah Valley Medical Center, 94 beds.

Schools: 4 elementary (K–5); 1 middle (6–8). Ukiah High School enrolls about 1,800, including 16% Hispanic, 7% Native American/Alaskan, 1% black. Selected as a California Distinguished School in 1988. 64% of graduates go on to college: 26% to a 4-year institution, 38% to junior college. Composite SAT scores for 1991: verbal, 448; math, 516. Mentoring program pairs students with community workers in numerous fields to explore careers. Mendocino College, a 2-year institution, enrolls about 5,000.

Educational level: 17.6% of Mendocino County residents have 16 or more years of formal education; state average, 19.6%. Per capita expenditure for public education, $622; state average, $461.

Library: Mendocino County Library has 144,000 books, 171 periodicals.

Recreation: 4 city parks include swimming pool, tennis courts, ball fields, picnic areas. 18-hole, par 70 municipal golf course. Lake Mendocino, just north of city, is recreational focal point including campsites, boat-launching ramps, beach, hiking trail, amphitheaters. Squaw Valley ski area is 4–5 hour drive east in the Sierra Nevada range.

3 BR, 2 BA house: $150,000 to $200,000 in the city.

Cost of electricity: $.10 to $.14 per kilowatt hour.

Cost of natural gas: $.49 to $.82 per therm.

Sales tax: 6.25%.

State income tax: Graduated 1% to 9.3%.

Churches: 30. Denominations: Assemblies of God, Baha'i, Baptist, Calvary Way, Christadelphians, Christian Science, Church of Christ, Church of God of Prophecy, Church of Jesus Christ of Latter-day Saints, Community, Episcopal, Evangelical Free, First Christian, Foursquare Gospel, Glad Tidings Gospel, Gospel Tabernacle, Lutheran-Evangelical, Lutheran Missouri Synod, Nazarene, Presbyterian, Religious Science, Roman Catholic, Seventh-Day Adventist, United Methodist, United Pentecostal, Victory Word Center.

Ukiah is the Native American word for "deep valley." This deep valley in the Coast Ranges has attracted settlers for 150 years—Forty-Niners, loggers, grape-growers, and, increasingly, fugitives from the thickly settled counties down toward San Francisco Bay, and beyond. Some residents commute to jobs in Santa Rosa, 70 miles south.

How Ukiah grows depends on planning—already in motion—and new jobs. With the future of forest products uncertain, and with the wineries being squeezed by subdivisions, some people say there's a need for more manufacturing. But don't count the grape-growers out—not yet, anyway.

What residents say . . .

John Parducci, vintner: "We're an old family, five generations living here right now. I grew up in the business. This is my 58th year of wine production. . . . We were isolated back then, three miles out of town. Now they're wanting to subdivide. . . . This is the last of the West. We're proud to live here but we hate to see what's happening to it. I'm predicting within 10 years it will be almost impossible for us to survive. . . . We're going to fight to the finish."

Gary Nix, realtor: "Many of our buyers are from out of the area. I would not want to say it's becoming cosmopolitan, but it's more cosmopolitan than it was. For a small community it's not so closed-minded as many are. . . . I'm involved right now in the Growth Management Steering Committee, a city commission formed for the purposes of reviewing what's happening to Ukiah, looking into the future. There are 33 members on the Committee. . . . It's a cross-section . . . Native American, people from all different socioeconomic groups. It's nice to see everybody recognize that growth is here and what we need to do is plan well for it. . . . We're very fortunate Ukiah has a good water source. It supplied us both through the severe drought in the '70s and the recent drought. Our water comes from wells along the Russian River. . . . We're in a similar situation to many counties in the state having financial problems. We're fortunate to have a very good school system. I like Ukiah. I want to see it grow but not bust wide open."

Chet Hardin, retired assistant principal, Ukiah High School: "I had flown over this country when I was in the Navy. It looked beautiful from 20,000 feet. We came up

335

here in 1957. . . . I handled all the discipline in the high school. In 19 years we had only one student seriously injured, never had a lawsuit. . . . There are four types of people here: After World War II, lots of people came out from the Midwest to work in the logging woods. Then we have lots of old Italian people, the ones who established the grapes here. Then we have lots of natives, born and raised here. Then we're getting more and more migrant Mexican-Americans becoming permanent members of the community. They fit in, there's no conflict. . . . This is your grape country. Kids in agricultural classes learn how to plant and care for wine grapes. We have a good little "ag" program. . . . Where else can you stand on a high school athletic field and see deer grazing? One day I saw two wild turkeys walking. . . . We are growing about three percent a year in student population. Many come here from southern California. Lots of them from the Bay Area. They keep adding sections of freeway up to Santa Rosa, a bedroom area for San Francisco. I think our growth is going to be limited by prospects of employment. . . . My wife and I have no children. We came here and taught in the system. Now we're retired. I've taken that book *Retirement Places Rated.* We went up in Washington to Puget Sound. Then to Phoenix, Sedona, and Prescott. Flew to Atlanta, got a car and drove to Brevard, Hendersonville, Asheville. Then to Arkansas, Hot Springs Village. Then to Branson in Missouri. All beautiful places. But we kind of feel Ukiah is the best place, for two reasons. One is the weather and setting. But second, this place is just filled with a hell of a lot of nice people."

Carole Hester, freelance writer: "Before I started working for the newspaper I was president of the Republican Women's Club, president of Business and Professional Women. I'm on the board of the American Heart Association, chairman of the Mendocino County National Women's Political Caucus. . . . I've only lived here six years. . . . It has its trade-offs. That which makes it wonderful to live here is also its greatest detriment. The charm of the people, the pristine quality, the small-town atmosphere . . . you don't have to use your ID to cash a check . . . it also means people are tunnel-sighted and myopic. It's difficult for people to have a vision about community growth, land growth, growth of any kind. . . . So far we've been able to stick our heads in the sand and enjoy what's here. . . . I interviewed people and asked, 'What do you see as the future of our town?' One of the exciting things because it gives me hope . . . people said it won't die for lack of a tax base or lack of jobs . . . because there just aren't any jobs here. . . . In the '60s, a lot of bright intellectuals moved up here into the hills. They don't participate in community activity. Some of us help support this community with our life blood. These people get the benefits without contributing. . . . We are part of the Emerald Triangle: Humboldt, Mendocino, and Del Norte counties. There are places you cannot walk because there are known growers of marijuana. You don't have to drive too far out for it to be unpleasant. . . . I am continually amazed at the talent here . . . a ballet company, a community theater, a civic light-opera company. . . . Living in a small town is a civics lesson. Politically, you can see more in a small town. . . . We've lived in lots of places. This is the first place where on a daily basis one is confronted with the homeless and the destitute. Highway 101 is a corridor for the poor and homeless. It used to be an easy mark for them to stop in churches along the road. Many churches now refer all requests to the community center, so churches are changing their role. We moved here from Fresno, where we lived on the poor side of the tracks. Yet I never saw a poor person, not once. Here they are part of you. It makes me never forget to be thankful. It helps me to have to wrestle with my conscience."

Stan Hildreth, *retired:* "I just stepped down from chairman of the California Pear Growers. They made me chairman emeritus . . . I'm the third generation. My grandfather came across the plains from Missouri, a Forty-Niner. My grandfather on my mother's side was sheriff. He chased Black Bart. My mother and dad were born here. . . . My father bought some property in the valley where I was born. My son is now there . . . I moved off the ranch. Now we're looking at the valley as a bedroom community for Santa Rosa. We're trying to maintain agriculture. . . . The competition between urban and agriculture is pretty intense. I'm not sure how long agriculture is going to be able to survive." ■

Vernal, UT 84078

Location: 171 miles east of Salt Lake City, 320 miles west of Denver, on the central portion of the Outlaw Trail, in northeastern Utah.

Population: 6,644 (1990).

Growth rate: 7% loss since 1980 with decline in oil production.

Per capita income: $8,447 (1985), 99% of state average ($8,535).

Geography/climate: Semi-arid high country, elevation 5,331 feet, ringed by Diamond Mountain, Blue Mountain, Green River Gorge. Wide seasonal changes in weather tempered by mountain ranges. Annual rainfall, 8 inches; snowfall, 25 inches. January high temperatures average 31; low, 5. July high, 90; low, 50. Low humidity, sunny.

Economic base: Area overlies the Uintah Basin, rich with deposits of crude oil, oil shale, tar sands; uintaite, tradenamed Gilsonite. Farming community, chiefly grain and hay. Vernal now developing alternatives to roller-coaster oil economy: tourism, light manufacturing. Major payrolls: Uintah County School District, 520; Ute Indian Tribe, 300; Deseret Generation, Ashley Valley Medical Center, Chevron Resources, American Gilsonite. Seat of Uintah County.

Newspaper: *The Vernal Express*, 54 N. Vernal Avenue, Vernal, UT 84078. 801-789-3511. Wednesdays. Steve Wallis, editor. $31 a year.

TV, radio: 1 local AM, 2 FM stations. Cable carries network-TV stations, PBS from Salt Lake City, Denver.

Health care: Ashley Valley Medical Center, 39 beds. 13 physicians, 7 dentists in local practice.

Schools: 6 elementary (K–5); 1 middle (6–7); 1 junior high (8–9). Uintah High School enrolls 1,150, sends 45% to higher education. 1990 composite ACT, 20.2. Ashley Valley High School, an alternative school, enrolls 80–90 students, including young mothers, adult education. Utah State University satellite campus.

Educational level: 12% of Uintah County residents have 16 or more years of formal education; state average, 19.1%. Per capita expenditure for public education, $587; state average, $508.

Library: Uintah County Library, 48,684 volumes. Circulation, 184,000. Largest national collection of material on outlaws housed in Outlaw Trail History Center, part of library.

Recreation: 4 city parks with 15 baseball diamonds, pavilions, playgrounds, volleyball court, 10 tennis courts, horseshoe pits, year-round swimming pool. Western Park is site of fairgrounds, arena, convention center. 18-hole public golf course. Bowling alley. 4 movie theaters including drive-in. Community theater. Camping north of town at Red Fleet, Steinaker state parks. Ouray National Wildlife Refuge, 23 miles south. Visitor Center of Dinosaur National Monument, 10 miles east. Uintah Arts Council sponsors annual Outlaw Trail Festival, July.

3 BR, 2 BA house: $35,000 to $65,000.

Cost of electricity: $.071 per kilowatt hour.

Cost of natural gas: $.47 per therm.

Sales tax: 6%.

State income tax: 2.55% to 7.2%.

Churches: 41, 28 of which are Church of Jesus Christ of Latter-day Saints. Other denominations: Assemblies of God, Baptist, Independent Baptist, Southern Baptist, Christian, Episcopal, Jehovah's Witnesses, Lutheran, Nazarene, Nondenominational, Pentecostal, Roman Catholic, United Church of Christ.

Vernal is the town that ordered a solid-brick bank delivered by parcel post. "The Parcel Post Bank," today called Zions First National Bank, stands at the corner of Main Street and Vernal Avenue. Built in 1916, the present bank replaced a wooden building that had worried the Mormon pioneers for some years. They were prospering in this remote corner of Utah, amassing substantial accounts in the hometown bank. The problem was a certain group of nondepositors who shared their lovely valley: Butch Cassidy and his Wild Bunch.

"Butch and his men used to ride boldly down the street with their six-shooters gleaming in the sun," Virginia Houston recounts in a history. "They would laugh and joke with each other as they passed the old frame bank and then would look back at it enviously. . . . Vernal folks were worried about the vulnerable state of their bank." Mrs. Houston's father, W. H. Coltharp, took the initiative, proposing a two-story, solid-brick bank. The only problem was the brick. No railroad served Vernal. The nearest kiln was 135 miles over roads more like ruts, and delivery by private wagon was going to cost too much—15 cents per brick, or about $7,500.

But Coltharp, who "had a lot of pioneer shrewdness about him," discovered that the bricks could be delivered by the U.S. Postal Service for about seven cents apiece, so long as no single package weighed more than 50 pounds. Thus, 5,000 packages of bricks were dispatched one day by parcel post from Salt Lake City to Vernal, over an official postal route measuring 407 miles. The rural Star Route delivery system struggled for weeks under this early example of banking by mail, and when Postal Headquarters in Washington got the news, rules governing parcel post were promptly rewritten. But imaginative solutions to difficult problems are still in style around Vernal, Utah.

What residents say . . .

Ken Bassett, city manager: "Back in the early and mid-1980s, when the federal government decided not to do a lot with oil reserves and synfuels, we went through a significant decline in our economy. A lot of speculators had been building multi-family complexes and expanding businesses. Lo and behold, when the federal government pulled their support, many people ended up losing what they had invested, and everything else. Government and anyone related to it was looked at as being the culprit . . . government didn't plan and foresee. We went through a time of very little cohesiveness and pride. People were licking their wounds. Then the community started realizing, we can wallow in our tears until hell freezes over but we're going to have to do something to make sure we don't get into this trouble again. A lot of that interest has gone into tourism. We are very proud of the new tourism program, which includes a brand new, major indoor arena. . . . Another community issue is education. The city has used a grant to purchase an existing office building and turn it into an extension center for Utah State University. They have always had a presence here but never had a home. Now they are able to beef up their educational opportunities here in Vernal. . . . We have been able to attract retail . . . Wal-Mart . . . K-Mart is just finishing up a major expansion. . . . One thing I've been trying to emphasize is the issue of community pride, making sure the community, as tough as things might be, always conveys an image of activity, of wellness, of liveliness. You do that in different ways. For example, we have a beautification project . . . close to 800 planters along Main Street, Highway 40. Every year, through an extremely successful volunteer effort, we plant all of these flowers in an hour and a half. . . . Once again, a feeling of wellness. When tourists come through this community we want them to think, 'Wow, am I really in rural Utah?'. . . Empty homes were a major problem. Developers came in and built condominiums, all on the come, all hoping this energy thing would go boom. It didn't, and they lost their

shirts. At one time we had over 700 single-family units not occupied. HUD came in and started auctioning them off. That created a problem for the market. If you wanted to leave Vernal, you had to give your home away. The home next to me . . . three-bedroom, family room, patio, nice big yard, sold for $10,500. The home across the street sold for $15,000. Finally, HUD got all their homes sold. . . . We are presently involved in a comprehensive planning project funded by the State of Utah to determine what are the needs, both social and economic, of an energy-impacted community. . . . When you go through these ups and downs, there is more divorce, more child-abuse and spouse-abuse, more educational problems. How do we cope with those? We're using Vernal as a demonstration. . . . We have, in fact, turned a corner. With added tourism, we're looking at a healthier city budget, a more vibrant community, more volunteerism, more festivals. . . . The turnaround has been very purposeful. It has come only from a community of residents who have changed their attitudes."

Alta Winward, chairman, Uintah Arts Council: "We decided to throw a summer project . . . about the lives of our local people dealing with outlaws. . . . We've had four different plays written. . . . The thing that's unique about us, it's all local people who write the scripts, write the music, do the performing. We feel like we're getting quite professional. This year, by the time we're through . . . 25,000 in the audience. For a small town, that's pretty good!"

Doris K. Burton, director, Outlaw Trail History Center: "The Outlaw Trail went right through Vernal. It came up through southern Utah to Robbers Roost, just 15 miles out of Vernal, where there was no law whatsoever. The outlaws even set up their own saloon . . . and the sheriff couldn't touch them. . . . There's a lot of outlaw history here. The Outlaw Trail History Center began a year and a half ago. We built a new room, part of the county library, and we're building on to the library right now to double the space. We provide the center for the National Outlaw Lawmen Association, the Western Outlaw Lawmen Association, and the Outlaw Trail History Association. . . . We have an 800 line so all the members can call in . . . Bill Webb from Kansas City, Ed Kirby from Connecticut . . . they're on our board of directors.

So, we're spread all over the country. [Kirby] is an authority on the Sundance Kid. . . . I was born here. This is predominantly a Mormon town but we have about every other church there is. The kids all go to school together. Everybody helps everybody. . . . It seems to me every 15 or 20 years we really have a boom. They overbuild and people move in. Then it goes bust. This has happened with us several times. . . . So we never worry. Maybe we should. You just figure it's going to come back pretty soon. But our library has kept growing. When people are laid off they can't afford to buy books. They use the library and we've just grown and grown and grown." ■

Warsaw, IN 46580

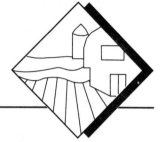

Location: 40 miles northwest of Fort Wayne, 47 miles southeast of South Bend, in north central Indiana.

Population: 10,968 (1990).

Growth rate: 3% since 1980.

Per capita income: $10,502 (1985), 5% higher than state average ($9,978).

Geography/climate: Generally flat terrain, 825 feet elevation. Continental climate—cold winters; hot, often humid summers. January average low temperature, 18; high, 33. 140 days at or below freezing. July average low, 62; high, 84. 14 days into the 90s across summer. Annual rainfall, 36 inches; snowfall, 31 inches.

Economic base: Headquarters of several manufacturers of orthopedic implants: Biomet, 473 employees; DePuy, 610; Othy, 268; Warsaw Orthopedic, 100; Zimmer, 2,100. Other large industrial payrolls: Creighton Brothers, eggs, 180; Da-Lite Screen, 400; Dalton Foundries, iron foundry, 704; Explorer Van, van conversions, 253; Jomac Products, gloves, rainwear, safety clothing, 117; Kimble Glass, ampules and vials, 300; R. R. Donnelley, printers, 1,700; Uniroyal, plastic extrusions, 225; Warsaw Coil, electrical coils, controls, 125; Sun Metal Products, wire spoke wheels, 150; Warsaw Foundry, gray iron castings, 100. Kosciusko County leads Indiana in dollar value of agricultural production and is among top 10 in U.S. Leading commodities: corn, eggs, hogs, soybeans. Largest duck producer in the world, Maple Leaf Farms, is located in Milford, 12 miles north. Warsaw is county seat, retail center.

Newspaper: *Times-Union,* corner of Market & Indiana (P.O. Box 1448), Warsaw, IN 46580. 219-267-3111. Daily, Monday through Saturday. Norman L. Hagg, editor. $77 a year.

TV, radio: Local AM/FM station. Cable carries network TV, PBS from Fort Wayne, Chicago. NPR from Fort Wayne.

Health care: Kosciusko Community Hospital, 113 beds. 46 physicians, 29 dentists in local practice.

Schools: 8 elementary (K–5); 1 middle (6–8). Warsaw High School enrolls 1,548, sends about 50% to higher education. 40% of students take SAT. 1990 average scores: math, 482; verbal, 431. Lakeland Christian Academy (7–12) enrolls 80. 3 private schools for pre-K through 6: Sacred Heart School, 190 enrollment; Warsaw Christian School, 174; Redeemer Lutheran, 65. Ivy Tech, state junior college, enrolls 940. Grace College and Theological Seminary, 1,100.

Educational level: 12.1% of Kosciusko County residents have 16 or more years of formal education; state average, 12.5%. Per capita expenditure for public education, $361; state average, $422.

Library: Warsaw Public Library, 91,374 volumes.

Recreation: 3 lakes within city limits; more than 100 lakes in county, including the deepest and largest lakes in Indiana. Numerous sites to fish, swim, boat. 10 city parks totaling 100 acres. Beaches, picnic areas, boat launches, lighted playing fields, game courts, trails, shelters, BMX race track. Racquet club, 7 golf courses in county. Bowling alley. 2 multi-screen cinemas, drive-in. Dinner theater. YMCA with pool, sauna, weight and fitness rooms, track, double gym, shuffleboard, horseshoes.

3 BR, 2 BA house: $80,000 to $200,000.

Cost of electricity: $.11 per kilowatt hour.

Cost of natural gas: $.55 per therm.

Sales tax: 5%.

State income tax: 3.4%.

Churches: 46. Denominations: Assemblies of God, Baptist, Independent Baptist, Reformed Baptist, Southern Baptist, Bible, Brethren, Charismatic, Christian, Christian & Missionary Alliance, Christian Science, Church of Christ, Church of God, Church of Jesus Christ of Latter-day Saints, Community, Foursquare Gospel, Free Methodist, Grace Brethren, Independent, Independent Fundamental, Jehovah's Witnesses, Lutheran, Mennonite, Missionary, Nazarene, Nondenominational, Pentecostal, Presbyterian, Roman Catholic, Salvation Army, Seventh-Day Adventist, Society of Friends, United Methodist, United Pentecostal, Wesleyan.

With a name like Warsaw in a county called Kosciusko, you'd expect a large Polish population. However, there are no more Poles than any other ethnic group in this northern Indiana town. The namesake of the county is Thaddeus Kosciusko, the Polish patriot who helped out with the Revolutionary War. He never got to Indiana, but Indiana was grateful, just the same. And to create a matched set of commemoratives, Warsaw was the obvious name for the county seat. Some other people of note did spend time in Warsaw and environs. James Whitcomb Riley, the Hoosier poet, painted signs in Warsaw. Ambrose Bierce, the novelist, was a reporter at the local newspaper. Theodore Dreiser went to school in Warsaw. Just as these early sons of Warsaw went forth to raise the human spirit; today, an unusual cluster of local factories improves the human condition. Warsaw is recognized as the world center for the production of orthopedic implants—knee and hip replacements and mechanical shoulders and elbows, among other ingenious substitutes for natural connections. Warsaw also is proud to provide a home base for the world's largest producer in three other categories: movie projection screens, spoked wheels, and rotogravure printing. But it all began with agriculture. Kosciusko County is endowed with almost 40 different soil types, including some of the best-producing crop land in the U.S. As elsewhere, the number of farms has been shrinking and average farm size growing as properties change hands. There were 1,327 farms in the county in 1987, with an average size of 202 acres and an average value of $239,496. Measured by dollar production, county farms consistently rank at the top in Indiana, and among the top 10 in the nation. Good soil is only part of the reason, a local expert explains. Much has to do with the simple idea of what you decide to do within available space.

What residents say ...

Paul Siebenmorgen, Sr., bank vice president, former county agricultural agent: "Versus a row crop, you can put 100,000 chickens on a couple of acres and generate large dollars. Maple Leaf Farms in Milford produces over half the ducks in the country. They also grow some of their own, plus contract with growers who use converted poultry houses. Then, North Manchester is sort of a hub of veal raising, I call them veal factories. Then we've got our fair share of confined hog houses and cattle operations. But I think it's these three items, ducks, eggs, and veal, that really hype the numbers. In the interest of fairness, we're the largest county in the state without a major metropolitan area in it. That also helps, more acres to produce crops on without having to take space for subdivisions.... The community's been insulated a little bit this time from the recession. In the orthopedic industry, a lot of their products are for elective-type surgery. When people think they're going to get laid off, they elect to have this surgery. So, going into a recession is even better for the orthopedic group. Another major industry we have here is Donnelley, the commercial printer, and typically people are advertising a little harder in a recession."

Jean Northenor, bank senior vice president, former county auditor: "I would describe Warsaw as a very young old town. Warsaw has been here a lot of years. Yet the people in Warsaw have never allowed it to become stagnant. You don't find many people here who believe the way things

used to be done is the only way, even though some of those youthful thinkers are not so young any more. I was the elected county auditor here for two terms, similar to a controller in industry, so I am very tuned in to the entire county. One other thing that makes Warsaw so strong is the county ... teamwork between the county and the town."

Barb Dagnall, executive director, Council on Aging: "One thing about Kosciusko County ... the people have a very strong spirit of volunteerism.... We run a mobile-meals program ... 400 volunteers take turns delivering noon meals Monday through Friday on 12 routes that go all over the county, and the county, as you have noted, is very large. The volunteers are not paid anything.... Some of our clients see this as a lifeline. They know someone will knock on their door Monday through Friday.... Some are not needy at all but choose to stay in their home rather than be institutionalized.... We have a beautiful gym at our Senior Opportunity Center. Seniors use it 9 A.M. to 4 P.M. Then the Boys Club and Girls Club have it to the late evening hours. It's a wonderful sense of being able to share. That building is used every day, all day long."

Neal Carlson, chairman, Warsaw Community Development Corporation: "We're trying to encourage second-story residential housing downtown. We've got four or five already finished.... The idea is to make downtown better." ■

Washington, IA 52353

Location: 110 miles southeast of Des Moines, 235 miles west of Chicago, in southeastern Iowa.

Population: 7,074 (1990).

Growth rate: 4% since 1986.

Per capita income: $11,659 (1985), 13% higher than state average ($10,096).

Geography/climate: Rolling agricultural prairie. Continental climate with severely cold winters and hot, humid summers. Averages: days freezing or below, 136; zero or below, 16; 90 or above, 22; snowfall, 30 inches; rainfall, 36 inches; thunderstorm days, 47. Average 100 days sunny and another 100 partly sunny.

Economic base: Seat of Washington County, one of the leading hog-producers nationally. Agriculture, 16% of employment; manufacturing, 18%; retail trade, 21%; services, 30%. Large payrolls: McCleery-Cumming Co., largest U.S. printer of advertising calendars, 350 workers; Washington County Hospital, 190; Crane Co., valves, 140; Kalona Plastics, 115; Modine Manufacturing, heat-transfer products, 111. 2 large, church-affiliated retirement homes bring the assets of an elderly population into town.

Newspaper: *Washington Evening Journal,* 111 N. Marion Avenue, Washington, IA 52353. 919-653-2191. Daily, Monday through Friday. Darwin Sherman, editor. $60 a year.

TV, radio: Local AM, FM stations. Cable carries 36 channels, including TV networks from Waterloo, Cedar Rapids. PBS from Iowa City, which also has NPR station, received off-air.

Health care: Washington County Hospital, 91 beds. 46 physicians, 7 dentists in local practice.

Schools: 2 elementary (K–3, 4–6); 1 junior high (7–9). Washington High School enrolls 345, sends 60% to higher education. Composite ACT, 1991: 21.9; 20-year average, 20.7.

Educational level: 11.8% of Washington County residents have 16 or more years of formal education; state average, 13.9%. Per capita expenditure on public education, $460; state average, $480.

Library: Washington Public Library, 85,000 volumes, 4,500 borrowers.

Recreation: Washington YMCA–YWCA is reputed to be largest in the world in a community under 7,000. Indoor pool, gym, 2 racquetball courts, weight-training room, Nautilus training, teen center, meeting rooms, men's and women's health club. 4 city parks with swimming pool, tennis courts. Summer weekly band concerts in Central Park. 4 golf courses in county. Lake Darling State Park, 20 miles southwest.

3 BR, 2 BA house: $65,000 to $80,000.

Cost of electricity: $.05 per kilowatt hour.

Cost of natural gas: $.35 per therm.

Sales tax: 4%.

State income tax: 0.4% to 9.98%.

Churches: 19. Denominations: Assemblies of God, Baptist, Berean, Christian, Church of Christ, Church of God, Church of the Nazarene, Jehovah's Witnesses, Lutheran, Mennonite, Presbyterian, Reformed Presbyterian, Roman Catholic, Seventh-Day Adventist, United Methodist.

Every year in Washington, Mike Zahs, state history teacher par excellence at the junior high school, leads at least one study-tour around the state for other junior high history teachers; Chuck Hotle, former feed and grain merchant turned writer, produces another historical novel on the southeast Iowa milieu; Gary McCurdy, leader of the Washington High School band and proprietor of the Tuba Materials Center, becomes "The Tubador," tooting his circa-1920 instrument at a hotel on the river; octogenarian David Elder goes off to a Canton, Missouri, summer stock to play cantankerous old men ("I am known as the resident curmudgeon, and I play butlers like crazy"); and Cathy Lloyd leads lines of two-wheelers on some eye-opening journeys.

What residents say . . .

Cathy Lloyd, director, Heartland Bicycle Tours: "We take people all over eastern Iowa on five-day bicycle tours, staying at country inns and bed-and-breakfasts . . . to the Amish Colonies, and Dyersville, the site of the movie *Fields of Dreams,* and with the arrival of riverboat gambling on the Mississippi, biking by day and casino at night. . . . I've been a biker for a lot of years, and I knew there were more bikers in the Midwest than turned out for the RAGBRAI . . . the 'Register Annual Great Bike Ride Across Iowa.' I went on the RAGBRAI for 13 years before starting my own company. This is our fifth year. . . . We've attracted people from all over the country. People are always stunned if they've never been to Iowa before. They think we are totally flat and have no atmosphere. They're always just amazed that we can speak English, are intelligent, and have a sense of humor."

David R. Elder, retired former owner of the local newspaper: "The paper was begun as *The Daily Hustler* in 1893. Frankly, I wish they'd kept the name. There are a thousand *Evening Journals* but only one *Daily Hustler.* . . . My father bought it in 1900. . . . I grew up with it, went into the business right after college. . . . My father had a partner, Ralph Shannon. They each had a son. Bill Shannon and I succeeded as major stockholders. My father died, Ralph Shannon died. I became publisher . . . until I began to grow long in the tooth. . . . It was our dream it should remain a locally owned, independent paper, and we sold it to three employees. But they couldn't get along. . . . A company in Kansas City owns it now. . . . Like almost all smaller, midwestern towns, we find it difficult to keep our most talented young people because there is no suitable employment. However, we have quite a number of father-and-son businesses. . . . The two remarkable things about this town, the two things other towns our size do not have . . . one is an exceptional YMCA-YWCA. The other is the McCleery Auditorium, which is in the community-center building. . . . In late 1974, Richard McCleery, the owner of one of the largest calendar factories in the United States, who had been very active in YMCA Men's Club plays, called a group of us together one night and said, 'If I give you half a million dollars, will you raise a quarter million locally, and we'll build us a theater.' By the time of its opening in 1976, he had put in over $600,000, we had raised over $300,000, not penny of it tax money or foundation money, all from local donations. Thousands of people participated. Well, it's magnificent. Towns five times our size envy us that theater. . . . I was president of the board when the theater was built. . . . Farmers nowadays in this county are not the bib–overall type. They're likely to be Ames graduates and active in all sorts of things politically and socially."

Harvey Holden, mayor, retired farmer:
"I've been mayor for three years, but I was on the City Council since 1978. I still own a farm . . . daughter and her husband run it . . . corn, soybeans, and livestock, 380 acres, one-half mile outside the city limits. . . . The difference between being a farmer and mayor is you have contact with people. I'm enjoying that. Ninety-nine and a half percent of the people are so nice. It's amazing to me the range of people's perceptions of the problem. For some people, a dog running across their yard is a problem. City government is challenged by being responsive. . . . You can't do everything people want you to. Right now we

are in the throes of deciding what to do about a new water-treatment plant, to spend millions of dollars or even to do it. We find that is less controversial among the people than a discussion of stop-signs. . . . We think we are having a little boom in the housing area . . . two subdivisions, one with 27 lots in it, and eight or 10 are now sold. We think we are attracting professional people from Iowa City. That hasn't happened before. . . . Yes, there are poor people in Washington. We see more transient people than we used to, Hispanic people and minorities. . . . The regular federal and county agencies have been exhausted, and the churches are helping out."

The Rev. George Bishop, minister, United Presbyterian Church: "Culture shock has kind of hit Washington. We have suddenly had to deal with things like racial prejudice. It revolves mainly around Iowa Beef Producers building a plant at Columbus Junction. They thought they could staff the plant with a greater degree of local workers, but ended up going to Chicago, Texas, New Mexico, even Mexico itself. We've had a large influx of Hispanics moving into town, to a degree with false expectations . . . that furnished housing would be awaiting them. . . . IBP set up a trailer court on the edge of town and these Hispanics have clustered in that area . . . very simple, unfurnished trailer homes. They move in there without money. It is a burden . . . and I don't mean burden as a negative thing . . . helping these people get located . . . furniture, stoves, bedding. For the most part they do not speak English. Along with the Hispanics we have had a rather significant influx of blacks. This, too, is a new experience for us. Washington is just now being forced to catch up

347

with the real world. We are now facing things we have been reading about in the paper. Do not hear this as a negative commentary on the community. I'm thrilled by the way the community has been rallying to meet this. The churches have helped form what is called a Cross-Cultural Commission to help deal with families' needs.

We have also the Friendship Emergency Fund . . . a product of a consortium of churches . . . to buy a second-hand stove, pay a light bill, repair a roof. . . . So we've had numerous needs thrust upon us, both financial and social. . . . I'm saying all this to support your premise that Washington is a great little community." ∎

West Plains, MO 65775

Location: 201 miles southwest of St. Louis, 280 miles southeast of Kansas City, 15 miles north of the Arkansas state line, in south central Missouri.

Population: 8,913 (1990).

Growth rate: 8% since 1986.

Per capita income: $7,547 (1985), 73% of state average ($10,283).

Geography/climate: Ozark country. Rugged, low landscape of hardwood forests and spring-fed streams. Mild climate, relatively free of extremes. January lows average 32; highs, 44. Occasional ice, sleet. 8 inches of snow in December–March period. Total annual precipitation, 43 inches. July low average temperature, 78; high 90.

Economic base: Agriculture, light industry, retailing, county-seat services. West Plains is the largest settlement in a 100-mile radius. Agribusiness is mainly livestock— beef, swine, dairy production, with limited sheep ranching. Prosperous market for timber products. Major payrolls: Southwest Mobile Systems, missile launchers, 710 persons; Hy-Test Division of Florsheim, steel-toe shoes, 479; Marathon Electric, motors, 405; Bruce Hardwood Flooring, 263; Rojo Farms, processed poultry, 199; Amyx Industries, hardwood furniture, 170; Eaton Corporation, valves, switches, 165.

Newspaper: *West Plains Daily Quill,* 125 N. Jefferson Street, West Plains, MO 65775-0110. 417-256-9191. Daily, Monday through Friday. Frank L. Martin, III, editor and publisher, $49 a year.

TV, radio: 1 local AM, 2 FM stations. Cable carries network-TV stations, PBS from Springfield, Missouri. Nearest NPR station, at Rolla, reaches barely past Willow Springs, 20 miles north.

Health care: Ozarks Medical Center, 120 beds. 65 physicians, including 10 osteopaths; 12 dentists in local practice.

Schools: 1 elementary (K–6); 1 middle (7–8). West Plains Senior High School enrolls 1,057, sends 40% to college. 1990 composite ACT, 21. Southwest Missouri State University enrolls 1,000.

Educational level: 7.6% of Howell County residents have 16 or more years of formal education; state average, 13.9%. Per capita expenditure for public education, $400; state average, $378.

Library: West Plains Public Library, estimated "on the low side" at 45,000 volumes.

Recreation: 3 public parks with swimming pool, 9 tennis courts, walking–jogging tracks, 2 handball/racquetball courts. 9-hole public golf course, 18-hole private club. Little League, soccer league, Mighty Mite football program. Winter sports center. Bowling lanes. 3-screen movie theater. Shopping mall. $5 million civic center under construction will house small meetings and conventions, swimming pool, other new recreational facilities. Many places within 30-mile radius for water sports, fishing, hunting, boating, hiking. Sections of Mark Twain National Forest lie east and west. Mammoth Spring State Park, 20 miles southeast; Norfolk Lake, 30 miles southwest.

3 BR, 2 BA house: $78,000 to $90,000.

Cost of electricity: $.05 to $.07 per kilowatt hour.

Cost of propane heating fuel: $.71 per gallon.

Sales tax: 6.225%.

State income tax: 1.5% to 6%.

Churches: 37. Denominations: Assemblies of God, Baptist (9), Christian, Church of Christ, Church of God of Prophecy, Church of Jesus Christ of Latter-day Saints, Disciples of Christ, Episcopal, Full Gospel, Jehovah's Witnesses, Lutheran, Lutheran-ELCA, Mission, Nazarene, Pentecostal (4), Presbyterian, Roman Catholic, Seventh-Day Adventist, United Methodist.

West Plains has sent a number of stars into orbit. There was Preacher Roe, the spitball pitcher for the Brooklyn Dodgers. His father was a doctor and his brother, Glenn, served as mayor of West Plains. Bill Virdon, the baseball manager, is another native son. Porter Waggoner, the country-music star, is credited with launching Dolly Parton's career. Herbert Gibson, creator of the Gibson Stores chain, was a local boy. And Steven Thompson, an early aviator, is remembered for shooting down the first German plane in World War I. More recently, West Plains takes some of the credit for successfully launching Patriot missiles in defense against Saddam Hussein's rockets during the Gulf War. The Patriot's mobile-launching rig is manufactured in town. Ma Barker might have been impressed.

What residents say ...

Frank L. Martin, III, editor and publisher, **West Plains Daily Quill:** "What makes this town different, what gives it, I think, the unique character, is fostered by the fact that early settlers were very poor refugees from other poor parts of the world, principally Tennessee and Kentucky, who didn't have the wherewithal or the ambition to go further west to good, tillable land. Our agriculture here is limited to livestock because we have almost no topsoil. . . . The early settlers moved here from Appalachia only because the spaces were more open. They were very provincial, some would say backward. It was kind of an outlaw area. Jesse James has relatives in the area. Ma Barker's gang used to have a rest area. . . . We have the same pioneer spirit, the same mind-your-own-business kind of tolerance. But since the '60s a lot of people have moved to the area both to retire and get back to the land, New Age people. . . . The town has taken the best of the ideas that are brought in and managed to embrace them and work them into the culture rather than having them dilute the culture. So, you get the best of the old spirit and best of the new ideas. . . . A couple of years ago, I went to a university-sponsored discussion of the uniqueness of this part of the country. As a group we listed the best and worst traits of the typical Ozark native. . . .

Number One on the list of best was the fierce feeling of independence that natives have inherited as a tradition. . . . When we got around to the worst, it was the same item . . . resistance to change. The result is we have something between a fairly stable economy and planned progress. . . . This is one of the few communities I know of its size which retains its youth. . . . As a percentage, you find a lot more young people graduating, working away professionally, and coming back. We have a very interesting group of . . . they would be yuppies anywhere else but in a rural environment . . . people in the 40–50 age group who have had diverse experiences but have chosen to come back here and raise their families."

Russ Cochran, president, Russ Cochran, Publisher: "Everybody anymore collects something. Often people my age collect objects of their childhood. In my case it was comic books. I was a kid in the '40s. There was no TV in West Plains. . . . We got our entertainment from movies or comic books. . . . In 1964, I started to collect comic books. That was also the year I went to work as chairman of the physics department at Drake University. . . . I got the idea of republishing comic books. I located the original art in New York City and got license to *Tales From the Crypt, Weird Science, Mad, The Vault of Horror.* I started reprinting them as a sideline while I was teaching. Then it gradually took over. It had always been a dream of mine to move back to West Plains, but there are not too many things you can do in West Plains, Missouri, with a PhD in physics. . . . In 1974, I resigned and moved back. By that time I knew I could make as much money publishing as teaching. I have four chil-

dren and wanted them to grow up in this town. All their grandparents live here. Almost everyone I'm related to in the world lives here. . . . I have the best of both worlds. I go to New York two or three times a year. I go to California two or three times a year . . . when I need some big-city stuff. I enjoy the isolation in West Plains. It is a very positive thing. West Plains doesn't have traffic jams. There's no street crime. It's a relaxed atmosphere. If you've ever seen 'The Andy Griffith Show,' it's Mayberry."

Mrs. Dortha Reavis, clerk of the Municipal Court: "We're not big-city people and don't know big-city ways and don't want to. I guess we're part of what you'd call the 'Bible Belt.' I couldn't believe it when we first got to getting marijuana and cocaine, why would anybody want to fool with this stuff. Now, it's much more common. . . . I believe it was in June of '80 the biggest drug arrest in the United States . . . over a million dollars of Quaalude. I had my living room full of what looked like feed sacks, plastic bags full of these pills shipped into here from Colombia, South America. Five or six people were arrested. I guess they were just traveling through. They checked into a motel and had moved all this stuff into the room. We got a tip that they were going to carry away all the furniture. The officer on duty sent a reserve policeman in a van to the motel parking lot. But he parked so close that he couldn't talk very loud on the portable radio when they started carrying out all those bags of pills. . . . We confiscated over $32,000 cash and a brand new Cadillac. . . . I asked if I could keep one pill as a souvenir. I think I've still got it somewhere. I was going to have it fixed into a paperweight." ∎

West Point, MS 39773

Location: 142 miles northeast of Jackson, 137 miles northwest of Birmingham, 149 miles southeast of Memphis, Tennessee, on Alt. U.S. 45 in northeastern Mississippi.

Population: 8,489 (1990).

Growth rate: 4% decline since 1980.

Per capita income: $7,720 (1985), 3% higher than state average ($7,483).

Geography/climate: Rolling, black prairie hills at 337 feet above sea level. 4 seasons. Mild winters: January average temperature, 47 degrees. Long spring, long Indian summer. Hot, humid summers with 67 days at 90 or higher. Average rainfall, 47 inches. Trace of snow.

Economic base: Agriculture, industry. Needlecraft, chemicals, steel fabrication, wood products, meat-packing, poultry-processing. Largest payroll: Bryan Foods, 2,000. West Point is the seat of Clay County.

Newspaper: *West Point Daily Times Leader,* 227 Court Street, West Point, MS 39773. 601-494-1422. Published Tuesday through Friday, Sunday. Spanky Bruce, editor. $75 a year.

TV, radio: Local AM, FM, TV stations. Cable provides 29 channels, networks, PBS. NPR received off-air from Oxford.

Health care: 60-bed Clay County Medical Center, built 1985, affiliated with Northeast Mississippi Medical Center, largest hospital in state, in Tupelo. 12 physicians, 3 dentists in local practice.

Schools: 2 elementary (K–4); 1 middle (5–7); 1 junior high (8–9). West Point High School enrolls 680 students, sends 55% of graduates to college. Recent composite ACT, 18.7. Mary Holmes Junior College, founded 1892, enrolls 556 students.

Educational level: 10.6% of Clay County residents have 16 or more years of formal education; state average, 12.3%. Per capita expenditure for public education, $300; state average, $333.

Library: Bryan Public Library, built 1978 largely with Bryan family money, has 50,000 volumes and is headquarters of a 10-library district.

Recreation: City Recreation Center. 9 Little League and baseball fields, most with lights. 10 tennis courts, 2 swimming pools. Camping, boating, fishing along Tennessee–Tombigbee Waterway. Old Waverly Golf Course, designed by Jerry Pate and Bob Cupp, rated by PGA as most challenging in Mississippi. Annual Prairie Arts Festival on Saturday before Labor Day.

3 BR, 2 BA house: $50,000 to $60,000 in smaller subdivisions, up to $90,000s in "nicer" locations.

Cost of electricity: $.05 per kilowatt hour.

Cost of natural gas: $.47 per therm.

Sales tax: 6%.

State income tax: 3% to 5%.

Churches: 19. Denominations: Apostolic, Baptist, Christian, Church of Christ, Church of God, Church of Jesus Christ of Latter-day Saints, Episcopal, Lutheran, Methodist, Presbyterian, Roman Catholic.

West Point is the northern point of what they call "The Golden Triangle." The other two corners are larger places: Columbus, population 23,800, 17 miles southeast; and Starkville, population 18,458, 11 miles southwest. The three communities combine to make up the third-fastest-growing area of Mississippi—after Jackson and Gulfport-Biloxi. With nearby larger places growing rapidly, West Point could be excused for marking time. But that would not be in character.

Twenty years ago, West Point was in some need of repair. It was a weary-looking place after the civil-rights turbulence of the '60s. Housing had deteriorated. Streets were unpaved. Water-supply and sewage-treatment systems were chronically overburdened. Downtown was shabby and the county hospital was on the verge of closing.

West Point has made a remarkable comeback. The arrival of new industry has increased the industrial job-base by 30 percent. Substandard housing has been cut to one percent. Downtown has been revitalized. "It was just a matter of the people of West Point saying we want to take care of this problem," says Louise Campbell, executive director of the Clay County Economic Development Corporation. "It was civic pride, cooperation, plus a little friendly competition. One downtown merchant would paint his building, and it would make the next one look bad. That's the way we started."

What residents say . . .

Spanky Bruce, editor, **Daily Times Leader:** "My real name is Roy but everyone calls me Spanky. I guess that's the price you pay for growing up in a small town. . . . The newspaper was owned by the same family for many years. Now we're owned by one of the large chains. . . . I moved here when I was six weeks old. I'm 56 now. Except for two stints in the Army I've been here since. Worked for the newspaper a total of 25 years. . . . We're really a blue-collar town. Our work force makes good money. The big money is concentrated in a few families. . . . The Bryan Foods family just built Old Waverley, an 18-hole golf course rated the best in the state this year. It's a 12-to-14-million-dollar development on the Tenn-Tom Waterway and it really has been a boon for us. . . . I guess the most significant thing we have done lately is pass a school bond issue. It was a very close fight. . . . The city is 50–50 black and white. West Point has come much further in race relationships than many other places. Back in the early '60s we had some big problems. We've got an excellent public school system. We have a white academy that gets about 15 percent of the potential public school enrollment. It's an excellent school. . . . I don't know whether we can ever be a viable retail force again. Most of our trade dollars not spent in West Point go to Tupelo. As our older merchants die off they are either replaced by a chain or an office building."

Joann Houston, executive director, United Way of Clay County: "I guess people like what they like. I like a small town. It has a lot of conveniences. It takes me 10 minutes to get to work. I always have a place to park. I can order anything I want on the telephone. When I go to work, half the people I see I know their face and name and we speak. . . . It's an open town, a friendly town, a caring town. . . . Our United Way is just six years old and we have increased our giving every year. We won a 'Blueprint Grant' from the W.K. Kellogg Foundation, the smallest United Way in the country to receive it. I think what interested them was our training and leadership programs. . . . One of our greatest needs is homemaker services for the elderly, congregate meals for the elderly. . . . The over-65 population is our fastest growing. . . . And like most communities we have a lot of need for day care. In six years, our budget has grown from $54,000 to $235,000. I think that is pretty phenomenal growth. . . . People say, 'Gosh, they're out in the boonies. Whatever happens there?' It's not true. . . . In one week, I went to a Southeast Conference basketball game, a concert at Mississippi University for Women at Columbus, a movie and a musical concert at West Point. Nothing cost over $5, and I could park within a block at each one at no cost. . . . I've lived in cities and, you know, most of what happens in cities you just read about in the paper."

Toxey Haas, Mississippi Small Business Person of the Year, 1990: "The company is Haas Outdoors, Inc., and I am president. Our claim to fame is camouflage that hides you better than any other. We're not only for hunters. We do a lot to help outdoor photographers. . . . Those camouflage suits developed by the military are for use in warfare. They have bold color breaks to break up the outline. Military camouflage gives you away when you're hunting deer and turkey. We're trying to hide by blending in. . . . I was looking for a background color that would work everywhere. It's a dirt color. Some people call it brown, some green. I call it the primary color of nature. Our patterns are fully detailed and very, very realistic. We sell directly to the sporting-goods stores. No distributors or mass merchants. . . . We market it as 'Mossy Oak Camouflage' . . . a hobby that turned into a business for me. . . . I've lived here every day since I was born and I'm 31 now. I started full-time in the business in 1987, $120,000 sales and two employees. This year we're between $5 and $6 million, 30 employees. . . . It's easier to get into business in a small town. Your overhead is lower and people work harder. Everybody in the community is willing to jump in and help. . . . You can enjoy your success so much more in a small town."

Edmund Miller, Jr., MD, internist: "My father grew up in West Point, joined the Navy, and I grew up in many places, as much as anywhere in Fairfax, Virginia. I came to West Point after I completed my residency training in Rochester, Minnesota. The scholarship I had received was a stipend of $6,000 per year from the State of Mississippi. One-fifth of that was forgiven upon my return to a town of 10,000 or less, the remainder repaid with a very favorable interest rate. With intensely frugal living and loving parents, one was able to support himself and a small family through medical school. . . . I think small towns can live or die with a few very influential families. If those certain families who are leaders in the community are forward-thinking and good people, then there's a good chance the town will be hospitable and a nice place to live. . . . Coming from Rochester where the public schools are said to be some of the best in the nation, supported by a really well educated population, we were worried about some of the things we had heard about the public schools in Mississippi in general, and I do think Mississippi has some problems in that regard. In West Point, in my opinion, they are just outstanding. . . . Down here they say 'It's a sorry dog that won't wag its own tail.' I have a daughter who is the number one student in the state in problem-solving. She's won a trip to an international competition in St. Louis . . . made the highest score on the PSAT exam. . . . Point being, the quality of the school system certainly is sufficient to enable my one daughter in particular to argue with me all night long . . . and usually think she's won. . . . My grandmother told me something that had great wisdom. She made the point, we all have to live together and we might as well learn to do it when we're children. In Mississippi to a real significant degree, we're all learning to live together." ∎

Williamstown, MA 01267

Location: 140 miles west-northwest of Boston, 155 miles north-northwest of New York City, 15 miles south of Bennington, Vermont, in the northwest corner of Massachusetts.

Population: 8,220 (1990).

Growth rate: 1.5% since 1986.

Per capita income: $12,078 (1985), 97% of state average ($12,510).

Geography/climate: Elevation in-town, at Field Park, 725 feet; near peak of Mount Greylock, 5 miles southeast, 3,317 feet, highest point in Massachusetts. Berkshire Hills setting. Half dozen brooks and streams flow through community. Cold, snowy winters produce great skiing. Very pleasant summers. Temperature averages: January: high, 31; low, 11. July: high, 82; low, 56. Annual rainfall, 43 inches; snowfall, 56 inches.

Economic base: Williams College, with 700 faculty and staff, is largest employer and main economic engine. Tourism, retail trade broaden the base. Industrial payrolls: Carol Cable, 297; Steinerfilm, 245. Other large employers include Sweetbrook Nursing Home, Williamstown Medical Associates, Mount Greylock Regional School District.

Newspaper: *The Advocate*, 38 Spring Street, Williamstown, MA 01267. 413-458-5713. Weekly, Wednesday. William P. Densmore, editor and publisher. $60 a year.

TV, radio: Local AM, FM stations. Cable carries network TV from Boston, Albany. NPR received from Albany.

Health care: Nearest hospital, North Adams Regional, 5 miles east. 166 beds. 16 physicians, 4 dentists in local practice.

Schools: 1 elementary (K–6). Mount Greylock Regional High School (7–12) enrolls 640, sends 74% to 4-year college. SAT scores: verbal, 453; math, 485. Charles H. McCann Vocational-Technical (9–12), in North Adams, also offers post-graduate. Williams College, founded 1793, enrolls 2,000.

Education level: 16.3% of Berkshire County residents have 16 or more years of formal education; state average, 20% County per capita expenditure for public education, $441; state average, $454.

Library: Williamstown Public Library, 35,000 volumes. Residents also have access to collections at Williams College.

Recreation: 3 public recreation areas, 2 with swimming. Supervised summer recreation—arts, crafts, sports, swimming—for children in grades 1 through 7. Williamstown Youth Center schedules school-year activities for 6- to 18-year-olds including basketball, hockey, downhill skiing. Little League, soccer fields. Town has 1 tennis court, others at Williams College available for town use. Hopkins Memorial Forest, 2,250 acres, has cross-country ski trails, farm museum. 1 public, 1 semi-private 18-hole golf courses. 40 miles of hiking trails around Mount Greylock. Brodie Mountain and Jiminy Peak ski areas are 15 miles south.

3 BR, 2 BA house: $120,000 to $185,000.

Cost of electricity: $.09 per kilowatt hour.

Cost of fuel oil: $1.03 per gallon.

Sales tax: 5%.

State income tax: 5.95%.

Churches: 9. Denominations: Baptist, Community Bible, Congregational (3), Episcopal, Roman Catholic (2), United Methodist.

It's a wonder any serious work gets down in Williamstown considering all the lovely distractions of this quintessential college town. Williams College is literally and otherwise the center of the community. Campus lawns reach back from both sides of Main Street. The Williamstown Theatre Festival's home is down the block, behind the stunning white columns of Adams Memorial Theatre. Starlight Stage, for students age eight to 18, performs in the First Congregational Church, a town landmark. Including other theater companies in town and nearby, Williamstown's boosters claim a higher per capita rate of play production than New York City.

Out on South Street, one of the largest collections of Renoir and other Impressionists is housed in the Sterling and Francine Clark Art Institute. Respectable collections also are housed in the Williams College Museum of Art and the Hopkins Forest Farm Museum.

Tennis is virtually an industry. The college has 24 courts and is host to the National Junior Tennis Program and the Adidas Tennis Camp, as well as being a very popular place with town residents.

"Originally a farming community, real cows still graze on real fields," notes a publication of the Williamstown Board of Trade. "The town maintains the values of open land and small-scale commercial activity. Much local business is transacted, most of it on a first-name basis, as residents walk along Spring Street in the morning to pick up their mail (for example)."

Williamstown can be excused for bragging that it creates "cosmopolitan flair in rural New England." It really does, not to mention added diversions in nearby places like Tanglewood, Bennington, and Saratoga. Unfortunately, Williamstown also shares in the prevailing Northeast economy, a subject of considerable comment along Spring Street and elsewhere in town.

What residents say . . .

John Holden, president, Williamstown Board of Trade: "Williamstown has never had to mobilize before. This is the first time the area has seen a serious economic decline. . . . What we do next, nobody's quite sure, except that the development of an executive park seems a good fit. . . . Most everyone else is promoting industrial areas. But the only manufacturing that has a possibility in the Northeast is high value-added. The labor force is quite skilled, but also fairly expensive. An executive park probably fits better with people's sense of what Williamstown is . . . a credit-card operation or any sort of information-processing or service industry. . . . We've finally been successful in getting an up-to-date phone system. Just this summer they installed digital switching, so now you can have touch-tone phones. . . . The Board of Trade is a fairly small operation. 180 participating members. That gives us $15,000 a year. We have one part-time secretary and the rest are volunteers. I work in the physical plant department of the college, assistant director for operations."

Steven LeDoux, town manager: "I grew up outside Worcester, Massachusetts, in the central part of the state. After I graduated from Notre Dame I got an MPA from Cornell, worked three years as administrative assistant to a county board of supervisors in New York State. Then I was the manager of a small town in Michigan for four years, and I've been seven years in Williamstown. . . . The tourist industry is not doing all that great. Williams College makes us a little more recession-proof. Before the recession it was quite different. Property values were just skyrocketing, particularly in '85 and '86. And the state government was in good shape. . . . This year we took a major cut in local aid, like all towns in Massachusetts. We had a good town meeting. We had to cut some things, and we eliminated the grades-one-through-six French program, a town-planner position, and a police-officer position. We were able to cut and not really affect services. Next year we'll either cut more services or. . . . They have a provision to override Proposition 2½, which says you can't raise taxes over two and a half percent. My sense is override throughout the state is [being voted] down on a large scale. . . . It may come down to the basic question, what are the fundamental things that government has to provide? . . . Three years ago over a long weekend, the community built a playground at the elementary school. It was all done with volunteers, hammers

down and dirty, over a three-day period. Probably if you value the sweat equity, it was a $200,000 project. Four years ago, a freak blizzard hit with the foliage still on the trees. A lot of trees and limbs fell into the rivers and streams. . . . Volunteers with chain saws went around and cleared out the streams, made it safer when the high waters came in spring. . . . We just did a major bond issue for a new water tank and well field. But the interesting thing, in spite of the northeast economy and poor Massachusetts bond ratings, we maintained the same rating we had in '79, Double A."

Phil Kalker, town native, Williams College graduate, entrepreneur, semi-retired: "Williamstown hasn't changed in my memory, and I doubt that it will. I had been away some 37 years, and it stayed pretty much the same. . . . Probably we are suffering at the moment from a lack of change in the mix of population. Young people tend to go elsewhere. The City of North Adams, which was the industrial hub, is almost totally lacking in jobs now. Therefore, you don't have the flow of middle management, who are active participants in the community. . . . Williamstown is a very special place because of the lay of the land. It's at the confluence of three valleys . . . one leaving to the northwest, a valley coming in from the southwest, one from the east. Those thee valleys meet here. Very few places have this particular character and visual impact. . . . The town is controlled by nonprofit or public entities. Besides the college, which has several thousand acres, Mount Greylock Reservation is a big chunk. . . . Mount Greylock is almost not visible from most places in Williamstown. The famous view of The Hopper appears when you come up from the south." ■

Wilmington, OH 45177

Location: 62 miles southwest of Columbus, 50 miles northeast of Cincinnati, 36 miles southeast of Dayton, in southwestern Ohio.

Population: 11,199 (1990).

Growth rate: 7% since 1980.

Per capita income: $9,500 (1985), 8% below state average.

Geography/climate: Gently rolling farmlands. Continental, 4-season climate, but tempered by southern location in state. Average 20 days over 90 degrees, 110 days at freezing or below. Average rainfall, 36 inches; snowfall, 29 inches. Changeable weather.

Economic base: Airborne Express employs 3,500, many part-time, at its national hub in Wilmington. More than a thousand farms, averaging 227 acres. Diversified manufacturing. Major payrolls: Randall Company, auto door frames and fuel filters, 550 employees; Irwin Company, woodworking tools, 500; Ferno-Washington, hospital carts, 340; Cincinnati Milacron, metalworking tools, 325; Crysteco, silicon wafers, 180.

Newspaper: *Wilmington News-Journal*, 47 S. South Street, Wilmington, OH 45177. 513-382-2574. Daily, Monday through Saturday. Jay Carey, managing editor. Clarence Graham, publisher. $73 a year.

TV, radio: Local AM, FM stations. Cable brings in full network coverage.

Health care: Clinton Memorial Hospital, 152 beds. 29 physicians, 12 dentists in local practice.

Schools: 3 elementary (K–5); 1 6th-grade school; 1 junior high (7–8). Wilmington Senior High School enrolls 901. Composite ACT score, 21. 55% of graduates enroll in 4-year colleges, 20% attend 2-year institutions. Wilmington College, a 4-year institution founded in 1870, enrolls 1,000.

Educational level: 10.8% of Clinton County residents have 16 or more years of formal education; state average, 13.7%.

Library: Wilmington Public Library has about 60,000 volumes, 8,500 card holders.

Recreation: Caesar Creek State Park, 10 miles distant, has a 2,830-acre lake surrounded by 7,000 acres of land. Cowan Lake State Park, 7 miles distant, has 237 campsites and 27 cabins around a 700-acre lake, popular with sailors.

3 BR, 2 BA house: $50,000 to $90,000. There is a shortage of housing in this size range.

Cost of electricity: $.061 per kilowatt hour.

Cost of natural gas: $.095 to $.13 per therm.

Sales tax: 6%.

State income tax: .743% to 6.9%.

Churches: Denominations: AME, Assemblies of God, Baptist, Christian Disciples of Christ, Church of Christ, Church of God, Church of Jesus Christ of Latter-day Saints, Full Gospel, Independent, Jehovah's Witnesses, Lutheran, Nazarene, Presbyterian, Roman Catholic, Seventh-Day Adventist, Society of Friends, United Methodist.

Most small towns are happy to have one source of urban amenities within fairly easy reach. Wilmington has three: Columbus, Dayton, and Cincinnati, all about an hour's drive away. As they say in real estate, location is everything.

It was the strategic location of the old Clinton County Air Force Base, a mile southeast of Wilmington, that caught the attention of Airborne Express in the late 1970s. Airborne bought the decommissioned military base to serve as its main U.S. hub for overnight delivery service. And Airborne brought jobs, 350 to start, 3,500 today, adding fuel to the economy of a five-county region.

Wilmington was on the map long before Airborne. But there seems little doubt that the air-freight company has virtually guaranteed the small town's future. Preserving the small-town feel may be a challenge as Columbus, Dayton, and Cincinnati grow ever closer. As one lifelong resident remarks, "We have country living and yet all the necessities." Contemplating how much "country" may have to be traded for growth is "scary in a way," she adds.

What residents say ...

Clifford N. (Nick) Eveland, Jr., mayor and third-generation manager of a family-owned construction business: "My grandfather started the company in 1906. We've built within a 50-mile radius of Wilmington, but for the past 10 years we have not had to go outside town. . . . Our unemployment rate is 4.5 percent, and that's pretty good. We've been very diligent in making a wide range of occupations available, from common laborers to farm hands to doctors of science. When I graduated from high school in 1966, two-thirds of my class had to go elsewhere to get jobs. I thought if I ever had the opportunity to do something about that I would. We've pretty well gotten there. . . . I think growth is going to happen, frankly, whether we want it or not . . . optimally less than 3 percent a year. My major agenda is to make sure the qual-

ity of life is enhanced rather than diminished. . . . I take a lot of pride in being mayor of the town. . . . I logged the time it takes: 32 to 36 hours a week, a big commitment. But a lot of the things we do take place in the evening. You've got to look at it as a hobby or a second job. If you enjoy what you're doing, it's less work. I'm in my eighth year. I have filed to run again and have no opposition. It appears I may be reelected!"

Barry Martens, owner of The General Denver Hotel, at Main and Mulberry, downtown: "The hotel had been closed for 11 and a half years. I bought it and settled the condemnation suit with the city. . . . The present mayor's grandfather built the hotel in 1924. It's built like a tomb, one of the finest buildings I've seen in my life. Everything was replaced inside. We have 29 rental units including five suites. All of the major corporations in Clinton County are using it. A number of rooms are under contract with Airborne. . . . I would say right now we have about a four-star restaurant, everything from a low-priced menu to lobster tail. We call the bar Ye Olde English Pub. . . . When you go into recessionary times you find a lot of middle-class Waspish types looking towards getting into rural America to raise their kids. Dayton and Cincinnati right now are going through tremendous problems. . . . Homes don't stay on the market here more than 30 days."

Harry McKinley, retired from General Motors Institute, in Flint, Michigan: "I had the long-term objective of working 25 years for GM, then finding a small town with a liberal-arts college. I worked in student personnel at GMI. . . . First I worked in the career center at Wilmington College, then student personnel. We moved back to Flint after two years here but decided we didn't like Flint anymore. Our neighborhood and the town had changed. So we moved back here 10 months later. I decided I was going to learn about city government and started attending City Council meetings. I haven't missed a meeting since a year ago August. . . . My general impression is the people in Wilmington get better government than they deserve for their lack of interest in it. . . . There is a heavy Quaker influence here. It permeates an awful lot of things that happen. . . . The philosophy, the way decisions are arrived at, by consensus. . . . It's a friendly place, small enough you get to know a lot of people. Like every town, certain cliques or social groups are difficult for outsiders to break into. . . . There seems to be a general effort

to develop Wilmington in a planned manner. . . . One problem is a bypass to get heavy traffic out of downtown. They just solved another problem with installation of a new water supply coming from Caesar Creek Lake, 10 miles out of town."

Campbell Graf, semi-retired: "I'm 73 years old and I've retired three times. I came here in 1977 to work for the college, mostly as assistant to the president, then to Clinton Memorial Hospital. Before that I spent 12 years at Wilberforce University, the first black institution in the nation. I helped start a cooperative work-study program at Wilberforce. . . . We have the potential in Wilmington of being a rural base for an urban population that needs a rural base. . . . People from the cities can gather here away from the pressure that most urban people are under. . . . You can really begin to think 25 to 50 years into the future, the long-distance future. . . . The Japanese have studied us. . . . Their analysis tells them they're better to stay away from the urban situation, unionism. The rural-type youngster not experienced in the urban world is probably their ideal hire. . . . We have an economic force in Airborne Express. . . . So much of what Airborne does happens at night . . . part-time jobs, the ideal companion to an area that has a lot of farming. Farmers are getting health and accident insurance for the whole family even though they're only part-time workers."

Rita Carey, communication manager, Airborne Express, City Council member: "About 60 planes land every night . . . probably 450,000 to 500,000 packages . . . about 1.6 million pounds. Wilmington is the major hub. We have a 9,500-foot runway. Wilmington Airpark is the only privately owned, operated, and maintained Category II instrument-landing system in the country. . . . Wilmington is a rural farming community that has grown up. . . . Agribusiness is still the biggest business in the county. . . . Many small towns across the country begin to deteriorate because people like to go to shopping malls. We have three malls. Our downtown has not been as thriving as it once was. The new municipal building will add to the viability of downtown. The General Denver Hotel is open and vital. The Murphy Theatre, a nice old building. Plus the County Courthouse. . . . Maybe downtown could become a service center as much as a business center."

Mary Alexander, executive director, Murphy Theatre Community Center: "The community purchased the building in 1987 to save it from being converted into a twin cinema. It's a gorgeous old theater, built in 1918, very ornate. Mr. Charles Webb Murphy built it. He's quoted as saying he'd rather have a monument on Main Street than in the cemetery. . . . At that time it was a 1,000-seat house, in a town of about 5,000. People said it would never make any money, that it was a big white elephant. It was sold out on opening night. . . . Now it seats 817, plus we have six boxes that seat four each, a two-tiered balcony, a full orchestra pit. . . . We have our own season performance, the second year of that, and we rent it to the high schools for their musicals and some of the elementary schools for Christmas plays. . . . We're starting to show classic films there again . . . Bette Davis, Greta Garbo. . . . My husband and I moved here in 1986 from the Chicago area. We got involved as volunteers, and it evolved into this full-time position for me. . . . When we first moved here I didn't know if I would like it. I think we had an advantage . . . people we got to know immediately through the theater." ■

Winfield, KS 67156

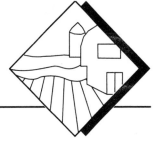

Location: At crossroads of U.S. 77 and 160, 50 miles southeast of Wichita, 120 miles northwest of Tulsa.

Population: 11,931 (1990).

Growth rate: 2.4% since 1986.

Per capita income: $10,201 (1985), 95% of state average ($10,684).

Geography/climate: Gently rolling Kansas farmlands subject to abrupt weather changes as warm Gulf air collides with polar cold on the Great Plains. Thunderstorms on average 55 days. Tornado country. 4 seasons with some torrid, hot midsummer days; mild winters. Average 37 inches rain, 12 inches snow.

Economic base: Winfield State Hospital & Training Center employs about 750; Rubbermaid, 500. Other major employers: Southwestern College, Binney and Smith (Crayolas).

Newspaper: *Winfield Daily Courier*, 201 E. 9th St., Winfield, KS 67156. 316-221-1100. Daily except Sunday. Frederick Seaton, publisher. $45.40 a year.

TV, radio: 2 local AM, FM stations. Cable brings in networks, premium channels, PBS, distant FM. NPR from Wichita.

Health care: William Newton Memorial Hospital, 99 beds. 17 physicians, 10 dentists, 1 orthodontist in local practice.

Schools: 3 elementary (K–5), each with 300–400 students; 1 middle school (6–8) with 350. Winfield High School enrolls 700. Also, 1 Roman Catholic school (1–6), Trinity Lutheran school (pre-K, K–6). Composite ACT score at high school, 21. 55% of graduates go to college.

Education level: 11.7% of Cowley County residents have 16 or more years of formal education; state average, 17%. Per capita expenditure for public education, $435; state average, $459.

Library: Winfield Public Library in 1990 moved out of cramped quarters in an old Carnegie building into former St. John's College library. 40,000 volumes, 10,600 card holders.

Recreation: 10 city parks totaling 215 acres. Winfield City Lake, the city water source, has 1,100 acres of water surface. Swimming, boating, fishing, marina. Hunting in area rated good to very good for field game. Municipal swimming pool, 13 tennis courts, 4 basketball courts, 18-hole golf course. 4-screen movie theater, 10-lane bowling alley, indoor ice-skating rink. Summer youth recreation program for ages 5–18.

3 BR, 2 BA house: $85,000 to $110,000.

Cost of electricity: $.062 per kilowatt hour.

Cost of natural gas: $.35 per therm.

Sales tax: 5.25%.

State income tax: 3.65% to 8.75%. Higher rates apply to persons deducting federal income tax.

Churches: 26. Denominations: American Methodist Episcopal, Apostolic, Assemblies of God, Baptist-American, Baptist-Bible Fellowship, Baptist-National, Baptist-Southern, Christian & Missionary Alliance, Church of Christ, Church of God, Episcopal, Evangelical Free, Jehovah's Witnesses, Lutheran, Methodist-Free, Methodist-United, Nazarene, Presbyterian, Reorganized Church of Latter-day Saints, Roman Catholic, United Pentecostal, Word of Life.

Anyone who has spent more than a little time picking at a guitar or a banjo or a dulcimer knows Winfield, Kansas, site of the annual Walnut Valley Festival, a sort of national convention of acoustic string musicians. Over a long weekend in September, the Winfield population practically doubles as performers and fans converge on the fair grounds for this remarkable event. It has been likened to Brigadoon—a village of musicians appearing out of the Kansas mists.

Big names have strummed in Winfield over the years: Watson, Berline, Flatt, and Blake, to name a few. More recent headliners include the likes of Dan Crary, John McCutcheon, Art Thieme, Northern Lights, and Spontaneous Combustion. At the 1990 festival, they set a world record by gathering 566 guitarists and getting them all to play the same tune—together.

The Rand McNally Road Atlas awards Winfield two special notes in red type, one for Southwestern College, a four-year institution founded in 1885; the other for Winfield's memorial to Kansans who died in the Vietnam War, styled after The Wall in Washington, D.C. If it weren't so much like Brigadoon, the music festival would rate a mention, too.

What residents say ...

Bob L. Redford, organizer of the Walnut Valley Festival: "The festival is always held on the third weekend in September. For the last 10 years we have had people come from every state in the Union and between 17 and 32 foreign countries every year. We are an international music festival. We are an acoustic festival. We host nine major contests here ... started with the International Flat Pick Guitar Championships ... and then we have a song-writing contest. Everybody in the country comes in and writes songs about Winfield .... 85 percent of the people who come to Winfield play an instrument, and 65 percent over the years have always brought their instruments. Imagine 6,000 people camped out on a fair grounds of about 120 acres, with about 300 camp fires going, five stages going in the middle of the arena. . . . If you double the size of the town for a few days you have problems to take care of. . . . It's hard to get all the porta-potties. . . . Essentially they camp out. Irregardless of rain it always comes off. We've had rain 16 out of 19 years, as much as 14 to 15 inches during the festival. . . . We start on Thursday and run through Sunday, generally from 9 o'clock in the morning. . . . You're looking at 150 to 200 hours of music every festival, 85 to 100 entertainers. . . . When the stage shuts down at midnight, that's when the good pickin' gets going. We are essentially in a dry county. Winfield is a dry town. It's a family affair."

Cheryl Higgins, news director, radio station KSOK, talk-show host: "When we had our 20th high school reunion, one of our classmates who had been to The Wall in Washington and was so moved by it suggested that we build a memorial along those lines . . . to Gary Bannon, who was killed in the Vietnam War. The project grew to include not just the names from our school but all those in the State of Kansas. We tried for a year to seek state and federal funding but failed. . . . In April 1989 we called the core committee together. We had always thought of ourselves as invincible. We wanted to have the wall constructed and dedicated by Veterans Day. . . . We raised $100,000, designed and constructed it by Veterans Day 1989. . . . There are 758 names there. It is a replica of The Wall, located in Memorial Park, in the center of town. . . . What is amazing, other communities have tried similar projects and failed. When I initiated our media campaign, I contacted a newspaper columnist in Wichita. The headlines on his column said, 'Anybody Got $93,000 for a Vietnam Memorial?' He more or less thought it wasn't possible and was surprised by our naive attitude. . . . Some of us were reaching back into our youth. . . ."

Lin Lewis, school-board president: "The magnet school is an extra school in town for grades three, four, five. It's a pretty neat program that began just this year. To be admitted, students have to be performing at grade level, and parents have to be willing to help teachers in grading,

going on field trips, doing the extra work. The teachers teach their strength, not necessarily one class. . . . We are one of the oldest orchestra programs in the nation . . . over 100 years of having an orchestra at the high school. We start them in about second or third grade. . . . We're starting negotiations with the teachers next week. . . . There were no raises last year. Instead, everyone received a single paid membership in Blue Cross. So this year we've got to do something. But the way the state looks, we're not going to have the money."

Richard E. (Rick) Cotton, city manager: "I don't know if you've heard the story of our purchasing a college campus. We used to have two colleges here. One was Southwestern, the other St. John's College, affiliated with the Lutheran Church Missouri Synod. The church had financial difficulties and unfortunately we were the short straw. The college closed in May of '86. It held a lot of sentiment with the community . . . a small but fairly good college. After they closed we had 19 acres and about 12 major buildings sitting empty in the middle of Winfield. There was a lot of apprehension. We looked for alternatives but nothing really developed. Then in January '89 the city purchased the buildings and grounds for $700,000. Now we have the old campus as a new town library . . . the gymnasium and fitness center . . . the former cafeteria as a large meeting room. Those three buildings alone we've had to insure for $2.4 million. . . . It has been renamed Baden Square, for the founder. . . . We're updating our comprehensive plan, using a citizen-task-force approach. It's just too much work for the planning commission by itself. We're striving to get input from residents, to build consensus for future projects."

Raymond King, retired president and CEO, First National Bank: "I'm a hometown boy. Served in the Navy in World War II, came back here and went to St. John's College for two years, graduated from OU— Oklahoma University. . . . They asked me to come up to the bank in 1954, and I retired here in February 1988. . . . I think Winfield is headed up. We've spent years and years preparing ourselves. We had a city manager back then who was very conservative, saved us up a lot of money. Then a few of us came along later and built a city lake, where our water supply now is, increased the electric power plant twice. So we've had that much growth, catering to what I call non-smokestack industry. . . . Back when I was mayor of Winfield we had an opportunity to get one of those big tire manufacturers. Would have employed 2,000 people. You can see what that would have done to the schools and the entire town. Some of us were so glad we didn't get it, though we didn't talk publicly about that, because of the impact it would have had. What you want is slow, orderly economic growth. . . . We used to be known as the city of trees before Dutch elm disease. Ninth Street was like driving a car through a tunnel. We've got a lot of redbuds on that street now. They just bloomed, and it sure looked beautiful." ■

York, NE 68467

Location: 52 miles west of Lincoln, 46 miles east of Grand Island, at the junction of I-80 and U.S. 81, in southeastern Nebraska.

Population: 7,884 (1990).

Growth rate: 2% since 1980.

Per capita income: $10,723 (1985), 2% higher than state average.

Geography/climate: Rolling prairie, elevation 1,609 feet. Winter cold air masses from Canada generally reach this area, along with 27 inches of snow on average. Long winters: 146 days at freezing or below, 17 zero-degree days. Spring can be short, summer long and hot, with 43 days at 90 or above. Annual rainfall, 28 inches. Growing season, 182 days average.

Economic base: Highly productive agricultural area produces corn, oats, alfalfa, milo, cattle, hogs. Countywide, agriculture employs 17%, retail trade, 17.5%; professional and related services, 20%; manufacturing, 12.6%. Large payrolls: Sundstrand Aerospace, aviation and aerospace components, 256; Champion Homebuilders, manufactured housing, 110; Nebraska Public Power District, 150. York is seat of York County and retail trading center.

Newspaper: *York News-Times*, 327 Platte Avenue, York, NE 68467. 402-362-4478. Daily except Sunday. David Sjuts, editor. $60 a year.

TV, radio: Local AM, FM stations. Cable carries TV networks from stations in Lincoln, Grand Island, Hastings; also PBS, NPR.

Health care: York General Hospital, 49 beds. 12 physicians, 12 dentists in local practice.

Schools: 3 elementary (K–6), 1 middle (7–8). York High School enrolls 423, sends 70% to college. 1990 composite ACT score, 21.1 (Nebraska, 19.6). York College, private, 4-year liberal-arts institution affiliated with Church of Christ, enrolls about 400.

Educational level: 13.6% of York County residents have 16 or more years of formal education; state average, 15.5%. County per capita expenditure for public education, $502; state average, $480.

Library: Kilgore Memorial Library, 40,000 volumes.

Recreation: 5 city parks include hiking and biking trails, picnic areas, playgrounds. Public swimming pool, 5 lighted softball and baseball fields, 2 lighted football fields, 10 lighted tennis courts. Community center has squash, handball courts, pool, workout areas. Soccer leagues enroll more than 300 children. 14-lane bowling alley, 18-hole private golf course, 3 movie theaters in town. Upland-game-hunting popular in fall, early winter.

3 BR, 2 BA house: $50,000 to $60,000.

Cost of electricity: $.06 per kilowatt hour.

Cost of natural gas: $.44 per therm.

Sales tax: 5%.

State income tax: 2% to 5.9%.

Churches: 17. Denominations: Assemblies of God, Baptist, Baptist-American, Disciples of Christ, Church of Christ, Jehovah's Witnesses, Lutheran, Nazarene, Nondenominational, Pentecostal, Presbyterian, Roman Catholic, United Methodist.

Travelers on Interstate 80 who are headed someplace else may know York only as a pit stop between Lincoln and Grand Island. But one magnificent procession of cars recently experienced something more. It was the Great American Road Race. York enticed the hundred-car, cross-country caravan of vintage autos to venture downtown with the promise of—a soothing ice massage of the neck. On a typical late June afternoon with Nebraska simmering in 100-degree heat, this chilling reception was a big hit with drivers, says Rotary Club president Sally Ruben.

For motorists who never leave the interchange of I-80 and U.S. 81, there is a cluster of service establishments all reportedly doing very well at dispensing a more familiar variety of Nebraska hospitality. Traffic counts keep rising, suggesting steady growth, perhaps more. "Sooner or later, somebody is going to figure out this is a perfect location," says Tom Robson, who has seen some others.

What residents say . . .

Tom Robson, general manager, KAWL AM & FM: "I'm a native of the town, married a local girl. My wife's name is Pat. It's a typical small-town kid's story. You think that happiness is seeing the town in the rear-view mirror, going off to find success. I went off to school in central Nebraska, worked for the Associated Press, covered Iowa, Nebraska, and South Dakota, got into TV with a CBS station in Missouri, from there to WOWT in Omaha. . . . In Baltimore, at WBAL-TV, I managed local and regional sales. We were there four years. I've been trying to buy [the York] station for the last 10 years. This was the very first commercial station I ever worked at, and really got hooked on radio. . . . We've lived in cities. Baltimore was a great experience. The kids were exposed to such cultural diversity in the schools . . . 23 different countries represented, far more than my parochial view of life. But we as parents realized they were growing up with

such a lack of space and freedom. . . . We've been back here about 30 days, just kind of getting settled. . . . It's tough, you try to get the kids involved in things. . . . We got a dog this morning, a springer spaniel."

Stan Schulz, director, Kilgore Memorial Library: "What I would say about York that makes it such a great town is the care and concern that people apparently have felt for the community. . . . Our current library building, which we moved into five years ago, was built from a single bequest . . . a million and two-thirds dollars, probably the largest library built from a single bequest in the United States . . . by Dr. Sherwood Kilgore, a lifelong York resident and physician, and his father had been a doctor here in York, as well. . . . And the same thing has happened with a number of other public facilities. A need was seen. . . . York County is one of the earliest sites where farmers tried deep-well irrigation, in the late 1920s and early 1930s. Almost all of the farmland here is irrigated, which, of course, is expensive but does give a certain financial stability to farm income. . . . Very few young people are financially situated to be able to continue farming. My daughter married a young man who wanted to farm but was also trained as an electrician. They have a farmstead . . . a few head of cattle, chickens, and ducks. . . . To make a living farming you've got to have a couple of hundred thousand dollars invested in machinery. If you have to borrow it, the margin isn't enough to cover the interest much less anything else. . . . One of my library staff is a farm wife. Her day is the kind of busy day a lot of people would find overwhelming. In the summertime when you're irrigating, the day starts at 4:30. They've got cattle, hogs and sheep . . . the sheep are her things, and a few chickens. The library opens at 12, so she comes to work then. Quite often she has various chores back home in the evening. She's a very well organized person! . . . A public library clientele always likes best-sellers and how-to-do-it kinds of things, and children's services are extremely important. . . . We probably have slightly more fiction and nonfiction published by religious publishing houses. There's a very strong interest in that. The southwestern portion of York County is largely settled by people from the Mennonite heritage. . . . York has a pretty good restaurant, a family-owned business called The Chances "R," with the *R* in quotation marks. It's good enough to draw Sunday traffic from Lincoln and Omaha. It even made the *Ford Times* a few years back."

C. G. "Kelly" Holthus, president, First National Bank of York; past president, American Bankers Association: "The year as president I spent 85 percent of my time on ABA business, attended 42 state conventions . . . over three years, 500,000 miles of travel and a lot of time in airports. . . . The bank will be 110 years old next April. During that time, only four groups have owned it. Very steady. Very dependable . . . $185 million in assets. In Nebraska we're 12th in size out of 400 banks. . . . York is a wealthy county . . . a lot of old money, third-generation money, strong agricultural base, and key businesses in very strong hands. . . . Country banks had their problems in the '80s when agriculture was in trouble, but by and large your smaller community banks are better able to roll with the punches. In a smaller community the decisions are made locally and you are able to react a little quicker. Decisions to lend are very close to the pocketbook of the bank's owners. . . . The thing that makes us really unique, with the world being so small, I can be in Washington, DC, for lunch and back in York in the evening, where I don't have to worry about locking my car. . . . We're on Interstate 80, which to me is like being on the railroad 100 years ago."

John Sozio, procurement quality engineer, soccer committee chairman: "All of a sudden two years ago, soccer started booming. Currently, 300 kids are in the league. . . . In the spring of 1993, soccer will be fully sanctioned at the high school, just like football and baseball. . . . You've got a school board watching their budget very carefully. You've got to convince them it's an opportunity. . . . I think part of the reason they voted for it, there were six of us who made the presentation. That really helped. They listened well. . . . You have to fight the resistance to change."

Sally Ruben, owner, Sally's Travel: "I came to York 27 years ago, when I was 22 years old, and planned to stay here one year. Then I'm going to live in Europe for awhile, I said. I've been to Europe lots of times but never stayed. I taught school for 13 years. . . . When I got to being 35, I thought Prince Charming had lost his way, obviously, so I quit teaching and started a travel agency. . . . Then Prince Charming came along, but I don't use his name. I started the agency not knowing anything about it . . . now have four or five people working for me. . . . I'm president of Rotary, the first woman president in York. I'm head of the Tree Board because I've been yakking about beautification. We're one of the American Tree Cities. York has always been fairly cosmopolitan. People travel. Last week I did somebody to Amman. I'm looking at Jakarta for another. We have several corporate accounts. . . . I'm not the typical woman in York. 49 years old and not married until 41. No children. But you can see I'm comfortable in York." ■

Yreka, CA 96097

Location: 291 miles north of San Francisco, 28 miles south of the Oregon state line, on I-5 at the top of California.

Population: 6,948 (1990).

Growth rate: 17% since 1980.

Per capita income: $9,443 (1985), 79% of state average ($11,885).

Geography/climate: North end of Shasta Valley at 2,595-foot elevation, surrounded by Klamath National Forest, 16 miles northwest of 14,162-foot Mt. Shasta. 4 seasons. Natives report interesting winter with 20 inches of snow; nice spring, warm summer, colorful fall. January average temperatures, 24–44; July, 52–92. May hit 100 in midsummer, but cools off at night. Fall starts in late October, onset of rainy season. Average year-round humidity at noon, 55%.

Economic base: Primarily a retail center. Timber-related agriculture is second in importance; government services, third. Major payrolls: U.S. Forest Service, 693; Siskiyou County, including schools, 675; Siskiyou General Hospital, 225; state government, 198; Hi-Ridge Lumber Co., 150. Yreka is county seat.

Newspaper: *Siskiyou Daily News*, 309 S. Broadway, Yreka, CA 96097. 916-842-5777. Daily except Sunday. Robert Diehl, editor. $67 a year.

TV, radio: Local AM, FM stations. Cable carries TV networks including PBS from Redding, California; and Medford, Oregon. NPR from Ashland, Oregon.

Health care: Siskiyou General Hospital, 57 beds. 26 physicians, 8 dentists in local practice.

Schools: 2 elementary (K–3); 1 middle (4–8). Yreka Union High School enrolls 750, sends 48%–53% to higher education, places at top of SAT scores in northern California. Wide range of advanced placement courses. Seventh-Day Adventist school (1–8). Satellite campus of College of the Siskiyous established in 1991.

Educational level: 14.0% of Siskiyou County residents have 16 or more years of formal education; state average, 19.6%. Per capita expenditure for public education, $579; state average, $461.

Library: Siskiyou County Public Library. Main branch in Yreka, 12 satellites. 200,000 volumes.

Recreation: 5 city parks, 4 playgrounds, swimming pool, tennis courts, athletic fields. Siskiyou County offers hunting, golfing, camping, hiking, Klamath River water sports. Mt. Shasta Ski Park, 45 miles south. Twin theater in town. Large community center for performing arts. The Blue Goose, historic steam engine, departs Yreka for Montague on a sightseeing run into Shasta Valley.

3 BR, 2 BA house: $65,000.

Cost of electricity: $.07 to $.08 per kilowatt hour.

Cost of propane: $1.48 per gallon.

Sales tax: 6.25%.

State income tax: 1% to 9.3%.

Churches: 18. Denominations: Assemblies of God, Baptist, Baptist-Southern, Berean Fundamental, Charismatic, Christian Science, Church of Christ, Church of Jesus Christ of Latter-day Saints, Community, Episcopal, Foursquare Gospel, Interdenominational, Jehovah's Witnesses, Lutheran, Nazarene, Pentecostal, Roman Catholic, United Methodist.

On a rainy March day in 1851, Abraham Thompson, a prospector down from Oregon, noticed particles of gold in the roots of grass pulled up by his pack animals as they grazed. Thompson might have shouted something like "Yreka!", but that is not part of the record. What is known is that within weeks some 2,000 miners rushed to the area surrounding Thompson's claim. The place was first named Shasta Butte City and then, the following year, Yreka. It is a Native-American word, pronounced "Wye-REE-ka" and meaning "white mountain," referring to Mt. Shasta, whose snow-white top dominates the southeastern horizon. By 1857, Yreka was a boom town of 5,000 and had gas-lit streets. It was a hustling, bustling center of opportunity, with more daily stagecoach arrivals and departures than anyplace else in California, according to local historians.

When the gold didn't pan out anymore, Yreka settled down as a logging and agricultural center, and base camp for some of the best hunting and fishing in the West. The economy provided a comfortable living for quite a number of people, whose legacy was at least 75 Victorian houses in the old town center.

What residents say . . .

Bernice Meamber, historian: "I helped organize and I'm the last remaining founder of the Siskiyou County Historical Society, founded in 1945. Mention Fred, too, we work together as a team. . . . In 1972, when we organized the Yreka Historic Preservation Corporation, we got four blocks on Third Street and three blocks on Miner Street on the National Register of Historic Places. That helped tourism a lot, to know we have a historic preservation group here. And the merchants had more pride in their buildings . . . then the rest of the town, when they saw what Third Street was doing. We started at a good time because it wasn't too hard then to get on the National Register. Right now we're having trouble with the three blocks on Miner . . . absentee owners, these city owners who think they can get the rents they charge in the cities. Therefore, we have some vacant stores on Miner Street again. I'm not sure what we'll do."

Robert Singleton, superintendent, Yreka Union School District: "I'm superintendent of elementary, kindergarten through eighth grade. We have about 1,250 students this year. Over the last three years we've been growing 30 to 40 students a year. This

year we kind of leveled off, about 20. . . .
We have a gifted and talented program for
our high achievers, and we just hired a
counselor at the elementary level, unique
in California. We have a lot of students at
risk, a lot of single-parent families. Because
we are the county seat, we also are the welfare center. There are several low-income
housing developments within the city. It's a
nice place to live while you're trying to pull
yourself together . . . with that comes your
share of at-risk students. We see larger families than 20 years ago . . . three or four
children . . . and young families doing everything they can to stay in this area, probably living on a lower standard than in an
urban area because they choose to stay here."

*Brian Reynolds, director, Siskiyou County
Public Library:* "Traditionally, our public
library service has been an example for
other rural areas. We've had very good support on the input side up until this fiscal
year. Right now we're taking a downturn.
The budget situation in the state is not
good. . . . One measure of a library's service is to add up all the branch-service
hours per year. We have been open more
than twice the hours of the nearest competi-
tor in our population group. The other
measure is spending. Our $17 to $18 per
capita is high for rural areas. . . . Yreka is
more friendly and interesting and cosmopolitan than you would guess . . . two theaters where live music and drama are put
on, close to Ashland [Oregon] where the
Shakespeare festival is . . . world-class entertainment no more than an hour away.
Yreka has a classic film series my wife and
I helped to start. . . . Tourism can be both
good and bad. I think tourism can over-
whelm a place if there is too much or it's
shoddy, but that hasn't happened here."

*Bob Marshall, manager, Yreka Community
Theater:* "The theater opened in October
1976 and I've been there since May of
1977. It's owned and operated by the City
of Yreka . . . a 307-seat house, traditional
proscenium arch. I do a seven-performance
series . . . a wide range of touring artists,
from operas and ballet to jazz and folk and
ethnic music. The series is called 'At Last!'
It took us several years to put together the
season we wanted. . . . Next season we've
got coming the Chinese Magic Review, a
group from Hong Kong; a folk group
from Mexico City; 'Juke Joints in Jubilee';
'Driving Miss Daisy,' with the New York
cast; a children's theater group out of New
York; a piano trio. . . . I have an artistic vision of the types of things and when I
want to expose my audience to them to
stretch them, hopefully, balanced with
things they will find entertaining and
intriguing. . . . I consider my audience very
sophisticated. The stigma of rural living
and the level of sophistication normally associated with it is not true. Our audiences
can discern quality. . . . We've got a first-
rate national identity. . . . Our type of programming has been used as a model.
We've been featured in '21 Voices,' 21 exemplary programs in the United States."

*Alan J. McMurry, retired general contractor,
writer:* "The main thing I recently wrote
involves lynchings in Siskiyou County from
start to finish. It's historical, called 'Just A
Little Lynching Now and Then.' Once they
did four at a time on the courthouse lawn.
It was the Wild West, no question about
it. . . . I finished that one last year. It's just
a hobby. I tried to get published but
couldn't get 'em interested. I had 500 cop-
ies printed. It's in the library. Since then
I've been working on 'This Is Alan.' That's

me. I haven't published it, just pass it around to my friends and relatives. . . . A real peculiar thing is happening here. In the last two years the darn town has increased about threefold in population. I don't know what all these people are doing. . . . We always used to say it was the typical small-town America. It's losing that appearance. It looks like an industrious town now."

Mark Dean, executive director, Chamber of Commerce: "Our influx of people is mainly from southern California and the Bay area, with an increase of folks from Seattle . . . disillusioned by the city but don't want to move back to cement and neon. With the electronic age, anybody can have improved quality of life and live anywhere they want." ■

TABLE 1. Towns Ranked by Growth Rate, 1980–90

The following table shows the population growth rate of the town between 1980 and 1990. **Source:** Population figures from the U.S. Bureau of the Census.

Town	Growth Rate	Town	Growth Rate
1. Plymouth, NH	45%	Jasper, IN	9
2. Elko, NV	40	Lebanon, NH	9
3. Glenwood Springs, CO	30	Red Wing, MN	9
4. Page, AZ	26	Smyrna, DE	9
5. Pikeville, KY	25	35. Arcadia, FL	8
6. Culpeper, VA	23	Bryan, OH	8
Littleton, NH	23	Crossville, TN	8
8. Anacortes, WA	21	Durango, CO	8
Boone, NC	21	39. Devils Lake, ND	7
Cartersville, GA	21	Greencastle, IN	7
11. Easton, MD	20	Hendersonville, NC	7
12. Rexburg, ID	19	Mount Airy, NC	7
13. Cedar City, UT	18	Lincoln City, OR	7
Hartselle, AL	18	Martinsburg, WV	7
Ukiah, CA	18	Pierre, SD	7
16. Yreka, CA	15	Silver City, NM	7
17. Bolivar, MO	14	Tahlequah, OK	7
Elkhorn, WI	14	Washington, IA	7
Essex, CT	14	Wilmington, OH	7
20. West Plains, MO	13	50. Cleveland, MS	6
21. Baraboo, WI	12	Hendersonville, NC	6
Stephenville, TX	12	Lewisburg, PA	6
23. Kalispell, MT	11	Newberry, SC	6
Newport, OR	11	Rolla, MO	6
25. Bardstown, KY	10	St. Helens, WA	6
Batesville, AR	10	56. Franklin, NH	5
Beaufort, SC	10	McPherson, KS	5
Mount Pleasant, TX	10	Moses Lake, WA	5
Winfield, KS	10	59. Elizabeth City, NC	4
30. Celina, OH	9	Harrison, AR	4

TABLE 1. Towns Ranked by Growth Rate, 1980–90 *(continued)*

The following table shows the population growth rate of the town between 1980 and 1990. **Source:** Population figures from the U.S. Bureau of the Census.

Town	Growth Rate	Town	Growth Rate
Marion, IL	4	Shippensburg, PA	1
62. Bemidji, MN	3	Somerset, KY	1
Brattleboro, VT	3	83. Carlinville, IL	0
Ft. Payne, AL	3	Grinnell, IA	0
Middlebury, VT	3	Houghton, MI	0
Tifton, GA	3	Penn Yan, NY	0
Warsaw, IN	3	Petoskey, MI	0
68. Crawfordsville, IN	2	88. Bath, ME	-4
Hastings, MI	2	Danville, KY	-4
Montrose, CO	2	Greeneville, TN	-4
Monroe, WI	2	West Point, MS	-4
Nevada, IA	2	92. Williamstown, MA	-5
Poteau, OK	2	93. Franklin, LA	-6
York, NE	2	94. Geneva, NY	-7
75. Bedford, VA	1	Georgetown, SC	-7
Carthage, TX	1	96. Marshall, MN	-8
Grand Rapids, MN	1	97. Bisbee, AZ	-12
Oxford, MS	1	98. Brewton, AL	-13
Rockland, ME	1	99. Douglas, WY	-16
St. Albans, VT	1	100. Lander, WY	-23

TABLE 2: Towns Ranked by Per Capita Income

Source: *County and City Data Book: 1988*, U.S. Bureau of the Census.

Town	Per Capita Income	Town	Per Capita Income
1. Essex, CT	$17,593	32. Shippensburg, PA	10,146
2. Monroe, WI	12,135	33. Nevada, IA	9,915
3. Williamstown, MA	12,078	34. Marshall, MN	9,818
4. Jasper, IN	11,879	35. Crawfordsville, IN	9,727
5. Page, AZ	11,847	36. Hartselle, AL	9,724
6. Glenwood Springs, CO	11,689	37. Stephenville, TX	9,682
7. Washington, IA	11,659	38. Ft. Payne, AL	9,652
8. Lebanon, NH	11,620	39. Bardstown, KY	9,650
9. Anacortes, WA	11,207	40. Lander, WY	9,628
10. Culpeper, VA	10,961	41. Durango, CO	9,624
11. Elko, NV	10,950	42. Petoskey, MI	9,598
12. Red Wing, MN	10,936	43. Newport, OR	9,577
13. Baraboo, WI	10,858	44. Douglas, WY	9,555
14. Beaufort, SC	10,802	45. Marion, IL	9,539
15. York, NE	10,723	46. Celina, OH	9,516
16. McPherson, KS	10,681	47. Wilmington, OH	9,500
17. Brattleboro, VT	10,667	48. Devils Lake, ND	9,455
18. Bryan, OH	10,664	49. Yreka, CA	9,443
19. Pierre, SD	10,663	50. Franklin, NH	9,373
20. Carthage, TX	10,625	51. Bedford, VA	9,356
21. Warsaw, IN	10,502	52. Ukiah, CA	9,327
22. Grinnell, IA	10,410	53. Penn Yan, NY	9,229
23. Easton, MD	10,378	54. Danville, KY	9,298
24. Kalispell, MT	10,358	55. Bath, ME	9,238
25. Greeneville, TN	10,350	56. Oxford, MS	9,222
26. Brewton, AL	10,348	57. Mount Pleasant, TX	9,214
27. Elkhorn, WI	10,323	58. Pikeville, KY	9,211
28. Montrose, CO	10,215	59. Grand Rapids, MN	9,174
29. Winfield, KS	10,201	60. Carlinville, IL	9,136
30. Hastings, MI	10,142	61. Rolla, MO	9,119
31. Cartersville, GA	10,138	62. St. Albans, VT	9,068

TABLE 2: Towns Ranked by Per Capita Income *(continued)*

Source: *County and City Data Book: 1988,* U.S. Bureau of the Census.

Town	Per Capita Income	Town	Per Capita Income
63. Geneva, NY	9,048	82. Greencastle, IN	8,045
64. Harrison, AR	9,010	83. Georgetown, SC	7,902
65. Batesville, AR	8,982	84. Rockland, ME	7,830
66. Littleton, NH	8,936	85. Bemidji, MN	7,792
67. Lincoln City, OR	8,929	86. West Point, MS	7,720
68. Mount Airy, NC	8,916	87. West Plains, MO	7,547
69. Martinsburg, WV	8,783	88. Franklin, LA	7,508
70. Middlebury, VT	8,762	89. Elizabeth City, NC	7,507
71. Moses Lake, WA	8,748	90. Bolivar, MO	7,497
72. Bisbee, AZ	8,595	91. Crossville, TN	7,415
73. St. Helens, OR	8,587	92. Cleveland, MS	7,384
74. Newberry, SC	8,554	93. Silver City, NM	7,316
75. Smyrna, DE	8,535	94. Plymouth, NH	7,235
76. Tifton, GA	8,488	95. Tahlequah, OK	7,201
77. Vernal, UT	8,447	96. Arcadia, FL	7,150
78. Somerset, KY	8,315	97. Cedar City, UT	7,095
79. Hendersonville, NC	8,312	98. Boone, NC	6,935
80. Lewisburg, PA	8,255	99. Houghton, MI	5,912
Poteau, OK	8,255	100. Rexburg, ID	5,733

TABLE 3. Towns Ranked by Proportion of Residents in 25–34 Age Group

The following table shows the proportion of residents in the 25–34 age group, for the county in which the town is located. **Source:** *County and City Data Book: 1988*, U.S. Bureau of the Census.

US Overall Average	*17.5%*	*US Overall Average*	*17.5%*
1. Glenwood Springs, CO	24.6	Lebanon, NH	17.1
2. Durango, CO	20.6	Littleton, NH	17.1
3. Douglas, WY	20.5	Plymouth, NH	17.1
4. Ukiah, CA	20.1	Bedford, VA	17.1
5. Elko, NV	19.8	34. Hartselle, AL	17.0
Lander, WY	19.8	Jasper, IN	17.0
7. Bath, ME	19.7	36. Hastings, MI	16.9
8. Kalispell, MT	19.4	Petoskey, MI	16.9
9. Beaufort, SC	19.3	Wilmington, OH	16.9
10. Page, AZ	19.2	Lincoln City, OR	16.9
Franklin, NH	19.2	Newport, OR	16.9
12. Brattleboro, VT	19.0	Culpeper, VA	16.9
13. Essex, CT	18.6	Cedar City, UT	16.9
14. Yreka, CA	18.5	York, NE	16.9
St. Helens, OR	18.5	44. Geneva, NY	16.8
16. Warsaw, IN	18.4	45. Bisbee, AZ	16.7
17. St. Albans, VT	18.2	Monroe, WI	16.7
18. Vernal, UT	18.0	47. Grinnell, IA	16.6
19. Rockland, ME	17.9	48. Grand Rapids, MN	16.5
20. Devils Lake, ND	17.6	49. Cartersville, GA	16.4
21. Smyrna, DE	17.5	Penn Yan, NY	16.4
22. Franklin, LA	17.4	Bryan, OH	16.4
Marion, IL	17.4	Shippensburg, PA	16.4
24. Montrose, CO	17.3	Georgetown, SC	16.4
Rexburg, ID	17.3	54. Nevada, IA	16.3
Anacortes, WA	17.3	Somerset, KY	16.3
27. Lewisburg, PA	17.2	Elizabeth City, NC	16.3
Middlebury, VT	17.2	Martinsburg, WV	16.3
29. Pikeville, KY	17.1	58. Pierre, SD	16.1

TABLE 3. Towns Ranked by Proportion of Residents in 25–34 Age Group (continued)

The following table shows the proportion of residents in the 25–34 age group, for the county in which the town is located. **Source:** *County and City Data Book: 1988*, U.S. Bureau of the Census.

US Overall Average	*17.5%*	*US Overall Average*	*17.5%*
Batesville, AR	16.1	West Point, MS	15.1
Crawfordsville, IN	16.1	81. Tifton, GA	14.9
Bardstown, KY	16.1	Williamstown, MA	14.9
62. Danville, KY	16.0	Crossville, TN	14.9
63. Washington, IA	15.9	Bemidji, MN	14.9
Mount Airy, NC	15.9	85. Marshall, MN	14.6
65. Harrison, AR	15.8	Boone, NC	14.6
66. Winfield, KS	15.7	Newberry, SC	14.6
Greeneville, TN	15.7	88. Carlinville, IL	14.5
Elkhorn, WI	15.7	89. Easton, MD	14.3
69. Brewton, AL	15.6	Cleveland, MS	14.3
Baraboo, WI	15.6	91. Greencastle, IN	14.1
71. Red Wing, MN	15.5	92. Silver City, NM	13.9
Carthage, TX	15.5	93. Poteau, OK	13.8
Mount Pleasant, TX	15.5	94. West Plains, MO	13.7
Moses Lake, WA	15.5	95. Rolla, MO	13.6
75. Celina, OH	15.4	Stephenville, TX	13.6
76. Tahlequah, OK	15.3	97. Bolivar, MO	13.0
77. Ft. Payne, AL	15.2	98. Arcadia, FL	12.8
McPherson, KS	15.2	99. Houghton, MI	12.7
79. Oxford, MS	15.1	100. Hendersonville, NC	10.8

TABLE 4. Towns Ranked by Percentage of Nonwhite Population

The following table shows the percentage of black and other nonwhite population of the county in which the town is located. **Source:** *County and City Data Book: 1988*, U.S. Bureau of the Census.

US overall average	*14.89%*	*US overall average*	*14.89%*
1. Cleveland, MS	64.6	31. Bardstown, KY	5.8
2. West Point, MS	54.3	32. Mount Airy, NC	5.3
3. Oxford, MS	48.0	33. Ukiah, CA	4.8
4. Georgetown, SC	44.9	34. Martinsburg, WV	4.7
5. Elizabeth City, NC	36.6	Essex, CT	4.7
6. Brewton, AL	35.3	36. York, NE	4.6
7. Franklin, LA	33.2	37. Devils Lake, ND	4.5
8. Beaufort, SC	31.9	38. Winfield, KS	4.4
9. Newberry, SC	31.0	39. Nevada, IA	4.3
10. Page, AZ	29.2	40. Williamstown, MA	4.1
11. Tifton, GA	29.0	41. Cedar City, UT	3.9
12. Tahlequah, OK	27.7	42. Durango, CO	3.7
13. Culpeper, VA	20.7	Grand Rapids, MN	3.7
14. Easton, MD	20.0	44. Moses Lake, WA	3.6
15. Smyrna, DE	19.3	45. Hendersonville, NC	3.4
16. Carthage, TX	18.9	Petoskey, MI	3.4
17. Arcadia, FL	17.7	47. Lewisburg, PA	3.3
18. Bemidji, MN	15.3	48. Batesville, AR	3.0
19. Mount Pleasant, TX	14.1	49. Douglas, WY	2.9
20. Lander, WY	13.2	50. Rolla, MO	2.8
21. Cartersville, GA	10.9	51. Anacortes, WA	2.7
22. Bedford, VA	10.6	Greeneville, TN	2.7
23. Hartselle, AL	10.5	53. Grinnell, IA	2.5
24. Poteau, OK	10.3	54. Shippensburg, PA	2.4
25. Vernal, UT	9.6	Wilmington, OH	2.4
26. Danville, KY	9.4	56. Greencastle, IN	2.3
27. Elko, NV	8.8	57. Lincoln City, OR	2.2
28. Bisbee, AZ	7.3	Newport, OR	2.2
29. Pierre, SD	6.3	59. Marion, IL	1.9
30. Yreka, CA	6.2	60. Ft. Payne, AL	1.8

TABLE 4.   Towns Ranked by Percentage of Nonwhite Population   (*continued*)

The following table shows the percentage of black and other nonwhite population of the county in which the town is located. **Source:** *County and City Data Book: 1988*, U.S. Bureau of the Census.

US overall average	*14.89%*	*US overall average*	*14.89%*
Kalispell, MT	1.8	West Plains, MO	1.0
62. Boone, NC	1.7	Montrose, CO	1.0
63. Geneva, NY	1.6	83. Glenwood Springs, CO	0.9
Elkhorn, WI	1.6	84. Bolivar, MO	0.8
65. Lebanon, NH	1.5	Washington, IA	0.8
Littleton, NH	1.5	Penn Yan, NY	0.8
McPherson, KS	1.5	Hastings, MI	0.8
Plymouth, NH	1.5	88. Baraboo, WI	0.7
St. Helens, OR	1.5	89. Crawfordsville, IN	0.6
70. Houghton, MI	1.4	Franklin, NH	0.6
Bath, ME	1.4	91. Pikeville, KY	0.5
Red Wing, MN	1.4	Bryan, OH	0.5
Stephenville, TX	1.4	Brattleboro, VT	0.5
74. Silver City, NM	1.3	Harrison, AR	0.5
St. Albans, VT	1.3	Rockland, ME	0.5
Marshall, MN	1.3	96. Middlebury, VT	0.4
Carlinville, IL	1.3	Monroe, WI	0.4
78. Somerset, KY	1.2	98. Jasper, IN	0.3
79. Rexburg, ID	1.1	Celina, OH	0.3
80. Warsaw, IN	1.0	100. Crossville, TN	0.2

TABLE 5. Towns Ranked by Crime Rate

The following table shows the number of serious crimes known to police per 100,000 population, for the county in which the town is located, as of July 1, 1985. "Serious crimes" are defined as murder, nonnegligent manslaughter, forcible rape, robbery, and aggravated assault. **Source:** *County and City Data Book: 1988*, U.S. Bureau of the Census.

US overall average	*5,242*	*US overall average*	*5,242*
1. Bolivar, MO	341	29. Mount Airy, NC	2,334
2. Elko, NV	813	30. Marion, IL	2,374
3. Celina, OH	871	31. West Plains, MO	2,400
4. Lewisburg, PA	1,150	32. York, NE	2,407
5. Carlinville, IL	1,155	33. Harrison, AR	2,473
6. Bedford, VA	1,162	34. Lebanon, NH	2,550
7. West Point, MS	1,238	Littleton, NH	2,550
8. Pikeville, KY	1,270	Plymouth, NH	2,550
9. Jasper, IN	1,399	37. Danville, KY	2,556
10. Grinnell, IA	1,492	38. Penn Yan, NY	2,562
11. Somerset, KY	1,671	39. Cleveland, MS	2,568
12. Greeneville, TN	1,673	40. Crawfordsville, IN	2,584
13. McPherson, KS	1,687	41. Crossville, TN	2,588
14. Poteau, OK	1,712	42. Hastings, MI	2,637
15. Ft. Payne, AL	1,822	43. Mount Pleasant, TX	2,646
16. Culpeper, VA	1,933	44. Hendersonville, NC	2,648
17. Bryan, OH	1,977	45. Baraboo, WI	2,661
18. Houghton, MI	2,008	46. Bardstown, KY	2,670
19. Shippensburg, PA	2,082	47. Boone, NC	2,683
20. Brewton, AL	2,111	48. Newberry, SC	2,696
21. Carthage, TX	2,113	49. Pierre, SD	2,754
22. Washington, IA	2,173	50. Franklin, NH	2,824
23. Cartersville, GA	2,182	51. Martinsburg, WV	2,847
24. Monroe, WI	2,193	52. Hartselle, AL	2,871
25. Grand Rapids, MN	2,221	53. Cedar City, UT	2,875
26. Marshall, MN	2,239	54. Wilmington, OH	2,886
27. Batesville, AR	2,255	55. St. Helens, OR	2,937
28. Red Wing, MN	2,281	56. Williamstown, MA	2,981

TABLE 5. Towns Ranked by Crime Rate *(continued)*

The following table shows the number of serious crimes known to police per 100,000 population, for the county in which the town is located, as of July 1, 1985. "Serious crimes" are defined as murder, nonnegligent manslaughter, forcible rape, robbery, and aggravated assault. **Source:** *County and City Data Book: 1988*, U.S. Bureau of the Census.

US overall average	*5,242*	*US overall average*	*5,242*
57. Winfield, KS	3,022	79. Ukiah, CA	4,225
58. Rockland, ME	3,088	80. Yreka, CA	4,308
59. Geneva, NY	3,116	81. Franklin, LA	4,431
60. Middlebury, VT	3,156	82. Petoskey, MI	4,443
61. Stephenville, TX	3,238	83. Nevada, IA	4,570
62. Bath, ME	3,315	84. Lincoln City, OR	4,663
63. Elkhorn, WI	3,351	Newport, OR	4,663
64. Warsaw, IN	3,374	86. Smyrna, DE	4,674
65. Douglas, WY	3,422	87. Tifton, GA	4,765
66. Easton, MD	3,424	88. Rolla, MO	4,821
67. Elizabeth City, NC	3,532	89. Moses Lake, WA	4,853
68. Tahlequah, OK	3,571	90. Durango, CO	4,882
69. Glenwood Springs, CO	3,622	91. Silver City, NM	4,883
70. Montrose, CO	3,688	92. Bemidji, MN	5,208
71. Devils Lake, ND	3,779	93. Arcadia, FL	5,216
72. Essex, CT	3,793	94. St. Albans, VT	5,222
73. Lander, WY	3,873	95. Kalispell, MT	5,547
74. Rexburg, ID	3,886	96. Page, AZ	5,753
75. Vernal, UT	3,893	97. Anacortes, WA	6,172
76. Georgetown, SC	3,908	98. Beaufort, SC	6,406
77. Bisbee, AZ	4,164	99. Oxford, MS	8,433
Greencastle, IN	4,164	100. Brattleboro, VT	8,673

TABLE 6. Towns Ranked by Number of Physicians in County

The following table shows the number of physicians per 100,000 resident population of the county in which the town is located. **Source:** *County and City Data Book: 1988*, U.S. Bureau of the Census.

US overall average	*197*	*US overall average*	*197*
1. Lebanon, NH	683	31. Geneva, NY	127
Littleton, NH	683	Culpeper, VA	127
Plymouth, NH	683	33. Page, AZ	126
4. Petoskey, MI	392	34. Middlebury, VT	125
5. Easton, MD	341	35. Yreka, CA	124
6. Williamstown, MA	240	36. Martinsburg, WV	123
7. Monroe, WI	231	Georgetown, SC	123
8. Essex, CT	216	38. Montrose, CO	122
9. Durango, CO	208	39. Oxford, MS	121
10. Danville, KY	198	Silver City, NM	121
11. Brattleboro, VT	197	41. Beaufort, SC	118
Anacortes, WA	197	42. Bath, ME	113
13. Ukiah, CA	196	43. Elko, NV	111
14. Rockland, ME	190	44. Newport, OR	109
15. Kalispell, MT	165	Lincoln City, OR	109
Franklin, NH	165	46. Rolla, MO	107
17. Lander, WY	161	Somerset, KY	107
18. Boone, NC	160	Winfield, KS	107
19. Smyrna, DE	157	49. Crossville, TN	106
20. Harrison, AR	155	50. Mount Pleasant, TX	104
21. Arcadia, FL	149	Red Wing, MN	104
22. Hendersonville, NC	148	Wilmington, OH	104
23. Devils Lake, ND	146	53. Jasper, IN	101
24. Elizabeth City, NC	141	54. Hartselle, AL	98
25. Shippensburg, PA	139	55. Houghton, MI	95
26. Lewisburg, PA	136	56. Bryan, OH	94
Glenwood Springs, CO	136	57. Batesville, AR	93
28. Tifton, GA	135	Greeneville, TN	93
29. Pierre, SD	134	59. Rexburg, ID	92
Nevada, IA	134	60. Grand Rapids, MN	91

TABLE 6. Towns Ranked by Number of Physicians in County (*continued*)

The following table shows the number of physicians per 100,000 resident population of the county in which the town is located. **Source:** *County and City Data Book: 1988*, U.S. Bureau of the Census.

US overall average	*197*	*US overall average*	*197*
Baraboo, WI	91	81. Warsaw, IN	70
62. Grinnell, IA	90	82. Brewton, AL	69
Bemidji, MN	90	83. Hastings, MI	68
64. Penn Yan, NY	88	84. Douglas, WY	63
65. Marion, IL	87	85. Celina, OH	62
66. Moses Lake, WA	86	86. Bisbee, AZ	60
67. West Plains, MO	84	Cleveland, MS	60
68. Mount Airy, NC	83	88. West Point, MS	59
Elkhorn, WI	83	89. Greencastle, IN	57
70. St. Albans, VT	82	90. Bolivar, MO	54
71. Newberry, SC	81	91. Cartersville, GA	51
72. McPherson, KS	80	92. Carlinville, IL	49
73. Marshall, MN	79	93. Vernal, UT	47
Crawfordsville, IN	79	94. Bardstown, KY	44
York, NE	79	95. Washington, IA	40
76. Franklin, LA	76	96. Poteau, OK	39
Stephenville, TX	76	97. Ft. Payne, AL	38
78. Pikeville, KY	75	98. Carthage, TX	36
79. Tahlequah, OK	74	99. St. Helens, OR	35
Bedford, VA	74	100. Cedar City, UT	16

TABLE 7: Towns Ranked by Proportion of Residents with College Education

The following table shows the proportion of residents of the county in which the town is located who have 16 or more years of formal education.
Source: *County and City Data Book: 1988*, U.S. Bureau of the Census.

US overall average	*16.2*	*US overall average*	*16.2*
1. Nevada, IA	33.9	30. Hendersonville, NC	15.2
2. Pierre, SD	26.1	31. Bath, ME	15.1
3. Page, AZ	23.2	32. Rolla, MO	14.9
4. Oxford, MS	23.1	33. Grinnell, IA	14.8
5. Durango, CO	22.1	Stephenville, TX	14.8
6. Beaufort, SC	21.9	35. Shippensburg, PA	14.6
Lebanon, NH	21.9	36. Houghton, MI	14.4
Littleton, NH	21.9	Lincoln City, OR	14.4
Plymouth, NH	21.9	Newport, OR	14.4
10. Boone, NC	20.0	39. Lewisburg, PA	14.3
11. Middlebury, VT	20.5	40. Cleveland, MS	14.1
12. Essex, CT	20.4	41. Yreka, CA	14.0
13. Glenwood Springs, CO	20.2	42. Bisbee, AZ	13.8
14. Cedar City, UT	19.9	Geneva, NY	13.8
15. Franklin, NH	19.8	Montrose, CO	13.8
16. Brattleboro, VT	19.7	45. York, NE	13.6
17. Rexburg, ID	18.7	46. Douglas, WY	13.4
18. Easton, MD	18.1	47. Anacortes, WA	13.2
19. Tahlequah, OK	17.8	48. Devils Lake, ND	13.1
20. Petoskey, MI	17.6	49. Elko, NV	12.7
Ukiah, CA	17.6	50. Danville, KY	12.6
22. Bemidji, MN	17.3	Silver City, NM	12.6
23. Smyrna, DE	16.6	52. Grand Rapids, MN	12.4
24. Lander, WY	16.3	Marshall, MN	12.4
Williamstown, MA	16.3	54. Greencastle, IN	12.1
26. McPherson, KS	15.6	Warsaw, IN	12.1
27. Kalispell, MT	15.4	56. Newberry, SC	12.0
Rockland, ME	15.4	Vernal, UT	12.0
29. Elkhorn, WI	15.3	58. Red Wing, MN	11.9

TABLE 7: Towns Ranked by Proportion of Residents with College Education (continued)

The following table shows the proportion of residents of the county in which the town is located who have 16 or more years of formal education.
Source: *County and City Data Book: 1988*, U.S. Bureau of the Census.

US overall average	16.2	US overall average	16.2
59. Hartselle, AL	11.8	Harrison, AR	9.8
Washington, IA	11.8	81. Mount Pleasant, TX	9.7
61. Winfield, KS	11.7	82. Carthage, TX	9.5
62. Moses Lake, WA	11.5	83. St. Albans, VT	9.4
Tifton, GA	11.5	84. Franklin, LA	9.2
64. Culpeper, VA	11.4	85. Greeneville, TN	8.9
65. Baraboo, WI	11.2	86. Crossville, TN	8.6
66. Georgetown, SC	11.1	Penn Yan, NY	8.6
67. Crawfordsville, IN	10.9	88. Bryan, OH	8.3
Monroe, WI	10.9	Celina, OH	8.3
69. Wilmington, OH	10.8	90. Arcadia, FL	8.2
70. Elizabeth City, NC	10.7	Batesville, AR	8.2
71. Martinsburg, WV	10.6	92. Poteau, OK	8.0
West Point, MS	10.6	93. Carlinville, IL	7.9
73. Hastings, MI	10.4	94. West Plains, MO	7.6
Marion, IL	10.4	95. Brewton, AL	7.2
75. Bedford, VA	10.3	96. Somerset, KY	7.1
76. Jasper, IN	10.2	97. Cartersville, GA	6.3
77. Bardstown, KY	10.0	Mount Airy, NC	6.3
St. Helens, OR	10.0	99. Pikeville, KY	6.2
79. Bolivar, MO	9.8	100. Ft. Payne, AL	5.7

TABLE 8. Towns Ranked by Expenditures for Public Education

The following table shows local government expenditures per capita for public elementary and secondary education, for the county in which the town is located. **Source:** *County and City Data Book: 1988*, U.S. Bureau of the Census.

US overall average	$451	US overall average	$451
1. Douglas, WY	$1,012	30. Marshall, MN	493
2. St. Helens, OR	1,007	31. McPherson, KS	491
3. Bemidji, MN	974	32. Essex, CT	487
4. Lander, WY	895	33. Monroe, WI	486
5. Cedar City, UT	676	Petoskey, MI	486
6. Devils Lake, ND	637	35. Bath, ME	484
Silver City, NM	637	36. Durango, CO	483
8. Ukiah, CA	622	37. Penn Yan, NY	479
9. Red Wing, MN	616	38. Georgetown, SC	476
10. Lewisburg, PA	612	39. Lebanon, NH	473
11. Moses Lake, WA	608	Littleton, NH	473
12. Grand Rapids, MN	607	Plymouth, NH	473
13. Geneva, NY	593	42. Bryan, OH	471
14. Vernal, UT	587	43. Elkhorn, WI	467
15. Yreka, CA	579	44. Celina, OH	466
16. Glenwood Springs, CO	570	Arcadia, FL	466
17. Newport, OR	567	46. St. Albans, VT	464
Lincoln City, OR	567	47. Carlinville, IL	462
19. Page, AZ	563	48. Bisbee, AZ	461
20. Montrose, CO	536	49. Washington, IA	460
21. Elko, NV	535	50. Martinsburg, WV	459
22. Franklin, LA	529	51. Jasper, IN	458
23. Brattleboro, VT	528	52. Shippensburg, PA	452
24. Carthage, TX	512	53. Grinnell, IA	451
25. Baraboo, WI	504	Cartersville, GA	451
Kalispell, MT	504	55. Williamstown, MA	441
27. York, NE	502	56. Winfield, KS	435
28. Anacortes, WA	499	57. Poteau, OK	431
29. Wilmington, OH	494	58. Mount Pleasant, TX	426

TABLE 8. Towns Ranked by Expenditures for Public Education (*continued*)

The following table shows local government expenditures per capita for public elementary and secondary education, for the county in which the town is located. **Source:** *County and City Data Book: 1988*, U.S. Bureau of the Census.

US overall average	$451	US overall average	$451
59. Pierre, SD	424	80. Hartselle, AL	362
60. Middlebury, VT	414	81. Warsaw, IN	361
61. Bedford, VA	413	82. Newberry, SC	357
62. Smyrna, DE	410	83. Bolivar, MO	351
63. Cleveland, MS	407	84. Bardstown, KY	349
64. Culpeper, VA	405	85. Houghton, MI	347
65. Crawfordsville, IN	404	86. Rexburg, ID	343
66. Greencastle, IN	403	87. Danville, KY	342
Rockland, ME	403	88. Hastings, MI	341
68. Mount Airy, NC	401	89. Rolla, MO	337
69. West Plains, MO	400	90. Somerset, KY	323
70. Brewton, AL	396	91. Boone, NC	312
71. Marion, IL	394	92. Tifton, GA	310
72. Easton, MD	389	Harrison, AR	310
73. Franklin, NH	375	94. Crossville, TN	307
Tahlequah, OK	375	95. Greeneville, TN	305
75. Batesville, AR	374	96. Ft. Payne, AL	300
76. Elizabeth City, NC	373	West Point, MS	300
77. Nevada, IA	367	98. Beaufort, SC	283
78. Hendersonville, NC	363	99. Stephenville, TX	283
Pikeville, KY	363	100. Oxford, MS	278

Table 9. Summary—Towns Ranked by All Seven Selectors

The following table is a summation of Tables 2 through 8, the seven selectors used to identify towns, state by state, for inclusion among the 100. The score is the total of place-scores on tables measuring per capita income, proportion of residents in 25-to-34 age group, percentage of nonwhite population, crime rate, number of physicians, proportion of residents with college education, and expenditures for public education.

Town	Total Score	Town	Score
1. Elko, NV	158	28. Grand Rapids, MN	298
2. Essex, CT	172	Red Wing, MN	298
3. Page, AZ	176	30. McPherson, KS	300
4. Lebanon, NH	182	31. Smyrna, DE	301
5. Lander, WY	183	32. Bath, ME	302
6. Ukiah, CA	209	Montrose, CO	302
7. Glenwood Springs, CO	214	Franklin, NH	302
8. Durango, CO	225	35. Geneva, NY	315
9. Lewisburg, PA	233	36. Nevada, IA	316
10. Culpeper, VA	234	37. Newport, OR	317
11. Littleton, NH	240	38. Bedford, VA	323
12. Pierre, SD	245	39. Jasper, IN	325
13. Devils Lake, ND	253	40. Danville, KY	326
14. Kalispell, MT	254	41. Carthage, TX	332
15. Petoskey, MI	262	42. Hartselle, AL	338
16. York, NE	263	43. Wilmington, OH	339
17. Yreka, CA	264	44. Lincoln City, OR	341
18. Williamstown, MA	265	45. Cedar City, UT	346
19. Shippensburg, PA	266	46. Georgetown, SC	352
20. Anacortes, WA	267	47. Winfield, KS	353
21. Plymouth, NH	268	48. Middlebury, VT	358
22. Brattleboro, VT	270	Vernal, UT	358
23. Beaufort, SC	274	50. Elkhorn, WI	359
Monroe, WI	274	Rockland, ME	359
25. Grinnell, IA	280	52. Bryan, OH	362
26. Easton, MD	287	53. Bemidji, MN	363
27. Douglas, WY	292	54. Baraboo, WI	365

Table 9.   Summary—Towns Ranked by All Seven Selectors *(continued)*

The following table is a summation of Tables 2 through 8, the seven selectors used to identify towns, state by state, for inclusion among the 100. The score is the total of place-scores on tables measuring per capita income, proportion of residents in 25-to-34 age group, percentage of nonwhite population, crime rate, number of physicians, proportion of residents with college education, and expenditures for public education.

Town	Total Score	Town	Score
Cartersville, GA	365	78. Crawfordsville, IN	427
Marion, IL	365	79. Bardstown, KY	429
Martinsburg, WV	365	West Point, MS	429
58. Brewton, AL	368	81. Hastings, MI	436
59. Marshall, MN	374	82. Tifton, GA	437
60. Washington, IA	379	83. Celina, OH	439
Mount Pleasant, TX	379	Rexburg, ID	439
62. Franklin, LA	380	85. Pikeville, KY	441
Oxford, MS	380	86. Harrison, AR	444
64. Elizabeth City, NC	384	87. Silver City, NM	445
65. St. Helens, OR	385	88. St. Albans, VT	446
66. Greeneville, TN	391	89. Somerset, KY	453
67. Warsaw, IN	397	90. Poteau, OK	456
68. Bisbee, AZ	398	91. Arcadia, FL	459
Hendersonville, NC	398	Carlinville, IL	459
70. Cleveland, MS	410	93. Rolla, MO	461
71. Boone, NC	411	94. Houghton, MI	462
Penn Yan, NY	411	95. Stephenville, TX	471
73. Moses Lake, WA	414	96. Ft. Payne, AL	483
74. Batesville, AR	420	97. Greencastle, IN	515
75. Tahlequah, OK	422	98. West Plains, MO	522
76. Newberry, SC	425	99. Bolivar, MO	524
Mount Airy, NC	425	100. Crossville, TN	542